FROMMER'S

COMPREHENSIVE TRAVEL GUIDE

Rome

10th Edition

by Darwin Porter
assisted by Danforth Prince

MACMILLAN • USA

ABOUT THE AUTHOR

A native of North Carolina, **Darwin Porter** was a bureau chief for *The Miami Herald* when he was 21, and later worked in television advertising. A veteran travel writer, he is the author of numerous bestselling Frommer guides, notably to England, France, the Caribbean, Italy, Germany, and Spain. When not traveling (which is rare), he lives in New York City. He is assisted by **Danforth Prince**, formerly of the Paris bureau of *The New York Times.*

MACMILLAN TRAVEL

A Prentice Hall Macmillan Company
15 Columbus Circle
New York, NY 10023

ISBN 0-02-860052-5

ISSN 0899-319X

Design by Michele Laseau
Maps by Ortelius Design

Special Sales

Bulk purchases of Frommer's Travel Guides are available at special discounts. The Special Sales Department can produce custom editions to be used as premiums and/or for sales promotion to suit individual needs. Existing editions can be produced with custom cover imprints such as corporate logos. Fro more information write to: Special Sales, Prentice Hall, 15 Columbus Circle, New York, NY 10023.

Manufactured in the United States of America

Contents

4 ROME ACCOMMODATIONS 87

SPECIAL FEATURES

5 ROME DINING 121

SPECIAL FEATURES

APPENDIX   273

INDEX   281

List of Maps

What the Symbols Mean

★ **Frommer's Favorites**   Hotels, restaurants, attractions, and entertainments you should not miss

$ **Super-Special Values**   Really exceptional values

In Hotel and Other Listings

The following symbols refer to the standard amenities available in all rooms:

A/C   air conditioning
TEL   telephone
TV   television
MINIBAR   refrigerator stocked with beverages and snacks

The following abbreviations are used for credit cards:

AE   American Express
DISC   Discover
EU   Eurocard
CB   Carte Blanche
ER   en Route
MC   MasterCard
DC   Diners Club
V   VISA

Trip Planning with this Guide
USE THE FOLLOWING FEATURES:

What Things Cost In   To help you plan your daily budget

Calendar of Events   To plan for or avoid

Suggested Itineraries   For seeing the city

What's Special About Checklist   A summary of the city's highlights[md]which lets you check off those that appeal most to you

Easy-to-Read Maps   All the essentials at a glance: currency, emergencies, embassies, and more

Fast Facts   All the essentials at a glance: currency, emergencies, embassies, and more

Frommer's Smart Traveler Tips   Hints on how to secure the best value for your money

OTHER SPECIAL FROMMER FEATURES

Cool for Kids   Hotels, restaurants, and attractions

Did You Know . . . ?   Offbeat, fun facts

Famous People   The city's greats

Impressions   What others have said

In Their Footsteps   Tracking the lives of famous residents

Invitation to the Reader

In researching this book, I have come across many fine establishments, the best of which I have included here. I am sure that many
of you will also come across appealing hotels, inns, restaurants,
guesthouses, shops, and attractions. Please don't keep them to
yourself. Share your experiences, especially if you want to com-
ment on places that have been included in this edition that have
changed for the worse. You can address your letters to:

Darwin Porter
Frommer's Rome
c/o Macmillan Travel
15 Columbus Circle
New York, NY 10023

A Disclaimer

Readers are advised that prices fluctuate in the course of time and
travel information changes under the impact of the varied and
volatile factors that affect the travel industry. Neither the authors
nor the publisher can be held responsible for the experiences of
readers while traveling. Readers are invited to write to the publisher with ideas, comments, and suggestions for future editions.

Safety Advisory

Whenever you're traveling in an unfamiliar city or country, stay
alert. Be aware of your immediate surroundings. Wear a
moneybelt and keep a close eye on your possessions. Be particularly careful with cameras, purses, and wallets, all favorite targets
of thieves and pickpockets.

1

Introducing Rome

FAMOUS THROUGHOUT HISTORY AS A CENTER OF PRESTIGE, POWER, AND intrigue, Rome contains a greater number of historic buildings, monuments, and ruins than any other city in the world. The memorials date from every ruling power, from the Etruscans to the Catholic popes, with thousands of reminders of the 18th and 19th centuries as well as the Mussolini era thrown in. Palaces, parks, churches, museums, piazze, statues, and fountains abound. Ancient and massive ruins—mocking the ambitions of humankind for immortality—bask in the sun, and baroque grandeur adorns almost every street corner. The sheer volume of sights has crafted one of the most memorable urban landscapes in the world.

Today, despite the city's status as capital of both modern Italy and as the site of the Vatican center of the Catholic church, Rome seems permeated with the temperament and sensuality of southern Europe. Familiar with power from the time of its earliest inhabitants, the city is famous for its blasé acceptance of the inevitability of death, its *joie de vivre* (known locally as a *gioia di vivere*), and its stoic acceptance of the inevitable rise and fall of personal and political fortunes.

The city is simultaneously strident, romantic, and sensual, and has forever altered the Western world's standards of beauty and excellence in such fields as art, religion, and government. And although today the romantic poets would probably be horrified at the traffic, pollution, overcrowding, political discontent, and barely controlled chaos of modern Rome, the city endures and thrives in a way that has often been described as eternal.

Modern Italian society faces daunting problems, including insufficient housing, a rapid rise in the cost of living, impossible traffic, a bureaucracy that tends to strangle personal initiative, a rising crime rate, and pollution that has caused irreparable damage to many of the city's monuments. However, Rome still manages to live a relatively relaxed way of life. Romans, along with their southern cousins in Naples, are specialists in the *arte di arrangiarsi,* the art of coping and surviving with style, a mode that is pursued with both passion and a sense of tragic resignation. The Romans have humanity if not humor, a 2,000-year-old sense of cynicism, and a strong feeling of belonging to a particular place.

The city's attractions seem as old as time itself, and despite the frustrations of the city's daily life, Rome continues to lure new visitors every year to sample its ancient pleasures and temptations anew.

1 Geography & People

GEOGRAPHY   Rome lies on the Tiber River, some 17 miles northeast from its mouth on the Mediterranean. Set within the central part of the Italian peninsula, near its western shoreline, Rome lies about 16 miles inland from the Tyrrhenian Sea.

Rome, according to legend, was built on seven hills, or low mountain ridges. These hills are only 44 feet above sea level at the

Ancient Monuments
- The Roman Forum, ringed by the Palatine and Capitoline Hills, the hub of a great imperial city.
- The Colosseum, symbol of classical Rome, built in A.D. 80 by 20,000 slaves. Byron called it "the gladiator's bloody circus."
- Ostia Antica, the long-buried city at the mouth of the Tiber, once the seaport and naval base of ancient Rome.
- The Pantheon, the best preserved monument of ancient Rome, constructed by Hadrian around A.D. 120.

Religious Shrines/Museums
- St. Peter's, the world's greatest basilica, spiritual home for millions of Catholics.
- The Basilica of San Giovanni in Laterano, the cathedral of Rome.
- The Vatican, the papal residence for 600 years and the setting for 4½ miles of art, including Michelangelo's Sistine Chapel.

Parks & Gardens
- Villa Borghese, a public park with open-air cafes and the Borghese Gallery.
- Villa d'Este, at Tivoli, outside Rome, with one of the wonders of Italy—its 18th-century fountains.

Ace Attractions
- The Spanish Steps, the eternal center for tourists and expatriates, including everybody from Keats to Wagner.
- Piazza Navona, the finest of Rome's squares, the former stadium of Domitian, now filled with visitors ringing Bernini's Fountain of the Four Rivers.

Film Locations
- Three films helped put Rome on the postwar tourist map: *Roman Holiday*, Fellini's *La Dolce Vita*, and *Three Coins in the Fountain*, which launched the tradition of tossing a coin over your shoulder to assure a return visit to Rome.

Pantheon, rising to 462 feet above sea level at Monte Mario, present site of the deluxe Cavalieri Hilton hotel.

These seven hills rise from the marshy lowlands of the Campagna and are mostly on the left bank of the Tiber. They include the Quirinale (seat of the Italian government today), Esquiline, Viminal, Caelian, and Aventine—and all combine to form a crescent-shaped plateau of great historical fame. In its center rises the Palatine Hill, all-powerful seat of the imperial residences of ancient Rome, which looks down upon the ancient Forum and the Colosseum. To the northwest rises the Capitoline Hill. Some historians have suggested that Rome's geography—set above a periphery of marshy and sweltering hot lowlands—contributed to the fall of the Roman Empire because of its propensity to breed malaria-inducing mosquitoes.

The modern city of Rome is composed of 22 districts, covering an area of nearly 10 square miles. The Tiber makes two distinct bends within Rome, below the Ponte Cavour, one of the city's major bridges, and again at the history-rich island of Tiberina.

THE PEOPLE   With bloodlines including virtually every race ever encompassed by the borders of the ancient Roman Empire, the people of Rome long ago grew accustomed to seeing foreign influences come and go. Picking their way through the architectural and cultural jumble of Rome, they are not averse to complaining (loudly) of the city's endless inconveniences, yet they are probably the first to appreciate the historical and architectural marvel that surrounds them. Cynical but hearty, and filled with humanity, modern Romans seem to propel themselves through the business of life with an enviable sense of style.

The crowds of pilgrims and the vast numbers of churches and convents exist side by side with fleshier and more earthbound distractions, the combination of which imbues many Romans with an overriding interest in pursuing the pleasures and distractions of the moment. This sense of theatricality can be seen in Roman driving habits; in animated conversations and gesticulations in restaurants and cafes; in the lavish displays of flowers, fountains, food, and architecture—the nation's trademark; and in the 27 centuries of building projects dedicated to the power and egos of long-dead potentates.

Despite the crowds, the pollution, the heat, and the virtual impossibility of efficiency, Romans for the most part take life with good cheer and *pazienza*. (Translated as "patience," it seems to be the frequently uttered motto of modern Rome, and an appropriate philosophy for a city that has known everything from unparalleled glory to humiliations and despair.) Romans know that since Rome wasn't built in a day, its charms should be savored slowly and with an appreciation for the cultures that contributed to this panoply.

IMPRESSIONS

Italy: A paradise inhabited with devils.
—Sir Henry Wotton, Letter To Lord Zouche, June 1592

It is not impossible to govern Italians. It is merely useless.
—Benito Mussolini, Attrib.

2 | History & Politics

History

Many of the key events that shaped the rich and often gory tapestry of Italian history originated in Rome, a city which has since its founding been the most influential within a country studded with important cities.

Although parts of Italy (especially Sardinia and Sicily) were inhabited as early as the Bronze Age, the region of Rome was occupied relatively late within the history of Italy. Some historians claim that the presence of active volcanoes during the Bronze Age in the region of Rome prevented prehistoric tribes from living there, but regardless of the reason, Rome has unearthed far fewer prehistoric graves and implements than those in neighboring Umbria and Tuscany.

ROME'S EARLIEST TRIBES By around 700 B.C., tribespeople had established sheepherding and farming communities on several of the low-lying hills that later became the symbol of Rome. Drawing on primeval models, they coalesced the origins of what eventually become the empire's religion, worshipping such deities as Jupiter, Juno, Mars, Minerva, and Ceres. Except for public grazing areas, most land was privately owned in a strongly defined patriarchal system where rights of inheritance, vendettas, and punishment within family-related tribes seem to have been well understood.

THE ETRUSCANS The arrival around 800 B.C. of the Etruscans on the east coast of Umbria has never fully been understood by sociologists or historians. (The many inscriptions they left behind—mostly on graves—are of no help, since the Etruscan language has never been deciphered.) Their religious rites and architecture show an obvious contact with Mesopotamia; the Etruscans may have been refugees from Asia

Dateline

- **Bronze Age** Tribes of Celts, Teutonics, and groups from the eastern Mediterranean inhabit the Italian peninsula.
- **1200–1000 B.C.** The Etruscans migrate from the eastern Mediterranean (probably Mesopotamia) and occupy territory north and south of Rome.
- **800 B.C.** Sicily and southern Italy (especially Naples) flourish under Greek and Phoenician protection. Independent of most outside domination, Rome evolves as an insignificant community of shepherds with loyalties divided among several Latin tribes.
- **753 B.C.** Rome's traditional founding date.
- **660 B.C.** Etruscans occupy Rome and designate it the capital of their empire; the city grows rapidly and a major seaport (Ostia) opens at the mouth of the Tiber.
- **510–250 B.C.** The Latin tribes, still

▶

Dateline

centered in Rome, maintain a prolonged revolt against the Etruscans. During this period, alpine Gauls attack the Etruscans from the north while Greeks living in Sicily destroy the Etruscan navy.

- **250 B.C.** The Romans and their allies finally purge the Etruscans from Italy; Rome flourishes as a republic and begins the accumulation of a vast empire.
- **250–50 B.C.** Rome obliterates its chief rival, Carthage, during two Punic Wars. Carthage's defeat allows unchecked Roman expansion into Spain, North Africa, Sardinia, and Corsica.
- **40 B.C.** Rome and its armies control the entire Mediterranean world.
- **44 B.C.** Julius Caesar is assassinated. His successor, Augustus, transforms Rome from a city of brick to a city of marble, and solidifies Rome's status as a dictatorship.
- **3rd century A.D.** Rome declines under a series of incompetent and corrupt emperors.

➤

Minor who began to travel westward around 1200–1000 B.C. We know that the Etruscans arrived in Italy in large numbers and within two centuries had subjugated Tuscany and Campania (to the north and south, respectively, of the Roman region) and the Villanova tribes who lived there. They forced the indigenous Latin tribes to work the land for them and support them as an aristocratic class of princes.

While the Etruscans built temples at Tarquinia and Caere (present-day Cerveteri), the few nervous Latin tribes who remained outside their sway gravitated to the strategic position of what was later known as Rome. The site was especially profitable for whoever controlled it because of its location at a point where the ancient Salt Way (via Salaria) crossed the Tiber River.

From their base at Rome, the Latins remained free of the Etruscans until about 600 B.C., thanks mainly to the presence of the Greek colonies along the Italian coast, which tended to hold back Carthaginians (Phoenicians) on one side and Etruscans on the other. But the Etruscan advance was as inexorable as that of the later Roman Empire, and by 600 B.C., the Etruscans were able to establish a military stronghold in the hills above Rome. When the new overlords took complete control, they introduced such new art forms as gold tableware and jewelry, bronze urns, and terra-cotta statuary. They also exposed the Latin tribes to the Greek and Asia Minor art and culture and they made Rome the government seat of all Latium. Roma is an Etruscan name, and the kings of Roma had Etruscan names: Numa, Ancus, Tarquinius, even Romulus.

Under the combined influences of the Greeks and the Mesopotamian east, Roma grew enormously. A new port was opened at Ostia, near the mouth of the Tiber. Artists from Greece carved statues of Roman gods to resemble Greek divinities. In the army that was subsequently established, wealthy soldiers were expected to provide a greater share of horses, armor, and weapons, a condition that resulted in the amassing of both increased responsibility and (eventually) increased power into the hands of the society's richest citizens. It is easy to see how this classification by wealth, which also affected voting and law-making, stemmed from a democratic concept of the army but led to an undemocratic concept of society. From this enforced (and not always peaceable) mélange of the Latin tribes with the Etruscans grew the roots of what eventually became famous as the Republic of Rome.

THE ROMAN REPUBLIC Gauls from the alpine regions invaded the northern Etruscan territory around 600 B.C., and the Latin tribes revolted in about 510 B.C., toppling the Etruscan-linked rulers from their power bases and establishing the southern boundary of Etruscan influence at the Tiber. Greeks from Sicily ended Etruscan sea power in 474 B.C., during the battle of Cumae off the Italian coastline just north of Naples. By 250 B.C., the Romans and their allies in Campania had vanquished the Etruscans, wiping out their language and religion. Despite the Etruscan's political collapse, their manners, beliefs, and many of their art forms were respected and maintained by the Latins, and in many cases assimilated into the culture of the new society. Even today, certain Etruscan customs and bloodlines are believed to exist in Italy, especially within the race's former stronghold of Tuscany.

Tempered in the fires of military adversity, the stern Roman republic was characterized by belief in the gods, the necessity of learning from the past, strength of the family, education through books and public service, and most important, obedience. The all-powerful Senate presided as Rome defeated rival powers one after the other in a steady stream of staggering military successes.

As their population grew, the Romans gave to their Latin allies, and then to conquered peoples, partial or complete Roman citizenship, always with the

Dateline

- **4th century A.D.** Rome is fragmented politically as administrative capitals are established in such cities as Milan and Trier, Germany.

- **A.D. 395** The empire splits: Constantine establishes a "New Rome" at Constantinople (Byzantium); Goths successfully invade Rome's provinces in northern Italy.

- **410–455** Rome is sacked by barbarians—Alaric the Goth, Attila the Hun, and Galseric the Vandal.

- **475** Rome falls, leaving only the primate of the Catholic church in control. The pope slowly adopts many of the responsibilities and the prestige once reserved for the Roman emperors.

- **731** Pope Gregory II renounces Rome's spiritual and political link to the authorities in Constantinople.

- **900** Charlemagne is crowned Holy Roman Emperor by Pope Leo III; Italy dissolves into a series of small warring kingdoms.

- **1065** The Holy Land falls to the Muslim Turks; the Crusades are launched.

➤

Introducing Rome History & Politics

Dateline

- **1303–77** Papal schism: a rival pope is established at Avignon.
- **1377** The "antipope" is removed from Avignon, and the Roman popes emerge as sole contenders to the legacy of St. Peter.
- **Mid-1400s** Originating in Florence, the Renaissance blossoms throughout Italy. Italian artists receive multiple commissions within the ecclesiastical communities of Rome.
- **1508** Ordered by the pope, Michelangelo begins work on the ceiling of the Vatican's Sistine Chapel.
- **1527** Rome is attacked and sacked by Charles V, who—to the pope's rage—is elected Holy Roman Emperor the following year.
- **1796–97** Napoleon's military conquests of Italy arouse Italian nationalism.
- **1861** Rome is declared the capital of the newly established Kingdom of Italy. The Papal States (but not the Vatican) are absorbed into the new nation.

obligation of military service. Colonies of citizens were established on the borders of the growing empire and were inhabited with soldiers/farmers and their families. Later, as seen in the history of Britain and the Continent, colonies began to thrive as semiautonomous units of their own, heavily fortified, and linked to Rome by well-maintained military roads and a well-defined hierarchy of military command.

The final obstacle to the unrivaled supremacy of Rome was the defeat, during the 3rd century B.C., of the city-state of Carthage during the two Punic Wars. Located on the coast of Tunisia, and founded by the Phoenicians many centuries previously as a trading post, Carthage had grown into one of the premier naval and agricultural powers of the Mediterranean with strongly fortified positions in Corsica, Sardinia, and Spain. Despite the impressive victories of the Carthaginian general, Hannibal, Rome eventually eradicated Carthage in one of the most famous defeats in ancient history. Rome was able to immediately expand its power into Northern Africa, Sardinia, Corsica, and Iberia.

THE ROMAN EMPIRE   By 49 B.C., Italy ruled all of the Mediterranean world either directly or indirectly, with all political, commercial, and cultural pathways leading directly to Rome. The possible wealth and glory to be found in Rome lured many there, but drained other Italian communities of human resources. As Rome transformed itself into an administrative headquarters, imports into the city from other parts of the empire hurt local farmers and landowners. The seeds for civil discord were sown early in the empire's life, although as Rome was embellished with temples, monuments, and the easy availability of slave labor from conquered territories, many of its social problems were overlooked in favor of expansion and glory.

On the eve of the birth of Christ, Rome
➤ was a mighty empire whose generals had

brought all of the Western world under the influence of Roman law, values, and civilization. Only within the eastern third of the Mediterranean did the existing cultures—especially the Greek—withstand the Roman incursions. Despite its occupation by Rome, Greece, more than any other culture, permeated Rome with new ideas, values, and concepts of art, architecture, religion, and philosophy.

Meanwhile, the ideals of democratic responsibility within the heart of the empire had begun to break down. The populace began to violently object to a government that took little interest in commerce, and seemed interested only in foreign politics. As taxes and levies increased, the poor emigrated in huge and idle numbers to Rome and the rich cities of the Po Valley. Entire generations of war captives, forced into the slave-driven economies of large Italian estates, were steeped in hatred and ignorance.

Christianity, a new and (at the time) revolutionary religion, probably gained a foothold in Rome about 10 years after Christ's crucifixion. Feared far more for its political implications than for its spiritual presuppositions, it was at first brutally suppressed before moving through increasingly tolerant stages of acceptability.

After the death of Julius Caesar, all power became entrenched within the hands of a series of all-powerful emperors, whose sweeping strengths brought Rome to new, almost giddy, heights. Augustus transformed the city from brick to marble in some of the most grandiose building projects in history, but as corruption spread, Rome endured a steady decay in the ideals and traditions upon which the empire had been founded. As the uncorruptible Roman soldier of an earlier era became increasingly rare, the army became filled with barbarian mercenaries. The tax collector became the scourge of the countryside, often killing the incentive for economic development and causing many to abandon their farms altogether in favor of a life of impoverishment within the cities. For every good emperor (Augustus, Trajan, Vespasian, Hadrian, to name a few), there were three or four corrupt, debased, and possibly insane heads of state (Caligula, Nero, Domitian, Caracalla, and many more).

Dateline
- **1929** Signing of a concordate between the Vatican and the Italian government delineates the rights and responsibilities of both parties.
- **1935** Italian invasion of Abyssinia (Ethiopia).
- **1941** Italian invasion of Yugoslavia.
- **1943** General Patton lands in Sicily and soon controls the island.
- **1945** Mussolini killed by a mob in Milan.
- **1946** Establishment of Rome as the capital of the newly created Republic of Italy.
- **1960s** Rise of left-wing terrorist groups; flight of capital from Italy; continuing problems of the impoverished south cause exodus from the Italian countryside into such cities as Rome.
- **1980s** *Il Sorpasso* imbues Rome (and the rest of Italy) with dreams of an economic rebirth.
- **1994** Right-wing forces win in Italian national elections.

As the decay progressed, the Roman citizen either lived on the increasingly swollen public dole and spent his days at gladiatorial games and imperial baths, or was a disillusioned patrician at the mercy of emperors who might murder him for his property. The 3rd century A.D. saw so many emperors that it was common, as H. V. Morton tells us, to hear in the provinces of the election of an emperor together with a report of his assassination. Despite a well-intentioned series of reforms in the 4th century A.D. by Diocletian, the empire continued to weaken and decay. Although he reinforced imperial power, he paradoxically at the same time weakened Roman dominance and prestige by establishing administrative capitals of the empire at such outposts as Milan, Trier in Germany, and elsewhere.

This practice was followed by Constantine when he moved the administrative capital away from Rome altogether, an act which sounded a death knell for a city already threatened by the menace of barbarian attacks. The sole survivor of six rival emperors, Constantine recognized Christianity as the official religion of the Roman Empire, and built an entirely new, more easily defensible capital on the banks of the Bosporus. Named in his honor (Constantinople, or Byzantium), it was later renamed Istanbul by the Ottoman Turks. When he moved to the new capital, Constantine and his heirs took with him the best of the artisans, politicians, and public figures of Rome. Rome, reduced to little more than a provincial capital controlling the much-threatened western half of the once-mighty empire, continued to founder and decay. As for the Christian church, although the popes of Rome were under the nominal auspices of an exarch from Constantinople, their power increased slowly but steadily as the power of the emperors declined.

THE EMPIRE FALLS The eastern and western sections of the Roman Empire split in A.D. 395, leaving Italy without the support it had formerly received from east of the Adriatic. When the Goths moved toward Rome in the early 5th century, citizens in the provinces, who had grown to hate and fear the cruel bureaucracy set up by Diocletian and sustained by succeeding emperors, often welcomed the invaders. And then the pillage began.

Rome was sacked by Alaric in 410. After fewer than 40 troubled years, Attila the Hun laid siege. He was followed in 455 by Gaiseric the Vandal, who engaged in a two-week spree of looting and destruction. The empire of the west lasted for only another 20 years; finally, the sacking and chaos ended it in A.D. 476, and a burned-out, much humiliated Rome was left to the ministrations of the popes. Without Rome, Italy disintegrated into anarchy, with order maintained by family clans strong enough to maintain power within their fortified citadels. Into the vacuum stepped the authorities of the church and a handful of ruling families, whose authority eventually became closely intertwined.

THE HOLY ROMAN EMPIRE After the fall of the Western Empire, the pope took on more and more of the powers of the emperor, despite the lack of any political unity within Italy. Decades of mismanagement by the Roman emperors were followed by the often anarchic rule by barbarian Goths. These were followed by takeovers in different parts of the country by various strong warriors, such as the Lombards. Italy was thus divided into several spheres of control, but always with the permeating influence of the Roman popes.

In 731, Pope Gregory II renounced Rome's spiritual dependence on Constantinople. Papal Rome turned forever toward Europe, and in 800 a king of the barbarian Franks was crowned Holy Roman Emperor by Pope Leo III. The new emperor's name was Charlemagne, and he established a capital at Aachen (known today to the French as Aix-la-Chapelle). This coronation marked a major milestone whereby a Roman pope collaborated with (and later conflicted with) a temporal European power. Although Charlemagne pledged allegiance to the Catholic church, he launched northwestern Europe on a course of what would eventually become bitter political opposition to the meddling of the papacy in temporal affairs.

Meanwhile, the religious powers in Rome looked with dismay at the increasing fragmentation of Italy into war zones between Lombards, Franks, Magyars, Venetians, Saracens, and Normans. As Italy dissolved, the feudal landowners of Rome gained control of the papacy, and a series of questionably religious pontiffs endured a diminishment of their powers. Eventually, even the selection process for determining the election of the popes fell into the hands of the increasingly Germanic Holy Roman Emperor, although this power balance would very soon shift.

Rome during the Middle Ages was a quaint, rural town. Narrow lanes with overhanging buildings filled many of what were originally built as showcases of ancient imperial power, including the Campus Martius. Great basilicas built and embellished with golden-hued mosaics, forums, mercantile exchanges, temples, and expansive theaters of the imperial era slowly disintegrated and collapsed. The decay of ancient Rome was assisted by periodic earthquakes, centuries of neglect, and the growing need for building materials. The seat of the Catholic church, it was a state almost completely controlled by priests, who had an insatiable need for new churches and convents.

By the end of the 11th century, the popes shook off control of the Roman aristocracy, rid themselves of what they considered the excessive influence of the emperors at Aachen, and began an aggressive expansion of church influence and acquisitions. The deliberate and conscious organization of the church into a format modeled on the hierarchies of the ancient Roman Empire put the church on a collision course with the empire and the other temporal leaders of Europe, resulting in an endless series of power struggles.

IMPRESSIONS

The Romans would never have had time to conquer the world if they had been obliged to learn Latin first of all.
—Heinrich Heine, *Das Buch Le Grand, In Reisebilder,* 1826–31

THE MIDDLE AGES The papacy soon became essentially a feudal state, and the pope became a medieval (later Renaissance) prince engaged in many of the worldly activities that brought criticism upon the church in later centuries. The fall of the Holy Land to the Turks in 1065 catapulted the papacy into the forefront of world politics, primarily because of the Crusades, most of which were judged military and economic disasters, and many of which the popes directly caused or encouraged. During the 12th and 13th centuries, the bitter rivalries that rocked the secular and spiritual bastions of Europe took their toll on the stability of the Holy Roman Empire, which grew weaker as city-states buttressed by mercantile and trade-related prosperity grew stronger, and as France emerged as a potent nation in its own right. Each investiture of a new bishop to any influential post became a cause for endless jockeying for power among many political and ecclesiastical factions.

These conflicts achieved their most visible impasse in 1303 with the full-fledged removal of the papacy from Rome to the French city of Avignon. For more than 70 years, until 1377, viciously competing popes (one in Rome, another under the protection of the French kings in Avignon) made simultaneous claims to the legacy of St. Peter, underscoring as never before the degree to which the church was both a victim and a victimizer in the temporal world of European politics.

The seat of the papacy was eventually returned to Rome, where a series of popes were every bit as interesting as the Roman emperors they replaced. The great families—Barberini, Medici, Borgia— enhanced their status and fortunes impressively whenever one of their sons was elected pope.

THE RENAISSANCE Rome's age of siege was not yet over. In 1527, Charles V spearheaded the worst sack in the city's history. To the horror of Pope Clement VII (a Medici), the entire city was brutally pillaged by the man who was to be crowned Holy Roman Emperor the following year.

During the years of the Renaissance, Reformation, and the Counter-Reformation, Rome underwent major physical changes. The old centers of culture reverted to pastures and fields, while great churches and palaces were built with the stones of ancient Rome. This building boom, in fact, did far more damage to the temples of the Caesars than did any barbarian or Teutonic sack. Rare marbles were stripped from the imperial baths and used as altarpieces or sent to lime kilns. So enthusiastic was the papal destruction of imperial Rome that it's a miracle anything is left.

THE MOVE TOWARD A UNITED ITALY During the 17th, 18th, and 19th centuries, the fortunes of Rome rose and fell with the general political and economic situation of the rest of Italy. Since

IMPRESSIONS

Vile in its origin, barbarous in its institutions, a casual association of robbers and of outcasts became the destiny of mankind.
—Lady Morgan, *Italy*, 1820

IMPRESSIONS

Of Rome, in short, this is my opinion, or rather indeed my most assured knowledge, that her delights on earth are sweet, and her judgments in heaven heavy.
—Sir Henry Wotton, Letter To Lord Zouche, May 1592

There is a horrid Thing called the mal'aria that comes to Rome every summer, and kills one, and I did not care for being killed so far from Christian burial.
—Horace Walpole, Letter To The Hon. Henry Seymour Conway, July 1740

the end of the 13th century, Italy had been divided into a series of regional states, each with mercenary soldiers, their own judicial systems, and an interlocking series of alliances and enmities, which had created a network of intensely competitive city-states. (Some of these families had attained formidable power under such *signori* as the Esse family in Ferrara, the Medici in Florence, and the Sforza families in Milan.) Rome, headquarters of the Papal States, maintained its independence and (usually) the integrity of its borders, although at least some of the city's religious power had been quenched as increasing numbers of Europeans converted to Protestantism.

Napoleon made a bid for power in Italy beginning in 1796, fueling his propaganda machines with what was considered a relatively easy victory. During the Congress of Vienna, which followed Napoleon's defeat, Italy was once again divided among many different factions: Austria was given Lombardy and Venetia, and the Papal States were returned to the popes. Some duchies were put back into the hands of their hereditary rulers, while southern Italy and Sicily went to a newly imported dynasty related to the Bourbons. One historic move, which eventually assisted in the unification of Italy, was the assignment of the former republic of Genoa to Sardinia (which at the time was governed by the House of Savoy).

By now, political unrest had become a fact of Italian (and Roman) life. At least some of it was encouraged by the rapid industrialization of the north, and the almost total lack of industrialization in the Italian south. Despite these barriers, in 1861, the Kingdom of Italy was proclaimed and Victor Emmanuel of the House of Savoy, king of Sardinia, became head of the new monarchy. In 1861, the designated capital of the newly united country, following a 2,000-year-old precedent, became Rome. In a controversial move that engendered resentment many decades later, the borders of the Papal States were eradicated from the map as Rome was incorporated into the new nation of Italy. The Vatican, however, did not yield its territory to the new order, despite guarantees of nonintervention proffered by the Italian government, and relations between the pope and the political leaders of Italy remained rocky until 1929.

At that time, Mussolini defined the divisions that, until now, have separated the Italian government and the Vatican by signing a concordate that granted political and fiscal autonomy to Vatican City.

It also made Roman Catholicism the official state religion of Italy, although this designation was removed through revision of the concordate in 1978. In 1984, Bruno Craxi officially annulled the concordate of 1929.

WORLD WAR II & THE AXIS   With Rome now firmly entrenched as the seat of Italian power, the history of the city was now tightly linked to that of Italy as a whole. Mussolini's support of the Fascists during the Spanish civil war helped encourage the formation of the "Axis" between Italy and Nazi Germany.

Despite its outdated military equipment, Italy added to the general horror of the era by invading Abyssinia (Ethiopia) in 1935, supposedly to protect Italian colonial interests there. In 1941, Italy invaded neighboring Yugoslavia, and in 1942 thousands of Italian troops were sent to assist Hitler in his disastrous campaign along the Russian front. In 1943, General Patton, leading American and (with General Montgomery) British troops, controlled all of Sicily within a month of their first attack.

Faced with this defeat and humiliation, Mussolini fled from Rome after being overthrown by his own cabinet. The Allies made a separate deal with Italy's king, Vittorio Emanuele III. A politically divided Italy watched as battalions of fanatical German Nazis moved south to resist the Allied march northward up the Italian peninsula. The Nazis released Mussolini from his Italian jail cell to establish the short-lived Republic of Salo, headquartered on the edge of Lake Garda, hoping for a groundswell of popular opinion in favor of Italian fascism. Events quickly proved this nothing more than a futile dream.

In April, 1945, with almost half a million Italians rising in a mass demonstration against him and the German war machine, and Rome almost paralyzed by public insurgencies, Mussolini was captured by Italian partisans as he fled into Switzerland. With his mistress, Claretta Petacci, and several others of his intimates, he was shot and strung up upside down from the roof of a gasoline station in piazzale Loreto, a few blocks east of the central railway station of Milan.

MODERN ROME   Rome today serves as the capital of the Republic of Italy, which was formed in 1946 in the aftermath of World War II. In the 1950s, Italy became one of the leading industrialized nations of the world, a giant in the manufacture of automobiles and office equipment, and an agricultural breadbasket of international repute.

In the 1960s, Rome became the campaign ground for an increasingly powerful socialist party spearheaded by Aldo Moro, who was later assassinated by a left-wing terrorist group. Meanwhile, as the city's wealthy grew increasingly alarmed at the growing socialization of their country, Rome and the rest of Italy suffered an unprecedented flight of capital and an increase in bankruptcies, inflation (almost 20% during most of the 1970s), and unemployment.

IMPRESSIONS

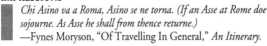

Chi Asino va a Roma, Asino se ne torna. (If an Asse at Rome doe
sojourne. As Asse he shall from thence returne.)
—Fynes Moryson, "Of Travelling In General," *An Itinerary.*

During the late 1970s and early 1980s, Rome was rocked by the
rise of terrorism instigated both by right-wing neo-fascists and by
left-wing intellectuals from the socialist-controlled universities of the
north.

In the 1990s some 6,000 businesspeople and politicians were
implicated in a billion-dollar government graft scandal. Such familiar
figures as Bettino Craxi, who headed the Socialist party, and Giulio
Andreotti, the seven-time prime minister, were accused of corruption.

Hoping for a renewal after all this exposure of greed, Italian voters
in March of 1994 turned to the right wing to head their government.
In overwhelming numbers, voters elected a former cruise ship singer
turned media billionaire, Silvio Berlusconi, its new leader. Berlusconi
swept to an unprecedented victory in national elections, emerging
as prime minister. His *Forza Italia* (Go, Italy) party formed an alliance
with the neo-fascist National Alliance and the secessionist Northern
League to sweep to victory. These elections were termed "the most
critical" for Italy in four decades. The new government was beset with
an almost hopeless array of new problems, including destabilization
caused by the Mafia and its underground economies. The city's
much-needed urban restoration is frequently stalled by the wishes of
art historians anxious to preserve ancient, medieval, and Renaissance
ruins. Despite its charms, the city continues to be plagued with
incessant traffic, a growing population, and an often disfunctional
physical plant where things simply do not always work very well.

Besides football (soccer), the family, and affairs of the heart, the
city's obsession today is with economic matters. As part of an almost
universal opinion shared by virtually every Italian, all levels of society
are actively engaged to some degree in withholding funds from the
government. Today, Italy's underground economy *(economia
sommersa)* competes on a monumental scale with the official
economy, with participation by all sorts of otherwise respectable
businesses and individuals. Complicating Italy's problems for
economists, the police, and politicians is the constant interference
of the Mafia, whose methods—even with numerous more or less
heartfelt crackdowns—continue today even more ruthlessly than ever.

Despite these burdensome problems, Rome is eager to play a role
in an increasingly complicated global economy, and the capital of
one of Europe's well-entrenched superpowers continues to hold an
irresistible fascination for the traveler.

Politics

Rome is the seat of a democratic government, which was established
in Italy in 1946. The Italian Parliament is composed of the Chamber
of Deputies and the Senate of the Republic. The Republic of Italy is

divided into 20 regions comprising 94 provinces and more than 8,000 communes. The president of the republic is elected by the members of both chambers of Parliament, who vote by secret ballot.

Political parties in Italy are numerous, and party loyalties fluctuate, since it is difficult for any one group to round up sufficient votes for election victory without gathering support from other organizations. Since 1948, Christian Democrats, originally supported by the United States and the Catholic church, led 52 coalition governments to victory. But in 1993, disgraced by charges of corruption, they changed their name to the Popular Party. Even so, they didn't prove popular in the spring elections of 1994, when Italian voters turned to a right-wing coalition, the Forza Italia party, led by Silvio Berlusconi. This media billionaire formed an alliance with the neo-fascist party, the National Alliance, and the separatist Northern League. The former Communist Party is now officially known as the Democratic Party of the Left, although a splinter group, the hard-line Communist Refounding Party, has also emerged. Other minor parties include the Greens and the anti-Mafia Le Rete Party.

3   Famous Romans

St. Alban   (3rd or 4th century) Roman soldier and first British martyr, he was beheaded at Verulamium (now St. Albans), England, for sheltering the Christian priest who had converted him.

Antonioni, Michelangelo   (b. 1912) Film director who began his career making documentaries, he is considered one of the best-known cinematists in Italian history. His films deal with the boredom, despair, and alienation of the upper-middle classes in Italy. He is best remembered for a trilogy of films consisting of *La Notte* (1960), *L'Avventura* (1960), and *L'Eclisse* (1961).

Apuleius, Lucius   (2nd century A.D.) The works of this Roman satirist are the only extant examples of Latin-language prose fiction. His most famous work is *The Golden Ass* (also known as *Metamorphoses*).

Aretino, Pietre   (1492–1556) Sponsored and supported by such royal patrons as Emperor Charles V and Francis I of France, he is one of the best-remembered political satirists of the Renaissance. Known as the "scourge of princes," he invariably fell into disgrace as his satirical arrow drove deep.

Augustus   (originally Gaius Octavius, later Gaius Julius Caesar Octavianus) (63 B.C.–14 A.D.) Grandnephew of Julius Caesar, who adopted him as his son and heir, he was considered the first Roman

IMPRESSIONS

Rome reminds me of a man who lives by exhibiting to travellers his grandmother's corpse.
—James Joyce, Letter to Stanislaus Joyce, September 1906

In Rome you have to do as the Romans do, or get arrested.
—Geoffrey Harmsworth, *Abyssinian Adventure*, 1935

emperor, enjoying absolute control of most of the known world after 27 B.C. He defeated Brutus and Cassius, slayers of his mentor, and also Mark Anthony.

Bellini, Vincenzo   (1801–35) During his short life, he elevated to a status never before heard the opera form of *bel canto.* Some of the pieces he wrote for coloratura soprano remain among the most sought-after by operatic divas the world over. His operas (*Norma, La Sonnambula,* and *I Puritani*) are noted for their beauty of melody rather than for the complexity of their harmonies, or the dramatic intensities of their plots.

Bernini, Giovanni Lorenzo   (1598–1680) This Renaissance sculptor and architect changed forever the architecture of Rome, designing many of its fountains (including those within the piazza Navona). Even more famous are his designs for the colonnade and piazza in front of St. Peter's, as well as the canopy whose corkscrew columns cover the landmark's principal altar.

Borgia, Cesare   (1476–1507) The name of this Italian adventurer and churchman is synonymous with cruelty and treachery, thanks to his ruthlessness in organizing the cities of central Italy under his rule.

Caruso, Enrico   (1873–1921) Born in Italy, the most famous operatic tenor of his era achieved his greatest success at New York's Metropolitan Opera. His interpretations of *Rigoletto, Pagliacci,* and *La Bohème* helped to spread the allure of opera to the New World.

Cellini, Benvenuto   (1500–1571) The most famous goldsmith in history, and a notable sculptor (*Perseus with the Head of Medusa*) as well, he was the author of a famous *Autobiography,* which, when first published in 1728, established him as one of the greatest rakes of the Renaissance.

Clement[s]   Clement was the consistently most popular name for a series of Roman popes and anti-popes who ruled—usually more or less despotically—with some interruption from 88 A.D. (Clement I) to 1774 (Clement XIV). Among the most famous of these not-always-clement princes of the church were Clement V (dubbed the anti-pope by his legions of enemies) and Clement VII (Giulio de'Medici).

Donizetti, Gaetano   (1797–1848) He was an Italian composer of some of the most famous—and singable—operas anywhere, including *Lucia di Lammermoor, L'Elisir d'Amore,* and *The Daughter of the Regiment.*

Eustachi, Bartolommeo   (1520–74) He was an Italian biologist whose painstaking dissections analyzed the ligaments, bones, tendons, nerves, and vessels of the human body. Named in his honor were the eustachian tubes, whose pressure-regulating abilities are vital to the functioning of the human ear. One of his contemporaries and competitors was **Gabrielo Fallopio** (1523–62), who identified and named in his own honor the fallopian tubes.

Fellini, Federico   (1920–1993) This neorealist film director was known for his zany, visually striking, and sometimes grotesque interpretations of social and psychological dilemmas. Examples of his work include *La Strada, La Dolce Vita* (whose title was adopted by an entire generation of fun-loving Italians as their mode of living), *8¹/₂, Juliet of the Spirits,* and his ode to the debaucheries and insanities of ancient Rome, *Satirycon.*

Fermi, Enrico   (1901–54) Roman physicist, and resident of the U.S. after 1939, he postulated the existence of the atomic particle identified as the neutrino, and produced element 93, neptunium. He was awarded the Nobel Prize for physics in 1938, and his work contributed heavily to the later development of the atomic bomb.

Gregory XIII   (1502–85) Roman pope from 1572 until his death, he launched the Counter-Reformation and departed from the policies of earlier popes by maintaining an unassailable (or at least discreet) personal comportment. One of his accomplishments was to develop a modern calendar, which is today in common usage throughout the Western world.

Machiavelli, Niccolò   (1469–1527) Political philosopher and Italian statesman, he is probably the world's most visible and oft-quoted defender of political conduct with a cynical and deliberate disregard for the moral issues involved. He is best remembered for his treatise on the art of ruling, *Il Principe* (The Prince).

Magnani, Anna   (1908–1973) This fiery Italian actress—whom Tennessee Williams once called "my favorite"—was making films in Italy in the 1930s and 1940s, long before she won an Academy Award in 1955 for *The Rose Tattoo,* written by Williams and co-starring Burt Lancaster. Dubbed in countless languages, her films were shown around the world, including the 1960 *The Fugitive Kind* opposite Marlon Brando and the 1968 *The Secret of Santa Vittoria.*

Maipighi, Marcello   (1628–94) Personal physician to Pope Innocent XII, he is considered the founder of microscopic anatomy.

Matteotti, Giacomo   (1885–1924) He was an Italian socialist whose murder by the Fascists is regarded as the removal of the final obstacle to Mussolini's complete control of Italy.

Menotti, Gian-Carlo   (b. 1911) Italian-born, and resident of the U.S. from 1928, he is known as a composer of highly melodic and sometimes satirical operas in the Italian *opera buffa* tradition. These include *The Medium, Amahl and the Night Visitors,* and *The Saint of Bleecker Street.*

Montessori, Maria   (1870–1952) Physician and educational theorist, she developed a method of education for young children that directs the child's energies into becoming the adult he or she wants to be within an environment of pedagogical freedom. In 1894, she became the first woman to receive an M.D. in Italy. Her most widely distributed work is *Pedagogical Anthropology.*

4   Art, Architecture, Literature & Music

ART   The mysterious **Etruscans,** whose earliest origins lay probably somewhere in Mesopotamia, brought the first truly impressive art to mainland Italy. Many of their finely sculpted sarcophagi rest today in Italian museums; the best collection is at the National Museum of the Villa Giulia in Rome. Several of the most frequently visited of the Etruscans' enigmatic tombs can be visited during day-trips from Rome (see "Easy Excursions from Rome," Chapter 10).

During the **Roman Empire,** the Romans discovered Greek art, fell in love with that country's statuary, and—as Roman influence throughout the Hellenistic world expanded—looted much of it. Unique to ancient Rome, however, was the execution of naturalistic portrait busts whose detailing reached a high point in a society whose leaders were eager to leave their portraits for posterity. Also unique to the Romans is a certain style of propaganda art, whose manifestations include both the construction and the sculptural adornment of the city's many triumphal arches.

The Romans were also adept at the adornment of their temples and villas with mosaics and painted frescoes. Noted for their naturalistic portrayal of flora and fauna, the ruined splendor and intricate detailing of these mosaics can still be admired in museums and excavations throughout Italy.

The aesthetic concepts of the Roman Empire eventually evolved into **early Christian and Byzantine art.** More concerned with moral and spiritual values than with the physical beauty of the human form or the celebration of political grandeur, early Christian artists turned to the supernatural and spiritual world for their inspiration, often glorifying churches rather than imperial palaces and pagan temples. Painting, meanwhile, depicted the earthly suffering (and heavenly rewards) of martyrs and saints.

The artistic expressions that followed the collapse of the Roman Empire manifested itself more aggressively within architecture rather than within the fields of painting or sculpture. In its many variations this style (identified today as **"Romanesque"**) flourished between A.D. 1000 and A.D. 1200. What might be the most notable forms of art from this early medieval period are the sculptures that ornamented the era's stone churches. Usually incorporated as bas-reliefs (i.e., low-relief carvings), and noted for their lack of polish and fluidity, they depicted ecclesiastical subjects, often with the intention of educating the worshipers.

Early in the 1300s, artists such as Cimabue and Giotto blazed new trails and brought emotional realism into their work in what was later seen as a complete break from Byzantine gloom and rigidity, and an early harbinger of the Renaissance. However, artists in Rome continued to retain reminders of ancient Rome in their work.

The **Italian Renaissance** was born in Florence during the 15th century and almost immediately spread throughout the rest of Italy.

Ghiberti defeated Brunelleschi in a contest to design bronze doors for the Baptistery of the Cathedral in Florence, and in reaction, Brunelleschi designed a dome for the cathedral, which has been hailed ever since as "a miracle of design." Keenly competitive with events in Florence, ecclesiastical planners in Rome hired Urbino-born Donato Bramante to work on a design for an amplified version of St. Peter's Basilica, the most significant and imposing building of the High Renaissance. Its interior required massive amounts of sculpture and decoration. To fill the void, artists, including Michelangelo, flooded into Rome from throughout Italy.

Perhaps it was in painting, however, that the Renaissance excelled. Artistic giant Raffaello Santi was commissioned to fresco the apartments of Pope Julius II in Rome. Simultaneously, Michelangelo painted the ceiling frescoes of the Sistine Chapel, an assignment that took four backbreaking years to complete. Italy—with infinite input from the patrons and artists in Rome—remained Europe's artistic leader for nearly 200 years.

The transitional period between the Renaissance and the baroque came to be called **"mannerism."** Although Tintoretto remains the most famous of this group, out of this period emerged such other (Rome-based) artists as Giulio Romano, Perin del Vaga, Rosso Fiorentino, and Parmigianino. Although little remains of their work (Rome was sacked and many artworks destroyed or carried away in 1527 during the city's siege by Charles V), their restless and sometimes contorted style soon spread from Rome throughout the rest of Italy.

In the early 17th century and into the 18th century, the **baroque** (meaning absurd or irregular) age altered forever the architectural skyline of Rome (see "Architecture," below). Simultaneously, great artists emerged, such as Bernini, renowned both as a sculptor and painter; Carracci, who decorated the Roman palace of Cardinal Farnese; and Caravaggio, one of the baroque masters of earthy realism and dramatic tension.

Shortly thereafter, the even more flamboyant rococo grew out of the baroque style. The baroque age also represented the high point of *trompe l'oeil* (illusionistic painting) whereby ceilings and walls were painted with disturbingly realistic landscapes that fool the eye with architecturally sophisticated perspectives and angles.

During the 17th, 18th, and 19th centuries, the great light had gone out of art in Italy. Rome in particular, capitalizing on the vast ruins that lay scattered within its perimeter, became a magnet for the **neoclassical** craze sweeping through France, Britain, and Germany. Thousands of foreign and Italian artists descended upon Rome to feed off its 2,000 years of artistic treasures. The era's return to the aesthetic ideals of ancient Greece and Rome helped to fuel the growing sense of pan-Italian nationalism.

By the 19th century, the beacon of artistic creativity was picked up by France, who ushered in a wide array of different artistic traditions (including impressionism) whose tenets were for the most part ignored in Italy.

The **20th century** witnessed the creative apexes of several major Italian artists whose works once again captured the imagination of the world. De Chirico and Modigliani (the latter's greatest contribution lay in a new concept of portraiture) were only two among many. Today, the works of many of Italy's successful futurist and metaphysical painters can be seen within Rome's Galleria Nazionale d'Arte Moderna. Sadly, although many of the works contained therein are world-class art of international stature, they tend to be overlooked in a city whose artworks encompass two millennia of treasures.

ARCHITECTURE   Little remains of the architecture of either the early Latin tribes or the **Etruscans** who conquered them. Despite the lack of it, it's probable that the first exposure of the Romans to large-scale building projects was initiated by these mysterious newcomers from Mesopotamia, and it's highly probable that much of their actual construction was performed by slaves. Historical writings by the Romans themselves record descriptions of their powerful walls, bridges, and aqueducts, which were very similar to the Mycenaean architecture of Crete.

As Rome asserted its own identity and overpowered its Etruscan masters, it borrowed heavily from themes already established by Etruscan artists and architects. In time, however, the Romans discovered and imitated the graceful proportions and aesthetic principles of Greek architecture.

The Roman Empire's architecture flourished magnificently, advancing in size, majesty, and efficient functionalism far beyond the architectural examples set by the Greeks. Part of this is credited to the development of a primitive form of concrete, but even more important was the fine-tuning of the arch. Monumental buildings were erected, each an embodiment of the strength, power, and careful organization of the empire itself. Among the greatest of these were Trajan's Forum and Caracalla's Baths, both in Rome. Equally magnificent were Rome's Colosseum and a building that later greatly influenced the Palladians during the Renaissance, Hadrian's Pantheon.

Of course, these immense achievements were made possible by two major resources: almost limitless funds pouring in from all regions of the empire, and an unending supply of slaves captured during military campaigns abroad.

The engineering concepts that were developed for the empire's aqueducts, amphitheaters, bridges, and temples were adapted after the Christianization of Rome for the construction of early Catholic and Byzantine churches. Making ample use of marble columns and granite blocks pilfered from crumbling pagan temples, the city's architects adapted the vaults, domes, and half-domes of the collapsed empire.

The art and architecture that developed became known as early medieval or **Romanesque.** In its many thick-walled variations, it flourished between A.D. 1100 and A.D. 1200. In Rome, there developed the basilica, whose form permeated the construction of most churches until the beginning of the Gothic age. Basilicas, in the purest (i.e., earliest) forms, contained a broad nave flanked with columns and aisles that end in a semicircular apse. Wooden trussed roofs were later replaced with roofs of vaulted masonry, which sheltered interiors containing mosaics and/or painted frescoes.

As the appeal of Romanesque faded, the **Gothic** or late medieval style encouraged a vast increase in both the quantities and preconceptions of large-scale buildings. Although the Gothic age continued to be profoundly religious, many secular buildings, including an array of palaces intended to show off the increasing wealth and prestige of Italy's ruling families, were erected. However, in Rome, adherence to the tried and true inspiration of ancient Rome always seemed to hold a greater appeal.

The **Renaissance,** though it began in Florence, soon spread quickly through the psyches of the builders and architects of Rome. Fueled by competition with the other Italian city-states, and eager to entrench their authority with a stupendous physical setting, the Roman popes commissioned some of the most talented architects of their day (including Bramante, Michelangelo, and Bernini) to design St. Peter's Basilica. The most significant and imposing building of the High Renaissance, St. Peter's has remained ever since as the very symbol of the papacy itself.

During the early 17th century and into the 18th century, the extreme ornamentation and neoclassical inspiration of the **baroque movement** swept through Italian architecture. Its development was linked to the much-needed reforms and restructuring of the Catholic church that followed the Protestant Reformation. Many great Roman churches and palazzi were constructed during this period, many richly ornamented with swirls of stucco, plaster, and gilt, and many of them inspired by the dignity of the imperial architecture of ancient Rome.

The even more flamboyant **rococo,** where interiors seemed to shimmer within flickering flames of gilt, grew out of the baroque style. During this era, much of the skyline of Rome was altered forever as architects, such as Bernini, added their theatrical and much-copied flair to such monuments as the piazza Navona, the statues of the Ponte Sant'Angelo, and the piazza that prefaces the entrance to St. Peter's Basilica. Within about a century, such secular and much-visited monuments as the Trevi Fountain (completed in 1762) and the Spanish Steps perpetuated Rome's love affair with the baroque.

IMPRESSIONS

Neque protinus uno est Condita Roma die. (Rome was not built in a day.)
—Pietro Angelo Manzolli (Palingenius, Pseud.), *Zodiacus Vitae*

Oh! Rome, tremendous, who, beholding thee,
Shall not forget the bitterest private grief
That e'er made havoc of one single life?
—Fanny Kemble (Mrs. Butler), *A Year Of Consolation,* 1847

During the 19th century, architects based many of their designs on simplified versions of **neoclassical** models, which even today seem to permeate the terrain of Rome. This allegiance to grander days coincided gracefully with the passions of pan-Italian nationalism. Because neoclassicism was inspired by the landscapes of Rome itself, and because it had long ago become an international style much copied throughout the rest of Europe and the Americas, it did little to fundamentally alter the landscapes of Rome.

Despite the intense building program that was initiated in Rome following the establishment of the city as the capital of a unified Italy, only one 19th-century building stands out as inappropriate to its setting and circumstances: the much-ridiculed monument to Victor Emmanuel II. Pompously oversized, and in glaring contrast to the ruins of ancient Rome, which lie nearby, it dominated (and still dominates) its neighborhood with acres of snow-colored marble and sentimental reminders of the heroic age.

During the **20th century,** Rome endured many of the grandiose (some say egomaniacal) building schemes of Mussolini. At least part of the capital's layout is credited to the dictator's dreams for such triumphant promenades as the via della Conciliazione, the via Cavour, and the via dei Fori Imperiali, Mussolini's most enduring complex of buildings is the EUR (*Esposizione Universale Romana*), a grandiose project intended as a permanent showcase of the glory of Rome. Planned for an opening in 1942 (an event that was delayed by World War II), its construction began anew in 1952. Set four miles south of the city center, it now contains a permanent amusement park (Luna Park) and a sports stadium (the Palazzo dello Sport) built for the 1960 Olympics. The 330-foot span of its dome was designed by Italian architect and engineer Pier Luigi Nervi.

In recent times, Italy has become a leader in advanced and witty interpretations of modern architecture. One good example is Rome's Stazione Termini (Central Railway Station). Unfortunately, despite its use of cantilevered concrete, its virtues (and the virtues of almost every other modern building in Rome) are almost completely overshadowed by the glories of Rome's older, and more impressive, monuments.

LITERATURE   Since Dante first recorded *The Divine Comedy,* the Tuscan, rather than the Roman, dialect has been considered the most desirable of the Italian idioms for the transmission of literary ideas. Despite the victory of the Florentines in this regard, the history of Roman literature goes back to the earliest recorders of the exploits of the ancient generals. These men of letters included Virgil, whose epics have been judged equal to the epics of the earlier, Greek-born Homer. Virgil's most-studied work, *The Aeneid,* crafted a creation myth for Rome that was appropriate for the city's expanding military glory. (Linking Rome to the heirs of the demolished city of Troy, he hit upon an inspired subject of guaranteed interest to his readers.)

One of the early Roman republic's most respected (and believed) historians was Livy, whose history of early Rome is more or less accepted as the authorized version. Later, Julius Caesar himself (perhaps the most pivotal—and biased—eyewitness of these events) wrote accounts of his military exploits in Gaul and of his transformation of the Roman republic into a dictatorship.

Latin prose is said to have reached its most perfect form with the cadences of Cicero. His *De Re Publica* expounds on theories of government, while *Brutus* was especially appreciated by 18th- and 19th-century statesmen for its comments on the art of oratory. Catullus's poetry presented romantic passion in startlingly vivid ways, which continue to shock anyone who bothers to translate them. By around 170 A.D., Marcus Aurelius's stoic *Meditations* seemed to parallel during the decline of Rome the despair of the kings of France on the eve of the French Revolution ("après mor le déluge").

After the collapse of Rome, very little was written of any enduring merit, with the exception of Christian Latin-language writings. Dante Alighieri (1265–1321) broke the thousand-year silence with the difficult-to-translate *terza rima* of *The Divine Comedy*. Called the first masterpiece of the then-innovative national language, it places Dante in firm control as the founder of both the Italian language and Italian literature in general.

From this time onward, the history of literature in Rome gracefully parallels the development of Italian literature in general. Medieval Italian literature was represented by religious poetry, secular lyric poetry, and sonnets.

During the Renaissance, Andrea di Pietro (better known as Palladio) and Vasari wrote treatises on the theories of art and architecture, and Niccolò Machiavelli drafted the first completely secular exposition ever written on the art of politics; entitled *Il Principe* (The Prince), it was intended as a primer in statesmanship for a young Medici. Famous goldsmith and philanderer Benvenuto Cellini set new models for introspection in his *Autobiography*, while personalities, such as Leonardo da Vinci, Michelangelo, and Lorenzo de' Medici, wrote and recorded many dozens of sonnets, poems, songs, and observations.

Between 1600 and around 1850, as the reins of international power and creativity shifted from Italy toward France, Britain, Germany, Russia, and the U.S., the literature of Italy took a second tier to such other art forms as music, opera, and architecture. The publication by Alessandro Manzoni (1785–1873) of his romantic epic *I Promessi Sposi* (The Betrothed), published in 1827 and set in 17th-century Italy, signals the birth of the modern Italian novel.

Since the institution of the Nobel Prize for literature in 1901, five Italians have received the coveted prize: Giosuè Carducci, poet and professor of Italian literature at the University of Bologna, in 1906; Grazia Deledda, Sardinia-born writer who used her native island as the subject of her work, in 1926; Luigi Pirandello, Sicily-born dramatist, in 1934; Salvadore Quasimodo, a poet, also a native of Sicily, in 1959; and Eugenio Montale, a journalist, music critic, and poet, in 1975.

MUSIC   Late in the 900s, a Benedictine monk from Arezzo named Guido Monaco invented a musical scale that was used in monasteries for the notation of single-melody, unharmonized, religious chanting known as Gregorian chants. The hierarchies in Rome abundantly approved of these musical forms, and endorsed them as incentives to an understanding of God and an example of proper monastic behavior.

Later in the musical development of Italy, secular (i.e., nonreligious) works were tolerated by the priests and bishops, but rarely encouraged with the same passions that the popes showed for painting, sculpture, and architecture. Recognizing the power of the church, however, most composers were careful to intersperse their secular outpourings with ample doses of religiously inspired works.

A truly idiosyncratic version of Italian music only began to be defined in the late 1600s, perhaps as the church loosened its grip on Italy's creative arts. At that time, Corelli (1653–1713) originated a musical form known as the *concerto grosso* and founded a highly colorful style of violin playing. Scarlatti (1660–1725) refined thematic development of musical scores, popularized the concept of chromatic harmonies, and helped to define the makeup of the operatic orchestra. A few generations later, Boccherini (1743–1805) contributed greatly to sophisticated applications of the chamber orchestra.

Especially important was Venice-born Vivaldi (1678–1741), who was considered one of the most influential European composers of his day. Composer of more than 700 musical works, many of them suitable for performances in churches, he developed techniques that greatly influenced the later compositions of Bach.

Despite the rich body of religious music whose presuppositions were supported by Rome, most musicologists best remember Italy for its opera. In fact, many visitors to Italy consider the opera one of the country's prime tourist attractions. (The opera season in Rome begins in November and continues through May.) In Rome, the Teatro dell'Opera (piazza Beniamino Gigli 1; tel. 481601) is considered one of the city's finest 19th-century buildings, although during July and August many performances are held within the ruined Baths of Caracalla or in historically important churches around town.

Jacopo Peri's *Dafne* (first performed in 1597) is now regarded as the world's first opera. Claudio Monteverdi (1567–1643), however, is viewed as the father of modern opera; his masterpiece was *L'Incoronazione di Poppea* (1642). Later, even the previously mentioned Vivaldi, although best remembered for his orchestral works, composed 43 different operas, the most frequently performed of which is *Armida al campo d'Egitto* (1718).

From this rich musical tradition arose the *bel canto* (beautiful singing) method of the 18th and early 19th centuries. The movement's most famous adherent was Vincenzo Bellini (1801–35), whose masterpiece was *Norma* (composed just four years before his early death). During the 19th century, opera, particularly in its musically ornate Neapolitan version, spread around the world. Bellini was followed in the bel canto tradition by Rossini (1792–1868), who is best known for his sparkling and witty *The Barber of Seville.*

Romantic opera also flowered, particularly within the works of Donizetti, best known for his *Lucia di Lammermoor,* which many years later brought Joan Sutherland world-class fame at New York's Metropolitan Opera.

It was Giuseppe Verdi (1813–1901) who became the greatest Italian operatic composer. He is credited (along with Richard Wagner) with developing opera into a fully integrated art. In all, Verdi produced 26 operas, including *Il Trovatore, La Traviata, Rigoletto, Un Ballo in Maschere,* and *Aïda.*

Verdi's musical heir was Giacomo Puccini (1858–1924), who trained in Milan, which had become the operatic headquarters of Italy. His most popular operas include *Madame Butterfly, La Bohème, Tosca,* and the incomplete *Turandot* (completed after Puccini's death by his musical disciple, Franco Alfano). Enrico Caruso (1873–1921), one of the most famous operatic tenors of all time, based his career on his interpretations of Puccini operas.

In the early 1900s, Italy had one of the wealthiest traditions of folk music in the world. (Though Rome possessed a goodly share of dialectal songs, Naples was particularly productive—producing such globally popular songs as "O Sole Mio" and "Funicule Funicula.") However, the effect of television, radio, and cultural inroads from the rest of the world has obliterated at least some of these musical traditions.

In the 1950s and early 1960s, Ornella Vanoni and Gino Paoli, Domenico Modugno ("Volare"), Mine, and Peppino di Capri provided much of the music for the sybaritic but fleeting moment known ever after as *La Dolce Vita.* Then, Italy (and especially Rome) never seemed as carefree, stylish, and romantic as it enjoyed an economic boom and the devoted patronage of the world's most beautiful people.

Today, jazz, rock, blues, folk music, and (to a lesser degree) heavy metal flourish in Rome in patterns that frequently parallel similar developments in the U.S. and the rest of Europe. Italy always manages, however, to infuse the barrage of outside influences with its own particular expression of style.

5 Language & Cultural Life

LANGUAGE   Italian, of course, is the official language of Rome, but it's spoken with a particular dialect that has always given linguistic delight to anyone born within the city's precincts. Although the purest form of Italian is said to be spoken in Tuscany (a legacy of medieval author Dante Alighieri, who composed *The Divine Comedy* in the Tuscan dialect), the Romans have always maintained a fierce pride in the particular stresses, intonations, and vocabulary of their own native speech patterns.

Regardless of the dialect, Italian is probably more directly derived from Latin than any of the other Romance languages. Many older Italians had at least a rudimentary grasp of ecclesiastical (church) Latin because of the role of Latin in the Catholic mass. Today, however, as the vernacular Italian has replaced the use of Latin in most church services, the ancient tongue can be read and understood only by a diminishing number of academics and priests.

Linguists consider Italian the most "musical" and mellifluous language in the West, and the Italian language easily lends itself to librettos and operas. The language is a phonetic one; that means you pronounce a word the way it is written, unlike many other languages, including English. It has been said that if an Italian sentence sounds "off key," it is because the grammar is incorrect.

The Italian alphabet is not as extensive as the English alphabet in that it doesn't normally use such letters as *J, K, W, X,* and *Y.* However, Italians discovered the *J* with the advent of jeans during the postwar era, although they often pronounce the word "yeans."

Even as late as World War II, many Italian soldiers couldn't understand each other, as some men spoke only in their local dialects. But with the coming of television, more and more Italians speak the language with similarity.

CULTURAL LIFE   Rome is one of the world's leading cultural centers. It is a city of music, with concerts performed in venues that range from medieval churches and Renaissance palazzi to parks and cloisters to piazze and local auditoriums.

Even more popular with Romans is opera, which continues as a growth industry among new legions of the young every year. The most exciting operas are staged every summer at the Terme di Caracalla; the season lasts from the first of July to the middle of August. Nowhere on earth is Verdi's *Aïda* performed with more gusto than at these former imperial baths.

Pirandello and Goldoni in the theater remain perennial favorites, although Roman audiences are also quite familiar with the works of Shakespeare, particularly those plays using Italy as a background—especially *Romeo and Juliet.*

The RAI—Radio Televisione Italiana, the state network—dazzles Roman audiences with a symphony orchestra and chorus, rated among the finest on earth. The Rome orchestra most often performs its regular season at the Foro Italico. Annually a special concert is staged for the pope, either at St. Peter's or within the precincts of the Vatican.

There is no national theater; instead, different theater companies perform in repertory in Rome. Of course, you'll need to have a good understanding of the Italian language to appreciate these programs. Outstanding Roman theater companies include Teatro di Roma, Teatro di Genoa, and Centro Teatrale Bresciano.

6 Religion, Myth & Folklore

RELIGION   Rome is the world's greatest ecclesiastical center. Few regions on earth have been as religiously prolific as Italy has, and few regions have influenced Christianity the way Italy has.

Even before the Christianization of the Roman Empire, the ancient Romans artfully (and sometimes haphazardly) mingled their allegiance to the deities of ancient Greece with whatever religious fad happened to be imported at the moment. After its zenith, ancient Rome resembled a theological hodgepodge of dozens of religious and mystical cults, which found fertile soil amid a crumbling empire. Eastern (especially Egyptian) cults became especially popular, and dozens of emperors showed no aversion to defining themselves as gods and enforcing worship by their subjects.

In A.D. 313, the emperor Constantine signed the edict of Milan, stopping the hitherto merciless persecution of Christians. (He also converted to Christianity himself.) Since then, Italy has adhered in the main to Catholicism.

Today the huge majority (99%) of Italians describe themselves as Roman Catholic, although their form of allegiance to Catholicism varies widely according to individual conscience. Despite the fact that only about one-third of the country attends mass with any regularity, and only about 10% claim to receive the sacrament at Easter, the country is innately—to its very core—favored by the Catholic tradition. That does not always mean that the populace follows the dictates of the Vatican. An example of this is that, despite the pressure by the Holy See against voting in favor of Communist party members (in 1949, the Vatican threatened to excommunicate—*ipso facto*—any Italian who voted for Communist or Communist-inspired candidates), the Communist platform in Italy used to receive up to 33% of the popular vote in certain elections.

Modern Italy's adherence to Catholicism is legally stressed by a law enacted in 1848 by the Kingdom of Sardinia (later reaffirmed by the Lateran Treaty) that states "The Catholic apostolic and Roman religion is the sole religion of the (Italian) State." The same treaties, however, give freedom of worship to other religions, but identify Rome as "the center of the Catholic world and a place of pilgrimage," and confer onto the State of Italy the responsibility of safeguarding the security of the pope and his emissaries, and respecting church property and church law in the treatment of certain matters, such as requests for divorces or annulments.

Significantly, throughout history Italy has produced more upperechelon leaders to staff the Vatican than any other country in the world. Only recently, with the election of a Polish-born pope

IMPRESSIONS

Rome's just a city like anywhere else. A vastly overrated city, I'd say. It trades on belief just as Stratford trades on Shakespeare.
—Anthony Burgess, *Inside Mr. Enderby,* 1963

(John Paul II), has a pattern of almost complete domination of the papacy by Italian prelates been altered. Because of the sometimes inconvenient juxtaposition of the Vatican within the administrative capital of Italy, the Lateran Treaty of February 11, 1929, which was confirmed by Article 7 of the constitution of the Italian republic, recognizes the Vatican City State as an independent and sovereign state and established and defines its relationship to the Italian State. That treaty, originally signed by Mussolini, lasted until 1984.

MYTH   Although modern visitors know Rome as the headquarters of Catholicism, the city also developed some of the world's most influential bodies of mythology.

During the days when Rome was little more than a cluster of sheepherder's villages, a body of gods were worshiped whose characters remained basically unchanged throughout the course of Roman history. To this panoply, however, were added and assimilated the deities of other conquered territories (especially Greece) until the roster of Roman gods bristled with imports from around the Mediterranean. In its corrupted (later) version, the list of gods grew impossibly unwieldy as more-or-less demented emperors forced their own deification and worship upon the Roman masses.

After the Christianization of Europe, the original and ancient gods retained their astrological significance as literal positions within the starry firmament. They also provided poetic fodder for endless literary and lyrical comparisons.

A brief understanding of each of the major god's functions will enhance insights during explorations of the city's museums and excavations.

Apollo was the representative of music, the sun, prophecy, healing, the arts, and philosophy. He was the brother of **Diana** (symbol of chastity and goddess of the hunt, the moon, wild animals, and later, of commerce); and the son of **Jupiter** (king of the gods and god of lightning), by a lesser female deity named **Leto. Cupid (Eros)** was the god of falling in love.

Juno (Hera), the wife of Jupiter, was attributed with vague but awesome powers and a very human sense of outrage and jealousy. Her main job seemed to be wreaking vengeance against the hundreds of nymphs seduced by Jupiter, and punishment of the thousands of children he supposedly fathered.

Mars, the dignified but bloodthirsty god of war, was reputed to be the father of **Romulus,** cofounder of Rome.

Mercury (Hermes), symbol of such Geminis (twins) as Romulus and Remus, was one of the most diverse and morally ambiguous of the gods. He served as the guide to the dead as they approached the underworld, and as the patron of eloquence, travel, negotiation, diplomacy, good sense, prudence, and (to a very limited extent) thieving.

Neptune, god of the sea, was attributed with almost no moral implications, but represents solely the watery domains of the earth.

Minerva (Athena) was the goddess of wisdom, arts and crafts, and (occasionally) of war. A goddess whose allure was cerebral and whose discipline was severe, she wears a helmet and breastplate emblazoned with the head of **Medusa** (the snake-haired monster whose gaze could turn men into stone). During the Renaissance, she became a symbol much associated, oddly enough, with the wisdom and righteousness of the Christian popes.

Venus, whose mythological power grew as the empire expanded, was the goddess of gardens and every conceivable variety of love. She was reportedly the mother of **Aeneas,** mythical ancestor of the ancient Romans. Both creative and destructive, Venus's appeal and duality are as primeval as the earth itself.

Ceres (Dometer), goddess of the earth and of the harvest, mourned for half of every year (during winter) when her daughter **Proserpine** abandoned her to live in the house of **Pluto,** god of death and the underworld.

Vulcan (Haphaestos) was the half-lame god of metallurgy, volcanoes, and furnaces, whose activities at his celestial forge crafted superweapons for an array of military heroes beloved by the ancient Romans.

Finally, **Bacchus (Dionysos),** the god of wine, undisciplined revelry, drunkenness, and absence of morality, gained an increasing importance within Rome as the city grew decadent and declined.

FOLKLORE Perhaps the most formal manifestation of folk rituals in all of Rome is the Commedia dell'Arte. Although it greatly influenced theatrical styles of France in the 17th century, it is unique to Italy. The plots almost always develop and resolve an imbroglio where the beautiful wife of an older curmudgeon dallies with a handsome swain, against the advice of her maid, and much to the amusement of the husband's valet.

Italy, even before the Christian era, was a richly religious land ripe with legends and myths. Modern Italy blends superstition, ancient myths and fables, and Christian symbolism in richly folkloric ways. Throughout Rome, rites of passage, such as births, first communions, marriages, and deaths, are linked to endless rounds of family celebrations, feasts, and gatherings. Faithful Romans might genuflect when in front of a church, when entering a church, when viewing an object of religious veneration (a relic of a saint, for example), or when hearing a statement that might tempt the Devil to meddle in someone's personal affairs.

7 Food & Drink

MEALS & DINING CUSTOMS You'll find restaurants of international renown here and an infinite number of *trattorie* and *rosticcerie* where good meals are offered at moderate prices. The main meals are served from noon to 3pm and 8 to 11pm, but food can also be obtained at other hours at the more informal trattorie and rosticcerie. Many restaurants throughout the country offer fixed-price meals that include two courses, a dessert, a house wine, and service. For more details, refer to Chapter 5, "Rome Dining."

THE CUISINE   Many visitors from North America erroneously think of Italian cuisine as limited. Of course, everybody's heard of minestrone, spaghetti, chicken cacciatore, and spumoni ice cream. But the chefs of Italy hardly confine themselves to such a limited repertoire.

Throughout your Roman holiday, you'll encounter such savory viands as *zuppa di pesce* (a soup or stew of various fish, cooked in white wine and herb flavored), *cannelloni* (tube-shaped pasta baked with any number of stuffings), *riso col gamberi* (rice with shrimp, peas, and mushrooms, flavored with white wine and garlic), *scampi alla griglia* (grilled prawns, one of the best-tasting, albeit expensive, dishes in the city), *quaglie con risotto e tartufi* (quail with rice and truffles), *lepre alla cacciatore* (hare flavored with tomato sauce and herbs), *zabaglione* (a cream made with sugar, egg yolks, and marsala), *gnocchi alla romana* (potato-flour dumplings with a sauce made with meat and covered with grated cheese), *stracciatella* (chicken broth with eggs and grated cheese), *abbacchio* (baby spring lamb, often roasted over an open fire), *saltimbocca alla romana* (literally "jump-in-your-mouth"—thin slices of veal with cheese, ham, and sage), *fritto alla romana* (a mixed fry that's likely to include everything from brains to artichokes), *carciofi alla romana* (tender artichokes cooked with mint and garlic, and flavored with white wine), *fettuccine all'uovo* (egg noodles served with butter and cheese), *zuppa di cozze o vongole* (a hearty bowl of mussels or clams cooked in broth), *fritta di scampi e calamaretti* (baby squid and prawns fast-fried), *fragoline* (wild strawberries, in this case from the Alban Hills), and *finocchio* (or fennel, a celerylike raw vegetable, the flavor of anisette, often eaten as a dessert and in salads).

Incidentally, except in the south, Italians do not use as much garlic in their food as most foreigners seem to believe. Most northern Italian dishes are butter based. Virgin olive oil is preferred in the south. Spaghetti and meatballs, by the way, is not an Italian dish, although certain restaurants throughout the country have taken to serving it "for homesick Americans."

Rome also has many specialty restaurants that represent every major region of the country. The dishes they serve carry such designations as *alla genovese, alla milanese, alla napolitana, alla fiorentina,* and *alla bolognese.*

WINES & OTHER DRINKS   Italy is the largest wine-producing country in the world; as far back as 800 B.C. the Etruscans were vintners. It is said that more soil is used in Italy for the cultivation of grapes than for food. Many Italian farmers produce wine just for their own consumption or for their relatives in a big city. However, it wasn't until 1965 that laws were enacted to guarantee regular consistency in winemaking. Wines regulated by the government are labeled DOC (*Denominazione di Origine Controllata*). If you see DOCG on a label (the "G" means *guarantita*), that means even better quality control.

Latium (Rome) is a major wine-producing region of Italy. Many of the local wines come from the Castelli Romani, the hill towns around Rome. Horace and Juvenal sang the praises of Latium wines even in imperial times. These wines, experts agree, are best drunk when young, and they are most often white, mellow, and dry (or else "demi-sec"). There are seven different types, including **Falerno** (yellowish straw in color) and **Cecubo** (often served with roast meat). Try also **Colli Albani** (straw-yellow with amber tints and served with both fish and meat). The golden-yellow wines of **Frascati** are famous, produced both in a demi-sec and sweet variety, the latter served with dessert.

Romans drink other libations as well. Perhaps their most famous drink is **Campari,** bright red in color and herb flavored, with a quinine bitterness to it. It's customary to serve it with ice cubes and soda.

Beer is also made in Italy and, in general, it is lighter than that served in Germany. If you order beer in a bar or restaurant, chances are it will be an imported beer, unless you specify otherwise, for which you will be charged accordingly. Some famous names in European beer making now operate plants in Italy, where the brew has been "adjusted" to Italian taste.

High-proof **grappa** is made from the "leftovers" after the grapes have been pressed. Many Romans drink this before or after dinner (some put it into their coffee). To an untrained foreign palate, it often appears rough and harsh; some say it's an acquired taste.

Italy has many **brandies** (according to an agreement with France, it is not supposed to use the word "cognac" in labeling them). A popular one is Vecchia Romagna.

Other popular drinks include several **liqueurs,** to which the Romans are addicted. Try herb-flavored Strega, or perhaps an Amaretto tasting of almonds. One of the best known is Maraschino, taking its name from a type of cherry used in its preparation. Galliano is also herb flavored, and Sambuca (anisette) is made of aniseed and is often served with a "fly" (coffee bean) in it. On a hot day, a true Roman orders a vermouth, Cinzano, with a twist of lemon, ice cubes, and a squirt of soda water.

8   Recommended Books, Films & Recordings

Books

GENERAL & HISTORY   Luigi Barzini's *The Italians* (Macmillan, 1964), should almost be required reading for anyone contemplating a trip to Rome. Critics have hailed it as the liveliest analysis yet of the Italian character.

Edward Gibbon's *The History of the Decline and Fall of the Roman Empire* is published in six volumes, but Penguin issues a passable abridgement. Gibbon issued the first volume in 1776. It has been hailed as a masterpiece and considered one of the greatest histories every written. No one has ever recaptured the saga of Rome's glory the way that Gibbon did.

Giuliano Procacci surveys the spectrum in his *History of the Italian People* (Harper & Row, 1973), which provides an encompassing look at how Italy became a nation.

If you like your history short, readable, and condensed, try *A Short History of Italy,* edited by H. Hearder and D. P. Waley (Cambridge University Press, 1963).

One of the best books on the long history of the papacy—detailing its excesses, triumphs, defeats, and most vivid characters—is Michael Walsh's *An Illustrated History of the Popes: Saint Peter to John Paul II* (St. Martin's Press, 1980).

The roots of modern Italy are explored in Christopher Hibbert's *Garibaldi and His Enemies: The Clash of Arms and Personalities in the Making of Italy* (Penguin, 1989).

In the 20th century, the most fascinating period in Italian history was the rise and fall of Fascism, as detailed in countless works. Try Vittorio De Fiori's *Mussolini, The Man of Destiny: Studies in Fascism, Ideology and Practice* (AMS Press, 1982). One of the best biographies of Il Duce is Denis M. Smith's *Mussolini: A Biography* (Random House, 1983). Eugen Weber writes of *Varieties of Fascism: Doctrines of Revolution in the Twentieth Century* (Krieger, 1982). Stein Larsen edited *Who Were the Fascists? Social Roots of European Fascism* (Oxford University Press, 1981). With the rise of fascists within the Italian government, this book is being read with even more interest in the 1990s.

One subject that's always engrossing is the Mafia, which is detailed in Pino Arlacchi's *Mafia Business: The Mafia Ethic and the Spirit of Capitalism* (Routledge, Chapman & Hall, 1987).

William Murray's *The Last Italian: Portrait of a People* (Prentice Hall, 1991) is the writer's second volume of essays on his favorite subject—Italy, its people and civilization. The *New York Times* called it "partly a lover's keen, observant diary of his affair."

ART & ARCHITECTURE   Giorgio Vasari's *The Lives of the Most Eminent Italian Architects, Painters, and Sculptors* was originally published in 1550 and was enlarged in 1568. In spite of some fanciful inventions, it remains the definitive work on Renaissance artists, from Cimabue to Michelangelo. Penguin Classics issues a paperback abridged version, called *Lives of the Artists* (1985).

T. W. Potter provides one of the best accounts of art and architecture of Rome in *Roman Italy* (University of California Press, 1987), which is also illustrated.

Another good book on the same subject is *Roman Art and Architecture,* by Mortimer Wheeler (World of Art Series, Thames & Hudson, 1990).

Rudolf Wittkower covers *Art and Architecture in Italy 1600–1750* (Penguin, 1980) rather exhaustively.

FICTION & BIOGRAPHY   John Hersey's Pulitzer Prize winner, *A Bell for Adano* (Knopf, 1944), is now a classic and is frequently reprinted. It is a well-written and disturbing story of the American invasion of Italy.

Benvenuto Cellini's *Autobiography,* also available in Penguin Classics, was first printed in Italy in 1728, although Cellini lived from 1500 to 1571. It's a Renaissance romp, filled with gossip and interesting details, so much so that it has been compared to a novel. It launched the tide of the romantic movement.

Irving Stone's *The Agony and the Ecstasy* (Doubleday, 1961), which was filmed with Charlton Heston playing Michelangelo, is the easiest to read and the most pop version of the life of this great artist; yet it contains much useful information, with a rather brilliant section on the creation of Michelangelo's most famous statue, *David.*

Dante's *The Divine Comedy* is famed throughout the world. It is a brilliant synthesis of the medieval Christian world view. *The Inferno* in Volume I was issued by Penguin in 1984, *Purgatory* in Volume II was published by Penguin in 1985, and *Paradiso* in Volume III was published by Penguin in 1986.

Giovanni Boccaccio (1313–75) has delighted readers ever since the publication of his *Decameron* (Norton, 1983), a collection of romantic and often racy tales.

Giorgio Bassani, born in 1916, provides the bourgeois milieu of a Jewish community under Mussolini in *The Garden of the Finzi-Contini* (Harcourt Brace Jovanovich, 1977).

The novels of Alberto Moravia, born in 1907, are classified as neorealism. Moravia is one of the best-known Italian writers read in English. Notable works include *Roman Tales* (Farrar, Straus, and Cudahy, 1957), *The Woman of Rome* (Penguin, 1957; also available in the Playboy paperback series), and *The Conformist* (Greenwood Press, 1975).

First published in 1959, when it caused a scandal, Pier Paolo Pasolini's *A Violent Life* (Pantheon, 1991) is a novel written by the controversial filmmaker. Once viewed with disdain, it is now considered a classic of postwar Italian fiction.

For the most recent look at one of the movers and shakers in Italy, you might enjoy Alan Friedman's *Agnelli and the Network of Italian Power* (Harrap, 1989).

TRAVEL   H. V. Morton's *A Traveler in Italy* (Methuen, 1964) is a towering work by one of the world's most widely read travel writers who has a rare sense of history.

Many great writers—when faced with the challenge of Italy—decided to become travel writers. These have included Charles Dickens who wrote *Pictures from Italy* (Ecco Press, 1988), a classic 19th-century account of the Grand Tour, going from Tuscany to Naples via Rome. Wolfgang Goethe's *Italian Journey* (Penguin, 1982) devotes more attention to Roman antiquities, and Henry James's *Italian Hours* (1909) is young James at his best, capturing the special atmosphere of Italy. It is currently issued by Ecco Press.

D. H. Lawrence and Italy (Viking Press, 1972) is three classic Italian travelogues collected in a single volume, including *Sea and Sardinia* and *Twilight in Italy.* It also includes *Etruscan Places,* which was published posthumously. Lawrence writes of a way of life that was disappearing even as he wrote the work.

Films

Italian films have never regained the glory they enjoyed in the postwar era. The "golden oldies" are still the best (often found in the classics section of your local video store and still shown on TV).

Roberto Rossellini's *Rome, Open City* (1946) influenced Hollywood's *films noirs* of the late 1940s. Set in a poor section of occupied Rome, the film tells the story of a partisan priest and a Communist who aid the resistance.

Vittorio De Sica's *Bicycle Thief* (1948) achieved world renown. Also set in one of Rome's poor districts, it tells of the destruction of a child's illusions and the solitude of a steel worker.

The late Federico Fellini burst into Italian cinema with his highly individual style, beginning with *La Strada* (1954) and going on to such classics as *Juliet of the Spirits* (1965), *Amarcord* (1974), and *The City of Women* (1980). *La Dolce Vita* (1961) helped to define an era.

Marxist, homosexual, and practicing Catholic, Pier Paolo Pasolini was the most controversial of Roman filmmakers until his mysterious murder in 1975. Explicit sex scenes in *Decameron* (1971) made it a world box-office hit.

Bernardo Bertolucci, once an assistant to Pasolini, achieved fame with such films as *The Conformist* (1970), based on the novel by Moravia. His *1900* is an epic spanning 20th-century Italian history and politics. One of his biggest international films was *Last Tango in Paris* (1971), starring Marlon Brando.

Michelangelo Antonioni swept across the screens of the world with his films of psychological anguish, including *La Notte* (1961), *L'Avventura* (1964), and *The Red Desert* (1964).

A Neapolitan director, Francesco Rosi became known for semidocumentary films, exploring such subjects as the Mafia in *Salvatore Giuliano* (1962) and the army in *Just Another War* (1970). His *Three Brothers* (1980) examines three different political attitudes, as the brothers have a reunion at their mother's funeral in Apulia.

Mediterraneo, directed by Gabriele Salvatores, was a whimsical comedy that won an Oscar for Best Foreign Language Film in 1991. It tells the story of eight Italian soldiers stranded on a Greek island in World War II.

Giuseppe Tornatore, who achieved such fame with *Cinema Paradiso,* which won the Academy Award for best foreign language film of 1989, directed one of three vignettes in the 1992 film *Especially on Sunday.*

The Taviani brothers, Paolo and Vittorio, both directors, created a stir in 1994 with the release of their film *Fiorile.* Set in their native Tuscany, it supposedly was a local folktale passed on by their mother. The film is a multigenerational saga.

Although directors more than stars have dominated Italian cinema, three actors have emerged to gain worldwide fame, including Marcello Mastroianni, star of such hits as *La Dolce Vita* (1961), and Sophia Loren, whose best film is considered *Two Women* (1961). Mastroianni was Fellini's favorite male actor and he starred him once again in *8¹/₂*. Anna Magnani not only starred in Italian films, but made many American films as well, including *The Rose Tattoo* (1955), with Burt Lancaster, and *The Fugitive Kind* (1960), with Marlon Brando.

Recordings

MEDIEVAL & RENAISSANCE MUSIC   Although the medieval Benedictine, Guido Monaco of Arezzo, was a musical theorist rather than a composer, his notational system was widely adopted by monasteries throughout medieval Italy. A recording that might expose you to the fruit of his labors is *Sunday Vespers/Vespers of the Madonna,* recorded by S. Giorgio Maggiore Schola Choir, G. Ernetti, conductor (Cetra Records LPU 0046). Religious music was greatly enhanced several centuries later by the compositions of Palestrina, whose work is admirably recorded in Missa de Beata Virgine (Three Motets) sung by the Spandauer Kantorei, conducted by Martin Behrmann (Turnabout TV 34-309).

Very few (if any) recordings of what is regarded as the world's first opera, *Dafne,* are easily available, but a more popular choral work by the same Renaissance composer, Jacopo Peri, is *Euridice,* sung by the Milan Polyphonic Chorus (I Solisti di Milano), conducted by Angelo Ephrikian (Orpheus Recordings OR 344-345-S).

One well-received interpretation of Monteverdi's famous vocal work *L'Incoronazione di Poppes* was recorded by the Concentus Musicus Wien, conducted by Nicholas Harnoncourt (Telefunken 6.35-247 HB). By the same composer, but in a different genre, is Monteverdi's *Seventh Book of Madrigals,* sung by an Italian vocal quartet known as the Ensemble Concerto (Tactus TAC 560 31103). An excellent collection of the late Renaissance's sonatas, canzonettas, and madrigals, played on original Renaissance instruments, is entitled *Music from the Time of Guido Reni,* (Guido Reni, born 1575 and died 1642, was a Renaissance painter who probably caused more public discord because of his philandering and political intrigues than any other in Italian history. He was eventually exiled from Rome in 1622.) This particular musical collection of works by this artist's musical contemporaries was recorded by the Aurora Ensemble (Tactus TAC 56012001).

A good collection of Italian cantatas composed by masters of the 18th century is *Il Lamento d'Olympia.* This includes vocal selections by Scarlatti and Bononcini, sung by mezzo-soprano Gloria Banditelli (Tactus TAC 67012001).

ORCHESTRAL & OPERATIC WORKS   The musical output of Italian composers greatly increased, and its orchestration grew more complex, beginning around 1700. One excellent (and exhaustive) overview of the work of Corelli is his *Complete Works,* recorded by the Academia Byzantina, conducted by Carlo Chiarappa (Europa Musica Eur 350-202).

Italy has produced stellar virtuoso performers who have become world-class experts on specific instruments. (Paganini, born 1782, on his violin; Bottesini, born 1821, on his double bass; and Cherubini, born 1760, on his harpsichord are good examples.) Bottesini's *Virtuoso Works for Double-Bass and Strings,* performed by I Solisti Agilani and conducted by Vittorio Antonelli (Nuova Era NUO 6810), might be one of the finest showcases for the double bass anywhere. Cherubini's *Harpsichord Sonatas Nos. 1–6,* performed by Laura Alvini, provides a highly genteel and attractively restrained insight into the work of a conservative Italian classicist who served for several years as court composer to King George III of England.

The best way for most novices to begin an appreciation of opera is to hear an assemblage of great moments of opera accumulated onto one record. A good example contains works by the most evocative and dramatic singer who ever hit a high "C" on the operatic stage, Maria Callas. *La Voce: Historic Recordings of the Great Diva* (Suite SUI 5002) brings together "La Callas's" spectacular arias from *Lucia di Lammermoor, La Traviata, Norma,* and *The Barber of Seville.*

Recordings of complete and unedited operas are even more rewarding. Excellent examples include the following: Bellini's *Norma,* featuring the divine and legendary Maria Callas, accompanied by the orchestra and the chorus of Milan's La Scala, is considered one of the world's great operatic events; Tullio Serafin conducts (Angel Records 3517C/ANG 35148-35150). Giuseppe Verdi's genius can be appreciated through *Nabucco,* performed with Placido Domingo by the Rydl Choir and Orchestra of the Dutch National Opera, conducted by Giuseppe Sinopoli (Deutsche Gramophone DDD 410 512-2-GH2). Also insightful for the vocal techniques of Verdi, his *Complete Songs* is recorded by Renata Scotto (soprano) and Paolo Washington (bass), accompanied by Vincenzo Scalera (piano) (Nuova Era NUO 6855). Rossini's great opera *Il Barbiere di Siviglia* and Puccini's *Tosca,* both recorded in their complete versions by the Turin Opera Orchestra and Chorus, are both conducted by Bruno Campanella (Nuova Era NUO 6760 and Foyer FOY 2023, respectively).

And no compendium of Italian opera would be complete without including the immortal tenor, Luciano Pavarotti, whose interpretations of Verdi's idealistic heroes have become almost definitive. One unusual version of *La Traviata* was recorded early in Pavarotti's meteoric rise to fame. Although later recordings might exhibit greater finesse, the version recorded at the Teatro Municipale in his hometown of Modena on February 7, 1965, is considered particularly memorable and passionate. Considered a classic, this version is still available on a two-cassette collection from C.I.M.E. (PTP-5123-4).

RECENT RELEASES   Only a handful of other countries can compete with Italy for richness of popular musical traditions. Although these traditions have been influenced by popular music from the U.S. and Britain, Italy still retains its distinctive musical flair. Some good examples of the peninsula's (musical) charm can be heard on *Musical Greetings from Italy;* this tuneful collection of Italian folk and folk-dance music is played by the Nordini Musette Orchestra (Standard Colonial Records COL 808). Specific regions of Italy are featured on other recordings, which include *From Sicily with Love (Favorite Sicilian Songs),* sung by local singers and recorded in Italy (Philips 4118); from Tuscany comes *Le Canzoni di Firenze (Traditional Songs of Florence),* by Odoardo Spadaro (RCA NL33027).

Within the field of jazz, Italy also competes effectively. Recorded in Milan, Chet Baker and Italian-born Mike Melillo, with an assemblage of Italian backup musicians, perform a haunting combination of piano and horn on *Symphonically* (Soul Note SN 11 34C). Another notable recording is the *Twin Peaks Soundtrack* by Italian native Angelo Badalamenti and David Lynch. Despite its original destiny as the musical accompaniment for a film, it survives beautifully without its cinematic visuals. It features what was described by critics as a "magical arrangemental blend" including lazy saxophone tracts imposed over finger-snapping rhythms (Warner Bros 7599-26316-1).

Italian pop is well defended in Alice Elisir's album *Alice Elisir* (EMI 64/74-87-014). Her torchy voice and upbeat modern tempos and arrangements evoke fire, tears, and laughter. Nino Buonocore brings a brooding and undeniably sexy male charm to *Le Cite tra le Mani* (EMI 64/79-02-044).

Finally, an album well suited to appeal to both Italian and American audiences is Jerry Vale's *Italian Album,* sung by Italian-American Jerry Vale and including such smile-inducing standbys as "Amore scusa mi" and "Oh Marie" (Columbia C12 30389).

2

Planning a Trip to Rome

THIS CHAPTER IS DEVOTED TO THE WHERE, WHEN, AND HOW OF YOUR TRIP—the advance-planning issues required to get it together and take to the road.

After deciding where to go, most people have two fundamental questions: What will it cost? and How do I get there? This chapter will answer both these questions and also resolve other important issues, such as when to go, what pretrip preparations are needed, where to obtain more information about Rome, and much more.

1 Information, Entry Requirements & Money

Information

Before you go, you can contact the **Italian National Tourist Office** at 630 Fifth Ave., Suite 1565, New York, NY 10111 (☎ **212/245-4822**); 500 N. Michigan Ave., Chicago, IL 60611 (☎ **312/644-0990**); or 12400 Wilshire Blvd., Suite 4550, Los Angeles, CA 90025 (☎ **310/820-0098**). In Canada, contact the Italian National Tourist Office at 1 Place Ville Marie, Montréal, QB H3B3M9 (☎ **514/866-7667**); and in England at 1 Princes St., London W1R 8AY (☎ **0171/408-1254**).

Entry Requirements

DOCUMENTS U.S., Canadian, British, Australian, New Zealand, and Irish citizens with a valid passport do not need a visa to enter Italy if they do not expect to stay more than 90 days and do not expect to work there. Those who, after entering Italy, find that they would like to stay more than 90 days can apply for a permit for an additional stay of 90 days, which as a rule is granted immediately. Check with your nearest Italian consulate.

CUSTOMS Most items designed for personal use can be brought to Rome duty-free. This includes clothing (new and used), books, camping and household equipment, fishing tackle, a sporting gun and 200 cartridges, a pair of skis, two tennis rackets, a portable type-writer, a record player with 10 records, a tape recorder or Dictaphone, baby carriage, two ordinary hand cameras with 10 rolls of film and 24 slides, one movie camera with 10 rolls of film, binoculars, per-sonal jewelry, portable radio set (subject to a small license fee), and 400 cigarettes (two cartons) or a quantity of cigars or pipe tobacco not exceeding 500 grams (1.1 lb.).

A maximum of two bottles of alcoholic beverages per person can be brought in duty-free. The bottles must be opened, however. Spe-cifically, overseas tourists arriving in Italy after having visited other countries will be allowed to carry with them, without any special formality except a verbal declaration, travel souvenirs purchased in said countries up to a total lire value equivalent to $500 (U.S.), in-cluding fine perfumes up to half a liter.

Upon leaving Italy, citizens of the United States who have been outside their own country for 48 hours or more are allowed to bring back home $400 worth of merchandise duty-free—that is, if they have claimed no similar exemption within the past 30 days. If you make purchases in Italy, it's important to keep your receipts. On gifts, the duty-free limit is $50. (For more information on sending gifts home, see Chapter 8, "Shopping A to Z.") **Note:** Antiques, with certification that they are at least 100 years old, are allowed in duty free.

A veterinarian's certificate of good health is required for dogs and cats, and should be obtained by owners in advance of entering Italy. Dogs must be on a leash or muzzled at all times. Other animals must undergo examination at the border or port of entry. Certificates for parrots or other birds subject to psittacosis must state that the country of origin is free of disease. All documents must be certified by a notary public, then by the nearest office of the Italian consulate.

Money

There are no restrictions as to how much foreign currency you can bring into Rome, although visitors should declare the amount brought in; this proves to the Italian Customs Office that the currency came from outside the country and therefore the same amount or less can be taken out. Italian currency taken into or out of Italy may not exceed 200,000 lire in denominations of 50,000 lire or lower.

The basic unit of Italian currency is the **lira** (plural: **lire**). Because of fluctuations in relative values of world currencies, I suggest that you contact any bank for the latest official exchange rate before going to Italy.

Coins are issued in denominations of 10, 20, 100, 500, and 1,000 lire, and bills come in denominations of 1,000 lire, 5,000 lire, 10,000 lire, 100,000 lire, and 500,000 lire.

TRAVELER'S CHECKS   Before leaving home, purchase traveler's checks and arrange to carry some ready cash (usually about $250, depending on your habits and needs). In the event of theft, if the checks are properly documented, the value of your checks will be refunded. Most large banks sell traveler's checks, charging fees that average between 1% and 2% of the value of the checks you buy, although some out-of-the-way banks, in rare instances, have charged as much as 7%. If your bank wants more than a 2% commission, it sometimes pays to call the traveler's check issuers directly for the address of outlets where this commission will cost less.

Issuers sometimes have agreements with groups to sell checks commission-free. For example, Automobile Association of America (AAA) clubs sell American Express checks in several currencies without commission.

American Express (☎ toll free **800/221-7287** in the U.S. and Canada) is one of the largest and most immediately recognized issuers of traveler's checks. No commission is charged to holders of certain types of American Express charge cards. The company issues checks denominated in U.S. dollars, Canadian dollars, British pounds sterling, Swiss francs, French francs, German marks, and Japanese yen. The vast majority of checks sold in North America are

The Lira, The Dollar & The Pound

At this writing, US$1 = approximately 1,670 Italian lire, and this was the rate of exchange used to calculate the dollar values given throughout this book, and within the table below. Depending on literally thousands of economic factors, this rate fluctuates from day to day and may not be the same when you travel to Italy.

Likewise, the ratio of British pounds to lire also fluctuates from time to time, according to complicated factors around the world and within the European Community. At presstime, £1 = approximately 2,450 lire, a ratio reflected in the chart below.

Lire	US$	Brit£	Lire	US$	Brit£
50	.03	2p	15,000	9.00	6.00
100	.06	4p	20,000	12.00	8.00
300	.18	12p	25,000	15.00	10.00
500	.30	20p	30,000	18.00	12.00
700	.42	28p	35,000	21.00	14.00
1,000	.60	40p	40,000	24.00	16.00
1,500	.90	60p	45,000	27.00	18.00
2,000	1.20	80p	50,000	30.00	20.00
3,000	1.80	1.20	100,000	60.00	40.00
4,000	2.40	1.60	125,000	75.00	50.00
5,000	3.00	2.00	150,000	90.00	60.00
6,000	3.60	2.40	200,000	120.00	80.00
7,500	4.50	3.00	250,000	150.00	100.00
10,000	6.00	4.00	500,000	300.00	200.00

denominated in U.S. dollars. For questions or problems that arise outside the U.S. or Canada, contact any of the company's many regional representatives.

Citicorp (☎ toll free **800/645-6556** in the U.S. and Canada, or **813/623-1709**, collect, from anywhere else in the world), issues checks in U.S. dollars, British pounds, German marks, and Japanese yen.

Thomas Cook (☎ toll free **800/223-9920** in the U.S. or **609/987-7300,** collect, from other parts of the world) issues MasterCard traveler's checks denominated in U.S. dollars, British pounds, French francs, German marks, Dutch guilders, Spanish pesetas, Australian dollars, Japanese yen, and Hong Kong dollars. Depending on individual banking laws in each of the various states, some of the above-mentioned currencies might not be available in every outlet.

Interpayment Services (☎ toll free **800/221-2426** in the U.S. or Canada, or **800/453-4284** from most other parts of the world) sells VISA checks sponsored by Barclays Bank and/or Bank of

America at selected branches around North America. Traveler's checks are denominated in U.S. or Canadian dollars, British pounds, Swiss francs, French francs, German marks, and Japanese yen.

Each of these agencies will refund your checks if they are lost or stolen, provided you produce sufficient documentation. When purchasing checks ask about refund hotlines; American Express and Bank of America have the greatest number of offices around the world.

CURRENCY EXCHANGE   For the best exchange rate, go to a bank, not to hotels or shops. Currency and traveler's checks (for which you'll receive a better rate than cash) can be changed at the airport and some travel agencies, such as American Express and Thomas Cook. Note the rates; it can sometimes pay to shop around.

Many hotels in Rome simply will not accept a dollar-denominated check, and if they do, they'll certainly charge for the conversion. In some cases they'll accept countersigned traveler's checks, or a credit card, but if you're prepaying a deposit on hotel reservations, it's cheapest and easiest to pay with a check drawn on an Italian bank.

This can be arranged by a large commercial bank or by a specialist like **Ruesch International,** 825 14th St. NW, Washington, DC 20005 (☎ **202/408-1200,** or toll free **800/424-2923**), which performs a wide variety of conversion-related tasks, usually for only $2 U.S. per transaction.

If you need a check payable in lire, call Ruesch's toll-free number, describe what you need, and note the transaction number given to you. Mail your dollar-denominated personal check (payable to Ruesch International) to their office in Washington, D.C. Upon receipt, the company will mail a check denominated in lire for the financial equivalent, minus the $2 charge. The company does not sell traveler's checks denominated in lire, but can help you with many different kinds of wire transfers and conversion of VAT (Value-Added Tax) refund checks. They'll mail brochures and information packets upon request.

Mutual of Omaha/Travelex, 1225 Frankin Ave., Garden City, NY 11530 (☎ toll free in the U.S. **800/377-0051**) provides foreign currency exchange at 30 airport locations in the U.S. or through the mail. With exchanges of $500 or more, they will guarantee to exchange back up to 30% at the same rate you originally exchanged with no service fee. Annual or short-term flight insurance policies are available starting at $5.

2 When to Go—Climate, Holidays & Events

Climate

The most pleasant times to be in Rome, weatherwise, are spring and fall. In the height of summer it can get quite hot and humid. The temperatures can stay in the 90s for days, but nights are most often comfortably cooler. The high temperatures begin in May, and often

What Things Cost in Rome	U.S. $
Taxi (from the central rail station to piazza di Spagna)	8.80
Subway or public bus (from any point within Rome to any other point)	.70
Local telephone call	.12
Double room at the Hassler (deluxe)	342.00
Double room at the Columbus (moderate)	147.00
Double room at the Hotel Aberdeen (budget)	114.00
Continental breakfast (cappuccino and croissant at most cafés and bars)	3.00
Lunch for one at Da Pancrazio (moderate)	27.00
Lunch for one at Trattoria l'Albanese (budget)	14.00
Dinner for one, without wine, at Relais le Jardin (deluxe)	75.00
Dinner for one, without wine, at Eau Vive (moderate)	32.00
Dinner for one, without wine, at Otello alla Concordia	23.00
Pint of beer	3.75
Glass of wine	2.00
Coca-Cola	1.30
Roll of color film, 36 exposures	5.90
Admission to the Vatican museums and Sistine Chapel	7.20
Movie ticket	7.95
Theater ticket at the Terme di Caracalla	25.00

last until October. Rome experiences its lowest average temperatures in December, 47°F; its highest in July, 82°F.

Rome's Average Daytime Temperature & Rainfall

Temperature °F

Month	Jan	Feb	Mar	Apr	May	June	July	Aug	Sept	Oct	Nov	Dec
Temperature	49	52	57	62	70	77	82	78	73	68	56	47

Rainfall (in inches)

Month	Jan	Feb	Mar	Apr	May	June	July	Aug	Sept	Oct	Nov	Dec
Inches of rain	3.6	3.2	2.9	2.2	1.4	0.7	0.2	0.7	3.0	4.0	3.9	2.8

Holidays

Offices and shops are closed on the following days: January 1 (New Year's Day); Easter Monday; April 25 (Liberation Day); May 1 (Labor Day); June 29 (Sts. Peter and Paul); August 15 (Assumption of the Virgin); November 1 (All Saints' Day); December 8 (Day of the Immaculate Conception); December 25 (Christmas); and December 26 (Santo Stefano).

Rome Calendar Of Events

January

- **Carnival,** in piazza Navona. This marks the last day of the children's market and lasts until dawn of the following day. Usually January 5.
- **Festa di Sant'Agnese,** at Sant'Agnese Fuori le Mura. In this ancient ceremony, two lambs are blessed and shorn. The wool is then used later for palliums. Usually January 17.

March

- **Festa di Santa Francesca Romana,** at piazzale del Colosseo near the Church of Santa Francesca Romana in the Roman Forum. It's a blessing of cars. Usually March 9.
- **Festa di San Giuseppe,** in the Trionfale Quarter, north of the Vatican. The heavily decorated statue of the saint is brought out at a fair with food stalls, concerts, and sporting events. Usually March 19.

April

- **Festa della Primavera.** The Spanish Steps are decked out with banks of flowers, and later orchestral and choral concerts are presented in Trinitá dei Monti. Dates vary.
- **Holy Week.** The most notable procession is led by the pope, passing the Colosseum and the Roman Forum up to Palatine Hill. A torchlit parade caps the observance. Sometimes at the end of March, but often in April.
- **Easter Sunday,** from a balcony of St. Peter's. The pope gives his blessing, and it's broadcast around the world.

May

- **International Horse Show,** at the piazza di Siena in the Villa Borghese. May 1–10 but dates vary.

June

- **Son et Lumière.** The Roman Forum and Tivoli are dramatically lit at night. Begins in early June and lasts until the end of September.
- **Festa di San Pietro,** in St. Peter's. The most significant Roman religious festival is observed with solemn rites. Usually around June 29.

July

⭐ La Festa Di Noiantri

Trastevere, the most colorful quarter of Old Rome, becomes a gigantic outdoor restaurant as tons of food and drink are consumed at tables lining the streets. Merrymakers and musicians provide the entertainment. **Where:** Trastevere. **When:** Mid-July, **Hours:** After reaching the quarter, find the first empty table and try to get a waiter. But guard your valuables. Details available from Ente Provinciale per il Turismo, via Parigi 11, Roma 00185 (☎ **06/488991**).

August

- **Festa della Catene,** in the Church of San Pietro in Vincoli. The relics of St. Peter's captivity go on display. August 1.

September

- **Sagra dell'Uva,** in the Basilica of Maxentius in the Roman Forum. During the harvest festival, musicians in ancient costumes entertain, and grapes are sold at reduced prices. Dates vary, usually early September.

November

- **Opera season** begins at Teatro dell'Opera and lasts until May.

December

- **Festa della Madonna Immacolata,** at the piazza di Spagna. Floral tributes to the Madonna by papal and government envoys. Usually December 8.
- **Midnight Mass,** at Santa Maria Maggiore. Veneration of metal and wood relics of the holy crib. December 24.
- **Blessing of the Pope,** from a balcony of St. Peter's. It's broadcast around the world. December 25 at noon.

3 Health & Insurance

HEALTH   You will encounter few health problems traveling in Rome. The tap water is generally safe to drink, the milk pasteurized, and health services good. Occasionally the change in diet may cause some minor diarrhea so you may want to take some antidiarrhea medicine along.

Carry all your vital medicine in your carry-on luggage and bring enough prescribed medicines to last you during your stay. Bring along copies of your prescriptions that are written in the generic—not brand-name—form. If you need a doctor, your hotel can recommend one or you can contact the your embassy or consulate. You can also obtain a list of English-speaking doctors before you leave from the **International Association for Medical Assistance to Travelers (IAMAT)** in the United States at 417 Center St., Lewiston, NY 14092 (☎ **716/754-4883**), in Canada at 40 Regal Rd., Guelph, ON N1K 1B5 (☎ **519/836-0102**).

If you suffer from a chronic illness or special medical condition, talk to your doctor before taking the trip. For conditions such as epilepsy, diabetes, or heart condition, wear Medic Alert's identification bracelet or necklace, which will immediately alert any doctor to your condition, and provide Medic Alert's 24-hour hotline phone number so that foreign doctors can obtain medical information for you. A lifetime membership costs $35, $45, or $60, depending on your choice of identification. Contact the **Medic Alert Foundation,** P.O. Box 1009, Turlock, CA 95381-1009 (☎ toll free **800/432-5378**).

INSURANCE   Before purchasing any additional insurance, check your homeowner's, automobile, and medical insurance policies as well as the insurance provided by credit-card companies and auto and travel clubs. You may have adequate off-premises theft coverage or your credit-card company may even provide cancellation coverage if the ticket is paid for with a credit card.

Remember, Medicare only covers U.S. citizens traveling to Mexico and Canada.

Also note that to submit any claim you must always have thorough documentation, including all receipts, police reports, medical records, and such.

If you are prepaying for your vacation or are taking a charter or any other flight that has cancellation penalties, look into cancellation insurance.

The following companies will provide further information:

Travel Guard International, 1145 Clark St., Stevens Point, WI 54481 (☎ **715/345-0505**, or toll free **800/826-1300**), offers comprehensive policies, including a seven-day policy that covers basically everything: emergency assistance, accidental death, trip cancellation and interruption, medical coverage abroad, and lost luggage. It costs $52. There are restrictions, however, which you should understand before you accept the coverage. This company is the only one to offer "cancel for any reason coverage."

Travel Insurance Pak, Travelers Insurance Co., Travel Insurance Division, 1 Tower Sq., Hartford, CT 06183-5040 (☎ toll free in the U.S. **800/243-3174**) is another supplier. Travel accident and illness coverage starts at $10 for 6 to 10 days; $500 worth of coverage for lost, damaged, or delayed baggage costs $20 for 6 to 10 days; and trip cancellation goes for $5.50 for $100 worth of coverage (written approval is necessary for cancellation coverage above $10,000).

Mutual of Omaha (Tele-Trip Company, Inc.), 3201 Farnam St., Omaha, NE 68131 (☎ toll free **800/228-9792**), offers travel insurance packages, which feature travel assistance services, trip cancellations, trip interruption, flight and baggage delays, accident medical, sickness, 24-hour accidental death and dismemberment, and medical evacuation coverages. Application for insurance can be taken over the phone for major credit-card holders.

HealthCare Abroad (MEDEX), Wallach & Co., 107 W. Federal St., P.O. Box 480, Middleburg, VA 22117-0480

(☎ **703/687-3166**, or toll free **800/237-6615**), offers a policy, good for 10 to 120 days, costing $3 a day, including accident and sickness coverage to the tune of $100,000. Medical evacuation is also included, along with a $25,000 accidental death and dismemberment compensation. Trip cancellation and lost or stolen luggage can also be written into this policy at a nominal cost.

Access America, 6600 W. Broad St., Richmond, VA 23230-1188 (☎ **804/284-3300**, or toll free **800/284-8300**), has a 24-hour hotline in case of an emergency and offers medical coverage for 9 to 15 days costing $49 for $10,000 worth of coverage. If you want medical plus trip cancellation, the charge is $89 for 9 to 15 days. A comprehensive package for $111 grants 9- to 15-day blanket coverage, including $50,000 worth of death benefits.

Insurance for British Travelers   Most big travel agents offer their own insurance and will probably try to sell you their package when you book a holiday. Think before you sign. Britain's Consumers' Association recommends that you insist on seeing the policy and reading the fine print before buying travel insurance.

You should also shop around for better deals. You might contact **Columbus Travel Insurance Ltd.** (☎ **0171/375-0011**) or, for students, **Campus Travel** (☎ **0171/730-3402**). If you're unsure about who provides what kind of insurance and the best deal, contact the **Association of British Insurers,** 52 Gresham St., London EC2V 7HQ (☎ **0171/600-333**).

4   What to Pack

Always pack as lightly as possible. Sometimes it's hard to get a porter or a baggage cart in train stations and airports. Also, airlines are increasingly strict about how much luggage you can bring, both carry-on and checked items. Checked baggage should not be more than 62 inches (width plus length plus height), or weigh more than 70 pounds. Carry-on luggage shouldn't be more than 45 inches (width plus length plus height) and must fit under your seat or in the bin above.

Note, also, that conservative middle-aged Romans tend to dress up rather than down, and that they dress very well indeed, particularly at theaters and concerts. Nobody will bar you for arriving in sports clothes, but you may feel awkward, so include at least one smart suit or dress in your luggage.

Some restaurants demand that men wear ties and that women not wear shorts or jogging attire, but those are the only clothing rules enforced.

Pack clothes that "travel well" because you can't always get pressing done at hotels. Be prepared to wash your underwear, or other garments, in your bathroom and hang them up to dry overnight.

The general rule of packing is to bring four of everything: four pairs of socks, four pairs of slacks, four shirts, and four sets of underwear. At least two of these will always be either dirty or in the process of drying. Often you'll have to wrap semiwet clothes in a plastic bag as you head for your next destination.

Take at least one outfit for chilly weather and one outfit for warm weather. Even in the summer, you may experience suddenly chilly weather, particularly if you go exploring in the hills. Always take two pairs of walking shoes in case one pair gets wet.

5 Tips for the Disabled, Seniors, Singles, Families & Students

FOR THE DISABLED   Before you go, there are many agencies that can provide advance-planning information.

For example, contact **MossRehab,** 1200 W. Tabor Rd., Philadelphia, PA 19141 (☎ **215/456-9603**). This service is not a travel agency. For assistance with your travel needs, call the number above. MossRehab provides information to telephone callers only.

You can also obtain a copy of **Air Transportation of Handicapped Persons,** published by the U.S. Department of Transportation. It's free if you write to Free Advisory Circular No. AC12032, Distribution Unit, U.S. Department of Transportation, Publications Division, M-4332, Washington, DC 20590.

You may also want to consider joining a tour for disabled visitors. Names and addresses of such tour operators can be obtained by writing to the **Society for the Advancement of Travel for the Handicapped,** 347 Fifth Ave., New York, NY 10016 (☎ **212/447-7284**). Annual membership dues are $45, or $25 for senior citizens and students. Send a stamped, self-addressed envelope.

FEDCAP Rehabilitation Services (formerly known as the Federation of the Handicapped), 211 W. 14th St., New York, NY 10011 (☎ **212/727-4268**), operates summer tours to Europe and elsewhere for its members. Membership costs $6 yearly.

For the blind, the best information source is the **American Foundation for the Blind,** 15 W. 16th St., New York, NY 10011 (☎ **212/620-2000**, or toll free in the U.S. **800/232-5463**).

Tips for Disabled British Travelers   RADAR (the Royal Association for Disability and Rehabilitation), 25 Mortimer St., London W1N 8AB (☎ **0171/637-5400**), publishes an annual holiday guide for the disabled, "Holidays and Travel Abroad" (£3.50 in the U.K., £5.26 in Europe, £7 in other destinations). RADAR also provides a number of holiday fact sheets on such subjects as sports and outdoor holidays, insurance, financial arrangements, and accommodations with nursing care for groups or for the elderly. There is a nominal charge for all these publications.

Another good resource is **Holiday Care Service,** 2, Old Bank Chambers, Station Rd, Horley, Surrey RH6 9HW (☎ **0293/774-535;** fax 0293/784-647), a national charity that advises on accessible accommodations for elderly and disabled people. It provides a free reservation service offering discounted rates.

If you're flying around Europe, the airline and ground staff will help you on and off planes, and reserve seats for you with sufficient leg room, but it is essential to arrange for this assistance *in advance* by contacting your airline.

The **Airport Transport Users Council,** 2/F Kingsway House, 103 Kingsway, London WC2B 6QX (☎ **0171/242-3883**), publishes two free pamphlets: "Flight Plan—A Passenger's Guide to Planning and Using Air Travel," which is packed with information, and "Care in the Air," which is specifically designed to help the disabled traveler.

FOR SENIORS   Many senior discounts are available, but note that some may require membership in a particular association.

For information before you go, write for a booklet—distributed free—called **"101 Tips for the Mature Traveler,"** available from Grand Circle Travel, 347 Congress St., Suite 3A, Boston, MA 02210 (☎ **617/350-7500,** or toll free **800/248-3737**).

SAGA International Holidays, 222 Berkeley St., Boston, MA 02116 (☎ toll free in the U.S. **800/343-0273**), runs all-inclusive tours for seniors, preferably for those 60 years old or older. Insurance is included in the net price of their tours.

In the United States, the best organization to belong to is the **American Association of Retired Persons,** 601 E St. NW, Washington, DC 20049 (☎ **202/434-AARP**). Members are offered discounts on car rentals, hotels, airfares. The association's group travel is provided by the AARP Travel Experience from American Express. Tours may be purchased through any American Express office or travel agent, or by calling toll free 800/927-0111. Flights to the various destinations are handled by the toll-free number as part of land arrangements.

Information is also available from the **National Council of Senior Citizens,** 1331 F St. NW, Washington, DC 20005-1171 (☎ **202/347-8800**), which charges $12 per person or per couple, for which you receive a monthly newsletter, part of which is devoted to travel tips. Reduced discounts on hotel and auto rentals are available.

Elderhostel, 75 Federal St., Boston, MA 02110 (☎ **617/426-7788**), offers an array of university-based summer educational programs for senior citizens throughout the world, including Rome. Most courses last around three weeks and are remarkable values, considering that airfare, accommodations in student dormitories or modest inns, all meals, and tuition are included. Courses include field trips, involve no homework, are ungraded, and emphasize liberal arts.

Participants must be over 60, but each may take an under-60 companion. Meals consist of solid, no-frills fare typical of educational institutions worldwide. The program provides a safe and congenial environment for older single women, who make up some 67% of the enrollment.

Golden Companions, P.O. Box 754, Pullman, WA 99163 (☎ **208/858-2183**), might provide the answer if you're between

45 and 89 and need a travel companion. A research economist, Joanne R. Buteau, founded this helpful service and is quick to point out that it's not a dating service. Travelers meet potential companions through a confidential mail network. Members, once they have "connected," make their own travel arrangements. Created in 1987, this organization draws members from many walks of life. Members also receive a bimonthly travel newsletter, *The Golden Gateways.* Membership for a full year costs $85 per person.

Tempo Travelers, 938 N. 70th St., #125, Lincoln, NE 68605, is another company catering to solo seniors, 50 years old or older, seeking compatible traveling companions. Catering to single, widowed, or divorced travelers, it responds to requests for written information.

Uniworld, 16000 Ventura Blvd., Encino, CA 91436 (☎ **818/382-7820,** or toll free in the U.S. **800/733-7820**), specializes in single tours for the mature person. They either arrange for you to share an accommodation with another single person, or else get you a low-priced single supplement. They specialize in travel to certain districts of England, France, Spain, Italy, or Scandinavia, including Rome.

Tips for British Seniors   Wasteels, Victoria Station, opposite platform 2, London SW1V 1JY (☎ **0171/836-8541**), currently provides an over-60s Rail Europe Senior Card. Its price is £5 to any British person with government-issued proof of his or her age, and £19 to anyone with a certificate of age not issued by the British government. With this card, discounts are sometimes available on certain trains within Britain and the rest of Europe.

FOR SINGLES   Unfortunately for the 85 million single Americans, the travel industry is far more geared toward couples, and singles often wind up paying the penalty. It pays to travel with someone, and one company that resolves this problem is **Travel Companion,** which matches single travelers with like-minded companions. It's headed by Jens Jurgen, who charges between $36 and $66 for a six-month listing in his well-publicized records. People seeking travel companions fill out forms stating their preferences and needs and receive a minilisting of potential travel partners. Companions of the same or opposite sex can be requested. A bimonthly newsletter averaging 34 large pages also gives numerous money-saving travel tips of special interest to solo travelers. A sample copy is available for $4. For an application and more information, contact Jens Jurgen, Travel Companion, P.O. Box P-833, Amityville, NY 11701 (☎ **516/454-0880**; fax 516/454-0170).

Singleworld, 401 Theodore Fremd Ave., Rye, NY 10580 (☎ **914/967-3334**, or toll free in the U.S. **800/223-6490**), is a travel agency that operates tours for solo travelers. Some, but not all, are for people in the 20s and 30s age range. Annual dues are $25.

Another agency to check is **Grand Circle Travel,** 347 Congress St., Suite 3A, Boston, MA 02210 (☎ **617/350-7500**, or toll free in the U.S. **800/248-3737**), which offers escorted tours and cruises for retired people, including singles.

Tips for British Singles   Single people sometimes feel comfortable traveling with groups composed mostly of other singles. One tour operator whose groups are usually composed of at least 50% of un-attached persons is **Explore, Ltd.** (☎ **0252/344-161**), with a well-justified reputation for offering offbeat tours. Groups rarely include more than 16 participants, and children under 14 are not allowed.

Dedicated independent travelers may want to check out **The Globetrotters Club,** BCM/Roving, London WCIN 3XX, which enables members to exchange information and generally assist each other in traveling as cheaply as possible. Persons wishing to join in the U.K. for one year pay £12 for the first year, £9 for each year's renewal.

FOR FAMILIES   Advance planning is the key to a successful family vacation in Rome. If you have very small children you should discuss your vacation plans with your family doctor and take along such standard supplies as children's aspirin, a thermometer, BandAids, and the like.

On airlines, a special menu for children must be requested at least 24 hours in advance, but if baby food is required, bring your own and ask a flight attendant to warm it to the right temperature. Take along a "security blanket" for your child, such as a pacifier, a favorite toy or book, or, for older children, something to make them feel at home in different surroundings, such as a baseball cap, a favorite T-shirt, or some good luck charm.

Make advance arrangements for cribs, bottle warmers, and car seats if you're driving anywhere.

Ask the hotel if it stocks baby food, and, if not, take some with you and plan to buy the rest in local supermarkets.

Draw up guidelines on bedtime, eating, keeping tidy, being in the sun, even shopping and spending—they'll make the vacation more enjoyable.

Babysitters can be found for you at most hotels, but you should always insist, if possible, that you secure a babysitter with at least a rudimentary knowledge of English.

Family Travel Times is published 10 times a year by **TWYCH, Travel with Your Children,** and includes a weekly call-in service for subscribers. Subscriptions cost $55 a year and can be ordered by writing to TWYCH, 45 W. 18th St., 7th Floor, New York, NY 10011 (☎ **212/206-0688**). TWYCH also publishes two nitty-gritty information guides, *Skiing with Children* and *Cruising with Children,* which sell for $29 and $22, respectively. A description of TWYCH's publications that includes a recent sample issue is available by sending $2 to the above address.

Families Welcome!, 21 West Colony Place, Suite 140, Durham, NC 27705 (☎ **919/489-2555**, or toll free in the U.S. **800/326-0724**), a travel company specializing in worry-free vacations for families, offers "City Kids" packages to Rome, featuring accommodations in family-friendly hotels or apartments. Some hotels include a second room for children free at a reduced rate during certain time periods. Packages can include car rentals, train and ferry passes, and special air prices, and are individually designed for each family. A welcome kit is distributed, containing "insider's information" for families traveling in Rome—reliable babysitters, where to buy Pampers, and advice such as that. A list of restaurants suitable for visiting with children is also included.

Romans adore *bambini,* especially their own, but they are most tolerant of other people's youngsters. Even on shopping expeditions, store owners are fond of giving children candy while parents make their purchases. So definitely take your children with you to Rome, but warn them repeatedly to stay out of the way of cars.

Tips for British Families   The best deals for families are often package tours put together by some of the giants of the British travel industry. Foremost among these is **Thomsons Tour Operators.** Through its subsidiary, **Skytours** (☎ **0181/200-8733**), they offer dozens of air/land packages to Italy where a predesignated number of airline seats are reserved for the free use of children under 18 who accompany their parents. To qualify, parents must book airfare and hotel accommodations lasting two weeks or more, and book as far in advance as possible. Savings for families with children can be substantial.

FOR STUDENTS   The largest travel service for students is **Council Travel,** a subsidiary of the Council on International Educational Exchange, 205 E. 42nd St., New York, NY 10017 (☎ **212/661-1450**), which provides details about budget travel, study abroad, working permits, and insurance. It also sells a number of publications for young people considering traveling abroad. For a copy of *Student Travels* magazine, providing information on all of Council Travel's services and CIEE's programs and publications, send $1 in postage. The organization issues to bonafide students for $16 an International Student Identity Card. Council Travel offices are located throughout the United States. Call toll free 800/GET-ANID to find out where the closest office is to you.

The **IYHF (International Youth Hostel Federation)** was designed to provide bare-bone overnight accommodations for serious budget-conscious travelers. For information contact **HI-AYH (Hostelling International/American Youth Hostels),** 733 15th St. NW, Suite 840, Washington, DC 20005 (☎ **202/783-6161**). Membership costs $25 annually except for those under 18, who pay $10, and those over 54, who pay $15.

Tips for British Students   **Campus Travel,** 52 Grosvenor Gardens, London SW1W 0AG (☎ **0171/730-3402**), provides a wealth of information and offers for the student traveler, ranging from route planning to flight insurance, including railcards.

The International Student Identity Card (ISIC) is an internationally recognized proof of student status that will entitle you to savings on flights, sightseeing, food, and accommodation. It costs only £5 and is well worth the cost. Always show your ISIC when booking a trip—you may not get a discount without it.

Youth hostels are the place to stay if you're a student. You'll need an International Youth Hostels Association card, which you can purchase from the youth hostel store at 14 Southampton St., London WC2 (☎ **0171/836-8541**) or Campus Travel (☎ **0171/730-3402**). Take both your passport and some passport-size photos of yourself, plus your membership fee. In England and Wales, this is £3 (for those under 18) or £9 (for those over 18). In Scotland, the fee is slightly less: £2.50 for those under 18, and £6 for everyone else.

The Youth Hostel Association puts together *The Hostelling International Budget Guide,* listing every youth hostel in 31 European countries. It costs £5.99 when purchased at the Southampton Street store in London (see above). Add 61p postage if it is being delivered within the United Kingdom.

If you're traveling this summer, many youth hostels on the continent will be full. To avoid disappointment, it's best to book ahead. In London you can make advance reservations at the hostel called **"Oxford Street,"** 14–18 Noel St., London W1 (☎ **0171/734-1618**) or at the hostel **"City of London,"** 36 Carter La., EC4 (☎ **0171/236-4965**), or, better yet, the membership department at 14 Southampton St. (see above).

6 Getting There

By Plane

"All roads lead to Rome," in ways the emperors never dreamed of. But of all the various ways of reaching Rome, the airplane is the best … and the cheapest.

If you're already in Europe, you'll have an easy time booking a flight to Rome. Alitalia flies to all the major capitals of Europe, while each of the national carriers of the various countries (such as Air France, British Airways, and Lufthansa) fly to Rome and/or Milan. However, for Americans and Canadians, it's sometimes expensive to book these fares once you're in Europe; it's cheaper to have Rome or Milan written into your ticket when you first book your flight to Europe from North America.

THE MAJOR AIRLINES

Any information about fares or even flights in the highly volatile airline industry is not writ in stone; even travel agencies with banks of computers have a hard time keeping abreast. For last-minute conditions, including a list of the carriers that fly to Rome, check with a travel agent or the individual airlines. Here is a rundown on the current status.

Frommer's Smart Traveler: Airfares

1. Take off-peak flights, which would include autumn to spring departures, and also flights on Monday through Thursday.

2. Don't make any last-minute changes in your itinerary (if you can help it) to avoid penalties.

3. Keep checking the airlines and their fares. Timing is everything. A recent spot check of one airline revealed that in just 7 days it had discounted a New York to Rome fare by $195.

4. Shop all airlines that fly to your destination.

5. Always ask for the lowest fare, not just a discount fare.

6. Ask about frequent-flyer programs to gain bonus miles when you book a flight.

7. Check "bucket shops" for last-minute discount fares that are even cheaper than their advertised slashed fares.

8. Ask about air/land packages. Land arrangements are often cheaper when booked with an air ticket.

9. Fly free (rarely) or at a heavy discount (usually) as a "courier."

From North America

American Airlines (☎ toll free in the U.S. **800/433-7300**) was among the first North American–based carriers to fly into Italy. From Chicago's O'Hare Airport, American flies nonstop every evening to Milan, where there are frequent connections into Rome. Flights from all parts of American's vast network fly regularly into Chicago.

TWA (☎ toll free in the U.S. **800/221-2000**) offers daily nonstop flights from New York's JFK to both Rome and Milan. In summer, the airline steps up its service, with two daily flights from New York to Rome, and maintains its daily nonstop flights to Milan unchanged. Because of the frequency of flights, it's often convenient and cost-effective to fly into Rome, and depart from Milan, or vice-versa, depending on your travel plans.

Delta (☎ toll free in the U.S. **800/241-4141**) flies from New York's JFK to both Milan and Rome. Separate flights depart every evening for both destinations, with fine links to the rest of Delta's rapidly growing network of domestic and international destinations. For a few months in midwinter, service to one or both of these destinations might be reduced to six flights a week.

For anyone interested in combining a trip to Italy with a stopover in, say, Britain or Germany along the way, there are sometimes attractive deals offered by **British Airways** (☎ toll free in the U.S. **800/AIRWAYS**) and **Lufthansa** (☎ toll free in the U.S. **800/645-3880**). Depending on any special promotions being offered (and with the understanding that all segments of a flight would be booked simultaneously from North America), flights into Rome might be attractively priced and offer a few days' holiday in London, Manchester, Munich, Düsseldorf, Hamburg, or Frankfurt along the way. British Airways, for example, maintains three and four flights a day from London to Rome and Milan, respectively, and often offers promotional deals to London (with discounted stopovers in London hotels) that are inexpensive.

Canada's second-largest airline, Calgary-based **Canadian Airlines International** (☎ toll free in Canada **800/426-7000**) flies every day of the week during summer, and a bit less frequently in winter, from Toronto to Rome. Two of the flights are nonstop, while the others touch down en route in either Montréal or Milan, depending on the schedule. Many other Canadians opt for transfers from their nearest international airport through such hubs as New York, Chicago, London, or Paris on such other carriers as Delta, British Airways, or American.

United (☎ toll free in the U.S. **800/538-2929**) also has air routes into Italy. From its hub at Dulles Airport in Washington, D.C., it flies every day nonstop into Rome, and then offers continuing service from Rome on to Milan. Passengers embark and disembark in both cities, according to their itineraries. Service is on wide-bodied 767s.

One well-known Italian specialist, **Alitalia** (☎ toll free in the U.S. **800/223-5730**), flies nonstop to both Rome and Milan from five different North American cities. These include New York's JFK, Boston, Chicago, Miami, and Los Angeles. The airline also runs joint flights with Malev (the national airline of Hungary) to Italy from Newark, New Jersey. Schedules are carefully designed to facilitate easy air transfers to such cities as Venice and Palermo. The airline also offers periodic promotions whose details change frequently, but which sometimes feature bargains. For example, one recent promotion involved a free round-trip ticket from Rome or Milan to many of the European cities serviced by Alitalia. To qualify, passengers needed to fly transatlantic on Alitalia before an agreed-upon date in early spring, but usually were able to include a short visit to Paris, London, or Berlin as an unexpected add-on to their holiday in Italy. Other promotions involved two-for-the-price-of-one tickets (or free upgrades to business or first class) during predesignated periods if passage was charged to an American Express credit card. Alitalia, incidentally, participates in the frequent-flyer programs of other airlines, including Continental and USAir.

Be aware that Alitalia's (and most other airlines') cheapest tickets are nonrefundable. Alitalia's sole exception to this rule is in the event of your hospitalization or the death of someone in your close family. Air travel between Monday and Thursday will save you money, since fares are higher for weekend (Friday to Sunday) travel.

From Great Britain

Both **British Airways** (☎ in London **0181/897-4000**) and **Alitalia** (☎ in London **0181/745-8200**) have frequent flights from London's Heathrow Airport to Rome, Milan, Venice, Pisa (the gateway to Florence), and Naples. Flying time from London to these cities is anywhere from 2$^{1}/_{2}$ to 3 hours. BA also has one direct flight a day from Manchester to Rome, which is convenient for passengers who live in the Midlands.

REGULAR FARES

Most of the major airlines that fly to Rome charge approximately the same fare, but if a price war should break, fares could change overnight. Specific fares and restrictions, of course, should be carefully understood before you make your final plans.

The key to getting a budget fare is "advance booking." The number of seats allocated to low-cost "advance purchase" fares is severely limited (sometimes to less than 25% of the capacity of a particular plane), so you have to make your reservations early to book a low-cost seat.

A large number of discounts are also available for passengers who can travel either midweek or midwinter in either direction. High season on most airlines' routes to Rome usually stretches from June 1 until September 15 (this could vary), and it is both the most expensive and the most crowded time to travel. So you should try to plan your departure for the low season, which falls between September and May.

All of the major carriers offer an **APEX** ticket, which is generally their cheapest transatlantic option. Usually such a ticket must be purchased between 14 and 21 days in advance and a stopover in Italy must last at least 7 days but not more than 30. Changing the date of departure from North America within 21 days of departure will sometimes entail a penalty of around $100 with some APEX tickets, while with others, no changes of any kind are permitted.

A more flexible (but more expensive) option is the **regular economy fare.** This offers the same seating and the same services as passengers using an excursion ticket, but is usually purchased by those who need to return to North America before spending their obligatory seven days in Europe—the number usually required for an APEX ticket. One of the most attractive benefits of a regular economy-class ticket is the absolute freedom granted to a passenger (if space is available) regarding last-minute changes in flight dates.

Business and **first class** are both ideal for long-legged and well-heeled passengers who prefer wide, roomy comfort, free drinks, savory meals served on fine linen and china, and (in first class) extra-wide seats that convert into sleepers.

OTHER GOOD-VALUE CHOICES

Alitalia clusters the price of tickets to its destinations in Italy into four different zones, each centered around the cities of Milan, Rome, Naples, and Palermo. If you intend to fly from North America to local airports at, say, Genoa, Venice, Rimini, or any of the towns of Sardinia or Sicily, you can add on a connecting flight from the main airport of that region to a secondary airport within the same region without any additional charge. (Alitalia calls these "common-rated" fares, meaning that it costs no more to fly to Venice from New York than it would have cost to fly to Milan from New York). Considering the distance between Milan and Venice, or the distance from Rome to Pisa or Florence, and the extra expense you'd have encountered on the train or highway, it's an attractive offer.

And for students, or anyone aged 12 to 24, special extensions are granted on the length of time a passenger can stay abroad. Alitalia's youth fare permits a stay abroad for up to one year. The round-trip high-season fare from New York to Rome is currently $958. With the year-long validity of the return half of the ticket, a North American student could, say, complete two full semesters at the University of Bologna and still fly home at a substantial savings over equivalent fares on some other airlines.

BUCKET SHOPS   The name originated in the 1960s in Britain, where mainstream airlines give that (their pejorative) name to resalers of blocks of unsold tickets consigned to them by major transatlantic carriers. "Bucket shop" has stuck as a label, but it might be more polite to refer to them as "consolidators." In its purest sense, a bucket shop acts as a clearinghouse for blocks of tickets that airlines discount and consign during normally slow periods of air travel.

Charter operators (see below) and bucket shops used to perform separate functions, but their offerings in many cases have been blurred in recent times, and many outfits perform both functions.

Tickets are sometimes—but not always—priced at up to 35% less than the full fare; perhaps your reduced fare will be no more than 20% off the regular fare. Terms of payment can vary—say, anywhere from 45 days prior to departure to last-minute sales offered in a final attempt by an airline to fill an empty aircraft.

Since dealing with unknown bucket shops might be a little risky, it's wise to call the Better Business Bureau in your area to see if complaints have been filed against the company from which you plan to purchase a fare.

Bucket shops abound from coast to coast, but to get you started, here are a few listings:

In New York, try **TFI Tours International,** 34 W. 32nd St., 12th Floor, New York, NY 10001 (☎ **212/736-1140** in New York State, or toll free **800/745-8000** elsewhere in the U.S.).

For the Midwest, explore the possibilities of **Travel Avenue,** 10 S. Riverside Plaza, Suite 1404, Chicago, IL (☎ toll free in the U.S. **800/333-3335**), a national agency whose headquarters are here. Its tickets are often cheaper than most bucket shops, and it charges the customer only a $25 fee on international tickets, rather than taking the usual 10% commission from an airline. Travel Avenue rebates most of that back to the customers—hence, the lower fares.

In New England, a possibility is **TMI** (Travel Management International), 39 JFK St. (Harvard Square), 3rd Floor, Cambridge, MA 02138 (☎ toll free in the U.S. **800/245-3672**), which offers a wide variety of discounts, including youth fares, student fares, and access to other kinds of air-related discounts as well. Among others, its destinations include Rome.

One of the biggest U.S. consolidators is **Travac,** 989 Sixth Ave., New York, NY 10018 (☎ **212/563-3303,** or toll free in the U.S. **800/TRAV-800**), which offers discounted seats throughout the U.S. to most cities in Europe, including Rome, on airlines that include TWA, United, and Delta.

UniTravel, 1177 North Warson Rd., St. Louis, MO 63132 (☎ toll free in the U.S. **800/325-2222**), offers tickets to Rome and elsewhere in Europe at prices that may or may not be reduced from the price clients would get if they had phoned the airlines directly. UniTravel is best suited to providing discounts for passengers who decide (or need) to get to Europe on short notice.

One final option suitable only for clients with supremely flexible travel plans is available through **Airhitch,** 2790 Broadway, Suite 100, New York, NY 10025 (☎ toll free in the U.S. **800/326-2009**). Prospective travelers inform Airhitch of any five consecutive days in which they're available to fly to Europe. Airhitch agrees to fly its passengers within those five days from any of three regions of the U.S. (These regions include the East Coast, the West Coast, and Midwest/Southeast.) Attempts will be made to fly passengers to and from the cities of their choice, but no guarantee is made.

CHARTER FLIGHTS   Strictly for reasons of economy (and never for convenience), some travelers are willing to accept the possible uncertainties of a charter flight to Rome.

In a strict sense, a charter flight occurs on an aircraft reserved months in advance for a one-time-only transit to some predetermined point. Before paying for a charter, check the restrictions on your ticket or contract. You may be asked to purchase a tour package and pay far in advance. You'll pay a stiff penalty (or forfeit the ticket entirely) if you cancel. Charters are sometimes canceled if the plane doesn't fill up. In some cases, the charter-ticket seller will offer you an insurance policy for your own legitimate cancellation (hospital certificate, death in the family, whatever).

There is no way to predict whether a proposed flight to Rome will cost less on a charter or less in a bucket shop. You'll have to investigate at the time of your trip.

Some charter companies have proved unreliable in the past. Among reliable charter-flight operators is **Council Charter,** 205 E. 42nd St., New York, NY 10017 (☎ **212/661-0311,** or toll free in the U.S. **800/800-8222**). This company can arrange "charter seats on regularly scheduled aircraft" to most major European cities.

One of the biggest New York charter operators is **Travac,** 989 Sixth Ave., New York, NY 10018 (☎ **212/563-3303,** or toll free in the U.S. **800/TRAV-800**).

REBATORS   To confuse the situation even more, rebators also compete in the low-cost airfare market. These outfits pass along to the passenger part of their commission, although many of them assess a lot for their services. Most rebators offer discounts that range from 10% to 25% (but this could vary from place to place), plus a $25 handling charge. They are not the same as travel agents, although they sometimes offer similar services, including discounted land arrangements and car rentals.

Some rebators include **Travel Avenue,** 641 W. Lake St., Suite 201, Chicago, IL 60606-3691 (☎ **312/876-6866,** or toll free in the U.S. **800/333-3335**); and **The Smart Traveller,** 3111 SW 27th Ave., Miami, FL 33133 (☎ **305/448-3338,** or toll free in the U.S. **800/448-3338**). The Smart Traveller also offers discount tours, hotel packages, and fly-drive packages.

STANDBYS   During their heyday in the 1960s and 1970s, discounted standby tickets were a favorite of spontaneous travelers with no scheduled demands on their time. They left a departure to the whims of fortune and the hopes that a last-minute seat would become available because of the no-show of a scheduled passenger. In recent years, however, the number of airlines offering standby tickets has greatly diminished.

At presstime, none of the airlines polled for this review offered standby fares to Italy. **Virgin Atlantic Airways** (☎ toll free **800/862-8621**) offered a variation on the standby theme, an "Instant Purchase Late Saver fare." It's usually offered only between New York and London, and only in winter, usually between late October and late March, with occasional extensions and variations. At presstime, tickets must be booked within 48 hours of a flight's departure, although a firm return date within 30 days of departure could, at the passenger's option, be scheduled at the time of purchase. The cost, subject to availability, was $189 each way, New York to London. (Once you land in London, however, you'll find that it's a long, long way by rail or bus to Italy, and the price of an intra-European flight from London to Rome or Milan might be appallingly expensive.) All in all, it's probably better to make your best deal for a ticket with a firm date of departure, so you can schedule your other commitments, such as hotel reservations, accordingly.

GOING AS A COURIER   This cost-cutting technique may not be for everybody. You travel as a passenger and courier, and for this service you'll secure a greatly discounted airfare or sometimes, although rarely, even a free ticket.

You're allowed one piece of carry-on luggage only, your baggage allowance is used by the courier firm to transport its cargo (which, by the way, is perfectly legal). As a courier, you don't actually handle the merchandise you're "transporting" to Europe you just carry a manifest to present to Customs.

Upon arrival, an employee of the courier service will reclaim the company's cargo. Incidentally, you fly alone, so don't plan to travel with anybody. (A friend may be able to arrange a flight as a courier on a consecutive day.) Most courier services operate from Los Angeles or New York, but some operate out of other cities.

Courier services are often listed in the yellow pages or in advertisements in travel sections of newspapers.

For a start, check **Halbart Express,** 147-05 176th St., Jamaica, NY 11434 (☎ **718/656-8189** from 10am to 3pm daily); or

Now Voyager, 74 Varick St., Suite 307, New York, NY 10013 (☎ **212/431-1616** daily from 10am to 5:30pm; at other times you'll get a recorded message announcing last-minute special round-trip fares).

The **International Association of Air Travel Couriers,** P.O. Box 1349, Lake Worth, FL 33460 (☎ **407/582-8320**), for an annual membership of $35, will send you six issues of its newsletter, *Shoestring Traveler,* and about half a dozen issues of *Air Courier Bulletin,* a directory of air-courier bargains around the world. Other advantages of membership are photo identification cards, and the organization acts as a troubleshooter if a courier runs into difficulties. As a subscriber, you have access to the company's 24-hour fax-on-demand system, containing daily updates of last-minute courier flights. For example, a recent New York to Rome round-trip ticket sold for only $100.

TRAVEL CLUBS   Another possibility for low-cost air travel is the travel club, which supplies an unsold inventory of tickets offering discounts in the usual range of 20% to 60%

After you pay an annual fee, you are given a "hotline" number to call to find out what discounts are available. Many of these discounts become available several days in advance of actual departure, sometimes as long as a week and sometimes as much as a month. It all depends. Of course, you're limited to what's available, so you have to be fairly flexible.

Some of the best of these clubs include the following:

Discount Travel International, Ives Building, 114 Forrest Ave., Suite 203, Narberth, PA 19072 (☎ **215/668-7184**), charges an annual membership of $45.

Moment's Notice, 425 Madison Ave., New York, NY 10017 (☎ **212/486-0500**), has a members' 24-hour hotline (regular phone toll charges) and a yearly fee of $45 per family.

Sears Discount Travel Club, 3033 S. Parker Rd., Suite 1000, Aurora, CO 80014 (☎ toll free in the U.S. **800/255-1487**), offers members, for $49, a catalog (issued four times a year), maps, discounts at select hotels, and a 5% cash bonus on purchases.

Encore Travel Club, 4501 Forbes Blvd., Lanham, MD 20706 (☎ toll free in the U.S. **800/638-8976**), charges $49 a year for membership in a club which offers 50% discounts at well-recognized hotels, sometimes during off-peak periods. It also offers substantial discounts on airfare, cruises, and car rentals through its volume purchase plans. Membership includes a travel package outlining the company's many services, and use of a toll-free phone number for advice and information.

A Note for British Travelers

A regular fare from the U.K. to Italy is considered extremely high, so savvy Brits usually call a travel agent for a "deal"—either a charter flight or some special air travel promotion. These so-called deals are always available, because of great interest in Italy as a tourist destination. If one is not possible for you, then an APEX ticket might be the way to keep costs trimmed. These tickets must be reserved in advance. However, a PEX ticket offers a discount without the usual booking restrictions. You might also ask the airlines about a "Eurobudget ticket," which requires restrictions or length-of-stay requirements.

British newspapers are always full of classified advertisements touting "slashed" fares to Italy. One good source is *Time Out,* a magazine published in London. London's *Evening Standard* has a daily travel section, and the Sunday editions of almost any newspaper will run many ads. Recommended companies include **Trailfinders** (☎ 0171/937-5400) and **Avro Tours** (☎ 0181/543-0000), which operates charters.

In London, there are many bucket shops around Victoria and Earl's Court that offer cheap fares. Make sure that the company you deal with is a member of the IATA, ABTA, or ATOL. These umbrella organizations will help you out if anything goes wrong.

CEEFAX, a British television information service included on many home and hotel TVs, runs details of package holidays and flights to Europe, including Rome. Just switch to your CEEFAX channel and you'll find a menu of listings that includes travel information.

Make sure you understand the bottom line on any special deal you purchase—that is, ask if all surcharges, including airport taxes and other hidden costs—are cited before committing yourself to purchase. Upon investigation, some of these "deals" are not as attractive as advertised. Also, make sure you understand what the penalties are if you're forced to cancel at the last minute.

By Train

Rome lies at the heart of a vast rail network, with train connections throughout continental Europe, including all the leading cities of Italy. Trains arrive throughout the day from Florence, and the trip takes $3^{1}/_{2}$ hours. A regular fare is 22,000 lire ($13.20); however, there is a supplement of 9,300 lire ($5.60) for *rapido* trains. Nine trains per day arrive from Venice, taking five hours and costing 40,200 lire ($24.10), plus a supplement of 14,800 lire ($8.90) for *rapido* trains.

If you're already on the Continent—in France, for example—you can take the *Napoli Express* train from the Gare de Lyon station in Paris at 8:56pm, arriving in Rome at 2:35pm the next day. A Rome-bound train leaves Munich nightly at 8:30pm, arriving in Rome at 8:12am the next morning. From Zurich, a daily train leaves at 11:03am, arriving in Rome at 8:50pm. Eurailpasses are good on these trains.

By Bus from the U.K.

Eurolines is the leading operator of scheduled coach services across Europe. Its comprehensive network of services includes regular departures to destinations throughout Italy, including Turin, Milan,

Bologna, Florence, and Rome; plus summer services to Verona, Vicenza, Padua, and Venice.

Eurolines services to Italy depart from London's Victoria Coach Station and are operated by modern coach, with reclining seats and a choice of smoking or non-smoking areas. Return tickets are valid for up to six months, and for added flexibility passengers may also leave their return date open.

Information and credit card reservations can be made by telephoning **0582/404511.** Alternatively, passengers may book in person at Eurolines, 52 Grosvenor Gardens, Victoria, London SW1 (opposite Victoria Rail Station). A round-trip ticket from London to Rome costs £139, or £90 one way.

By Car

If you're already on the Continent, particularly in a neighboring country such as France or Austria, you may want to drive to Rome. However, arrangements should be made in advance with your car-rental company.

It is also possible to drive from London to Rome, a distance of 1,124 miles via Calais/Boulogne/Dunkirk or 1,085 miles via Oostende/Zeebrugge, not counting Channel crossings. You can cross over from England to France, using either one of the ferries or else the Chunnel, the new tunnel under the English Channel inaugurated in 1994. Once you arrive on the northern coast of France by whatever mode of transport you selected, you still face a 24-hour drive to Rome. Most drivers play it safe and budget a leisurely three days for the journey.

Most of the roads from western Europe leading into Italy are toll free, with some notable exceptions. If you use the Swiss superhighway network, you'll have to purchase a special tax sticker at the frontier. You'll also pay to go through the St. Gotthard Tunnel into Italy. Crossings from France can be through the Mont Blanc Tunnel, for which you'll pay, or you can leave the French Riviera at Menton (France) and drive directly into Italy along the Italian Riviera in the direction of San Remo.

If you don't want to drive such distances, ask a travel agent to book you on a Motorail arrangement where the train carries your car. This service, however, is good only to Milan, as there are no car-and-sleeper expresses running the some 390 miles south to Rome.

Organized Tours

Many travelers are more comfortable traveling with an organized tour, and they appreciate the advantages a tour group offers. First, you know ahead of time just what your visit will cost. You won't have to arrange your own transportation in places where language might be a problem, or look after your own luggage, or cope with reservations and payment at individual hotels, or face other "nuts and bolts" requirements of travel that can make or break your enjoyments of a Roman holiday. Although a sampling of the best-rated tour companies follows, you should consider consulting a good travel agent for advice.

SIGHTSEEING TOURS

A tour operator that seems to meet with consistent approval from its participants is a family-operated company for three generations named **Perillo Tours,** 577 Chestnut Ridge Rd., Woodcliff Lake, NJ 07675-9888 (☎ **201/307-1234,** or toll free in the U.S. **800/431-1515**). Since it was established in 1945, it has sent more than a million travelers to Italy in comfort. As one of the world's largest Italy operators, it uses more first-class hotel rooms in Italy than any other company in America. Known and well respected for the value it offers, Perillo's tours cost much less than the assembled elements of each tour if each component had been arranged separately. Guides tend to be well qualified, well informed, and sensitive to the needs of tour participants.

Perillo operates hundreds of departures year-round. Between April and October, five different itineraries are offered, ranging from 10 to 14 days each, covering broadly different regions of the peninsula. Between November and April, the Off-Season Italy tour covers three of Italy's premier cities, including Rome. All tours include airfare from North America (usually on Alitalia), overnight accommodation in first-class hotels, breakfast and dinner daily, and all baggage handling and taxes. Also included are all sightseeing fees, transfers, and tours by deluxe motorcoach. Most buses contain their own lavatory. Tours begin at around $1,650 per person, double occupancy, for one of the off-season short tours, to around $2,499 for a two-week visit to Rome, Florence, and Venice.

Another contender for package tour business in Italy is **Italiatour,** member of the Alitalia Group (☎ **212/765-2183,** or toll free in the U.S. **800/845-3365**), which offers a widely varied selection of tours through all parts of the peninsula. The company's strongest appeal is to the free-at-heart (i.e., clients who don't want any semblance of a tour at all). Catering to the reluctance of many travelers to commit themselves too rigidly to group travel in a bus, the company specializes in tours for independent travelers who ride from one destination to another by train or by rental car. They offer a wide choice of loosely structured itineraries to Italy's best-known cities. In most cases, the company sells pre-reserved hotel accommodations that, because of their volume purchases, are usually less expensive than what you'd pay if you had reserved the accommodations yourself. A choice of accommodations in several different price ranges is available to the urban centers of Italy as well as to such less-often visited cities as Orvieto, Lucca, Viterbo, Mantua, and Perugia. With any of these tours, there is a strong incentive to book air passage from North America at the same time as the hotel nights, but because of the company's close link with Alitalia, the prices quoted for air passage are sometimes among the most reasonable on the retail market. Repeat travelers to Italy sometimes opt for one of the Fly-Drive programs, where discounted prices on rental cars are combined with airfare from North America.

Italiatour's longest offering is a loosely supervised 12-day/10-night jaunt through the major art cities of Italy, with accommodations in luxury hotels. Prices begin at $1,625 per person. Airfare is extra, but the price includes hotel accommodations (double occupancy), breakfasts, transfers between cities, some city tours, and a gondola ride in Venice.

OPERA TOURS

Dailey-Thorp, 330 W. 58th St., Suite 610, New York, NY 10019-1817 (☎ **212/307-1555**), in business since 1971, is probably the best-regarded organizer of music and opera tours operating in the U.S. Because of its "favored" relations with box offices, it's often able to purchase blocks of otherwise unavailable tickets to operas in Rome. Tours range from 7 to 21 days and include first-class or deluxe accommodations and meals in top-rated European restaurants.

EDUCATIONAL/STUDY TRAVEL

Courses for foreign students are available at several centers in Rome covering not only the Italian language and literature but also the country's history, geography, and fine arts. You can write for information. In Rome, a leading center for studying the language and literature is **Italiadea,** piazza della Cancelleria 85, 00186 Roma (☎ 06/68307620), offering courses throughout the year.

The **Roman Cookery School,** Chalet del Lago, via Reginaldo Belloni, Anguillara Sabazia (Rome) 00061 (☎ and fax **06/9968364**), is a cooking school on the beachfront of the Lake of Bracciano, with views over the old town of Anguillara, 16 miles from Rome. In this one-time fishing village, two English-speaking hosts, Alice Pugh and Audris Louw d'Aragona, conduct classes in Italian regional cuisine, featuring all the regions of Italy. Accommodation can be arranged where needed at a small hotel across from their school.

3

Getting to Know Rome

THE POPULATION OF ROME IS COMPOSED MAINLY OF THE ROMANS AND THE visitors—the two are virtually inseparable. The city almost seems at times to exist as a host to its never-ending stream of sightseers. It wines them, dines them, and entertains them.

Rome is also a city of images, beginning at dawn, which is best seen from Janiculum Hill; with its bell towers and cupolas, the silhouette of Rome comes into view. It is a city of sounds, as the first peal of bells calls the faithful to an early-morning mass. As the city wakes up, office-workers rush into cafes for their first cappuccinos of the day, often passing by fruit and vegetable stands (the Romans like their produce fresh).

By 10am the tourists are on the street battling city traffic in their quest for a contact with art and history. Renaissance palaces and baroque facades give way eventually to what is left from the ruins of antiquity, the heritage of a once-great empire.

In Chapter 6, I'll take you on seemingly endless treks through ancient monuments and basilicas. But monuments are not the total picture. In Rome, you'll find yourself embracing life with intensity. In other words, "When in Rome . . ."

1   Orientation

Arriving

BY PLANE   Chances are that you'll arrive in Italy at Rome's **Leonardo da Vinci International Airport** (☎ **06/65951**), popularly known as Fiumicino, from the town located adjacent to the airport, 18$^1/_2$ miles from the center of the capital. Domestic flights arrive at one terminal, international ones at the other. (If you're flying by charter, you might arrive at Ciampino Airport, a military airport with tight security.)

The least expensive way into Rome from Fiumicino is via a small train departing from the terminal in front of the airport and taking you in about 20 minutes to Ostiense, a suburban rail station. Departures are about every 30 minutes, and the cost is 6,000 lire ($3.60). At Ostiense, you can connect on the lower level with Metropolitana Line B, Piramide station, of the subway system, which will take you to Stazione Termini at the center of Rome. Of course, it helps greatly if you're not loaded down with luggage. Visitors arriving on night flights can take a bus operated by Rome transit authorities, which delivers passengers in the early hours to piazzale dei Partigiani, from which they can walk the short distance to the Ostiense rail station.

Should you arrive on a charter flight at **Ciampino** (☎ **06/79340297**), take an ACOTRAL bus, departing every 30 minutes or so, which will deliver you to the Anagnina stop of Metropolitana Line A. At Anagnina you can take Linea A to the Stazione Termini, the rail station in the heart of Rome, where your final connections can be made. Trip time is about 45 minutes, and the cost is 1,500 lire (90¢).

Rome Orientation

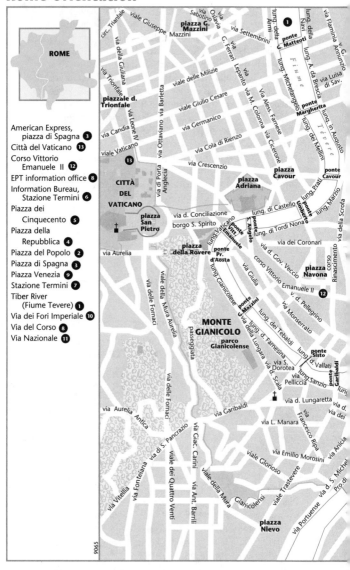

ROME

Taxis from Fiumicino are quite expensive—65,000 lire ($39) and up—and therefore not recommended for the trip from the airport.

If you arrive at Ciampino, you're closer to the city, which is usually reached in less than half an hour. Because of the shorter distance, you pay the amount shown on the meter if you go by taxi (not double, as some drivers may insist).

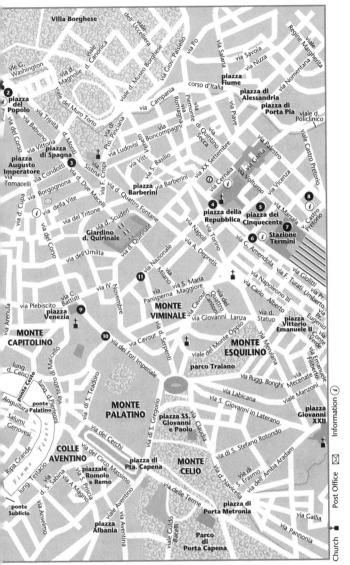

Information (i)   Post Office ⊠   Church ∎∎

800 m
0
880 y

BY TRAIN   Trains arrive in the center of old Rome at the **Stazione Termini,** piazza dei Cinquecento (☎ **4775**), the train and subway transportation hub for all of Rome. Many hotels lie near the station, and you can walk to your hotel if you don't have too much luggage. Otherwise, an array of taxi, bus, and subway lines await you.

If you're taking the Metropolitana (Rome's subway network), follow the illuminated *M* sign in red, which points the way. To catch a bus, go straight through the outer hall of the termini and enter the sprawling bus lot of the piazza dei Cinquecento. Taxis are also found here.

The train station is filled with services. At a branch of the Banca Nazionale delle Communicazioni (between Tracks 8–11 and Tracks 12–15) you can exchange money. Information on rail travel to other parts of Italy is dispensed at Informazioni Ferroviarie, in the larger outer hallway. There is also a Tourist Information Booth here, along with baggage services, barbershops, day hotels, gift shops, restaurants, and bars. But beware of pickpockets, often young children.

BY BUS   Arrivals are at the **Stazione Termini** (see above) where all the same facilities awaiting train passengers are also available to bus passengers. Information on buses is dispensed at a booth operated by ATAC, the city bus company, at piazza dei Cinquecento, which is open daily from 7:30am to 7:30pm. The main office of ATAC is at via Volturno 65 (☎ **06/46951**).

BY CAR   From the north, the main access route is the **A1 (Autostrada del Sole),** cutting through Milan and Florence, or you can take the coastal route, SSI Aurelia, from Genoa. If you're driving north from Naples, you take the southern lap of the **Autostrada del Sole (A2).** All these autostrade join with the **Grande Raccordo Anulare,** a ring road that encircles Rome, channeling traffic into the congested city. Long before you reach this ring road, you should study a map carefully to see what part of Rome you plan to enter and mark your route accordingly. Route markings along the ring road tend to be confusing.

Tourist Information

Tourist information is available at the **Ente Provinciale per il Turismo,** via Parigi 5, 00185 Roma (☎ **06/48899228**), open daily from 8:15am to 7:15pm. There's another **information bureau** at the Stazione Termini (☎ **06/487-1270**), open daily from 8:30am to 7pm.

City Layout

MAIN ARTERIES & STREETS   Your feet will probably first touch Roman soil at **Leonardo da Vinci International Airport,** near the mouth of the Tiber River, 18 1/2 miles from the center of Rome. The drive in to the city is rather uneventful until you pass through the city wall, the remarkably intact **Great Aurelian Wall,** started in A.D. 271 to calm Rome's barbarian jitters. Suddenly, ruins of imperial baths loom on one side and great monuments can be seen in the middle of blocks. Inside the walls, you'll find a city designed for a population that walked to get where it was going. Parts of Rome actually look and feel more like an oversize village than the former imperial capital of the Western world.

The Stazione Termini faces a huge piazza, **piazza dei Cinquecento,** which in many ways is an embodiment of the city. It's named after 500 Italians who died heroically in a 19th-century battle in Africa. There are certainly many more attractive sites in Rome, but this piazza has several noteworthy aspects. First, it is next to the modern railroad station. Immediately next to the sculptured-concrete cantilevered roof of the station facade is a remnant of the Servian Wall, built nearly six centuries before the birth of Christ by an ancient Roman king. If that isn't enough, the far side of the piazza is bordered by the ruins of the Baths of Diocletian, a former bastion of imperial luxury whose crumbling brick walls were once covered with the rarest of colored marbles and even now enclose marble and bronze statuary.

Most of the old city and its monuments lie on the east side of the **Tiber River (Fiume Tevere),** which meanders through town between 19th-century stone embankments. However, several important monuments are on the other side: **St. Peter's Basilica** and the **Vatican,** the **Castel Sant'Angelo** (formerly the tomb of the emperor Hadrian), and the colorful section of town known as **Trastevere.** The bulk of ancient, Renaissance, and baroque Rome lies across the Tiber from St. Peter's on the same side as the Stazione Termini. The various quarters of the city are linked by large boulevards (large at least in some places) that have mostly been laid out since the late 19th century.

Starting from the **Victor Emmanuel monument,** a highly-controversial pile of snow-white Brescian marble whose quarrying and construction must have employed whole cities, there's a street running practically due north to the **piazza del Popolo** and the city wall. This is **via del Corso,** one of the main streets of Rome—noisy, congested, always crowded with buses and shoppers, called simply "Corso." Again from the Victor Emmanuel monument, the major artery going west (and ultimately across the Tiber to St. Peter's) is **corso Vittorio Emanuele.** To go in the other direction, toward the Colosseum, you take **via del Fori Imperial,** named for the excavated ruins of the imperial forums that flank this avenue. This road was laid out in the 1930s by Mussolini, who was responsible for much of the fine archeological work in Rome, if perhaps for the wrong reasons. Yet another central conduit is **via Nazionale,** running from **piazza della Repubblica** (also called the piazza Esedra), ending again right by the Victor Emmanuel monument at **piazza Venezia,** which lies in front of it. The final lap of the via Nazionale is called via Quattro Novembre.

For 2½ millennia before these boulevards were built, the citizens had to make their way through narrow byways and curves that

IMPRESSIONS

At Florence, you think; at Rome, you pray; at Venice, you love; at Naples, you look.
—Italian Proverb, Quoted By Maurice Baring, *Round The World In Any Number Of Days,* 1913

All roads lead to Rome.
—Traditional

defeated all but the best senses of direction. These streets—among the most charming aspects of the city—still exist in large quantities, mostly unspoiled by the advances of modern construction. However, this tangled street plan has one troublesome element: automobiles. The traffic in Rome is awful! When the claustrophobic street plans of the Dark Ages open unexpectedly onto a vast piazza, every driver accelerates full throttle for the distant horizon, while groups of peripatetic tourists and Romans flatten themselves against marble fountains for protection or stride with firm jaws right into the thick of the howling traffic.

The traffic problem in Rome is nothing new. Julius Caesar was so exasperated by it that he banned all vehicular traffic during the daylight hours. Sometimes it's actually faster to walk than to take a bus, especially during any of Rome's four daily rush hours (that's right, four: to work, home for lunch/siesta, back to work, home in the evening). The hectic crush of urban Rome is considerably less during the month of August, when many Romans are out of town on holiday. If you visit at any other time of year, however, be prepared for the general frenzy that characterizes your average Roman street.

FINDING AN ADDRESS   Finding an address in Rome can be a problem because of the narrow, often cobbled streets of old Rome and the little, sometimes "hidden" piazzas or squares. Numbers usually run consecutively, with odd numbers on one side of the street and even numbers on the other side. However, in the old districts, a different system is sometimes followed, although it is rare. These ancient streets begin their numbering on one side, running in order until the end, then running back in the opposite direction on the other side. Therefore, no. 50 could be opposite no. 308.

STREET MAPS   Arm yourself with a detailed street map, not the general overview often handed out free at tourist offices. Even if you're in Rome for only a day or two, and plan to see only the major monuments, you'll still need a detailed street map to find such attractions as the Trevi Fountain. The best ones are published by **Falk,** and they're available at most newsstands and kiosks in Rome. The best selections of maps are sold in the travel department of various bookstores. See "Bookstores" under "Shopping A to Z," Chapter 8.

NEIGHBORHOODS IN BRIEF

Here are the main districts of interest, and some of their more important attractions. Often a district will be named for a major square or monument, such as the piazza di Spagna or the piazza Navona districts.

Ancient Rome   This is the district that most visitors come to Rome to explore, for it includes the Colosseum, Palatine Hill, the Roman Forum, the Fori Imperiali (Imperial Forums), and Circus Maximus.

The Appian Way   Via Appia Antica is a 2,300-year-old road that has witnessed much of the history of the ancient world. By 190 B.C. it extended from Rome to Brindisi, and its most famous sights today are the catacombs, the graveyards of patrician families. It was here, according to legend, that Christ had the famous exchange with St. Peter ("Lord, wither goest thou?"). Christ explained that he was returning to Rome to be crucified again, since Peter had abandoned the Christians in their hour of need. Peter returned to Rome and his own martyrdom.

Città del Vaticano [Vatican City]   This is a small "city-state," but its influence extends around the world. The Vatican Museums and St. Peter's take up most of the land area and the popes have lived here for six centuries.

Medieval Rome [piazza Navona and the Pantheon]   One of the most alluring areas of Rome centers around piazza Navona and the Pantheon. The district is a maze of narrow streets and alleys from the Middle Ages and is filled with churches and palaces built during the Renaissance era, often with materials stripped from ancient Rome, including rare marbles. The only way to explore it is on foot.

Monte Mario   On the northwest precincts of Rome, this residential area offers panoramic views over the eternal city, especially from Villa Madama, which was launched by Raphael but is closed to the public. Monte Mario is the site of the deluxe Cavalieri Hilton where you can stop in for a drink.

Parioli   This is the most elegant residential section of Rome, framed by the green spaces of Villa Borghese to the south and Villa Glori and Villa Ada to the north. It is a setting for some of the city's finest restaurants, hotels, and nightclubs.

Piazza di Spagna   Ever since the 17th century these steps—former site of the Spanish ambassador's residence—have been the center of tourist Rome. Keats lived in a house opening onto the steps, and some of Rome's most prestigious shopping streets fan out from it, including via Condotti.

Prati   Known only to the connoisseurs of Rome, this district is really a middle-class suburb, lying north of Castel Sant'Angelo and Vatican City. It is becoming increasingly patronized by budget travelers because of its low-cost *pensioni* (boardinghouses). The flower market in the Trionfale Quarter to the west is worth the trip.

Renaissance Rome   Many buildings in this district, south of corso Vittorio Emanuele, were constructed in Renaissance times as private homes. Much of the section centers around the Palazzo Farnese. Walk via Giulia with its antiques stores, interesting hotels, and modern-art galleries.

Stazione Termini   The station adjoins the piazza dei Cinquecento and, for many, this is their introduction to Rome. Much of the area is seedy and filled with gas fumes from all the buses and cars, but there is still much here to interest the visitor, including the Basilica da Santa Maria Maggiore and the Baths of Diocletian. Many good hotels remain.

Trastevere   This is the most authentic district of Rome, lying "across the Tiber," and its people are of mixed ancestry, including Jewish, Roman, and Greek, and speak their own dialect. The area centers around the ancient churches of Santa Cecilia in Trastevere and Santa Maria in Trastevere.

Via Vittorio Veneto   In the 1950s and early 1960s this was the haunt of the *La Dolce Vita* set, as King Farouk of Egypt and Swedish actress Anita Ekberg paraded up and down the boulevard to the delight of the aggressive cameramen. The street is still there, still the site of luxury hotels, elegant cafes, and restaurants, although it no longer has the allure it did in its heyday.

2   Getting Around

By Public Transportation

BY SUBWAY   The **Metropolitana,** or **Metro** for short, is the fastest means of transportation in Rome. It has two underground lines: Line A goes from via Ottaviano, near St. Peter's to Anagnina, stopping at piazzale Flaminio (near piazza del Popolo), piazza Vittorio Emanuele, and piazza San Giovanni in Laterano. Line B connects the Rebibbia district with via Laurentina, stopping at via Cavour, piazza Bologna, Stazione Termini, the Colosseum, Circus Maximus, the Pyramid of C. Cestius, St. Paul's Outside the Walls, the Magliana, and the EUR. A big red letter M indicates the entrance to the subway. The price is 1,200 lire (70¢). A booklet of 10 tickets costs 6,000 lire ($3.60).

Tickets are available from vending machines at all stations. These machines accept 50 lira, 100 lira, and 200 lira coins. Some stations have managers, but they will not make change. Booklets of tickets are available at *tabacchi* (tobacco) shops and in some terminals. Some machines change 1,000-lire (60¢) notes into coins.

Building an underground system for Rome has not been easy, since every time workers start digging, they discover an old temple or other archeological treasure and heavy earth-moving has to cease for a while.

BY BUS/TRAM   Roman buses are operated by an organization known as ATAC, or **Azienda Tramvie e Autobus del Comune di Roma,** via Volturno 65 (☎ **46951** for information).

For only 1,200 lire (70¢), you can ride to most parts of Rome (but not outlying districts) on quite good bus hookups. The ticket is valid for 1¹/₂ hours, and you can get on many buses during that time period using the same ticket. At Stazione Termini, you can purchase a special tourist bus pass, costing 4,000 lire ($2.40) for one day or 18,000 lire ($10.80) for a week. This allows you to ride on the ATAC network without bothering to purchase individual tickets. This tourist pass is also valid on the subway. Never ride the trains when the Romans are going to or from work, or you'll be mashed flatter than fettuccine. On the first bus you board, you place your ticket in a small machine that prints the day and hour you boarded. And you do the same on the last bus you take during the validity period of the ticket.

Buses and trains stop at areas marked FERMATA, and in general they are in service from 6am to midnight daily. After that and until dawn, service, on main-line stations only, is very marginal. It's best to take a taxi in the wee hours—if you can find one.

At the bus information booth at piazza dei Cinquecento, in front of Stazione Termini, you can purchase a directory complete with maps summarizing the particular routes. Ask there about where to purchase bus tickets, or buy them in a tobacco shop or at a bus terminal. You must have your ticket before boarding the bus, as there are no ticket-issuing machines on the vehicles.

Take extreme caution riding the overcrowded buses of Rome—pickpockets abound! This is particularly true on bus no. 64, a favorite of tourists because of its route through Rome's historic districts and also a favorite of Rome's vast pickpocketing community. Bus 64 has earned various nicknames: "The Pickpocket Express" or "The Wallet Eater."

By Taxi

If you're accustomed to hopping a cab in New York or London, then do so in Rome. If not, take less-expensive means of transport. Avoid paying your fare with large bills—invariably taxi drivers don't have change. The driver will also expect a 15% tip. Don't count on hailing a taxi on the street or even getting one at a stand. You can usually get one at Stazione Termini or piazza San Silvestro. If you're going out, have your hotel call one. At a restaurant, ask the waiter or cashier to dial for you. If you want to phone yourself, try one of these numbers: **3570, 4944,** or **3875.**

The meter begins at 6,400 lire ($3.80), plus another 300 lire (20¢) for every 800 feet. On Sunday, a 1,000 lire (60¢) supplement is assessed, plus another 3,000-lire ($1.80) supplement from 10pm to 7am. There's yet another 500-lire (30¢) supplement for every suitcase. From Fiumicino airport to town, you pay the price on the meter, plus another 14,000-lire ($8.40) surcharge. The driver might be heading home for dinner, but you pay the supplement regardless.

By Car

All roads may lead to Rome if you're driving, but don't count on actually do much driving once you get there. Since reception desks of most Roman hotels have at least one English-speaking person, it is wise to call ahead to find out the best route into Rome from wherever you're starting out.

To the neophyte, Roman drivers will appear like the chariot racers in *Ben Hur.* When the light says green, go forth with caution. Many Roman drivers go through the red light. Roman drivers in traffic gridlock move bravely on, fighting for every inch of the road.

To complicate matters, many zones, such as that around piazza di Spagna, are traffic free, and other traffic-free zones are being tried out in various parts of Rome.

RENTALS   It is virtually impossible to drive around Rome, but if you plan to take many excursions from the city—for example, into the hill towns—you'll find a car a most reliable and convenient means of transport.

Renting a car is easy. All drivers in Rome must have nerves of steel, a sense of humor, a valid driver's license, a valid passport, and in most cases, must be between the ages of 21 and 70. In all cases, payment and paperwork are simple if you present valid credit cards with your completed rental contract. If that isn't possible, the payment of a substantial cash deposit will probably be required in advance. Insurance on all vehicles is compulsory in Italy. A *carta verde* or "green card" is valid for 15, 30, or 45 days and should be issued to cover your car before your trip to Italy. Beyond 45 days, you must have a regular Italian insurance policy.

You'll find a bewildering assortment of car rental kiosks at the airports and railway stations of Rome, and agencies are also located downtown. **Hertz** has its main office near the parking lot of the Villa Borghese, via Vittorio Veneto 156 (☎ **547991**, or toll free **800/654-3001**). The **Budget** headquarters are at via Boncompagni 14C (☎ **484810**, or toll free **800/472-3325**). The downtown **Avis** office, which is usually considered closest to most of Rome's hotels, is at piazza Isquilino 1C (☎ **4701216**, or toll free **800/331-2112**). **Maggiore,** an Italian company, has an office at via di Tor Cervara (☎ **229351**); however, billing errors are more easily resolved if you stick to an affiliate of one of North America's larger companies. All toll-free numbers are for calls made in the U.S. or Canada.

At presstime, all three of the major car-rental companies charge approximately the same for their least expensive vehicles. Budget Rent-a-Car seemed especially lenient about permitting a vehicle to be returned at a location different from that of the original pickup. Each of the major companies will quote two tiers of rental prices which either include or do not include collision-damage insurance; this extra protection will eliminate all financial responsibility to a renter in the event of an accident. Each of the companies, for an additional charge of between $12 and $20 a day, will sell a renter a collision-damage waiver (CDW). This extra protection will cover all or part of the repair-related costs if there's an accident. In some cases, even if you purchase the CDW, you'll still pay around $300 per accident. Asking a few pertinent questions before you rent might save a lot of anxiety later. Know in advance that if you don't purchase the waiver, you are likely to be responsible for the full value of the car. Credit-card companies, including American Express, offer to pay the cost of any deductible damage to a rented car in certain countries *if the imprint of the credit card is made on the original rental contract.* Check with your credit-card company before you decide to handle your coverage in this way.

Depending on the company, purchase of the above-mentioned CDW may not include the value of damage and/or loss caused by attempted break-ins. At Avis and Budget, purchase of an additional theft policy is mandatory; at Hertz, it is strongly recommended. Such policies are usually priced at around $11 per day, and even if there is a break-in (or if the car is stolen), you might still have to pay a deductible of between $100 and $200. Many travelers, however, consider the best insurance against theft is the practice of *never* leaving luggage visible through the windows of a parked car.

For a week-long midsummer rental of a cramped but peppy Peugeot 106 or Fiat Mirabella, each of the companies charges between $150 and $310, depending on the season and the circumstances. For pickups at most airports in Italy, all three of the companies are obligated to impose a 10% government tax. To avoid that charge, consider pickup of your car at any of the inner-city locations that each of the companies maintains throughout Italy.

As the size and comfort level of cars increase, so do the rental costs, although at the midsized level, all three of the companies tend to charge roughly equivalent rates. Special promotions, which come and go frequently, tend to favor one or another company over its competitors. As always, it pays to phone around before committing yourself. The smallest available cars at all three of the companies tend to be small, very cramped, and not suitable for large or long-legged renters, or for clients with lots of luggage. To these rates is added the unavoidable 19% government tax (different from the airport pickup tax), plus the cost of any optional medical insurance. Discounts of 10% are sometimes offered to members of the American Automobile Association (AAA) or the American Association of Retired Persons (AARP).

If you want just a short holiday in the countryside, try to plan your visit for a weekend, when some companies, most notably Hertz, offer values for short-term weekend rentals. Hertz defines a weekend as any time between 9am on Thursday and 9am on Monday.

These prices can—and almost certainly will—change by the time of your arrival in Rome. One thing is certain, however: The best prices are almost always available at any company for clients who reserve their car at least two business days in advance from a telephone in North America.

GASOLINE   Gas stations—called *staziones di servizio* in Italian—are located throughout central Rome. Usually they are identified by the scallop-shaped logo of Shell or by the fire-breathing black dragon of AGIP, the major oil company of Italy. Only a few gas stations accept credit cards; all prefer cash.

Gasoline is much more expensive in Italy than in North America. Depending on market conditions and the octane level, gasoline (known as *benzina* in Italy) ranges from $4 to $5 a gallon. Filling the tank of a medium-sized car can cost from $35 and up, something to seriously consider when you're planning your budget.

DRIVING RULES   The Italian Highway Code follows the Geneva Convention, and Italy uses international road signs. Driving is on the right, passing on the left. Violators of the highway code are fined; serious violations may also be punished by imprisonment. In Rome, the speed limit is 50 kilometers per hour (kmph) or 31.25 miles per hour (m.p.h.). Seat belts are compulsory.

U.S. and Canadian drivers are requested to carry an International Driver's License when touring Italy. Drivers without such a license may present a valid U.S. or Canadian driver's license to obtain a declaration from the Automobile Club d'Italia entitling them to drive on Italian roads. The declaration is available from any ACI frontier or provincial office. U.S. and Canadian licenses are valid in Italy if accompanied by an official translation.

The **Automobile Club d'Italia (ACI)** is the equivalent of the AAA (American Automobile Association). Its head office is at via Marsala 8, 00185 Roma (☎ **06/4998389**). The office is open Monday through Saturday from 8:30am to 1:30pm. The Information and Assistance Centre (CAT) of the ACI is at via Magenta 5, 00185 Roma (☎ **06/4477**), and it is open around the clock. Both offices are close to the main railway station (Termini).

ROAD MAPS   A good map of Rome and its environs is published by **Grande Carta Stradale d'Italia.** The best touring maps are published by the **Automobile Club d'Italia** (ACT) and the **Italian Touring Club,** or you can purchase the maps of the **Carta Automobilistica d'Italia** covering Italy in two maps on the scale of 1:800,000 (1cm = 8km). These maps are sold at certain newsstands and at all major bookstores in Rome, especially those with travel departments. Many travel bookstores in the U.S., Canada, and Britain also carry them. If U.S. outlets don't have these maps, they often offer Michelin's red map (no. 988) of Italy, which covers all of Italy in some detail.

BREAKDOWNS/ASSISTANCE   In case of car breakdown and for any tourist information, foreign motorists can call **116** (nation-wide telephone service). For road information, itineraries, and all sorts of travel assistance, call **06/49981** (ACI's information center). Both services operate 24 hours a day.

PARKING   Find out if your hotel has a garage. If not, you are usually allowed to park your car in front of the hotel long enough to unload your luggage. Someone at the hotel—a doorman, if there is one—will direct you to the nearest garage or place to park.

By Bicycle, Motorscooter & Motorcycle

St. Peter Moto Renting & Selling, via di Porta Castello 43 (☎ **6874909**), open Monday through Saturday from 9am to 1pm and 3:30 to 7pm, rents Mopeds. Rates range from 150,000 lire ($90) per day. Renters must post deposits ranging from a low of 300,000 lire ($180) to a high of 1,200,000 lire ($720), depending on the type of vehicle rented. For motorcycles, the minimum age for a renter is 18, and a valid driver's license is required. Only the most experienced should rent a motorcycle, as it is dangerous riding because of traffic. Take the Metro to Ottaviano.

Bicycles are rented at many places throughout Rome. Ask at your hotel for the nearest rental location, or go to **I Bike Rome,** via Veneto

156 (☎ **3225240**), which rents bicycles from the underground parking garage at the Villa Borghese. Most rentals cost 5,000 lire ($3) per hour, or 15,000 lire ($9) per day. It's open daily from 9am to 8pm.

On Foot

Much of the inner core of Rome is traffic free—so you'll need to walk whether you like it or not. Walking is the perfect way to see Rome, especially the ancient, narrow, cobbled streets of Old Rome. However, walking in many parts of the city is hazardous and uncomfortable, because of overcrowded streets, heavy traffic, and too-narrow sidewalks. Sometimes sidewalks don't exist at all, and it becomes a sort of free-for-all with pedestrians competing for space against vehicular traffic, with the traffic always seeming to win. If you're going to another district—and chances are that your hotel will be outside of Old Rome—you can take the bus or Metro. For such a large city, Rome is covered amazingly well on foot, because so much of what will interest a visitor lies in various clusters.

Fast Facts: Rome

American Express The offices of American Express are at piazza di Spagna 38 (☎ **67641**). The travel service is open Monday through Friday from 9am to 5:30pm and on Saturday from 9am to 12:30pm. Hours for the financial and mail services are Monday through Friday from 9am to 5pm and on Saturday from 9am to noon. The tour desk is open during the same hours as those for travel services and also on Saturday afternoon from 2 to 2:30pm only, from May through October.

Area Code The telephone area code for Rome and its environs is **06**.

Babysitters Most hotel desks in Rome will help you secure a babysitter, or you can call a local agency, **Centro Bimbi** (☎ **6873508**). You should ask for an English-speaking sitter if available.

Bookstores See "Shopping A to Z," Chapter 8.

Business Hours In general, banks are open Monday through Friday from 8:30am to 1:30pm and 3 to 4pm. Some banks keep afternoon hours ranging from 2:45 to 3:45pm. The American Service Bank is at piazza Mignanelli 5 (☎ **6786815**). Two other favorite U.S. banks are Chase Manhattan, via Michele Mercati 39 (☎ **866361**), and Citibank, via Boncompagni 26 (☎ **4713**). Shopping hours are governed by the siesta. Most stores are open year-round Monday through Saturday from 9am to 1pm and then 3:30 or 4pm to 7:30 or 8pm. Most shops are closed on Sunday except for some barbershops that are open Sunday morning. Hairdressers are closed Sunday and Monday.

Camera/Films   U.S.-brand film is available in Rome, but it's expensive. Take in as much as Customs will allow if you plan to take a lot of pictures.

Car Rentals   See "Getting Around" earlier in this chapter.

Cigarettes   Seek out stores called *tabacchi*. Some bars also sell cigarettes. For a package of U.S. cigarettes in your familiar brand, you'll pay more than for an Italian variety; however, the taste of the Italian brands may be unfamiliar and may require some getting used to. American and British contraband cigarettes are sold freely on the streets for much less than you'll pay in the shops. Although purchasing them is illegal, it seems to be the custom.

Climate   See "When to Go" in Chapter 2.

Crime   See "Safety" below.

Currency Exchange   This is possible at all major rail and airline terminals in Rome, including the Stazione Termini where the *cambio* (exchange booth) beside the rail information booth is open daily from 8am to 8pm. At some cambios you'll have to pay a commission, often 1.5%. Banks, likewise, often charge commissions. One that doesn't is **Frama,** via Torino 21B (☎ **4817632**), off via Nazionale near Stazione Termini. It's open Monday through Friday from 8:30am to 6pm and on Saturday from 9am to 1pm. Many so-called money changers will approach you on the street, but often they're pushing counterfeit lire—they offer very good rates for their fake money!

Dentist   To secure a dentist who speaks English, call the U.S. embassy in Rome, via Vittorio Veneto 121 (☎ **46741**). You may have to call around in order to get an appointment. There is also the 24-hour G. Eastman Dental Hospital, viale Regina Elena 287 (☎ **4453220**).

Doctor   Call the American embassy (see "Dentist" above), which provides you with a list of doctors who speak English. All big hospitals in Rome have a 24-hour first-aid service (go to the emergency room). You'll find English-speaking doctors at the privately run Salvator Mundi International Hospital, viale delle Mura Giancolensis 67 (☎ **588961**). For medical assistance, the International Medical Center is on 24-hour duty at via Amendola 7 (☎ **4882371**).

Driving Rules   See "Getting Around" earlier in this chapter.

Drug Laws   Penalties are severe and could lead to either imprisonment or deportation. Selling drugs to minors is dealt with particularly harshly.

Drugstores   A reliable pharmacy is Farmacia Internazionale, piazza Barberini 49 (☎ **4825456**), open day and night. Most pharmacies are open from 8:30am to 1pm and 4 to 7:30pm. In general, pharmacies follow a rotation system so that several are always open on Sunday. The concierge at your hotel can usually direct you to the nearest drugstore.

Electricity It is generally 220 volts, 50 Hz AC, but it might be 125 volt outlets, with different plugs and sockets for each. It is recommended that any visitor carrying electrical appliances obtain a transformer either before leaving the U.S. or Canada or in any electrical appliance shop in Rome. Check the exact local current with the hotel where you are staying. Plugs have prongs that are round, not flat; therefore an adapter plug is needed.

Embassies/Consulates The consular and passport services of the **United States** are at via Vittorio Veneto 119A (☎ **46741**), open Monday through Friday from 8:30am to 12:30pm and 2 to 4:30pm; for **Canada,** at via Zara 30 (☎ **445981**), open Monday through Friday from 10am to noon and 2 to 4pm. For the **United Kingdom,** offices are at via Francesco Crispi 122 (☎ **66311**), open in summer, Monday through Friday from 8am to 1:30pm and in off-season, Monday through Friday from 9am to 12:30pm and 2 to 4:30pm. For **Australia,** the embassy is at via Alessadria 215 (☎ **852721**), open Monday through Thursday from 8:30am to 12:30pm and 1:30 to 5:30pm, and on Friday from 8:30am to 1:15pm. The Australia Consulate is around the corner in the same building at corso Trieste 25. For **New Zealand,** the office is at via Zara 28 (☎ **4402928**), and hours are Monday through Friday from 8:30am to 12:45pm and 1:45 to 5pm. In case of emergency, embassies have a 24-hour referral service.

Emergencies The police "hot line" number is **212121**. Usually, however, dial **113** for the police, to report a fire, or summon an ambulance.

Etiquette Women in sleeveless dresses and men with bare chests are not welcome in the best bars and restaurants of Italy and may be refused service. Also, persons so attired are ordered to cover up when they visit museums and churches.

Eyeglasses Try Vasai, piazza della Repubblica 22 (☎ **4814505**), which lies adjacent to the Grand Hotel and is a very large shop with lots of choices and a central location.

Gasoline See "Getting Around" earlier in this chapter.

Hairdresser/Barbers Romans are considered great hair stylists for both men and women. Sometimes large hotels have these services on the premises, and all neighborhoods have them. Just ask at the reception desk of your hotel for a good one. Otherwise, women can patronize Gracia, via Frattina 75 (☎ **6792046**). Handling both men and women, Sergio Valente is an elegant choice at via Condotti 11 (☎ **6794515**). Both these establishments are in the center of Rome.

Holidays See "When to Go" in Chapter 2.

Hospitals A private clinic with English-speaking doctors is Salvator Mundi International Hospital, viale delle Mura Gianicolensis 67 (☎ **588961**). You might also prefer the services of the Rome American Hospital, via Emilio Longoni 69 (☎ **225571**).

The International Medical Center, via Giovanni Amendola 7 (☎ 4882371), is staffed with English-speaking doctors, and operates 24 hours a day. It can arrange appointments with anybody from a general doctor to a cardiologist, from a pediatrician to a surgeon.

Hotlines   Dial **113**, which is a general SOS to report any kind of danger, such as a rape attack. You can also dial **112**, the police emergency number. For a personal crisis, call Samaritana, via San Giovanni in Laterno 250 (☎ 70454444), open daily from 1 to 10pm.

Information   See "Tourist Information" earlier in this chapter.

Language   The official language of Italy, of course, is Italian, a Romance tongue derived from Latin. Numerous dialects were common throughout parts of Italy until the Tuscan dialect became Italy's literary language in the 14th century. The best phrase book is Berlitz *Italian for Travellers.* Another way of communicating if you don't speak Italian is through Quickpoint, a visual translator, allowing you to point at pictures to communicate. This three-panel brochure contains some 400 color illustrations of everyday items such as a pay phone or gasoline. You just point to the corresponding picture. Single copies cost $6 and can be ordered by calling **703/548-8794** in the U.S., or writing to Gaia Communications Inc., Dept. 102, P.O. Box 239, Alexandria, VA 22313-0239.

Laundry/Dry Cleaning   First-class and deluxe hotels provide this service, often on the same day, but you'll pay for the extra convenience. All neighborhoods in Rome have laundries (not self-service) and dry-cleaning establishments. Most laundries have minimum-load requirements ranging from 3 to 4 kilograms (6½ to 9 lb.). A central laundry is found at Sarti, via di Ripetta (☎ 3219409). For dry cleaning, try Bologna, via della Lungara 141 (☎ 6875762).

Legal Aid   The consulate of your country is the place to turn, although offices cannot interfere in the Italian legal process. They can, however, inform you of your rights and provide a list of attorneys. You'll have to pay for the attorney out of your pocket, however, as there is no free legal assistance. If you're arrested for a drug offense, about all the consulate will do is notify a lawyer about your case and perhaps inform your family.

Libraries   There's the British Council Library, via Quattro Fontane 20 (☎ 4826641), open Monday and Thursday from 10am to 1pm and 2 to 7pm, on Tuesday from 10am to 1pm and 2 to 6pm, and on Wednesday from 10am to 6pm.

Liquor Laws   Wine with meals has been considered a normal part of family life for hundreds of years in Italy. There is no legal drinking age for buying or ordering alcohol, and alcohol is sold day and night throughout the year.

Lost Property   Usually lost property is gone forever. But you might try checking at Oggetti Rinvenuti, via Nicolò Bettoni 1 (☎ 5816040), which is open Monday through Saturday from 9am to noon. A branch at the Stazione Termini off Track 1 (☎ 4730682) is open daily from 7am to midnight.

Luggage Storage/Lockers   These are available at the Stazione Termini, piazza dei Cinquecento.

Mail   Post office boxes in Italy are red and are attached to walls. One slot is for letters intended just for the city (on the left). On the right is a slot for letters for all other destinations. Vatican City post office boxes are blue, and you can buy special stamps at the Vatican City Post Office. It is said that letters mailed at Vatican City reach North America or Britain much more quickly than does mail sent from within Rome.

The Vatican post office is adjacent to the information office in St. Peter's Square. It is open Monday through Friday from 8:30am to 7pm and on Saturday from 8:30am to 6pm.

Maps   See "Getting Around" earlier in this chapter.

Newspapers/Magazines   In Rome, it is possible to find the *International Herald Tribune* or *USA Today* as well as other English-language newspapers and magazines at hotels and news kiosks, including *Time* and *Newsweek*.

Pets   A veterinarian's certificate of good health is required for dogs and cats, and should be obtained by owners before entering Italy. Dogs must be on a leash or muzzled at all times. Other animals must undergo examination at the border or port of entry. Certificates for parrots or other birds subject to psittacosis must state that the country of origin is free of disease. All documents must be certified first by a notary public, then by the nearest Italian consulate.

Police   The all-purpose number for police emergency assistance in Italy is **113**.

Radio/TV   Most radio and television broadcasts are on RAI, the Italian state radio and TV network. Occasionally, especially during the tourist season, the network will broadcast special programs in English. Announcements are made in the radio and TV guide sections of local newspapers. Vatican Radio also carries foreign-language religious news programs, often in English. Shortwave transistor radios pick up broadcasts from the BBC (British), Voice of America (United States), and CBC (Canadian). RAI television and private channels broadcast only in Italian. More expensive hotels often have TV sets in the bedrooms with cable subscriptions to the CNN news network.

Religious Services   Catholic churches abound in Rome. Several of these conduct services in English, including San Silvestro, piazza San Silvestro 1 (☎ 679775), and Santa Susana, via XX Settembre 14 (☎ 4882748). The American Episcopal Church is St. Paul's, via Napoli 58, at via Nazionale (☎ 4883339). The Jewish temple, Sinagoga Ebraica, is at lungotevere dei Cenci (☎ 6564648). "Pro Unione" Ecumenical Gatherings, conducted by the Franciscan Friars of the Atonement for non–Roman Catholics visiting Rome, include background briefings, slide presentations, and excursions to some of the most important places of ecumenical interest in Rome, including St. Peter's Basilica, Santa Sabina, San Clemente, the Colosseum, the Roman Forum, the Vatican Gardens, and the Catacombs (where eucharistic liturgies and prayer services can be arranged for groups). Through these services, the Centro Pro Unione hopes to offer an opportunity for encounter and dialogue. All services are free, but a voluntary contribution is requested. "Pro Unione" Ecumenical Gatherings take place at the Centro Pro Unione which is located on the first floor of the Palazzo Doria Pamphilj, via Santa Maria dell'Anima, 30 (Piazza Navona). For information, call **6833631**.

Restrooms   Facilities are found near many of the major sights, often with attendants, as are those at bars, nightclubs, restaurants, cafes, and hotels, plus the airports and the railway station. You're expected to leave 200 to 500 lire (10¢ to 30¢) for the attendant. If you're not checking into a hotel in Rome but going on by train elsewhere, you can patronize the Albergo Diurno, a hotel without beds at the Stazione Termini. It has baths, showers, and well-kept toilet facilities.

Safety   Whenever you're traveling in an unfamiliar city or country, stay alert. Be aware of your immediate surroundings, and wear a moneybelt. This will minimize the possibility of your becoming a victim of crime. Every society has its criminals. It's your responsibility to be aware and alert even in the most heavily touristed areas. The most common menace in Rome is the plague of pickpockets and roving gangs of gypsy children who virtually surround you, distract you in all the confusion, and rob your purse or wallet. Never leave valuables in a car, and never travel with your car unlocked. A U.S. State Department travel advisory warns that every car—whether parked, stopped at a traffic light, or even moving—can be a potential target for armed robbery.

Shoe Repair   Many department stores have these services, and each Rome neighborhood has its favorite shoe-repair place. Ask at your hotel reception desk, or go to Leotta, via del Boschetto (☎ **4819177**).

Taxes   As a member of the European Union, Italy imposes a tax on most goods and services. It is a "value-added tax," called IVA in Italy. For example, the tax affecting most visitors is that imposed at hotels, which ranges from 9% in first-class and second-class hotels and pensions to 13% in deluxe hotels.

Telegram/Telephone/Telex/Fax   For telegrams, ITALCABLE operates services abroad, transmitting messages by cable or satellite. Both internal and foreign telegrams may be dictated over the phone (dial **186**).

You can also send telegrams from all post offices during the day and from the telegraph office at the central post office in piazza San Silvestro, off della Mercede, at night.

A public telephone is always near at hand in Rome, especially if you're near a bar. Local calls from public telephones require the use of tokens (*gettone*) or coins. To make your call, deposit a 200-lire token in the slot but don't release it until after the number has been dialed and the party has answered. Tokens can be purchased at all tobacco shops and bars.

Thanks to ITALCABLE, international calls to the U.S. and Canada can be dialed directly. Dial 00 (the international code from Italy), then the country code (1 for the U.S. and Canada), the area code and the number you are calling. Calls dialed directly are billed on the basis of the call's duration only. A reduced rate is applied from 11pm to 8am Monday through Saturday and all day Sunday.

If you wish to make a collect or credit-card call, dial **170**. An ITALCABLE operator will come on and will speak English. If you make a long-distance call from a public telephone, there is no surcharge. *However, hotels have been known to double or triple the cost of the call, so be duly warned.*

Your hotel will probably send a telex or fax for you. If your hotel doesn't have a fax, go to Capitalexpress, via Bresadola 55 (☎ **2585404**), Monday through Friday from 8:30am to 6:30pm.

Taxis   See "Getting Around" earlier in this chapter.

Time   In terms of standard time zones, Rome is six hours ahead of eastern standard time in the United States. Daylight saving time goes into effect in Italy each year from May 22 to September 24.

Tipping   This custom is practiced with flair in Italy—many people depend on tips for their livelihoods. In hotels, the service charge of 15% or 18% is already added to a bill. In addition, it's customary to tip the chambermaid 1,000 lire (60¢) per day; the doorman (for calling a cab), 1,000 lire (60¢); and the bellhop or porter, 2,000 lire ($1.20) per bag. A concierge expects 3,000 lire ($1.80) per day, as well as tips for extra services performed, which could include help with long-distance calls, newspapers, or stamps.

In restaurants, 15% is added to your bill to cover most charges. An additional tip for good service is almost always expected. Know that it is customary in certain fashionable restaurants in Rome to leave an additional 10%, which, combined with the assessed service charge, is a very high tip indeed. The sommelier expects 10% of the cost of the wine. Checkroom attendants now expect 1,500 lire (90¢), although in simple places Romans still hand washroom attendants 200 to 300 lire (10¢ to 20¢), more in deluxe and first-class establishments. Restaurants are required by law to give customers official receipts.

In cafes and bars, tip 15% of the bill, and give a theater usher 1,500 lire (90¢). Taxi drivers expect at least 15% of the fare.

Tourist Offices   See "Tourist Information" earlier in this chapter.

Transit Information   For airport information at Leonardo da Vinci International Airport, phone **65951**; for Ciampino Airport, phone **79340297**. For bus information, phone **46951**, and for rail information, call **4775.**

Visas   See "Information, Entry Requirements & Money" in Chapter 2.

Water   Rome is famed for its drinking water, which is generally safe; nevertheless, Romans traditionally order bottled mineral water in restaurants.

Yellow Pages   Unless you're fluent in Italian, better forget these. Ask at your hotel for assistance if you're seeking a particular establishment, such as the nearest dry-cleaning store.

3 Networks & Resources

FOR STUDENTS   The Rome center for budget student travel is **Centro Turistico Studentesco e Giovanile (CTS),** via Genova 16 (☎ **46791**). Air, sea, train, and bus discounts are available here and you can pick up a helpful brochure, "Young Rome." An accommodation-booking service is also available, including low-cost hotels in other Italian cities. On the bulletin board young people post notices offering or seeking rides (which is a better arrangement than hitchhiking). The office is open Monday through Friday from 9am to 1pm and 4 to 7pm, and on Saturday from 9am to 1pm.

FOR GAY MEN & LESBIANS   Before you go to Italy, men can order *Spartacus,* the international gay guide, $29.95, from Giovanni's Room, 1145 Pine St., Philadelphia, PA 19107 (☎ **215/923-2960**). Both lesbians and gay men might want to pick up a copy of *Ferrari's Places of Interest* ($14.95) at the same outlet.

Once in Rome, look for a copy of *Rome Gay News* for more information about the gay and lesbian scene there.

The gay and lesbian liberation center is **Circolo Mario Mieli,** via Ostiense 202 (☎ **5413985**), a center where gay men and women meet. Various activities take place here, and shows are often presented. Friday night is disco night here. Office hours are Monday through Friday from 10am to 6pm.

FOR WOMEN   A feminist bookstore and a clearinghouse for "what's happening" is **Al Tempo Ritrovato,** piazza Farnese 103 (☎ **68803749**). Here you'll find an array of international publications appealing to women's interests. It's open Tuesday through Sunday from 10am to 1:30pm and 3:30 to 8pm.

FOR SENIORS   Visit the tourist office in Rome (see "Tourist Information" in "Orientation" above) and ask about any special discounts for older travelers that might be available on transportation, hotels, cultural events, and museums during the time of your visit.

Rome Accommodations

AFTER A LONG AND CAREFUL PROCESS OF ELIMINATION, I OFFER THIS LIST OF recommended hotels. Although they come in several different price categories, they all share something in common—style. I've looked for places with architectural grace and a relaxed ambience, establishments where the management is alert and understanding, where the facilities provide all necessary comforts. But more specifically I've sought out those hotels with personality, hotels that treat you like a guest instead of a walking traveler's check.

My selections are divided into five major categories: very expensive, expensive, moderate, inexpensive, and budget. Rome's poshest hotels, while no bargain, are among the most luxurious in Europe. The bulk of this chapter, however, concerns moderately priced hotels, where you'll find rooms with private bath. The final group is budget hotels, and a charming group they are; each one has been judged clean and cheerful and offers surprisingly more in services and facilities than you would expect from the prices charged. In the two less expensive categories, you'll find a few pensions.

HOTELS   Italy controls the prices of its hotels, designating a minimum and a maximum rate. The difference between the two may depend on the season, the location of the room, or even its size. Hotels are classified by stars in Italy, indicating their category of comfort: five stars for deluxe, four stars for first class, three stars for second class, two stars for third class, and one star for fourth class. Government ratings do not depend on sensitivity of decoration or on frescoed ceilings, but rather on facilities, such as elevators and the like. Many of the finest hostelries in Rome are rated second class because they only serve breakfast (a blessing really, for those seeking to escape the board requirements).

Hotels in Rome today are divided on the question of whether breakfast is included in the room price. Usually the more expensive establishments charge extra for this meal, which most often consists of cappuccino (coffee with milk) and croissants, with fresh butter and jam. First-class and deluxe establishments serve what is known as either an English breakfast or an American breakfast—meaning ham and eggs—but this must nearly always be ordered from the à la carte menu. Many smaller hotels and pensions serve only continental breakfast. If you're really watching your lire, always determine exactly what is included and what is extra.

PENSIONS   The *pensione* is generally more intimate and personal than a hotel—in one, the nature and quality of the welcome depend largely on the host or hostess, who might also be the cook and chief maid or maintenance man. As a general rule, a first-class pension in Rome is the equivalent of a second-class hotel. A third-class hotel is the equivalent of a second-class pension. In most of these pensions, you'll be asked to take half-board arrangements, although not always.

BED & BREAKFASTS   In Rome, these establishments are commonplace, and they offer the best accommodation value. Finding a suitable one, however, may be tricky. Often B&B places are family homes or apartments, so don't count on hotel services, or even private baths. Sometimes, however, B&Bs are in beautiful private homes, lovely guest houses, or restored mansions. Prices range from $20 to $50 per person nightly, including breakfast. Sometimes arrangements can be made for you to order an evening meal. Tourist offices generally keep a list of this type of accommodation.

HOME EXCHANGES An increasingly popular and economical way to travel is to exchange your home with that of a Roman family, often with a car included, provided you extend the same privilege. Several U.S.-based organizations specialize in this unique form of vacationing.

Intervac U.S. is part of the largest worldwide exchange network. It publishes three catalogs a year, containing more than 9,000 homes in more than 36 countries. Members contact each other directly. The $62 cost, plus postage, includes the purchase of all three of the company's catalogs (which will be mailed to you), plus the inclusion of your own listing in whichever one of the three catalogs you select. If you want to publish a photograph of your home, it costs $11 extra. Hospitality and youth exchanges are also available. The organization can be contacted at P.O. Box 590504, San Francisco, CA 94119 (☎ **415/435-3497,** or toll free in the U.S. **800/756-HOME**).

The Invented City, 41 Sutter St., Suite 1090, San Francisco, CA 94104 (☎ **414/673-0347**), is another international home-exchange agency. Home-exchange listings are published three times a year, in February, May, and November. A membership fee of $50 allows you to list your home, and you can also give your preferred time to travel, your occupation, and your hobbies.

Vacation Exchange Club, P.O. Box 650, Key West, FL 33041 (☎ **305/294-1448,** or toll free in the U.S. **800/638-3841**), will, for $60, send you four directories a year—in one of which you're listed.

RELAIS & CHATEAUX Most member hotels of this association are in France, but many of these prestigious (and invariably expensive) hotels also exist in Rome. Instead of sterile modern hotels, you'll frequently get places steeped in atmosphere and quality, often palaces or ancient castles converted to receive guests.

Prices for a double room can range anywhere from $200 to as much as $1,000 a night. To qualify for membership within the organization, all participating hotels must satisfy a demanding set of criteria for food, accommodations, and service.

For an illustrated catalog of these establishments worldwide, send $10 to Relais & Châteaux, 11 E. 44th St., Suite 707, New York, NY 10017 (☎ **212/856-0115**). For reservations, each individual hotel or inn must be contacted directly.

RELIGIOUS INSTITUTIONS Convents, monasteries, and other religious institutions in Rome offer accommodations, generally of the fourth-class hotel or pension category. Some are just for men; others are for women only. Many, however, accept married couples. Italian tourist offices generally have abbreviated listings of these accommodations.

Rome Accommodations

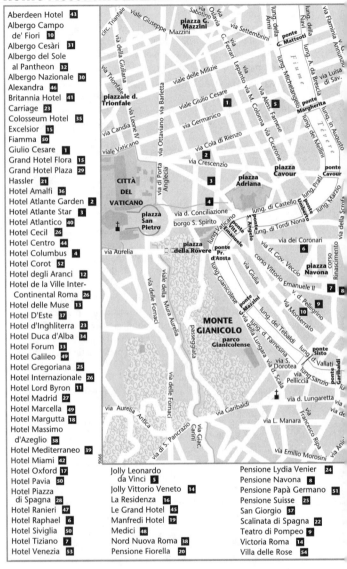

Aberdeen Hotel 43
Albergo Campo de' Fiori 10
Albergo Cesàri 31
Albergo del Sole al Pantheon 32
Albergo Nazionale 30
Alexandra 46
Britannia Hotel 41
Carriage 23
Colosseum Hotel 35
Excelsior 15
Fiamma 50
Giulio Cesare 1
Grand Hotel Flora 15
Grand Hotel Plaza 29
Hassler 21
Hotel Amalfi 36
Hotel Atlante Garden 2
Hotel Atlante Star 3
Hotel Atlantico 40
Hotel Cecil 26
Hotel Centro 44
Hotel Columbus 4
Hotel Corot 52
Hotel degli Aranci 12
Hotel de la Ville Inter-Continental Roma 26
Hotel delle Muse 13
Hotel D'Este 37
Hotel d'Inghliterra 23
Hotel Duca d'Alba 34
Hotel Forum 33
Hotel Galileo 49
Hotel Gregoriana 25
Hotel Internazionale 26
Hotel Lord Byron 11
Hotel Madrid 27
Hotel Marcella 49
Hotel Margutta 18
Hotel Massimo d'Azeglio 38
Hotel Mediterraneo 39
Hotel Miami 42
Hotel Oxford 17
Hotel Pavia 50
Hotel Piazza di Spagna 28
Hotel Ranieri 47
Hotel Raphael 6
Hotel Siviglia 50
Hotel Tiziano 7
Hotel Venezia 53

Jolly Leonardo da Vinci 5
Jolly Vittorio Veneto 14
La Residenza 16
Le Grand Hotel 45
Manfredi Hotel 19
Medici 48
Nord Nuova Roma 38
Pensione Fiorella 20

Pensione Lydia Venier 24
Pensione Navona 8
Pensione Papà Germano 51
Pensione Suisse 25
San Giorgio 37
Scalinata di Spagna 22
Teatro di Pompeo 9
Victoria Roma 14
Villa delle Rose 54

VILLAS & APARTMENTS   In Rome, information on villas and apartments is available in daily newspapers or through local real-estate agents. The following organizations deal in the rental of villas or apartments in both Rome and Italy.

Rent a Vacation Everywhere, Inc. (RAVE), 383 Park Ave., Rochester, NY 14607 (☎ **716/256-0760**), offers moderately priced to

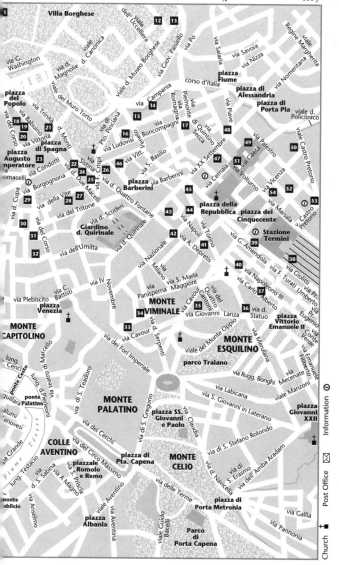

deluxe apartments and villas throughout Italy, in Veneto, Tuscany, Liguria, Umbria, and along the Amalfi coast, plus apartments in Florence and Rome. Partners Gloria Gioia and Annette Waldman have, for the most part, personally visited the villas they represent.

Hideaways International, 767 Islington St. (P.O. Box 4433), Portsmouth, NH 03802 (☎ **603/430-4433**), represents an

Italy-based real-estate management company that makes available several hundred villas scattered throughout Italy. A catalog listing color photos of each property is available upon request for $15.

Another reputable company renting privately owned accommodations in Italy, including apartments and villas, is **Hometours, Inc.,** 1170 Broadway, New York, NY 10001 (☎ **212/689-0851,** or toll free in the U.S. **800/689-0679** outside New York State). The company offers rentable dwellings in Umbria, along the Amalfi coast, in Tuscany, and in or around such cities as Livorno, Lucca, and Grosseto. There are also apartments in central Rome, Siena, Venice, and Florence, and a handful of large and echoing baroque palaces suitable for up to a dozen occupants at a time. Units are rented for a minimum of seven days. Unlike many other travel outfits, Hometours can also arrange bed-and-breakfast accommodations in simple, family-run one-, two-, and three-star hotels throughout Italy. To obtain their 180-page color catalog with descriptions and pictures, send $6 for postage and handling, $2 for their bed-and-breakfast catalog of small family-run hotels, or else $2 for descriptive literature about any other locations.

YOUTH HOSTELS   The Italian Youth Hostel Association operates more than 50 hostels throughout Italy, and they are likely to be overcrowded in summer, particularly at popular tourist meccas. Reservations can be made by writing directly to the individual youth hostel. The headquarters, **Italiana Alberghi per la Gioventù,** via Cavour 44, 00184 Roma (☎ **06/4871152**), provides details. You must be a member. In the U.S. you can join before you go by contacting **Hostelling International/American Youth Hostels** (HI-AYH), 733 15th St. NW, #840, Washington, DC 20005 (☎ **202/783-6161**). Membership is $25; if you're under 18 the charge is $10, and if you're over 54 it's $15.

FYI   Before I begin describing my choices, I'm going to warn you about some customs and situations in Italian hotels that you won't find in the States. Number one is that rooms vary substantially in the same hotel, even though the prices wouldn't seem to indicate it. It is perfectly acceptable to ask to see the room first, before you check in. Often you'll be sent up with a bellboy who has several keys, and you can choose the room that suits you best—unless, of course, only one room is vacant. Second, Rome tends to be noisy and so, unfortunately, are its hotel rooms, so be prepared.

As for hotel bills, everything is "à la carte," as it were. You have a bathless room? Then be prepared to pay extra for a shower. It's hot outside? Then that air conditioner in your room will probably cost quite a bit *extra* on top of the room price. It's cold outside? Sometimes even heat is charged for, although rarely these days. The next thing you should know is that some hotels have off-season rates; if you're traveling between November and Easter, ask at the desk and you may be in for a nice surprise. As for tipping, far too many foreign visitors think that because "service" is added onto their bills, the chambermaid has been taken care of. Not entirely true. In all but deluxe hotels, the service charge covers only pension funds and the like, and gives nothing to the maid.

PARKING   It is rare for hotels to have private garages; many were constructed before the advent of the automobile. Others built after the automobile didn't find enough room in overcongested Rome for garage space. Hotel reception desks will advise about nearby garages (usually in the same neighborhood as the hotel). Fees range from 4,000 to 60,000 lire ($2.40 to $36) per night.

RESERVATIONS   It's always a good idea to make reservations before you go, and this can be done through a travel agent or by writing or faxing directly to the hotel (some establishments require deposits, and this takes a great deal of time, especially considering how slow the Italian mails are). Some of the more expensive hotels have toll free 800 numbers in North America. You can call the hotel of your choice and give them your credit-card number. It's invariably easy to obtain an expensive room at any time of the year, but low-cost accommodations are generally heavily booked.

In case, however, you haven't made reservations, you're bound to find some place that can put you up for the *first night*. My advice, in that event, is to time your arrival for shortly before 9am and head straight for your first choice of hotel. If there is any space to be had, you'll be assured of getting first chance at it.

TAXES   All Italian hotels impose an IVA (Imposta sul Valore Aggiunto) tax. This tax is in effect throughout the other European Union countries. It applies only to the "value added" to products and services as they progress from source to consumer. It replaces some 20 other taxes and is an effort to streamline the tax structure.

What that means for you is an actual increase in the price you'll pay for a hotel room. Deluxe hotels will slap you with a whopping tax of 13%, while first-class, second-class, and other hotels will impose 9%. Most hotels will quote you an inclusive rate, covering this tax. However, other establishments prefer to add it on when you go to pay the bill. To know exactly what you're going to pay for a room, ask to be quoted an all-inclusive rate—that is, with service, even a continental breakfast (which is often obligatory)—when you check in. It will help you to avoid unpleasant surprises later.

The concierge of your hotel, incidentally, is a usually reliable dispenser of information.

THE PRICE CATEGORIES   In hotels rated very expensive, you can spend from 450,000 lire ($270) and up for a double room. Hotels judged expensive charge from 300,000 to 450,000 lire ($180 to $270) for a double room; those in the moderate category ask 210,000 to 300,000 lire ($126 to $180) for a double. Anything from 80,000 lire ($48) all the way up to 210,000 lire ($126) is judged "Inexpensive," at least by the inflated Roman standards of hotel pricing. A double room—most often without bath—that rents for under 80,000 lire ($48) is definitely in the "Budget" classification.

Unless otherwise specified, breakfast is of the continental variety.

1 Near Stazione Termini

Very Expensive

⭐ **Le Grand Hotel,** via Vittorio Emanuele Orlando 3, 00185 Roma.
☎ **06/4709,** or toll free **800/221-2340** in the U.S., or
800/955-2442 in Canada. Fax 06/4747307. 168 rms, 36 suites. A/C
MINIBAR TV TEL **Metro:** Piazza della Repubblica.
Rates: 320,000–350,000 lire ($192–$210) single; 470,000–520,000 lire
($282–$312) double; from 800,000 lire ($480) suite. Breakfast 26,000
lire ($15.60) extra; 13% IVA tax extra. AE, DC, MC, V. **Parking:** 40,000–
60,000 lire ($24–$36).

The Grand Hotel, just off the piazza della Repubblica, is one of the
great hotels in Europe. When it was inaugurated by its creator, César
Ritz, in 1894, Escoffier, the world's greatest chef, presided over a
lavish banquet, and the note of grandeur that was then struck has
never died away. Its roster of guests has included some of the greatest names in European history, including royalty, of course, and such
New World moguls as Henry Ford and J. P. Morgan. Only a few
minutes from via Veneto, the Grand looks like a large, late Renaissance palace, its five-floor facade covered with carved loggias, lintels,
quoins, and cornices. Inside, the floors are covered with marble and
Oriental rugs, the walls are a riot of baroque plasterwork, and crystal
chandeliers, Louis XVI furniture, potted palms, antique clocks, and
wall sconces complete the picture. The spacious bedrooms are conservatively decorated with matching curtains and carpets, and
equipped with dressing rooms and fully tiled baths. Every accommodation is different. While most are traditional, with antique head-
boards and Venetian chandeliers, some are modern. Every room is
soundproof.

 Dining/Entertainment: The hotel's Le Grand Bar is an
elegant meeting place for the elite. Tea is served every afternoon,
accompanied by harp music. At Le Pavillon, a buffet, you can enjoy
quick meals amid potted plants, or try Le Restaurant, the hotel's more
formal dining room. Dietetic and kosher foods can be arranged with
advance notice. Service is first rate.

 Services: 24-hour room service, babysitting, laundry and valet
service.

 Facilities: Beauty salon, garage available.

Expensive

Hotel Massimo d'Azeglio, via Cavour 18, 00184 Roma.
☎ **06/4880646,** or toll free **800/223-9832** in the U.S.
Fax 06/4827386. 210 rms. A/C MINIBAR TV TEL **Metro:** Stazione
Termini.
Rates (including breakfast): 245,000 lire ($147) single; 330,000 lire
($198) double. AE, DC, MC, V. **Parking:** 35,000–45,000 lire ($21–$27).

This up-to-date hotel near the train station and opera was established
as a small restaurant by one of the founders of an Italian hotel

Frommer's Smart Traveler: Hotels

Value-Conscious Travelers Should Ask about the Following:

1. The price you pay in inexpensive hotels depends on the plumbing. Rooms with showers are cheaper than rooms with private baths. For a bath, you'll have to use the corridor bathroom, but you'll save a lot of money.

2. Consider a package tour (or book land arrangements with your air ticket). You'll often pay at least 30% less than individual "rack" rates (off-the-street independent bookings).

3. If Rome hotels are full, forget it. But if they're not, a little on-the-spot bargaining can bring down the cost of a hotel room. Be polite. Ask if there's a "businessperson's rate," or if school-teachers get a discount. This is a face-saving technique. Sometimes it works and sometimes it doesn't—but you can try. The technique is best at night, when the hotel faces up to 40% vacancy and wants to fill some of those empty rooms.

4. At cheaper hotels that take credit cards, ask if payment by cash will get you a reduction.

5. If you're going to spend at least a week in Rome, ask about long-term discounts.

Questions to Ask If You're on a Budget:

1. Is there a garage? What's the charge?

2. Is there a surcharge on either local or long-distance calls? There usually is in some places and it might be an astonishing 40%. Make your calls at the nearest post office.

3. Does the hotel include service charge in the rates quoted, or will it be added on at the end of your stay?

4. Are all taxes included in the price or will they be added on?

5. Is breakfast (continental) included in the rates?

dynasty more than a century ago. In World War II it was a refuge for the king of Serbia and also a favorite with Italian generals. Today this centrally located hotel is the "Casa Madre," or Mother House, of the Bettoja chain. Run by Angelo Bettoja and his charming wife, who hails from America's southland, it offers clean, comfortable accommodations, plus an adjacent bar and a well-trained staff. Its facade is one of the most elegant neoclassical structures in the area, and its lobby has been renovated, with light paneling. The restaurant is covered separately in the dining chapter.

Hotel Mediterraneo, via Cavour 15, 00184 Roma. ☎ **06/4884051,** or toll free **800/223-9832** in the U.S. Fax 06/4744105. 272 rms, 10 suites. A/C MINIBAR TV TEL **Metro:** Stazione Termini.

Rates (including breakfast): 285,000 lire ($171) single; 380,000 lire ($228) double; from 460,000 lire ($276) suite. AE, DC, MC, V.

Parking: 35,000–45,000 lire ($21–$27).

The Hotel Mediterraneo is one of Rome's most vivid manifestations of Italian art deco styling. Because of the war, it wasn't completed until 1944, but its blueprints were executed from 1936 to 1938 in anticipation of the hoped-for World's Fair of 1942. Because its position lay beside what Mussolini planned as his triumphant passageway through Rome, each of the local building codes was deliberately violated, and approval was granted for the creation of an unprecedented 10-floor hotel. Its height, coupled with its position on one of Rome's hills, provides panoramic views from its roof garden and bar, which is especially charming at night.

Mario Loreti, one of Mussolini's favorite architects, was the man who planned for an interior sheathing of gray marble, the richly allegorical murals of inlaid wood, and the art deco friezes ringing the ceilings of the enormous public rooms. Don't overlook the gracefully curved bar, crafted from illuminated cut crystal, or the ships' figureheads that ring the ceiling of the wood-sheathed breakfast room. The lobby is also decorated with antique busts of Roman emperors, part of the Bettoja family's collection. Each bedroom is spacious and pleasantly furnished, containing lots of exposed wood, solidly dependable furniture, and a radio.

Moderate

Britannia Hotel, via Napoli 64, 00184 Roma. ☎ **06/4883153.** Fax **06/4882343.** 32 rms (all with bath). A/C MINIBAR TV TEL **Bus:** Nos. 57, 64, or 75.

Rates (including breakfast): 230,000 lire ($138) single; 270,000 lire ($162) double. AE, DC, MC, V. **Parking:** Free.

The Britannia Hotel takes its name from its location next to an Anglican church on a street right off via Nazionale, within walking distance of the main railroad station. Its elaborately detailed Victor Emmanuel facade is graced with plant-filled upper terraces, each of which adds a note much like that of a private garden. Inside is one of the neighborhood's most stylish renovations. The bar contains a labyrinth of banquettes, each padded with plush cushions and amplified with mirrors and lots of plants. Upstairs, the bedrooms are outfitted in monochromatic schemes of gray, blue, or pink, and filled with carpeting and modern paintings. Each unit has a radio; personal safe; fire alarm; and bath with radio, hairdryer, scales, and a sunlamp. Some of the rooms have wide private terraces.

$ **Hotel Atlantico**, via Cavour 23, 00184 Roma. ☎ **06/4744105,** or toll free **800/223-9832** in the U.S. Fax 06/4824976. A/C MINIBAR TV TEL **Metro:** Stazione Termini.

Rates (including breakfast): 200,000 lire ($120) single; 275,000 lire ($165) double. AE, DC, MC, V. **Parking:** 35,000–45,000 lire ($21–$27).

The comfortable Hotel Atlantico, a leading selection in its price bracket, has an old-fashioned aura but has been considerably modernized and updated, making it one of the finer properties within a few blocks of the railway station. This is one of the smaller hotels of the family-run Bettoja chain, so if it's full, one of the polite employees will direct you to another of their nearby hotels. There's a pleasant lobby and comfortable spacious bedrooms filled with upholstered furniture. The hotel connects with the Mediterraneo "21" Restaurant, and is air-conditioned throughout.

Hotel d'Este, via Carlo Alberto 4B, 00185 Roma. ☎ **06/4465607.** Fax 06/446501. 40 rms (all with bath). A/C MINIBAR TV TEL **Metro:** Piazza Victor Emmanuel.

Rates: 110,000 lire–200,000 lire ($66–$120) single; 130,000 lire–250,000 lire ($78–$150) double. Breakfast 30,000 lire ($18) extra. AE, DC, MC, V. **Parking:** 25,000 lire ($15).

In 1986, what had been a flea-bitten pension from the late 1800s was radically renovated into the well-kept hotel you'll find today. Rising four stories from a position five blocks west of the Stazione Termini, near the front entrance of the Basilica of Santa Maria Maggiore, the hotel is owned by the Italian-Canadian husband-and-wife team of Giuseppe Gaudio and Ellin Bessner. Bedrooms in front have double-paned windows to protect from street noise; bedrooms in back overlook a garden. Each contains a safety-deposit box and comfortable, conservative furniture. Since its new ownership, the hotel has been used as a backdrop for several scenes in made-for-TV movies catering to the Italian market. On the premises is a rooftop bar and cafe and laundry facilities. The hotel also contains a restaurant whose tables spill out onto the piazza in front during warm weather. Lunches and dinners cost from around 35,000 lire ($21) each.

Hotel Marcella, via Flavia 106, 00187 Roma. ☎ **06/4746451.** Fax 06/4815832. 68 rms (all with bath). A/C MINIBAR TV TEL **Metro:** Piazza Barberini.

Rates (including breakfast): 180,000 lire ($108) single; 260,000 lire ($156) double; 320,000 lire ($192) triple. AE, DC, MC, V. **Parking:** 28,000–38,000 lire ($16.80–$22.80).

The Marcella is an attractive hotel in a residential and commercial neighborhood not far from piazza della Repubblica. After its premises were thoroughly renovated in the 1980s, it won an award from the Rome Tourist Board, and has continued lesser renovations every year since then. The lobby is stocked with lattices and verdant plants, a theme that is repeated on the flower-ringed sun terrace on the building's roof. (Two elevators will help you make the climb.) From the comfortable chairs there, you'll have a distant panorama over Rome as far away as St. Peter's. Bedrooms are simple but comfortable, and contain separate sun alcoves raised on a dais, as well as radios. The hotel has a bar but no restaurant.

Medici, via Flavia 96, 00187 Roma. ☎ **06/4827319.** Fax 06/4740767. 68 rms (all with bath). MINIBAR TV TEL **Metro:** Piazza della Repubblica.

Rates (including breakfast): 170,000 lire ($102) single; 220,000 lire ($132) double. AE, DC, MC, V. **Parking:** 28,000–35,000 lire ($16.80–$21).

The Medici, built in 1906, is a substantial hotel that has easy access to the railway terminal and the shops along via XX (Venti) Settembre. Many of its better rooms overlook an inner patio garden, with Roman columns and benches, and posts holding up greenery and climbing ivy. The patio is often filled with Vespas (motor scooters) and hotel deliveries, so breakfast is served downstairs below the bar. The lounge, with its white coved ceiling, has many nooks, all connected by wide white arches. Furnishings are traditional, with lots of antiques. Likewise, the generous-size bedrooms are also attractively furnished. The few rooms that are air conditioned carry a 20,000 lire ($12) supplement to the rates quoted above.

Nord Nuova Roma, via G. Amendola 3, 00185 Roma.
☎ **06/4885441,** or toll free **800/223-9832** in the U.S. Fax 06/48117163. 159 rms (all with bath). A/C MINIBAR TV TEL **Metro:** Stazione Termini.
Rates (including breakfast): 175,000 lire ($105) single; 235,000 lire ($141) double. AE, DC, MC, V. **Parking:** 35,000–45,000 lire ($21–$27).

The Nord Nuova Roma, near the railway station, is the best bargain in the family-run Bettoja chain. It has garage parking for 100 cars, and a small, intimate bar. Its well-maintained and most comfortable rooms are standard and modernized, making the hotel a good family choice. A most satisfying fixed-price lunch or dinner can be arranged at the nearby Massimo d'Azeglio Restaurant, beginning at 30,000 lire ($18).

San Giorgio, via G. Amendola 61, 00185 Roma. ☎ **06/4827341,** or toll free **800/223-9832** in the U.S. Fax **06/4883191.** 186 rms (all with bath), 5 suites. A/C MINIBAR TV TEL **Metro:** Stazione Termini.
Rates (including breakfast): 215,000 lire ($129) single; 290,000 lire ($174) double; 405,000 lire ($243) suite. AE, DC, MC, V. **Parking:** 35,000–45,000 lire ($21–$27).

A four-star first-class hotel built in 1940, the San Giorgio is constantly being improved by its founders, the Bettoja family (in 1950 it became the first air-conditioned hotel in Rome, and is now also soundproof). The San Giorgio is connected to the Massimo d'Azeglio, so guests can patronize that establishment's fine restaurant without having to walk out on the street. The hotel is ideal for families, as many of its corner rooms can be converted into larger quarters. Each bedroom has a radio, along with other amenities, which often lie behind the wood-veneer doors. Breakfast is served in a light and airy room. The staff is most helpful in easing your adjustment into the Italian capital.

Inexpensive

Aberdeen Hotel, via Firenze 48, 00184 Roma. ☎ **06/4821092.** 26 rms (all with bath or shower). MINIBAR TV TEL **Metro:** Stazione Termini.
Rates (including breakfast): 140,000 lire ($84) single; 190,000 lire ($114) double. AE, DC, MC, V. **Parking:** 25,000 lire ($15).

A completely renovated hotel near the Roma Opera House, this is centrally located for most of the landmarks and for rail and bus connections at the main station. It's in a quiet and safe area of Rome, as it lies in front of the Ministry of Defense. Rooms are furnished with sleek modern styling and have such amenities as hairdryers and radios. For 25,000 lire ($15), air conditioning is available. Only a breakfast buffet is served, although many inexpensively priced trattorie lie nearby.

Fiamma, via Gaeta 61, 00185 Roma. ☎ **06/4883859.** Fax 06/4883511. 79 rms (all with bath or shower). TV TEL **Metro:** Stazione Termini.

Rates (including breakfast): 100,000–125,000 lire ($60–$75) single; 140,000–165,000 lire ($84–$99) double. AE, DC, MC, V.

Fiamma, on the far side of the Baths of Diocletian, is a renovated old building with five floors of shuttered windows and a ground floor faced with marble and plate-glass windows. The lobby is long and bright, filled to the brim with a varied collection of furnishings, including overstuffed chairs, blue enamel railings, and indirect lighting. On the same floor (made of marble, no less) is a monklike breakfast room. Air conditioning is available in some of the comfortably furnished bedrooms.

Hotel Centro, via Firenze 12, 00184 Roma. ☎ **06/4828002.** Fax 06/4871902. 38 rms (all with bath), 3 suites. A/C TV TEL **Metro:** Piazza della Repubblica.

Rates (including breakfast): 140,000–170,000 lire ($84–$102) single; 180,000–210,000 lire ($108–$126) double; 250,000 lire ($150) suite. AE, DC, MC, V. **Parking:** 30,000 lire ($18).

The Hotel Centro, on a quiet street near busy via Nazionale, facing the opera house, offers reasonably priced accommodations and pleasant surroundings. Each of its comfortable rooms contains a safe and radio, among other amenities. The hotel has its own parking garage nearby. Room service, laundry, and valet service are available.

Hotel Corot, via Marghera 15–17, 00185 Roma. ☎ **06/44700900.** Fax 06/44700905. 20 rms (all with bath). A/C MINIBAR TV TEL **Metro:** Stazione Termini.

Rates (including breakfast): 120,000–140,000 lire ($72–$84) single; 150,000–170,000 lire ($90–$102) double; 165,000–195,000 lire ($99–$117) triple; 180,000–$205,000 lire ($108–$123) quad. 15% discounts to clients staying two nights anytime from Fri to Sun. AE, DC, MC, V.

Modernized and comfortable, this hotel occupies the second and third floors of a turn-of-the-century building that contains a handful of private apartments as well as another hotel that offers fewer amenities. Guests register in a small, paneled area on the building's street level, then take an elevator to their respective floors. Bedrooms are airy, high-ceilinged, and filled with simple but traditional furniture and soothing colors. Bathrooms are modern and contain hairdryers. There's a residents' bar near one of the sun-flooded windows in one of the public rooms.

$ **Hotel Galileo**, via Palestro 33, 00185 Roma. ☎ **06/4441207.**
Fax 06/4441208. 40 rms (all with bath). A/C TV TEL **Metro:** Castro
Pretorio.

Rates (including breakfast): 139,000 lire ($83.40) single; 192,000 lire
($115.20) double. AE, DC, MC, V. **Parking:** 28,000 lire ($16.80).

The Hotel Galileo, renovated in 1993, receives high marks in its
category for good value, comfortable accommodations, and a desirable location. Its entrance lies to the side of a buff- and cream-colored
19th-century palace, at the end of a cobblestone passage whose pavement is set in patterns of papyrus leaves. Inside, an intimate bar stands
a few steps from the modern reception area. An elevator leads to the
often-sunny and clean bedrooms, each a bit larger than you might
expect and filled with angular but attractive furniture. A few units
offer private terraces. No meals are served other than breakfast, which
in good weather is offered on a flower-garden terrace several floors
above street level.

Hotel Miami, via Nazionale 230, 00184 Roma. ☎ **06/485827.** Fax
06/484562. 22 rms (all with bath), 3 suites. MINIBAR TV TEL
Metro: Piazza della Repubblica.

Rates (including breakfast): 130,000 lire ($78) single; 150,000 lire ($90)
double; from 190,000 lire ($114) suite. AE, DC, MC, V.

The Hotel Miami, a former duchess's palace, is conveniently situ-
ated in the heart of a major shopping artery. What used to be a
fifth-floor pension is now nicely done over with warmly tinted marble
floors, olive-green wall coverings, and comfortable, low-slung chairs
in the conservatively elegant sitting room. From the high-ceilinged
street-level lobby, you'll ride an elevator up to the reception area. The
spacious and simple bedrooms are filled with lots of sunlight, warm
colors, and chrome accents, and each has a handsome tiled bath. The
quieter rooms get a little less sunlight, as they look out on a
courtyard. Air conditioning is available in the rooms for an additional
20,000 lire ($12) per day.

Hotel Pavia, via Gaeta 83, 00185 Roma. ☎ **06/483801.** Fax
06/4819090. 50 rms (all with bath or shower). A/C MINIBAR TV
TEL **Metro:** Stazione Termini.

Rates (including breakfast): 100,000–145,000 lire ($60–$87) single;
120,000–165,000 lire ($72–$99) double. AE, DC, MC, V. **Parking:**
10,000–20,000 lire ($6–$12).

The Hotel Pavia is a popular choice on this quiet street near the gardens of the Baths of Diocletian and the railway station. Established
in the 1980s, it occupies a much-renovated century-old building.
You'll pass through a wisteria-covered passageway that leads to the
recently modernized reception area of what used to be a private villa.
The public rooms are tastefully covered in light-grained paneling with
white lacquer accents and carpeting. The staff is attentive. Each room
is quiet, often with a good view, and is attractively furnished with
simple, modern wood furniture and calming colors.

Hotel Ranieri, via XX Settembre 43, 00187 Roma. ☎ **06/4814467.**
Fax 06/4818834. 40 rms (all with bath or shower). MINIBAR TV
TEL **Metro:** Piazza della Repubblica.

> **Rates** (including breakfast): Mon–Thurs 158,000 lire ($94.80) single;
> 210,000 lire ($126) double. Fri–Sat 128,000 lire ($76.80) single; 170,000
> lire ($102) double. AE, MC, V.

This winning three-star hotel occupies a very old building that was
completely renovated in 1990. The location is good: From the hotel
you can stroll to the Rome Opera, the piazza della Repubblica, and
via Vittorio Veneto. The public rooms, the lounge and the dining
room, are attractively decorated, in part with contemporary art. This
hotel offers good, comfortable bedrooms. Guests can arrange for a
home-cooked meal in the dining room.

Hotel Siviglia, via Gaeta 12, 00185 Roma. ☎ and fax 06/4441195.
41 rms (all with bath). A/C MINIBAR TV TEL **Metro:** Stazione
Termini or Castro Pretorio.

> **Rates** (including breakfast): 100,000–120,000 lire ($60–$72) single;
> 140,000–180,000 lire ($84–$108) double. AE, DC, V. **Parking:** 6,000
> lire ($3.60).

The Hotel Siviglia was built as a private villa late in the 19th century
in a Victor Emmanuel style of cream-colored pilasters and neoclassical detailing. After World War II, it was transformed into a hotel.
Inside is a combination of antique grandeur and modern comfort.
Bronze lampbearers ornament the stairs leading to the simply furnished but high-ceilinged bedrooms, a few of which have sun terraces. Breakfast is served either in a tavernlike basement dining room
or in a small side garden under the shade of a venerable palm.

$ Hotel Venezia, via Varese 18, 00185 Roma. ☎ **06/4457101.**
Fax 06/4457687. 61 rms (all with bath or shower). A/C MINIBAR
TV TEL **Metro:** Stazione Termini.

> **Rates** (including breakfast): 160,000 lire ($96) single; 215,000 lire
> ($129) double. AE, DC, MC, V. **Parking:** 30,000 lire ($18).

The Hotel Venezia, near the intersection of via Marghera, is the type
of place that restores one's faith in moderately priced hotels. The
location is good—it's three blocks from the railroad station, in a
part-business, part-residential area dotted with a few old villas and
palm trees. The Venezia had a total renovation in 1991, which transformed it into a good-looking and cheerful hostelry with a charming collection of public sitting rooms. The floors are brown marble.
The rooms are bright, often furnished with 17th-century reproductions. All units have Murano chandeliers, and almost all
are air-conditioned from July through September. Some
accommodations have a balcony for surveying the action on the street
below. The housekeeping is superb—the management really cares.

Villa delle Rose, via Vicenza 5, 00185 Roma. ☎ **06/4451788.** Fax
06/4451639. 38 rms (all with bath). A/C TV TEL **Metro:** Stazione
Termini or Castro Pretorio.

> **Rates** (including breakfast): 130,000 lire ($78) single; 185,000 lire
> ($111) double. AE, DC, MC, V.

Set less than two blocks north of the railway station, behind a digni-fied cut-stone facade inspired by the Renaissance, this hotel was originally built as a private home in the late 1800s. Despite many renovations, the ornate trappings of the wealthy family who built the place are still visible, including a set of Corinthian marble columns in the lobby, and a flagstone-covered terrace that fills part of a ver-dant garden in back. Much of the interior, however, has been stripped down to a functionally modern 1960s kind of minimalism, with com-fortable but boxy furniture and not a great deal of charm. Morning breakfasts in the garden, however, where rows of pink and red roses bloom (and give the hotel its name) do a lot to add country flavor to an otherwise very urban location. The English-speaking staff is helpful and tactful.

Budget

Pensione Papà Germano, via Calatafimi 14A, 00185 Roma. ☎ **06/486919.** 13 rms (2 with bath). TEL **Metro:** Stazione Termini.
Rates: 35,000 lire ($21) single without bath, 45,000 lire ($27) single with bath; 55,000 lire ($33) double without bath, 65,000 lire ($39) double with bath; 23,000 lire ($13.80) per person quad. 10% discounts Nov–Feb. MC, V.

It's about as basic and simple as anything you're likely to read about in this guidebook. This 1892 Belle Époque building was renovated last in 1987. Chances are that your fellow guests will arrive, back-pack in tow, directly from the main station, four blocks to the south. Located on a block-long street immediately east of the Baths of Diocletian, the pension offers simple but clean accommodations with battered furniture, a high-turnover clientele of European and North American students, and well-maintained showers. The energetic owner, Gino Germano, offers advice on sightseeing attractions to anyone who asks. No breakfast is available, although dozens of cafes nearby serve steaming cups of *caffè con latte* beginning early in the day. English is spoken.

2 Near the Parioli District, Via Veneto & the Villa Borghese

Very Expensive

Excelsior, via Vittorio Veneto 125, 00187 Roma. ☎ **06/4708,** or toll free **800/221-2340** in the U.S., **800/955-2442** in Canada. Fax 06/4826205. 327 rms (all with bath), 45 suites. A/C MINIBAR TV TEL **Metro:** Piazza Barberini.
Rates: 300,000–330,000 lire ($180–$198) single; 460,000–510,000 lire ($276–$306) double; from 1,400,000 lire ($840) suite. Breakfast 26,000 lire ($15.60) extra; 13% IVA extra. AE, DC, MC, V. **Parking:** 30,000 lire ($18).

The Excelsior (pronounced "Ess-*shell*-see-or") is a limestone palace whose boutique corner tower, which looks right over the U.S. Embassy, is a landmark in Rome. Guests enter a string of cavernous reception rooms with thick rugs, marble floors, gilded garlands and plasters decorating the walls, and Empire furniture (supported by winged lions and the like).

The guest rooms are either new (the result of a major renovation) or traditional. Doubles are spacious and elegantly furnished, often with antiques and silk curtains. The furnishings in singles are also of high quality. Most of the bedrooms are different, many with a sumptuous Hollywood-style bath—marble-walled with a bidet and a mountain of fresh towels.

The palatial hotel once attracted some of the stellar lights of the "Hollywood on the Tiber" era—notably Shelley Winters, Elizabeth Taylor, Ingrid Bergman, and Roberto Rossellini. Nowadays, you're more likely to bump into international financiers and Arab princesses.

Dining/Entertainment: The Excelsior Bar, open daily from 10:30am to 1am, is perhaps the most famous on via Veneto, and La Cupola is known for its national and regional cuisine, with dietetic and kosher food prepared on request.

Services: Room service, babysitting service, laundry and valet service.

Facilities: Beauty salon, barbershop, sauna.

★ **Hotel Lord Byron**, via G. de Notaris 5, 00197 Roma.
☎ **06/3220404.** Fax 06/3220405. 28 rms, 9 suites. A/C MINIBAR TV TEL **Metro:** Piazzale Flaminio. **Bus:** No. 52.
Rates (including breakfast): Apr–June and Sept–Oct, 350,000 lire ($210) single; 430,000–540,000 lire ($258–$324) double. Nov–Mar and July–Aug, 300,000 lire ($180) single; 350,000–420,000 lire ($210–$252) double. Suites from 750,000 lire ($450) year round. AE, DC, MC, V.

This art deco villa is set on a residential hilltop in Parioli, an area of embassies and exclusive town houses at the edge of the Villa Borghese. From the curving entrance steps off the staffed parking lot in front, you'll notice design accessories that attract the most sophisticated clientele in Italy. In a niche in the reception area is an oval Renaissance urn in chiseled marble. Flowers are everywhere, the lighting is discreet, and everything is on a cultivated small scale that makes it seem more like a well-staffed (and extremely expensive) private home than a hotel.

Each of the rooms is different, most often with lots of mirrors, upholstered walls, spacious bathrooms with gray marble accessories, big dressing rooms/closets, and all the amenities.

Dining/Entertainment: On the premises is one of Rome's best restaurants, Relais le Jardin, covered separately in the dining chapter. The hotel's piano bar, Il Salotto, is a chic gathering spot, with live music beginning at 7pm.

Services: 24-hour room service, laundry and valet service, concierge desk.

Facilities: Car-rental desk.

Expensive

Grand Hotel Flora, via Vittorio Veneto 191, 00187 Roma.
☎ **06/489929,** or toll free **800/44-UTELL** in the U.S.,
800/268-7041 in Ontario and Québec. Fax 06/4820359. 175 rms,
8 suites. A/C MINIBAR TV TEL **Metro:** Piazza Barberini.

Rates (including buffet breakfast): 280,000 lire ($168) single; 380,000
lire ($228) double; from 600,000 lire ($360) suite. AE, DC, MC, V.

The Grand Hotel Flora, a "grand hotel" styled like a palazzo, stands
at the gateway to the Borghese Gardens. The public rooms are furnished with well-selected reproductions and antiques, with Oriental
carpets and crystal chandeliers. All accommodations are well furnished and well maintained. A focal point of social get-togethers is
the Empire Bar. Room service, laundry, and valet are provided.

Jolly Vittorio Venito, corso d'Italia 1, 00198 Roma. ☎ **06/8495,** or
toll free **800/221-2626** in the U.S., **800/237-0319** in Canada. Fax
06/8841104. 200 rms (all with bath), 3 suites. A/C MINIBAR TV
TEL **Bus:** No. 910.

Rates (including American breakfast): 270,000 lire ($162) single;
310,000 lire ($186) double; 450,000 lire ($270) suite. AE, DC, MC, V.
Parking: 38,000 lire ($22.80).

The Jolly Vittorio Veneto lies between the Villa Borghese gardens
and via Veneto. Totally ignoring the traditional, the hotel's architects opted for modern in metal and concrete, with bronze-tinted
windows. Try to get a room with a garden view. To register, you
descend a grand staircase that leads to the sunken lobby. The rooms
here are bold in concept, compact in space, and contemporary in
furnishings. Room service is offered daily from 7am to 11pm.

Victoria Roma, via Campania 41, 00187 Roma. ☎ **06/473931.** Fax
06/4871890. 110 rms (all with bath), 4 suites. A/C MINIBAR TV
TEL **Bus:** No. 910.

Rates (including breakfast): 180,000–220,000 lire ($108–$132) single;
280,000–320,000 lire ($168–$192) double; from 350,000 lire ($210)
suite. AE, DC, MC, V.

The Victoria Roma will fool you. As you sit on wrought-iron chairs
on its roof garden, drinking your apéritif in a forest of palms and
potted palms—all overlooking the Borghese gardens—you'll think
you're at a country villa. But via Veneto's just across the way. Even
the lounges and living rooms retain that country-house decor, with
soft touches that include high-backed chairs, large oil paintings, bowls
of freshly cut flowers, provincial tables, and Oriental rugs. The Swiss
owner, Alberto H. Wirth, has set unusual requirements of innkeeping
(no groups), and has attracted a fine clientele over the years—including diplomats, executives, and artists. The bedrooms are well furnished and maintained. Meals can be taken à la carte in the elegant
grill room, which serves the best of Italian and French cuisine. A
fixed-price meal costs 35,000 lire ($21).

Moderate

Alexandria, via Vittorio Veneto 18, 00187 Roma.
☎ **06/4881943.** Fax 06/4871804. 39 rms (all with bath), 6 suites.
A/C MINIBAR TV TEL **Metro:** Piazza Barberini.

Rates (including breakfast): 150,000–160,000 lire ($90–$96) single;
220,000–230,000 lire ($132–$138) double; 280,000–320,000 lire
($168–$192) suite. AE, DC, MC, V. **Parking:** 35,000 lire ($21).

Set behind the dignified stone facade of what was originally a
19th-century private mansion, this hotel offers clean, comfortable
accommodations filled with antique furniture and modern conveniences. Rooms facing the front are exposed to the roaring traffic and
animated street life of the via Veneto; those in back are quieter but
with less of a view. No meals are served other than breakfast, although
the hall porter or a member of the polite staff can carry drinks to
clients seated in the reception area. The breakfast room is especially
appealing. Inspired by an Italian garden, it was designed by the noted
architect Paolo Portoghesi.

Hotel Degli Aranci, via Barnaba Oriani 9–11, 00197 Roma.
☎ **06/8085250.** Fax 06/8070202. 54 rms (all with bath or shower),
3 suites. A/C MINIBAR TV TEL **Bus:** No. 3 from Stazione Termini.

Rates (including breakfast): 157,000 lire ($94.20) single; 240,000 lire
($144) double; 400,000 lire ($240) suite. AE, MC, V. **Parking:** Free.

This former private villa stands on a tree-lined residential street,
surrounded by similar villas now used, in part, as consulates and
ambassadorial town houses. Most of the accommodations have tall
windows opening onto city views, and are filled with provincial
furnishings or English-style reproductions. The public rooms have
memorabilia of ancient Rome scattered about, including
bisque-colored medallions of soldiers in profile, old engravings of
ruins, and classical vases highlighted against the light-grained
paneling. A marble-top bar in an alcove off the sitting room adds a
relaxed touch. From the glass-walled breakfast room, at the rear of
the house, you can see the tops of orange trees.

Hotel Oxford, via Boncompagni 89, 00187 Roma. ☎ **06/4828952.**
Fax 06/4815349. 57 rms (all with bath), 2 suites. A/C MINIBAR TV
TEL **Bus:** No. 3, 56, 58, or 62.

Rates (including breakfast): 170,000 lire ($102) single; 230,000 lire
($138) double; 320,000 lire ($192) suite. 15% reductions Jan–Mar 15.
AE, DC, MC, V. **Parking:** 40,000 lire ($24)

The centrally located Hotel Oxford, off via Veneto, is adjacent to
the Borghese gardens. Recently renovated, the Oxford is now
air-conditioned, centrally heated, and fully carpeted throughout.
There is a pleasant lounge and a cozy bar (which serves snacks), plus
a dining room offering a good Italian cuisine. The hotel is on the
American embassy's preferred list of moderately priced hotels in
Rome that can be confidently recommended to U.S. visitors.

La Residenza, via Emilia 22–24, 00187 Roma. ☎ **06/4880789.** Fax 06/485721. 27 rms (all with bath or shower), 6 suites. A/C MINIBAR TV TEL **Metro:** Piazza Barberini.

Rates (including breakfast): 120,000 lire ($72) single; 235,000 lire ($141) double; 265,000 lire ($159) suite. MC, V. **Parking:** 4,000 lire ($2.40).

La Residenza successfully combines the intimacy of a generously sized town house with the elegant appointments of a well-decorated hotel. The location is superb—in the neighborhood of via Veneto, the American embassy, and the Villa Borghese. The converted villa has an ocher-colored facade, an ivy-covered courtyard, a quiet location, and a labyrinthine series of plushly upholstered public rooms decorated with Oriental rugs, Empire divans, oil portraits, and warmly accommodating groupings of rattan chairs with cushions. Each bedroom has a radio in addition to other amenities. A series of terraces is scattered strategically throughout the hotel, which combines to make this one a favorite stopover for many international visitors.

Inexpensive

$ Hotel delle Muse, via Tommaso Salvini 18, 00197 Roma. ☎ **06/8088333.** Fax 06/8085749. 61 rms (all with bath or shower). TV TEL **Bus:** No. 4.

Rates (including buffet breakfast): 113,000 lire ($67.80) single; 147,000–157,000 lire ($88.20–$94.20) double. AE, DC, MC, V. **Parking:** 25,000–35,000 lire ($15–$21).

This three-star establishment is not far from the Villa Borghese. Furnishings are modern and come in a wide range of splashy colors. In summer the hotel operates a restaurant in the garden, where you can enjoy a complete meal for 25,000 lire ($15). A bar is open 24 hours a day (in case you get thirsty at 5am). There's also a TV room, plus a writing room and two dining rooms, along with a garage for your car. A bus that stops nearby runs to all parts of the city.

3   Near the Spanish Steps & Piazza del Popolo

Very Expensive

★ Hassler, piazza Trinità dei Monti 6, 00187 Roma. ☎ **06/6782651,** or toll free **800/223-6800** in the U.S. Fax 06/6789991. 85 rms, 15 suites. A/C MINIBAR TV TEL **Metro:** Piazza di Spagna. **Bus:** 497 from Stazione Termini.

Rates: 400,000 lire ($240) single; 590,000–750,000 lire ($354–$450) double; from 1,400,000 lire ($840) suite. Breakfast 28,000 lire ($16.80) extra. AE, DC, MC, V.

The Hassler, the only deluxe hotel in this old part of Rome, uses the Spanish Steps as its grand entrance. The original 1885 Hassler was rebuilt in 1944 and was used as headquarters of the American Air Transport Command for the last year of World War II. In 1947 the hotel reopened its doors and became an immediate success, regaining its original glory, and today its reputation is almost legendary; the lush hotel, with its ornate decor, has been favored by such Americans as the Kennedys, Eisenhowers, and Nixons—and by titled Europeans and movie stars. The brightly colored rooms, the lounges with a mixture of modern and traditional furnishings, and the bedrooms with their "Italian Park Avenue" trappings, all strike a 1930s note.

The bedrooms have a personalized look—Oriental rugs, tasteful draperies on the French windows, brocade furnishings, comfortable beds, and (the nicest touch of all) bowls of fresh flowers. Some rooms have balconies with views of the city. All accommodations contain a private bath, usually with two sinks and a bidet. A Presidential Suite (next to the restaurant) and a Paradise Penthouse are also available, and are, of course, more expensive.

Dining/Entertainment: The Hassler Roof Restaurant, on the top floor, is a great favorite with visitors and Romans alike for its fine cuisine and panoramic view. The Hassler Bar is ideal for an apéritif or a drink; in the evening, it has piano music. In summer, breakfast and lunch are served in a flower-bedecked courtyard.

Services: Room service (daily 7am to 11:30pm), telex and fax services, limousine, in-room massages, in-house laundry.

Facilities: There is parking in front for only two cars (always taken), so arrangements can be made at a nearby garage.

Hotel de la Ville Inter-Continental Roma, via Sistina 67–69, 00187 Roma. ☎ **06/67331,** or toll free **800/327-0200** in the U.S. or Canada. Fax 06/6784213. 192 rms, 23 suites. A/C MINIBAR TV TEL **Metro:** Piazza di Spagna or Barberini.

Rates (including breakfast): 470,000–490,000 lire ($282–$294) single; 540,000–590,000 lire ($324–$354) double; from 760,000 lire ($456) suite. AE, DC, MC, V. **Parking:** 35,000 lire ($21).

This hotel looks deluxe (even though it's officially rated first class) from the minute you walk through the revolving door, which is attended by a smartly uniformed doorman. Once inside this palace built in the 19th century on the site of the ancient Lucullus's Gardens, you'll see Oriental rugs, marble tables, brocade-covered furniture, and a staff that speaks English. There are endless corridors leading to what at first seems a maze of ornamental lounges, all elegantly upholstered and hung with their quota of crystal lighting fixtures. Some of the public rooms have a sort of 1930s elegance; others are strictly baroque, and in the middle of it all is an open courtyard.

The bedrooms and the public areas have been completely rehabilitated in a classic yet up-to-date way. The higher rooms with balconies have the most panoramic views of Rome, and all guests are free to use the roof terrace with the same view.

Dining/Entertainment: La Piazzetta de la Ville Restaurant, serving Italian and international cuisine, is on the second floor and overlooks the garden. Meals cost from 60,000 lire ($36) and are served only to clients of the hotel. The hotel also has an American bar.

Frommer's Cool for Kids: Hotels

Hotel Venezia   (see p. 101) At this good, moderately priced family hotel near the Stazione Termini, rooms are renovated and most are large enough for extra beds for children.

Cavalieri Hilton   (see p. 120) This hotel is like a resort at Monte Mario, with a swimming pool, gardens, and plenty of grounds for children to run and play, yet it's only 15 minutes from the center of Rome, reached by the hotel shuttle bus.

Hotel Massimo d'Azeglio   (see p. 94) Near the Stazione Termini, this has long been a family favorite. Rooms are large, well kept, and comfortable, and the well-trained staff is solicitous of children.

San Giorgio   (see p. 98) Near the railway station, this family-owned hotel is ideal for parents traveling with children. Many of its corner rooms can be converted into larger quarters by opening doors.

Services: 24-hour room service, babysitting, laundry, valet.
Facilities: Roof terrace.

Expensive

Hotel d'Inghilterra, via Bocca di Leone 14, 00187 Roma.
☎ **06/672161.** Fax 06/6840828. 102 rms (all with bath), 12 suites. A/C MINIBAR TV TEL **Metro:** Piazza di Spagna.
Rates: 260,000–295,000 lire ($156–$177) single; 350,000–420,000 lire ($210–$252) double; 500,000–800,000 lire ($300–$480) suite. Breakfast 22,000 lire ($13.20) extra. AE, DC, MC, V.

The Hotel d'Inghilterra nostalgically holds onto its traditions and heritage, even though it has been completely renovated. Considered the most fashionable small hotel in Rome, it's been the favorite of many a discriminating "personage"—Anatole France, Ernest Hemingway, Alec Guinness. (In the 19th century, the king of Portugal met here with the pope.) The bedrooms have mostly old pieces—gilt and much marble, along with mahogany chests and glittery mirrors—as well as modern conveniences. The hotel's restaurant, the Roman Garden, serves excellent Roman dishes. The main salon of the hotel is dominated by a gilt mirror and console, surrounded by Victorian furniture. The preferred bedrooms are higher up, opening onto a tile terrace, with a balustrade and a railing covered with flowering vines and plants. The English-style bar is a favorite gathering spot in the evening, with its paneled walls, tip-top tables, and old lamps casting soft light.

★ **Scalinata di Spagna**, piazza Trinità dei Monti 17, 00187 Roma.
☎ **06/6793006.** Fax 06/69940598. 15 rms (all with bath or shower), 1 suite. A/C MINIBAR TV TEL **Metro:** Piazza di Spagna.
Rates (including breakfast): 250,000 lire ($150) single; 350,000 lire

($210) double; 400,000 lire ($240) triple; 550,000 lire ($330) suite. AE, MC, V.

Scalinata di Spagna was the most appealing pension near the Spanish Steps before its conversion in 1988 into a three-star hotel. It's right at the top of the steps, directly across the small piazza from the deluxe Hassler. This is a delightful little building—only two floors are visible from the outside—done up in mustard-yellow and burgundy-red paint and nestled between much larger structures. You'll recognize the four relief columns across the facade and the window boxes with their bright blossoms. The interior is like an old inn—the public rooms are small with bright print slipcovers, old clocks, and low ceilings.

The decorations vary radically from one room to the next; some have low, beamed ceilings and antique-looking wood furniture, while others have loftier ceilings and more average appointments. Everything is spotless and most pleasing to the eye. In season, breakfast is served on the roof garden terrace with its sweeping view of the dome of St. Peter's across the Tiber. Reserve well in advance.

Moderate

Carriage, via della Carrozze 36, 00187 Roma. ☎ **06/6990124.** Fax 06/6788279. 24 rms (all with bath), 2 suites. A/C MINIBAR TV TEL **Metro:** Piazza di Spagna.

Rates (including breakfast): 220,000 lire ($132) single; 270,000 lire ($162) double; 350,000 lire ($210) triple; 450,000 lire ($270) suite. AE, DC, MC, V.

The aptly named Carriage caters to the "carriage trade," which in today's sense means staff members of the British and French embassies, plus an occasional movie star or film director. The 18th-century facade covers some charming, although small, accommodations (if you reserve, ask for one of the two rooftop bedrooms). Antiques have been used tastefully, creating a personal aura, even in the bedrooms with their matching bedcovers and draperies. Each bedroom has a radio and other amenities. To meet your fellow guests, head for the Renaissance-style salon, which is called an American bar, or the roof garden. There is no dining room in the hotel.

Hotel Gregoriana, via Gregoriana 18, 00187 Roma.
☎ **06/6794269.** Fax 06/6784258. 19 rms (all with bath or shower). A/C TV TEL **Metro:** Piazza di Spagna.

Rates (including breakfast): 180,000 lire ($108) single; 280,000 lire ($168) double. No credit cards. **Parking:** 40,000 lire ($24).

This small, elite hotel is favored by members of the Italian fashion industry who book rooms here for visiting friends from out of town. The ruling matriarch of an aristocratic family left the building to an order of nuns in the 19th century, but they eventually moved to other quarters. Today there might be a slightly more elevated spirituality in Room C than in the rest of the hotel, as it used to be a chapel. Throughout the establishment, however, the smallish rooms provide comfort and Italian designs. The elevator cage is a black-and-gold

art deco fantasy, and the door to each accommodation has a reproduction of an Erté print whose fanciful characters indicate the letter
designating that particular room.

Hotel Internazionale, via Sistina 79, 00187 Roma.

☎ **06/69941823.** Fax 06/6784764. 42 rms (all with bath), 2 suites.
A/C MINIBAR TV TEL **Bus:** No. 492 from Stazione Termini.

Rates (including breakfast): 185,000 lire ($111) single; 260,000 lire
($156) double; 600,000 lire ($360) suite. AE, MC, V. **Parking:** 40,000
lire ($24).

The Hotel Internazionale emerged from the combination of several
old palaces, and traces of their past splendor can be seen in a few of
the public rooms. Just half a block from the top of the Spanish Steps,
the Internazionale has been a favorite of knowledgeable travelers since
the 1920s. The atmosphere is like that of a small inn, and service is
efficient. The rooms are furnished with old wooden pieces that can't
really be called antiques, yet are substantial and comfortable. Accommodations facing the narrow and often-noisy via Sistina now have
double windows. Bits and pieces of former elegance remain, especially in the Sala de Pranzo (dining room), whose ceiling is paneled.

Hotel Madrid, via Mario de' Fiori 94-95, 00187 Roma.

☎ **06/6991510.** Fax 06/6791653. 26 rms (all with bath), 7 suites.
A/C MINIBAR TV TEL **Metro:** Piazza di Spagna.

Rates (including breakfast): 170,000–180,000 lire ($102–$108) single;
220,000–235,000 lire ($132–$141) double; from 260,000 lire ($156)
suite for three; from 300,000 lire ($180) suite for four. AE, DC, MC, V.

The Hotel Madrid evokes *fin-de-siècle Roma*. The interior has been
redone, and many modern comforts have been added. The hotel
appeals to the individual traveler who wants a good standard of service. Guests often take their breakfast amid ivy and blossoming plants
on the roof terrace. The view of the rooftops and the distant dome
of St. Peter's is scenic. Some of the doubles are really quite large,
equipped with small scatter rugs, veneer armoirs, and shuttered windows. All accommodations contain radios. The hotel is an ocher
building with a shuttered facade on a narrow street practically in the
heart of the boutique area centering around via Frattina, near the
Spanish Steps.

Hotel Piazza di Spagna, via Mario de' Fiori 61, 00187 Roma.

☎ **06/6796412.** Fax 06/6790654. 16 rms (all with bath). A/C
MINIBAR TV TEL **Metro:** Piazza di Spagna. **Bus:** No. 61, 71, 81, or
85.

Rates (including breakfast): 170,000 lire ($102) single; 220,000 lire
($132) double. AE, MC, V.

Set about a block from the downhill side of the Spanish Steps, this
hotel was a rundown pensione until members of the Giocondi family radically renovated it in 1991. Originally built in the early 1800s,
the building enjoys a pleasant location.

Scattered over three floors are well-scrubbed, simply furnished bedrooms with high ceilings, cool terrazzo floors, and views over the street

outside. There's no elevator, but an ornate wrought-iron balustrade flanks the staircase leading upstairs. Although there's no bar and no restaurant inside, the neighborhood is filled with options for drinking and dining.

💲 Manfredi Hotel, via Margutta 61, 00187 Roma.
☎ **06/3207676.** Fax 06/3207736. 15 rms (all with bath). A/C MINIBAR TV TEL **Metro:** Piazza di Spagna.
Rates (including American breakfast): 200,000 lire ($120) single; 260,000 lire ($156) double. AE, MC, V.

The renovated Manfredi is only a few yards away from the Spanish Steps. All rooms are provided with excellent facilities and comforts. This cozy but refined hotel is on the third floor of a stately building on a street known for its art galleries.

Inexpensive

Hotel Margutta, via Laurina 34, 00187 Roma. ☎ **06/6798440.** 21 rms (all with bath). **Metro:** Flaminio.
Rates (including breakfast): 134,000 lire ($80.40) single or double; 170,000 lire ($102) triple. AE, DC, MC, V.

On a cobblestone street, the Margutta offers attractively decorated rooms and a helpful staff. The hotel is housed in a two-centuries-old building that was transformed into a small hotel in 1961. Located off the paneled lobby with a black stone floor is a simple breakfast room with framed lithographs. There are only double rooms; ask for one of the top-floor rooms with a view.

Pensione Lydia Venier, via Sistina 42, 00187 Roma.
☎ **06/6791744.** Fax 06/6797263. 30 rms (10 with bath, 10 with shower but no toilet). **Metro:** Piazza Barberini.
Rates (including breakfast): 75,000 lire ($45) single without shower or bath, 85,000 lire ($51) single with shower but no toilet, 95,000 lire ($57) single with bath; 107,000 lire ($64.20) double without shower or toilet, 130,000 lire ($78) with shower but no toilet, 215,000 lire ($129) double with bath. AE, MC, V.

This respectable but cost-conscious pensione is set on one of the upper floors of a gracefully proportioned apartment building on a street that radiates out from the top of the Spanish Steps. Bedrooms are a simple but dignified combination of slightly battered modern and antique, with understated furnishings and an occasional reminder (such as a ceiling fresco) of an earlier era.

Pensione Suisse, via Gregoriana 54, 00187 Roma. ☎ **06/6783649.** Fax 06/6781258. 14 rms (9 with bath). TEL **Metro:** Piazza Barberini.
Rates (including breakfast): 80,000 lire ($48) single without bath, 95,000 lire ($57) single with bath; 110,000 lire ($66) double without bath, 140,000 lire ($84) double with bath; 180,000 lire ($108) triple with bath. MC, V (but only for 50% of total bill).

Pensione Suisse is excellent, although small. It's run with efficiency and panache by Signora Jole Ciucci, who has been in the business for about 50 years, the last 30 of which have been here on via Gregoriana. The Suisse is a sparkling-clean affair, with rooms spread out over the third floor of a century-old patrician building. Halls and lobbies are muted beige, with high ceilings, leather chairs, and occasional throw rugs on the floors. There's also a visiting room with parquet floors, overstuffed leather easy chairs, and a Victorian chandelier. Furnished either in blond-toned modern pieces or antiques, many of the rooms are big, simple, and comfortable.

Budget

Pensione Fiorella, via del Babuino 196, 00187 Roma.
☎ **06/3610597.** 7 rms (none with bath). **Metro:** Flaminio.
Rates (including breakfast): 47,000–48,000 lire ($28.20–$28.80) single; 72,000–80,000 lire ($43.20–$48) double. No credit cards.

A few steps from the Piazza del Popolo is the utterly basic Pensione Fiorella. Antonio Albano and his family are one of the best reasons to visit this unstylish but comfortable pensione. They speak little English, but their humor and warm welcome make renting one of their well-scrubbed bedrooms a lot like visiting a light-hearted relative. The bedrooms open onto a high-ceilinged hallway.

4   Near Piazza Colonna

Expensive

Albergo Nazionale, piazza Montecitorio 131, 00186 Roma.
☎ **06/6789251.** Fax 06/6786677. 87 rms (all with bath), 15 suites. TV TEL **Bus:** No. 95.
Rates (including breakfast): 250,000 lire ($150) single; 380,000 lire ($228) double. AE, DC, MC, V.

The Albergo Nazionale faces one of Rome's most historic squares, piazza Colonna, with its Column of Marcus Aurelius, Palazzo di Montecitorio, and Palazzo Chigi. Because of its location next to the Parliament buildings, the albergo is frequently used by government officials and members of diplomatic staffs; in fact, it maintains the atmosphere of a club. There are many nooks conducive to conversation in the public lounges. The lobbies are wood-paneled, and there are many antiques throughout the hotel. Rooms are usually spacious, decorated in a traditional style, either carpeted or floored with marble.

Inexpensive

Albergo Cesàri, via di Pietra 89A, 00186 Roma.
☎ **06/6792386.** Fax 06/6790882. 50 rms (30 with bath or shower). A/C TV TEL **Bus:** 492 from Stazione Termini.
Rates: 70,000 lire ($42) single without bath, 135,000 lire ($81) single with bath; 125,000 lire ($75) double without bath, 165,000 lire ($99) double with bath; 190,000 lire ($114) triple with bath; 210,000 lire ($126) quad with bath. Breakfast 15,000 lire ($9) extra. AE, DC, MC, V.
Parking: 35,000 lire ($21).

The Cesàri, on a quiet street in the old quarter of Rome, has been around since 1787. Its overnight guests have included Garibaldi and Stendhal. Its well-preserved exterior harmonizes with the Temple of Neptune and many little antiques shops nearby. The completely renovated interior has mostly functional modern pieces in the bedrooms, although there are a few traditional trappings as well to maintain character. Breakfast (which costs extra) is the only meal available, and there is a parking garage.

Hotel Cecil, via Francesco Crispi 55a, 00187 Roma. ☎ **06/6797998.** Fax 06/6797996. 40 rms (all with bath or shower). TV TEL **Metro:** Piazza Barberini.

Rates (including breakfast): 138,000–184,000 lire ($82.80–$110.40) single; 195,000–264,000 lire ($117–$158.40) double. AE, MC, V. **Parking:** 25,000–30,000 lire ($15–$18).

Henrik Ibsen lived here in the 1860s while writing *Peer Gynt* and *Brand.* Today it's an attractively streamlined hotel with clean and comfortable bedrooms. Many units contain parquet floors and patterned wallpapers. The location is not far from via Sistina, which runs into the top of the Spanish Steps. There's a roof garden with bar service.

5   Near the Pantheon, Piazza Navona & Piazza Campo de' Fiori

Very Expensive

⭐ **Albergo del Sole al Pantheon,** piazza della Rotonda 63, 00186 Roma. ☎ **06/6780441.** Fax 06/69940689. 26 rms (all with bath), 4 suites. A/C MINIBAR TV TEL **Bus:** No. 56, 62, 64, or 70.

Rates (including breakfast): 300,000 lire ($180) single; 420,000 lire ($252) double; 500,000 lire ($300) suite. AE, DC, MC, V. **Parking:** 25,000–35,000 lire ($15–$21).

The Albergo del Sole al Pantheon, overlooking the Pantheon, is an absolute gem. The present-day albergo is one of the oldest hotels in the world; the first records of it as a hostelry appear in 1467. Long known as a retreat for emperors and sorcerers, the hotel has hosted such guests as Frederick III of the Hapsburg family. Mascagni celebrated the premiere of *Cavalleria Rusticana* here. Later, it drew such distinguished company as Jean-Paul Sartre and his companion, Simone de Beauvoir. Today the rooms are exquisitely furnished and decorated with period pieces and stylized reproductions. The hotel staff will direct you to a nearby garage.

Expensive

Grand Hotel Plaza, via del Corso 126, 00186 Roma. ☎ **06/69921111.** Fax 06/69941575. 207 rms, 5 suites. A/C TV TEL **Bus:** No. 2, 81, 90, or 115.

Rates: 257,000–278,000 lire ($154.20–$166.80) single; 346,000–375,000 lire ($207.60–$225) double; 750,000 lire ($450) suite. Breakfast 22,000 lire ($13.20) extra. AE, DC, MC, V.

Empress Carlota of Mexico received Pope Pius IX here in 1866, and in 1933 Pietro Mascagni composed his opera *Nerone* in one of its bedrooms. Vincent Price always stayed here while making "all those bad movies," and when you see the grand decor, you'll understand why. The hotel was partially renovated in 1993. The public rooms are vintage 19th century and contain stained-glass skylights, massive crystal chandeliers, potted palms, inlaid marble floors, and a life-size stone lion guarding the entrance to the ornate stairway leading upstairs. The bar seems an interminable distance across the parquet floor of the opulent ballroom.

The hotel contains well-furnished bedrooms, many quite spacious, and four suites. Some rooms have been modernized and others are old-fashioned. Many rooms have minibars. The Mascagni Restaurant serves Italian cuisine.

Hotel Raphael, largo Febo 2, 00186 Roma. ☎ **06/682831.** Fax 06/6878993. 55 rms, 15 suites. A/C MINIBAR TV TEL **Bus:** No. 64, 70, or 492.

Rates (including breakfast): 250,000 lire ($150) single; 385,000 lire ($231) double; 500,000 lire ($300) suite. AE, DC, MC, V. **Parking:** 35,000 lire ($21) nearby.

This tasteful hotel is known to the discerning who prefer a retreat hidden in the heart of Old Rome, a short walk from piazza Navona. Originally constructed as a convent, the building with its ivy-covered facade was converted into a hotel in 1961. The bedrooms, some of which have their own terraces, are individually decorated in aristocratic imperial decor, with bathrooms covered with travertine marble. The public rooms āre filled with antiques and art work, including a collection of Picasso ceramics. From the rooftop terrace, one of the most panoramic views of Old Rome can be seen.

Dining/Entertainment: The hotel dining room, Ristorante El Raffaellino, is one of the finest places to eat in the area. It offers an international menu, heavy on Italian specialties, that ranges from antipasti served on the buffet, to risotto cooked in champagne, to chateaubriand. The hotel bar is a chic rendezvous, and snacks, such as prosciutto or sandwiches, are served there.

Services: Room service, babysitting, laundry, car rentals, currency exchange.

Moderate

Teatro di Pompeo, largo del Pallaro 8, 00186 Roma. ☎ **06/68300170.** Fax 06/68805531. 12 rms (all with shower). **Bus:** No. 64.

Rates (including breakfast): 180,000 lire ($108) single; 210,000 lire ($126) double. AE, DC, MC, V.

Built on top of the ruins of the Theater of Pompey, this small charmer lies near the spot where Julius Caesar met his final fate. It's on a quiet piazzetta near the Palazzo Farnese and the Campo de' Fiori. The bedrooms are decorated in an old-fashioned Italian style with beamed ceilings and hand-painted tiles. There's no restaurant but breakfast is served. It's possible to exchange foreign currency here, and English is spoken.

Hotel Tiziano, corso Vittorio Emanuele 110, 00186 Roma.

☎ and Fax 06/6865019. 46 rms, 4 suites. A/C MINIBAR TV TEL **Bus:** No. 64, 65, 75, and 170.

Rates (including breakfast): 180,000 lire ($108) single; 240,000 lire ($144) double; 300,000 lire ($180) suites. Discounts of 15% offered Fri–Sun and in Aug. AE, DC, MC, V. **Parking:** 25,000 lire ($15).

This hotel occupies the central section of the Pacelli Palace, a 16th-century structure best known as the family home of Pope Pius XII. (Those sections of the palace to the left and right of the Tiziano are occupied by another hotel and by offices of the Italian government, respectively.) Despite many improvements and modernizations, the hotel retains its neoclassical allure and some of the dignity of the original structure. It enjoys a prominent position on a main thoroughfare between piazza Venezia and St. Peter's. It maintains a restaurant, open for lunch and dinner Monday to Friday, which charges from around 35,000 lire ($21) for a full meal, and which is popular with the neighborhood's business and government community. The hotel also maintains its own garage, set within a three-minute walk, where patrons may park their cars for a supplemental charge.

Inexpensive

Albergo Campo de' Fiori, via del Biscione 6, 00186 Roma.

☎ **06/68806865.** Fax 06/6876003. 27 rms (9 with bath or shower), 1 honeymoon suite. **Bus:** No. 64 from Stazione Termini to Museo di Roma; then arm yourself with a good map for the walk to this place.

Rates (including breakfast): 77,000 lire ($46.20) single without bath; 95,000 lire ($57) double without bath, 105,000 lire ($63) double with shower, 160,000 lire ($96) double with bath; 130,000 lire ($78) triple without bath, 180,000 lire ($108) triple with bath or shower; 160,000 lire ($96) suite. MC, V.

This seems to be everybody's favorite budget hideaway. Lying in the historical center of Rome at a market area that has existed since the 1500s, this cozy, narrow six-story hotel offers rustic rooms, many quite tiny and sparsely adorned, others with a lot of character. The best of them have been restored and are on the first floor. Yours might have a ceiling of clouds and blue skies along with mirrored walls. The best accommodation is the honeymoon retreat on the sixth floor, with a canopied king-size bed. Honeymooners beware: There is no elevator.

Guests can enjoy the panorama from the terrace overlooking the fruits and vegetables below, and, in the distance, St. Peter's. There is no restaurant or bar.

Pensione Navona, via dei Sediari 8, 00186 Roma. ☎ **06/6864203.**
Fax 06/68803802. 22 rms (10 with shower). **Bus:** No. 64.

Rates (including breakfast): 70,000 lire ($42) single without bath;
103,000 lire ($61.80) double without bath, 113,000 lire ($67.80) double
with bath. AE.

Although the individual accommodations within it are not as glamorous as the exterior of the palace that contains it, this pensione offers clean and decent accommodations, some of which are open to
views of the building's central (and quiet) courtyard. Run by an
Australian-born family of Italian descent, the place has tiled bathrooms, ceilings high enough to relieve the midsummer heat, and an
array of architectural oddities, which remain the legacy of the con-
tinual construction this palace has endured since its foundation was
first laid in the 1300s. The pensione lies on a small street that radiates out from the southeastern tip of the piazza Navona.

6   Quartiere Prati

Expensive

Giulio Cesare, via degli Scipioni 287, 00192 Roma. ☎ **06/3210751.**
Fax 06/3211736. 86 rms (all with bath). A/C MINIBAR TV TEL
Bus: No. 280.

Rates (including breakfast): 280,000 lire ($168) single; 380,000 lire
($228) double. AE, DC, MC, V. **Parking:** Free.

Located in a sedate part of Rome, across the Tiber from piazza del
Popolo, is the tasteful Giulio Cesare, an elegant villa that was the
former house of Countess Paterno Solari. In the guest salon, where
the countess once entertained diplomats from all over the globe, are
mostly antique furnishings and Oriental carpets. In the public rooms
are tapestries, Persian rugs, mirrors, ornate gilt pieces, and crystal
chandeliers. In yet a smaller salon, guests gather for drinks in an atmosphere of fruitwood paneling and 18th-century furnishings.

The carpeted bedrooms look like part of a lovely private home;
some contain needlepoint-covered chairs. Other facilities include a
garden where breakfast is served, a snack bar, a piano bar, and parking
space in the courtyard for 10 cars.

Jolly Leonardo da Vinci, via dei Gracchi 324, 00192 Roma.
☎ **06/32499,** or toll free **800/221-2626** in the U.S., **800/237-0319**
in Canada. 245 rms (all with bath), 7 suites. A/C MINIBAR TV TEL
Metro: Lepanto.

Rates (including breakfast): 240,000–270,000 lire ($144–$162) single;
320,000–370,000 lire ($192–$222) double, from 500,000 lire ($300)
suite. AE, DC, MC, V. **Parking:** 35,000 lire ($21).

The Jolly Leonardo da Vinci stands in the Quartiere Prati, on the
Vatican side of the Tiber (across the bridge from piazza del Popolo).
This modern hotel has large public lounges furnished with
leather-covered, deep armchairs. The buffet breakfast is called
buongiorno Jolly. Politicians and film and TV stars who live in Rome

are regular clients of the outstanding men's hair stylist, Amleto, at this hotel.

Dining/Entertainment: The hotel has a pleasant American bar, a restaurant, a grill, and a snack bar. Meals in the Vivaldi & Giovannini Restaurant start at 50,000 lire ($30).

Services: Room service, laundry and valet service.

Facilities: Men's and women's hairdresser, underground garage.

7 Near St. Peter's

Very Expensive

★ **Hotel Atlante Star,** via Vitelleschi 34, 00193 Roma.
☎ **06/6873233.** Fax 06/6872300. 80 rms, 10 suites. A/C MINIBAR TV TEL **Metro:** Ottaviano. **Bus:** No. 64, 81, or 492.

Rates (including breakfast): 365,000 lire ($219) single; 420,000 lire ($252) double; 580,000 lire ($348) suite. AE, DC, MC, V. **Parking:** 50,000 lire ($30).

This first-class hotel lies a short distance from St. Peter's Basilica and the Vatican. The tastefully renovated lobby is covered with dark marble, chrome trim, and lots of exposed wood, while the upper floors somehow give the impression of being inside a luxuriously appointed ocean liner. This stems partly from the lavish use of curved and lacquered surfaces, walls upholstered in freshly colored printed fabrics, modern bathrooms, and wall-to-wall carpeting. Even the door handles are art deco–inspired.

The small but posh accommodations are outfitted with all the modern comforts, and there's also a royal suite with a Jacuzzi. The hotel has the most striking views of St. Peter's of any hotel in Rome. If there is no room at this inn, the owner will try to get you a room at his nearby Atlante Garden (see below).

Dining/Entertainment: The restaurant, Les Etoiles, is an elegant roof garden choice at night, overlooking a panoramic view of Rome, with an illuminated St. Peter's in the background. A flavorful cuisine—inspired in part by Venice—is served. A meal here begins at 100,000 lire ($60).

Services: 24-hour room service, laundry/valet, babysitting, express check-out.

Facilities: Roof garden, foreign-currency exchange, secretarial services in English, translation services.

Moderate

Hotel Atlante Garden, via Crescenzio 78, 00193 Roma.
☎ **06/6872361.** Fax 06/6872315. 43 rms (all with bath). A/C MINIBAR TV TEL **Metro:** Ottaviano.

Rates (including breakfast): 240,000 lire ($144) single; 290,000 lire ($174) double. AE, DC, MC, V. **Parking:** 50,000 lire ($30).

The Atlante Garden stands on a tree-lined street near the Vatican. The entrance takes you through a garden tunnel lined with potted palms, which eventually leads into a series of handsomely decorated public rooms. More classical in its decor than its neighbor under the same management (the Hotel Atlante Star, see above), Atlante Garden offers 19th-century bedrooms, which have been freshly papered and painted, and contain tastefully conservative furniture and all the modern accessories. The renovated baths are tiled.

Hotel Columbus, via della Conciliazione 33, 00193 Roma.
☎ **06/6865435.** Fax 06/6864874. 105 rms (all with bath or shower), 4 suites. A/C MINIBAR TV TEL **Bus:** No. 64.
Rates (including breakfast): 185,000 lire ($111) single; 245,000 lire ($147) double; 345,000 lire ($207) suite. AE, DC, MC, V. **Parking:** Free.

In a 15th-century palace, built some 12 years before its namesake set off for America, is the Hotel Columbus, a few minutes' walk from St. Peter's. It was once the private home of a wealthy cardinal who later became Pope Julius II, and who tormented Michelangelo into painting the Sistine Chapel. The building looks much as it must have those long-centuries ago—a severe time-stained facade, small windows, and heavy wooden doors leading from the street to the colonnades and arches of the inner courtyard. The cobbled entranceway leads to a reception hall with castlelike furniture, then on to a series of baronial public rooms. Note especially the main salon with its walk-in fireplace, oil portraits, battle scenes, and Oriental rugs. The hotel is conveniently located on the triumphal boulevard built by Mussolini in the 1930s to "open up" the Vatican after the Lateran Treaty of 1929, which created the Vatican state.

The bedrooms are considerably simpler than the tiled and tapestried salons, done in soft beiges and furnished with comfortable and serviceable modern pieces. All accommodations are spacious, but a few are enormous and still have such original details as decorated wood ceilings and frescoed walls. The hotel also contains a restaurant, serving lunch or dinner for 45,000 lire ($27).

8 Near the Circus Maximus, the Forum & the Colosseum

Expensive

Hotel Forum, via Tor de Conti 25-30, 00184 Roma. ☎ **06/6792446.**
Fax 06/6786479. 80 rms (all with bath), 6 suites. A/C TV TEL **Bus:** No. 27, 81, 85, or 87.
Rates (including breakfast): 200,000–230,000 lire ($120–$138) single; 300,000–350,000 lire ($180–$210) double; 400,000–450,000 lire ($240–$270) suite. AE, DC, MC, V. **Parking:** 30,000 lire ($18).

The Hotel Forum, built around a medieval bell tower off the Fori Imperiali, offers an elegance that captures the drama of Old Rome, as well as tasteful, sometimes opulent accommodations. At the peak of the *la dolce vita* heyday of the 1950s, this former convent was converted into a hotel. The bedrooms, which look out on the sights of the ancient city, are well appointed with antiques, mirrors, marquetry, and Oriental rugs. The hotel's lounges are conservatively conceived as a country estate, with paneled walls and furnishings that combine Italian and French provincial styles. Dining is an event in the roof garden restaurant. During the season, you can enjoy an *aperitivo* at the hotel's bar on the roof, surveying the timeless Roman Forum. Reserve well in advance.

Inexpensive

Colosseum Hotel, via Sforza 10, 00184 Roma. ☎ **06/4827228.** Fax 06/4827285. 50 rms (all with bath). TEL **Metro:** Cavour.

Rates (including breakfast): 123,000–140,000 lire ($73.80–$84) single; 170,000–180,000 lire ($102–$108) double. AE, DC, MC, V. **Parking:** 30,000 lire ($18).

Not far from the Santa Maria Maggiore basilica, the Colosseum Hotel offers baronial living on a miniature scale. Someone with insight and lira notes designed this hotel, which opened in 1965, in excellent taste, a reflection of the best in Italy's design heritage. The bedrooms are furnished with well-conceived antique reproductions (beds of heavy carved wood, dark-paneled wardrobes, leatherwood chairs)—and all with monklike white walls. Air conditioning is available on request for 20,000 lire ($12) per day. TV is also available for 10,000 lire ($6) per day. The drawing room, with its long refectory table, white walls, red tiles, and provincial armchairs, invites lingering. The reception room, with its parquet floors, arched ceilings, and Savonarola chair, makes a good impression.

Hotel Amalfi, via Merulana 278, 00185 Roma. ☎ **06/4744313.** Fax 06/4820575. 20 rms (all with bath). MINIBAR TV TEL **Metro:** Cavour.

Rates (including breakfast): 85,000–115,000 lire ($51–$69) single; 115,000–170,000 lire ($69–$102) double. AE, DC, MC, V.

In an offbeat but interesting section of Rome lies the Hotel Amalfi, only a short block from the Basilica of Santa Maria Maggiore. It stands behind a narrow and modernized storefront on a busy street. A pleasantly paneled reception area leads to well-scrubbed bedrooms. For the luxury of air conditioning, you pay a 25,000 lire ($15) supplement per day. Mimmo Nigro and his brother, Donato, are the helpful owners. On the premises is a cozy breakfast room and bar.

Hotel Duca d'Alba, via Leonina 14, 00184 Roma. ☎ **06/484471.** Fax 06/4884840. 26 rms (all with bath). A/C MINIBAR TV TEL **Metro:** Cavour.

Rates (including breakfast): 150,000–175,000 lire ($90–$105) single; 160,000–210,000 lire ($96–$126) double. AE, DC, MC, V. **Parking:** 30,000 lire ($18).

Close to the Roman Forums and the Colosseum, this hotel has been restored but maintains its aura of the 19th century, when it was built. Its facade was restored in 1994, and it's been renovated inside with modern, yet classic styling. This is a well-run hotel, with comfortably furnished bedrooms. The hotel has both a breakfast room and a bar. If no room is available at the Duca d'Alba, management will book you into their other hotel, the Hotel Britannia.

9 Monte Mario

Very Expensive

Cavalieri Hilton, via Cadlolo 101, 00136 Roma. ☎ **06/35091,** or toll free **800/445-8667** in the U.S. or Canada. Fax 06/35092241. 373 rms (all with bath), 17 suites. A/C MINIBAR TV TEL
Transportation: Free hotel shuttle bus goes back and forth to the city center.

Rates: 320,000–430,000 lire ($192–$258) single; 435,000–600,000 lire ($261–$360) double; from 1,000,000 lire ($600) suite. Breakfast 31,500 lire ($18.90) extra. AE, DC, MC, V. **Parking:** 5,000 lire ($3).

The Cavalieri Hilton combines all the advantages of a resort hotel with the convenience of being a 15-minute drive from the center of Rome. Overlooking Rome and the Alban Hills from its perch on top of Monte Mario, it is set in 15 acres of trees, flowering shrubs, and stonework. Its facilities are so complete that many visitors (obviously not first-timers to Rome) never leave the hotel grounds. The entrance leads into a marble lobby, whose sculpture, 17th-century art, and winding staircases are usually flooded with sunlight from the massive windows.

The guest rooms and suites, many with panoramic views, are designed to fit contemporary standards of comfort, quality, and style. Soft furnishings in pastel colors are paired with Italian furniture in warm-tone woods. Each unit has a keyless electronic lock, independent heating and air conditioning, color TV with in-house movies, radio, and bedside control for all electric apparatus in the room, as well as a spacious balcony. The bathrooms, sheathed in Italian marble, are equipped with large mirrors, hairdryer, international electric sockets, vanity mirror, piped-in music, and phone.

Dining/Entertainment: The hotel's stellar restaurant, La Pergola, is regarded as one of the finest in Rome. In summer, a garden restaurant, Il Giardino dell'Uliveto, with a pool veranda is an ideal choice.

Services: 24-hour concierge, room service (daily 7am to midnight), laundry/valet, a hotel bus makes frequent runs to the city center.

Facilities: Tennis courts, jogging paths, Turkish bath, sauna with massage, indoor arcade of shops, outdoor swimming pool, health club, facilities for the disabled.

5

Rome Dining

Rome is one of the world's greatest capitals for dining. From elegant, deluxe spots with lavish trappings to little trattorie opening onto hidden piazzas deep in the heart of Old Rome, the city abounds with good restaurants in all price ranges.

The better-known restaurants have menus printed in English. Even some of the lesser-known establishments have at least one person on the staff who speaks English a bit to help you get through the menu.

An Italian restaurant is either called a **trattoria,** or a **ristorante.** Supposedly there's a difference, but I've yet to discern one. Trattorie presumably are smaller and less formal, but sometimes in a kind of reverse snobbism, the management will call an elegant place a trattoria. A ristorante is supposed to be more substantial, but often the opposite is true.

Roman meals customarily include at least three separate courses: pasta, main course (usually a meat dish with vegetables or salad), and dessert. But if you're not that hungry, it's perfectly all right to order just the pasta à la carte and skip the meat course (even though the waiter might feign surprise). Meats, while tasty, are definitely secondary to the pasta dishes, which are much more generous and filling. The wine is so good (especially the white Frascati wine from the nearby Castelli Romani), and moderate in price, that I recommend you adopt a European custom and have it with lunch and dinner.

Meal hours are rather confining in Italy. In the rare event that you do not take continental breakfast at your hotel, you can have coffee and sweets at **tavola calda.** They're all over the city. The name literally means "hot table," and they're stand-up snack bar–type arrangements, open all day long. Restaurants generally serve lunch between 1 and 3pm in the afternoon, dinner between about 7:30 and 11pm; at all other times, restaurants are closed for business. Dinner, by the way, is taken late in Rome, so while the restaurant may open at 7:30, even if you get there at 8pm, you'll often be the only one in the place. Romans think in terms of "dinner" in the afternoon (*pranzo*) and "supper" in the evening (*cena*).

Further, I'd recommend that you leave a few hours free—and go to a different part of town for dinner each night. It's a great way to see Rome.

PRICES   Some restaurants offer a tourist menu or *menu turistico* at an inclusive price. The tourist menu includes soup (nearly always minestrone) or pasta followed by a meat dish with vegetables, topped off by dessert (fresh fruit or cheese), as well as a quarter liter of wine or mineral water, along with the bread, cover charge, and service (you'll be expected to tip something extra).

If you order from the tourist menu, you'll avoid the array of added charges that the restaurateur likes to tack on. You won't get the choicest cuts of meat, nor will you always be able to order the specialties of the house, but you'll probably get a quite good, filling repast if you pick and choose your restaurants carefully. But be warned. Even though a restaurant owner offers such a menu, the staff is often reluctant to serve it, since it is their least profitable item. Often the owner will advertise a tourist menu in the window, but it won't be featured on the menu you're shown by the waiter. You'll have to ask for it in most cases, and you won't win any "most beloved patron" contests when you do.

What about the *prezzo fisso?* A confused picture. A fixed-price meal might even undercut the tourist menu, offering a cheaper meal of the casa. On the other hand, it might not include wine, service, bread, or cover charge—for which you'll be billed extra. If you're on the most limited of budgets, make sure you understand what the prezzo fisso entails so as to avoid misunderstanding when you settle the tab.

Most restaurants will charge you a *pane e coperto* (bread and cover) charge which is unavoidable. It's a charge restaurants impose for the privilege of your patronizing their establishment. This charge ranges from about 1,000 to 3,000 lire (60¢ to $1.80) per person. A tip *(servizio),* ranging from 10% to 15%, is usually added to your bill, but it is customary to leave some small change as an extra reward, especially if the service has been good.

For our purposes, meals rated "Very Expensive" usually cost more than 120,000 lire ($72); "Expensive," 65,000 to 120,000 lire ($39 to $72); "Moderate," 40,000 to 65,000 lire ($24 to $39); and anything under 40,000 lire ($24) is considered "Inexpensive." These prices are computed on the basis of a three-course meal (not the most expensive items on the menu), including a carafe of the house wine, service, and taxes.

A FINAL CAVEAT   All Roman restaurants are closed at least one day a week—usually Sunday or Monday, but that varies. Also, beware of the month of August, when most Romans go on holiday. Scores of restaurants close down, displaying only a lonely *chiuso per ferie* sign. It's always best to call a restaurant (or ask one of the hotel staff to call for you) before you head there.

1   Near Stazione Termini

Moderate

Scoglio Di Frisio, via Merulana 256. ☎ 4872765.
Cuisine: NEAPOLITAN. **Reservations:** Recommended. **Bus:** No. 93 from Stazione Termini.
Prices: Appetizers 11,000–18,000 lire ($6.60–$10.80); main courses 18,000–22,000 lire ($10.80–$13.20); fixed-price menus 60,000–100,000 lire ($36–$60). AE, DC, MC, V.
Open: Dinner only, daily 7:30–11pm.

Scoglio di Frisio is the choice *suprême* to introduce yourself to the Neapolitan kitchen. While there, you should abandon your Yankee concepts and get reacquainted with genuine pizza (pizza pie is redundant). At night, you can begin with a plate-size Neapolitan pizza (crunchy, oozy, and excellent) with clams and mussels. After

Rome Dining

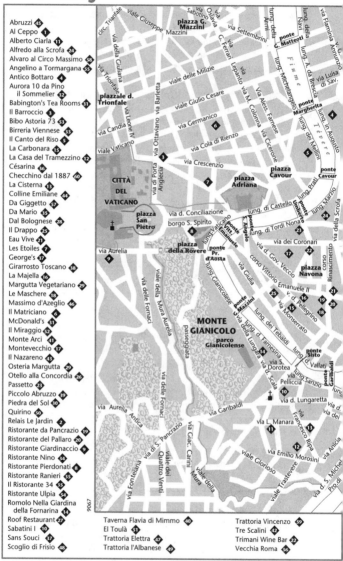

devouring the house specialty, you may then settle for chicken cacciatore (hunter's style), or veal scaloppine. Scoglio di Frisio also has entertainment—so it makes for an inexpensive night on the town. All the fun, cornball "O Sole Mio" elements spring forth in the evening—a guitar, mandolin, and a strolling tenor who is like Mario

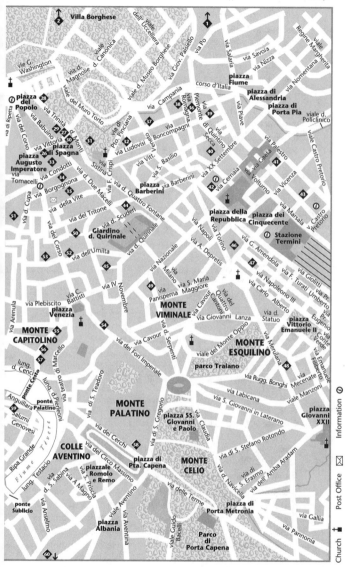

Lanza reincarnate. The decor's nautical in honor of the top-notch fish dishes—complete with a high-ceilinged grotto with craggy walls, fishermen's nets, crustaceans, and a miniature three-masted schooner hanging overhead. It lies on a broad street, south of the Stazione Termini.

Taverna Flavia di Mimmo, via Flavia 9. ☎ 4745214.

> **Cuisine:** ROMAN/INTERNATIONAL. **Reservations:** Recommended.
> **Metro:** Piazza della Repubblica.
> **Prices:** Appetizers 10,500–16,000 lire ($6.30–$9.60); main courses 18,000–40,000 lire ($10.80–$24). AE, DC, MC, V.
> **Open:** Lunch Mon–Sat 1–3pm; dinner Mon–Sat 7:30–1:30pm.

Taverna Flavia di Mimmo, just a block from via XX Settembre, is a robustly Roman restaurant where during the heyday of *La Dolce Vita* movie people used to meet over tasty dishes. The restaurant still serves the same food that used to delight Frank Sinatra and the "Hollywood on the Tiber" crowd. Specialties include a risotto with scampi and spaghetti al whisky. A different regional dish is featured daily, which might be Roman-style tripe. Exceptional dishes include ossobuco with peas, a seafood salad, and fondue with truffles.

Inexpensive

Monte Arci, via Castelfidardo 33. ☎ 4941220.

> **Cuisine:** ROMAN/SARDINIAN. **Reservations:** Recommended. **Bus:** No. 36 from Stazione Termini.
> **Prices:** Appetizers 7,000–10,000 lire ($4.20–$6); main courses 13,000–20,000 lire ($7.80–$12). AE, V.
> **Open:** Lunch Mon–Sat 12:30–3pm; dinner Mon–Sat 7–11:30pm.

Monte Arci, on a cobblestone street not far from the railway station, is set behind a sienna-colored facade, which also shelters a stately but faded apartment building. The restaurant features low-cost Roman and Sardinian specialties (you'll spend less money if you have pizza). Typical dishes include maloreddus (a regional form of gnocchetti), pasta with clams or lobster, pasta with pesto, and pasta with those delectable porcini mushrooms.

Il Nazareno, via Marghera 25. ☎ 4957782.

> **Cuisine:** ROMAN/ABRUZZI. **Reservations:** Recommended. **Metro:** Stazione Termini.
> **Prices:** Appetizers 8,500–13,500 lire ($5.10–$8.10); main courses 18,000–22,000 lire ($10.80–$13.20). AE, DC, MC, V.
> **Open:** Lunch daily noon–3pm; dinner daily 7–11pm.

Established in the 1920s, this is one of the most reliable restaurants near the railway station. Outfitted like a country trattoria, the place is a magnet for many of the entrepreneurs and hoteliers in this busy commercial neighborhood. The menu includes specialties from both Rome and Abruzzi, and the kitchen prides itself on its house specialty, roasted rack of lamb with herbs. Spaghetti with clams is one of the most frequently ordered main dishes.

Trattoria Elettra, via Principe Amedeo 72–74. ☎ 474-5397.

> **Cuisine:** ROMAN/ITALIAN. **Reservations:** Not required. **Metro:** Stazione Termini.
> **Prices:** Appetizers 8,000–10,000 lire ($4.80–$6); main courses 10,500–18,000 lire ($6.30–$10.80). AE, DC, MC, V.
> **Open:** Lunch Sun–Fri noon–3:30pm; dinner Sun–Fri 7–11:30pm.
> **Closed:** Aug 5–28.

This well-run family-style trattoria offers good food at reasonable prices. It's located between the Stazione Termini (about three blocks away) and the Basilica of Santa Maria Maggiore, quite close to via Manin. The place is bright and cheerfully unpretentious. The pasta is good; try the ravioli stuffed with ricotta, spinach, and salmon. You might also try risotto with asparagus in a cream sauce followed by one of the main meat or poultry dishes of the day, including ossobuco.

Trimani Wine Bar, via Cernaia 37b. ☎ **4469630.**

> **Cuisine:** CONTINENTAL. **Reservations:** Not required. **Metro:** Piazza della Repubblica or Castro Pretorio.
>
> **Prices:** Salads and platters of light food 12,000–19,000 lire ($7.20–$11.40); glasses of wine 5,000–15,000 lire ($3–$9), depending on the vintage. AE, DC, MC, V.
>
> **Open:** Lunch Mon–Sat 11:30am–3pm; dinner Mon–Sat 5:30pm–midnight. **Closed:** Three weeks in Aug and Dec 25–Jan 1.

Specifically conceived as a tasting center for French and Italian wines, spumantis, and liqueurs, this elegant wine bar lies at the edge of a historic district where traffic is partially restricted. Amid a post-modern, award-winning interior decor inspired by classical Rome, you'll find comfortable seating, occasional live music, and a staff devoted to pressurizing half-full bottles of wine between pours. Menu items are inspired by the cuisine of stylish bistros in Paris, and might include vegetarian pastas (in summertime only), salads niçoises, herb-laden bean (fagiole) soups, slices of quiche, Hungarian goulasch, gazpacho, and platters of French and Italian cheeses and pâtés.

Trimani, a family of wine brokers whose company was established in 1821, maintains a well-stocked shop about 40 yards from its wine bar, at via Goito (tel. 4469661), where an astonishing array of the oenological bounty of Italy is for sale.

2 Near the Parioli District, Via Veneto & the Villa Borghese

Very Expensive

George's, via Marche 7. ☎ **484575.**

> **Cuisine:** INTERNATIONAL. **Reservations:** Required. **Metro:** Piazza Barberini.
>
> **Prices:** Appetizers 13,000–18,000 lire ($7.80–$10.80); main courses 42,000–48,000 lire ($25.20–$28.80). AE, DC, MC, V.
>
> **Open:** Lunch Mon–Sat 7:30pm–midnight. **Closed:** Aug.

George's has been a favorite of mine ever since Romulus and Remus were being tended by the she-wolf. Right off via Veneto, it's not run by George, but by Michele Pavia, maître d' here for a quarter of a century before becoming its owner. Many guests drop in for a before-dinner drink to enjoy the music in the piano bar. They then proceed to an elegantly decorated and raised dining room with a rented ceiling. There is a relaxed clublike atmosphere, and English is spoken, of course. Oysters are a specialty, served in every form from fritters to "angels on horseback." The kitchen has an uncompromising dedication to quality, as reflected by the marinated mussels, smoked Scottish salmon, and sole George's; many veal and steak dishes are offered as well. From June to October, depending on the weather, the action shifts to the garden, suitably undisturbed because it was once part of a papal villa.

⭐ **Relais le Jardin,** in the Hotel Lord Byron, via G. de Notaris 5. ☎ **3613041.**

Cuisine: ROMAN. **Reservations:** Required. **Bus:** No. 52.
Prices: Appetizers 28,000–46,000 lire ($16.80–$27.60); main courses 42,000–56,000 lire ($25.20–$33.60). AE, DC, MC, V.
Open: Lunch Mon–Sat 1–3pm; dinner Mon–Sat 8–10:30pm. **Closed:** Aug.

Relais le Jardin is one of the best places to go in Rome for cuisine that's both traditional and creative. On the ground floor of one of the most elite small hotels of the capital (see my hotel recommendation in Chapter 4), the restaurant has an almost aggressively lighthearted decor, combining white lattice with cheerful pastel colors. Many of the cooks and service personnel were trained at foreign embassies or diplomatic residences abroad. Classified as a Relais & Châteaux, the restaurant serves a frequently changing array of dishes that might include seafood crêpes, noodle pie with salmon and asparagus, or fresh salmon with asparagus. Dessert may be a charlotte kiwi royal or "the chef's fancy."

⭐ **Sans Souci,** via Sicilia 20. ☎ **4821814.**

Cuisine: FRENCH. **Reservations:** Required. **Metro:** Piazza Barberini.
Prices: Appetizers 25,000–30,000 lire ($15–$18); main courses 48,000–56,000 lire ($28.80–$33.60). AE, DC, MC, V.
Open: Dinner only, Tues–Sun 8pm–1am. **Closed:** Aug 10–30.

Sans Souci is the most elegant and sophisticated dining choice in Rome, and it also serves some of the finest food. With this

---

Frommer's Smart Traveler: Restaurants

Value-Conscious Travelers Should Take Advantage of the Following:

1. When one is available, order a fixed-price meal in which everything—including tax, service, and cover charge—is included.
2. Watch the booze—tabs mount quickly. It's cheaper to ask for a carafe of the house wine.
3. Pastas, pizzas, and rice dishes (risotto) are exceptional bargains.
4. Standing up and eating at a cafe or rosticceria is less expensive than sitting down.
5. Make a picnic lunch and save the extra money for a really good dinner.

unbeatable combination, it's no wonder that it has a chic—and frequently famous—clientele. An additional plus is its location—right off via Veneto. To begin your evening, you'll enter the dimly lit small lounge/bar to the right at the bottom of the steps. Here, amid tapestries and glittering mirrors, the maître d' will present you with the menu, and you can leisurely make selections while sipping a drink. The menu is ever changing, as "new creations" are devised. But you are likely to be offered "Beggar's Purse" crêpes filled with seasonal delicacies, such as porcini mushrooms or fresh spring asparagus, and blended with ricotta and served with a white-truffle sauce. Fresh goose liver is sautéed with black truffles, and sea bass is grilled with fresh herbs. Salt-marsh lamb from Normandy appears en croûte with a thyme sauce. The dessert soufflés are seasonal, made with fresh fruit. In all, Sans Souci is the most elegant spot in Rome for dinner.

Moderate

Al Ceppo, via Panama 2–4. ☎ 8419696.

> **Cuisine:** ROMAN. **Reservations:** Highly recommended. **Bus:** 4, 52, or 53.
> **Prices:** Appetizers 12,000–18,000 lire ($7.20–$10.80); main courses 18,000–45,000 lire ($10.80–$27). AE, DC, MC, V.
> **Open:** Lunch Tues–Sun 1–3pm; dinner Tues–Sun 8–11pm. **Closed:** Last three weeks of Aug.

Although its location is somewhat hidden, Al Ceppo lies only two blocks from Villa Borghese, near piazza Ungheria. The clientele is likely to be Roman rather than foreign. "The Log" (its English name) features an open fireplace that's fed with wood on which the chef does lamb chops, liver, and bacon to charcoal perfection. The beefsteak, which hails from Tuscany, is also succulent. Other dishes on the menu include a delectable handmade pasta, taglioline monteconero, or else you can order monkfish with rosemary, garlic, and tomatoes, flavored with cayenne. Another specialty is rabbit à la Marchiginana, stuffed with veal, pine nuts, and pistachio nuts, or else a fish carpaccio (made with raw sea bass). Save room for such desserts as apple cobbler, a pear and almond tart, or especially the chocolate meringue hazelnut cake.

$ **Ambasciata d' Abruzzo**, via Pietro Tacchini 26. ☎ 8078256.

> **Cuisine:** ABRUZZI. **Reservations:** Recommended. **Bus:** 26, 52, 53, or 168.
> **Prices:** All you can eat 50,000 lire ($30). AE, DC, MC, V.
> **Open:** Lunch Mon–Sat 1–3:30pm; dinner Mon–Sat 7–11:30pm. **Closed:** Aug.

If you like ambitious portions on the all-you-can-eat basis, and tasty, well-cooked food that's a good value for the money, then strike out for this little, hard-to-find restaurant in the Parioli district. It's both superb value and great fun, providing you are ravenously hungry and enjoy bountiful dining. It accomplishes the seemingly impossible, not skimping on quality or quantity.

The atmosphere is exceedingly informal, and you may have to stand in line if you don't reserve a table. It's in the true tavern style, with strings of sausages, peppers, and garlic. The culinary parade commences with a basket overflowing with assorted sausages placed on your table; even a herb-flavored baked ham is presented, resting on a cutting board with a knife. Help yourself—but go easy, as there's more to come. Another wicker basket holds moist, crunchy peasant-style bread. Next, a hearty mass of spaghetti vongole (with baby clams) is placed before you. Then proceed to an overloaded antipasto table with selections including marinated artichokes, salads, whatever. Later, those still at the table are served a main dish, such as grilled fish. Then comes the large salad bowl, mixed to your liking, followed by an assortment of country cheeses, plus a basket brimming with fresh fruit. You're even given your choice of a dessert. A pitcher of the house wine is at your disposal, and the price not only includes coffee, but a chaser of Sambuca as well.

Aurora 10 da Pino Il Sommelier, via Aurora 10. ☎ 4742779.

Cuisine: ROMAN/SICILIAN. **Reservations:** Recommended. **Metro:** Piazza Barberini.

Prices: Appetizers 15,000–19,000 lire ($9–$11.40); main courses 18,000–29,000 lire ($10.80–$17.40). AE, DC, MC, V.

Open: Lunch Tues–Sun noon–3pm; dinner Tues–Sun 7–11:15pm. **Closed:** Aug 12–20.

Established in 1981 a few paces from the top of via Veneto, this restaurant lies within the vaulted interior of what was originally a Maronite convent. Its manager (and namesake) is Pino Salvatore, whose high-energy direction and attentive staff have attracted some of the capital's most influential diplomats and a scattering of film stars. The place is especially noted for its awesome array of more than 250 kinds of wine, collectively representing every province of Italy. Unusual for Rome, the restaurant features a large soup menu, along with a tempting array of freshly made antipasti. You can begin with a selection of your favorite pasta or risotto, then follow with perhaps a salad "Aurora," linguine with lobster, a Sicilian-style fish fry, swordfish in herb sauce, risotto with asparagus, or beef stew flambé.

Césarina, via Piemonte 109. ☎ 4880828.

Cuisine: EMILIA ROMAGNA/ROMAN. **Reservations:** Recommended. **Bus:** 56.

Prices: Appetizers 9,000–15,000 lire ($5.40–$9); main courses 14,000–25,000 lire ($8.40–$15). AE, DC, MC, V.

Open: Lunch Mon–Sat 12:30–3pm; dinner Mon–Sat 7:30–11pm.

Specializing in the cuisine of Rome and the region around Bologna (Emilia Romagna), this restaurant has grown since it was originally established by a well-meaning matriarch, Césarina Masi, around 1960. (Many tourist veterans of Rome remember Ms. Masi fondly because of her strict supervision of the kitchens, and because of the way she would lecture regular clients who didn't finish their tagliatelle.) Although she died in the mid-1980s, the restaurant perpetuates her culinary traditions in a newer incarnation of the original corner-in-the-wall. Today, with three dining rooms and more than 200 seats, the restaurant serves excellent versions of *bollito misto* (an array of well-seasoned boiled meats), which are rolled from table to table on a trolley; and a misto Césarina—three kinds of pasta, each handmade and served with a different sauce. Equally appealing is the saltimbocca and the *cotoletta alla bolognese*, a veal cutlet baked with ham and cheese. A dessert specialty is semifreddo Césarina. The staff is tactful and polite, the food is excellent, and the selection of antipasti is freshly made and very appealing.

Giarrosto Toscano, via Campania 29. ☎ 5821899.

Cuisine: TUSCAN. **Reservations:** Required. **Bus:** No. 90B, 95, 490, or 495.

Prices: Appetizers 12,000–18,000 lire ($7.20–$10.80); main courses 18,000–21,000 lire ($10.80–$12.60). AE, DC, MC, V.

Open: Lunch Thurs–Tues 12:30–3pm; dinner Thurs–Tues 7:30–11:30pm.

Girarrosto Toscano, facing the walls of the Borghese gardens, draws a crowd of guests from via Veneto haunts, which means that you may have to wait. Under vaulted ceilings in a cellar setting, some of the finest Tuscan specialties in Rome are served. Begin by enjoying an enormous selection of antipasti, which the waiters bring around: succulent little meatballs, vine-ripened melon with prosciutto, an omelet, mozzarella, and especially delicious Tuscan salami. You're then given a choice of pasta, such as fettuccine in a cream sauce. Priced according to weight, the bistecca alla fiorentina is the best item to order, although it's expensive; it's a grilled steak seasoned with oil, salt, and pepper. Oysters and fresh fish from the Adriatic are served every day. Of course, the beefsteak, fresh fish, or fresh oysters—all based on weight by the gram and also on daily market quotations—will be much more expensive than the prices indicated above. So order with care if you're on a strict budget. For dessert, I'd recommend what everybody has—an assortment of different flavors of ice cream, called *gelato misto*.

Piccolo Abruzzo, via Sicilia 237. ☎ 482-0176.

Cuisine: ABRUZZI. **Reservations:** Highly recommended. **Bus:** No. 490 or 495.

Prices: Appetizers 8,000–14,000 lire ($4.80–$8.40); main courses 13,000–22,000 lire ($7.80–$13.20). AE, MC, V.

Open: Lunch Mon–Fri 12:30–3pm; dinner Mon–Sat 7pm–midnight.

An imaginative array of antipasti and copious portions make Piccolo Abruzzo, a good stroll from via Veneto, one of the most popular restaurants in its neighborhood. Many regulars plan a meal either early or late to avoid the jam, as the place is small and popular. Full meals are priced according to what you take from the groaning antipasti buffet. You can follow with a pasta course, which might be samples of three different versions, followed by a meat course, then cheese and dessert. All this lively scene takes place in a brick- and stucco-sheathed room, perfumed with hanging cloves of garlic, salt-cured hams, and beribboned bunches of Mediterranean herbs.

3 Near the Spanish Steps & Piazza del Popolo

Very Expensive

El Toulà, via della Lupa 29B. ☎ **6873498.**

> **Cuisine:** ROMAN/VENETIAN. **Reservations:** Required for dinner. **Bus:** No. 26, 90, or 913.
> **Prices:** Appetizers 16,000–22,000 lire ($9.60–$13.20); main courses 33,000–52,000 lire ($19.80–$31.20); fixed-price menu 90,000 lire ($54). AE, DC, MC, V.
> **Open:** Lunch Mon–Fri 1–3pm; dinner Mon–Sat 8–11pm. **Closed:** Aug.

El Toulà offers the quintessence of Roman haute cuisine with a creative flair. The elegant setting, attracting the international set, is one of vaulted ceilings and large archways that divide the rooms. Guests stop in the charming bar to order a drink while deciding on their food selections from the impressive menu. The menu changes every month. In honor of the restaurant's Venetian origins, one section of the menu is devoted exclusively to culinary specialties of that city in the lagoons. Items include fegato (liver) alla Veneziana, the most classic dish of Venice, along with calamari stuffed with vegetables, bigoli pasta in squid ink, *bacalari* (codfish mousse served with polenta), and another Venetian classic, *broetto*, a fish soup made with monkfish and clams. The selection of sherbets depends on the availability of fruits—the cantaloupe and fresh strawberry versions are celestial concoctions. You can request a mixed plate if you'd like to sample several of them. El Toulà usually isn't crowded at lunchtime.

Expensive

Dal Bolognese, piazza del Popolo 1–2. ☎ **3611426.**

> **Cuisine:** BOLOGNESE. **Reservations:** Required. **Metro:** Flaminio.
> **Prices:** Appetizers 13,000–24,000 lire ($7.80–$14.40); main courses 18,000–28,000 lire ($10.80–$16.80). AE, DC.
> **Open:** Lunch Tues–Sun 12:45–3pm; dinner Tues–Sat 8:15–11pm.
> **Closed:** Aug 5–20.

This is one of those rare dining spots that's not only chic, but noted for its food as well. Young actors, models, artists from the nearby via Margutta, and even executives show up here, quickly booking the limited sidewalk tables. To begin your meal, I suggest the savory Parma ham, or perhaps the melon and prosciutto if you're feeling extravagant (try a little freshly ground pepper on the latter). For your main course, specialties include lasagne verde, tagliatelle alla bolognese, and a most recommendable cotolette alla bolognese. Instead of lingering in the restaurant, you may want to cap your evening by calling on the Rosati next door (or its competitor, the Canova, across the street), and enjoying one of the tempting pastries.

Moderate

Da Mario, via della Vite 55–56. ☎ **6783818.**

    Cuisine: ROMAN/FLORENTINE. **Reservations:** Recommended.
    Metro: Piazza di Spagna.
    Prices: Appetizers 10,000–14,000 lire ($6–$8.40); main courses 14,000–
    20,000 lire ($8.40–$12). AE, DC, MC, V.
    Open: Lunch Mon–Sat 12:30–3pm; dinner Mon–Sat 7:30–11pm.
    Closed: Aug.

Da Mario is noted for its moderately priced game specialties. It also offers excellent Florentine dishes, although the typical beefsteak is too costly these days for most budgets. You can dine in air-conditioned comfort on the street level or descend to the cellars. A good beginning is a wide-noodle dish, pappardelle, best when served with a game sauce (caccia). Capretto (kid) is served in the Florentine fashion, although you may prefer two roasted quail with polenta. I recommend the gelato misto, a selection of mixed ice cream.

Il Ristorante 34 (also A1 34), via Mario de' Fiori 34.
    ☎ **6795091.**

    Cuisine: ROMAN. **Reservations:** Required. **Metro:** Piazza di Spagna.
    Prices: Appetizers 10,000–20,000 lire ($6–$12); main courses 15,000–
    21,000 lire ($9–$12.60). AE, DC, MC, V.
    Open: Lunch Tues–Sun 12:30–3pm; dinner Tues–Sat 7:30–10:30pm.
    Closed: Aug 6–26.

Il Ristorante 34 is a very good and increasingly popular restaurant close to the most famous shopping district of Rome. Its long and narrow interior is sheathed in scarlet wallpaper, ringed with modern paintings, and capped with a vaulted ceiling. In the rear, stop to admire a display of antipasti proudly exhibited near the entrance to the bustling kitchen. Your meal might include noodles with caviar and salmon, risotto with chunks of lobster, pasta-and-lentil soup, meatballs in a sauce with fat mushrooms, two kinds of entrecôte, or pasta in a pumpkin-flavored cream sauce. The spaghetti with clams is among the best in Rome.

Osteria Margutta, via Margutta 82. ☎ **323-1025.**

    Cuisine: ROMAN. **Reservations:** Recommended. **Metro:** Piazza di
    Spagna.
    Prices: Appetizers 12,000–16,000 lire ($7.20–$9.60); main courses
    18,000–23,000 lire ($10.80–$13.80). AE, DC, MC, V.
    Open: Lunch Mon–Sat 12:30–3pm; dinner Mon–Sat 7:30–10:30pm.

Osteria Margutta is on a street that traditionally has housed the nucleus of Rome's art colony. It's most fun to visit on Sunday, when art shows are staged along the street, but you can visit the galleries and antiques shops any day of the week. Should you get hungry during your stroll, drop in at this rustic tavern, where art posters provide added style. You'll pass by tables of tempting antipasti, which are priced according to your choice. Try succulent versions of *carciofi* (artichokes) or marinated eggplant. Dishes include roast beef, lamb with green peppercorns, and various kinds of pasta. Steaks are also a choice.

Ristorante Nino, via Borgognona 11. ☎ 679-5676.

Cuisine: TUSCAN. **Reservations:** Recommended. **Metro:** Piazza di Spagna.
Prices: Appetizers 8,000–40,000 lire ($4.80–$24); main courses 16,000–60,000 lire ($9.60–$36). AE, DC, MC, V.
Open: Lunch Mon–Sat 12:30–3pm; dinner Mon–Sat 7:30–11pm.
Closed: Aug.

Ristorante Nino, off via Condotti a short walk from the Spanish Steps, is a tavern mecca for writers, artists, and an occasional model from one of the nearby high-fashion houses. Nino's enjoys deserved acclaim for its Tuscan dishes. The cooking is hearty and completely unpretentious. The restaurant is particularly known for its steaks shipped in from Florence and charcoal broiled, which are priced according to weight. A plate of cannelloni Nino is one of the chef's specialties. Other good dishes include grilled veal liver, two deviled quail, fagioli cotti al fiasco, codfish alla livornese, and zampone. For dessert, I suggest the Florentine cake called castagnaccio.

Ristorante Ranieri, via Mario de' Fiori 26. ☎ 6791592.

Cuisine: INTERNATIONAL. **Reservations:** Required. **Bus:** 52, 53, 56, 81, or 90.
Prices: Appetizers 15,000–20,000 lire ($9–$12); main courses 20,000–32,000 lire ($12–$19.20). AE, DC, MC, V.
Open: Lunch Mon–Sat 12:30–3pm; dinner Mon–Sat 7:30–11pm.

Ristorante Ranieri, off via Condotti, is well into its second century (it was founded in 1843). Neapolitan-born Giuseppe Ranieri, for whom the restaurant is named, was the chef to Queen Victoria. Long a favorite dining place of the cognoscenti, Ranieri still maintains its Victorian trappings. Nothing ever seems to change here. Many of the dishes on the good menu reflect the restaurant's ties with royalty—veal cutlet l'Impériale, mignonettes of veal à la Regina Victoria, and tournedos Enrico IV. The imperial veal cutlet dish—served with asparagus and mushrooms—was actually created some time in the 19th century for the queen herself. Most of the dishes are French and Italian, although the overall menu is international.

Inexpensive

Otello alla Concordia, via della Croce 81. ☎ 6791178.

Cuisine: ROMAN. **Reservations:** Not required. **Metro:** Piazza di Spagna.
Prices: Appetizers 8,000–14,000 lire ($4.80–$8.40); main courses 12,000–26,000 lire ($7.20–$15.60). AE, DC, MC, V.
Open: Lunch Mon–Sat 12:30–3pm; dinner Mon–Sat 7:30–11pm.

Set on a side street amid the glamorous boutiques near the northern edge of the Spanish Steps, this is one of the most popular and consistently reliable restaurants of Rome. Diners enter from a stone corridor that leads into a dignified building, the Palazzo Povero, choosing a table (space permitting) in either an arbor-covered courtyard or within a cramped but convivial series of inner dining rooms. Banks of fruit from the Roman countryside and displays of Italian bounty decorate an interior well-known to many of the district's shopkeepers from the surrounding fashion district. The spaghetti alle vongole veraci (spaghetti with clams) is excellent, as well as breast of turkey with mushrooms, abbacchio arrosto (roasted baby lamb), eggplant parmigiana, a selection of grilled or sautéed fish dishes (including swordfish), and several different preparations of veal.

4 Near Piazza Colonna, the Trevi Fountain & Quirinale Hill

Inexpensive

Colline Emiliane, via Avignonesi 22. ☎ 4817538.

> **Cuisine:** EMILIANA ROMAGNOLA. **Reservations:** Required. **Metro:** Piazza Barberini.
> **Prices:** Appetizers 8,000–14,000 lire ($4.80–$8.40); main courses 16,000–25,000 lire ($9.60–$15). No credit cards.
> **Open:** Lunch Sat–Thurs 12:30–2:45pm; dinner Sat–Thurs 7:30–10:45pm. **Closed:** Aug.

Colline Emiliane is a small restaurant, right off piazza Barberini, that serves the classic *cucina bolognese.* It's a family-run place where everybody helps out. The owner is the cook, and his wife makes the pasta, which, incidentally, is about the best you'll encounter in Rome. The house specialty is an inspired tortellini alla panna (cream sauce) with truffles. You might prefer one of the less expensive pastas, however, and all of them are excellent and handmade—maccheroncini al funghetto and tagliatelle alla bolognese. As an opener, I suggest culatello di Zibello, a delicacy from a small town near Parma that is known for having the finest prosciutto in the world. Main courses include braciola di maiale, boneless rolled pork cutlets that have been stuffed with ham and cheese, breaded, and sautéed. To finish your meal, I recommend budino al cioccolato, a chocolate pudding that is baked like flan.

Il Miraggio, vicolo Sciarra 59. ☎ 6780226.

> **Cuisine:** ROMAN/SARDINIAN. **Reservations:** Recommended. **Bus:** 56, 85, 87, or 90B.
> **Prices:** Appetizers 9,000–15,000 lire ($5.40–$9); main courses 12,000–24,000 lire ($7.20–$14.40). AE, V.
> **Open:** Lunch Mon–Sat 12:30–3:30pm; dinner Mon–Sat 7:30–10:30pm.

While shopping near piazza Colonna, you may want to escape the roar of traffic along the corso by dining at this informal, hidden-away "mirage" in a charming location on a crooked street. It's a cozy, neighborhood setting with fast service and mouth-watering food. The decor in the dining room includes a wine keg set in the wall. A specialty of the house is tortellini alla papalina. You might want to try filet of beef with truffles, rosetta di vitello modo nostro (veal "our style"), or spiedino all siciliana (rolls of veal with ham and cheese inside, onions and bay leaves outside, grilled on a skewer). Fresh seafood specialties are also featured.

Quirino, via delle Muratte 84. ☎ **6794108.**

Cuisine: ROMAN. **Reservations:** Required. **Metro:** Piazza Barberini.
Prices: Appetizers 10,000–14,000 lire ($6–$8.40); main courses 16,000–24,000 lire ($9.60–$14.40). AE, V.
Open: Lunch Mon–Sat 12:30–3:30pm; dinner Mon–Sat 7:30–10:30pm.
Closed: Aug 1–20.

Quirino is a good place to dine right after you've tossed your coin into the Trevi Fountain. Founded in 1958, the restaurant is housed in an 18th-century building that was originally the home of the Serafini family, scions of at least one pope. The atmosphere inside is typically Italian, with hanging Chianti bottles, a beamed ceiling, and muraled walls. The food is strictly in the "home-cooking" style of Roman trattorie. At times you can enjoy fresh chicory that is perfumed and bitter at the same time. All the ritual dishes of the Roman kitchen are here, including brains in butter. I'm also fond of a mixed fry of tiny shrimp and squid rings, which resemble onion rings. For an opening course, I recommend risotto, milanese style, or spaghetti with clams. The classic Sicilian pasta dish, pasta alla Norma, is served here—tomatoes, eggplant, and *salata* (a salted ricotta). You can also order *involtini alla Messinese,* a roulade of either fish or meat, according to your wishes, which is filled with cheese, grilled, and served with salad greens in the Sicilian style. For dessert, a basket of fresh fruit will be placed on your table.

5 Near the Pantheon, Piazza Navona & Piazza Campo de' Fiori

Expensive

Il Drappo, vicolo del Malpasso 9. ☎ **6877365.**

Cuisine: SARDINIAN. **Reservations:** Required. **Bus:** 46, 62, or 64.
Prices: Fixed-price dinner 75,000 lire ($45). AE.
Open: Dinner only, Mon–Sat 8pm–midnight. **Closed:** Aug.

Il Drappo, on a hard-to-find, narrow street off a square near the Tiber, is operated by brother-sister team Paolo and Valentina. The facade is graced with a modernized trompe-l'oeil painting above the stone entrance, which is flanked with potted plants. Inside, you'll have your choice of two tastefully decorated dining rooms festooned with yards of patterned cotton draped from supports on the ceiling. Flowers and candles are everywhere. Fixed-price dinners may include a wafer-thin appetizer called *carte di musica* (sheet music paper), which is topped with tomatoes, green peppers, parsley, and olive oil, followed by fresh spring lamb in season, a fish stew made with tuna caviar, or a changing selection of strongly flavored regional specialties that are otherwise difficult to find in Rome. Service is first rate.

Tre Scalini, piazza Navona 30. ☎ **6879148.**
   Cuisine: ROMAN. **Reservations:** Recommended.
   Prices: Appetizers 16,000–20,000 lire ($9.60–$12); main courses 22,000–35,000 lire ($13.20–$21). AE, DC, MC, V.
   Open: Lunch Thurs–Tues 12:15–3:30pm; dinner Thurs–Tues 7:15–11:15pm. **Closed:** Dec–Feb.

Established in 1882, this is the most famous and most respected restaurant on piazza Navona—a landmark for ice cream as well as more substantial meals. Although there's a cozy bar on the upper floor, outfitted with simple furniture, and with a view over the piazza, most visitors opt either for a seat in the ground-floor cafe or restaurant. Both areas expand their premises during warm weather with chairs and tables on the piazza. House specialties include *canfallo in passitte* (butterfly-shaped pasta in an herb and cheese sauce); *risotto con porcini;* risotto with pesto; spaghetti with clams; roast duck with prosciutto; many choices of fish, including a carpaccio of sea bass; saltimbocca; and roast lamb in the Roman style. No one will object if you order just a pasta and salad, unlike other restaurants nearby that oblige visitors to order several different courses. *Tartufo* (ice cream disguised with a coating of bittersweet chocolate, cherries, and whipped cream) and simpler versions of ice cream range from 5,000 lire ($3) to 10,000 lire ($6) each; whisky with soda costs from 10,000 lire ($6).

Moderate

Montevecchio, piazza di Montevecchio 22. ☎ **6861319.**
   Cuisine: ROMAN/ITALIAN. **Reservations:** Required. **Bus:** 70 or 492.
   Prices: Appetizers 12,000–15,000 lire ($7.20–$9); main courses 20,000–30,000 lire ($12–$18). AE, MC, V.
   Open: Lunch Tues–Sun 1–3pm; dinner Tues–Sun 8–11:30pm.
   Closed: Aug 10–25.

To visit, you must negotiate the winding streets of one of Rome's most confusing neighborhoods, around piazza Navona. The heavily curtained restaurant on this Renaissance piazza is where both Raphael and Bramante created many of their masterpieces and where Lucrezia Borgia spun many of her intrigues. The entrance opens onto a high-ceilinged, not particularly large room filled with rural mementos and bottles of wine. Your meal might begin with a strudel of funghi porcini (mushrooms), followed by the invariably good pasta of the day. Then select roebuck with polenta, roast Sardinian goat, or one of several veal dishes (on one occasion, served with salmon mousse).

Passetto, via Giuseppe Zanardelli 14. ☎ **68806569.**
   Cuisine: ROMAN/INTERNATIONAL. **Reservations:** Recommended.
   Bus: 70, 87, or 492.

Dining   Near the Pantheon, Piazza Navona & Piazza Campo de' Fiori

Prices: Appetizers 10,000–18,000 lire ($6–$10.80); main courses 16,000–50,000 lire ($9.60–$30). AE, DC, MC, V.

Open: Lunch Tues–Sat 12:30–3:30pm; dinner Tues–Sat 7:30–11:30pm.

Passetto, dramatically positioned at the north end of the landmark piazza Navona, draws patrons with its reputation for excellent Italian food. The surroundings are stylish—there are three rooms, one containing frosted-glass cylinder chandeliers. In summer, however, it's better to try one of the outside tables on the big terrace looking out on piazza Sant'Apollinare. Formally dressed waiters, crisp white linen, and heavy silverware add a touch of luxury. Pastas are exceptional, including penne alla Norma. One recommended main dish is orata (sea bass) al cartoccio (baked in a paper bag with tomatoes, mushrooms, capers, and white wine). Another house specialty is rombo passetto (a fish similar to sole) cooked in a cognac-and-pine-nut sauce. Fresh fish is often priced by its weight and tabs can soar quickly—be careful. Meals can be accompanied by a selection of fresh varied salads personally chosen from a service trolley. Fresh vegetables are abundant in summer, and a favorite dessert is seasonal fruits, such as lingonberries, raspberries, or blackberries with fresh thick cream.

Ristorante da Pancrazio, piazza del Biscione 92. ☎ 6861246.

Cuisine: ROMAN. **Reservations:** Recommended. **Bus:** 46 or 62.

Prices: Appetizers 12,000–16,000 lire ($7.20–$9.60); main courses 14,000–35,000 lire ($8.40–$21); fixed-price 25,000 lire ($15). AE, DC, MC, V.

Open: Lunch Thurs–Tues noon–3pm; dinner Thurs–Tues 7:30–11:15pm. **Closed:** Two weeks in Aug (dates vary).

Ristorante da Pancrazio is a dining oddity visited as much for its archeological interest as for its culinary allure. One of its two dining rooms is authentically decorated in the style of an 18th-century tavern. Another occupies the premises of Pompey's ancient theater, and as such is lined with marble columns, carved capitals, and bas-reliefs that would be the envy of many museums. Classified as a national monument, it's probably the only establishment that feeds the body as well as a visitor's sense of history. Menu items include the full range of traditional Roman dishes, and include risotto alla pescatore (rice with an assortment of seafood), mixed fish fry, several preparations of scampi, saltimbocca, and a Roman specialty, *abbacchio al forno*, a special preparation of roasted baby lamb with potatoes.

Inexpensive

Il Barroccio, via dei Pastini 13–14. ☎ 6793797.

Cuisine: ROMAN. **Reservations:** Recommended. **Bus:** 64 or 78.

Prices: Appetizers 11,500–13,500 lire ($6.90–$8.10); main courses 16,000–22,000 lire ($9.60–$13.20). AE, DC, MC, V.

Open: Lunch Tues–Sun 12:30–3pm; dinner Tues–Sun 7:30–11pm.

Il Barroccio, serving generous portions of reasonably priced Roman food, attracts a loyal following who crowd into the restaurant and grab a table in one of several small salons. The parade of dishes is served against a typical backdrop of horseshoes on the wall, dried corn, wagon-wheel lights, and bronze lanterns. In these busy surroundings, you'll often get haphazard service, but no one seems to mind, especially when itinerant musicians arrive to entertain you and then pass the hat. A la carte items range from a simple but good bean soup to the more elaborate seafood antipasto. At night, pizza is a specialty, as is an array of boiled mixed meats, served with a herb-flavored green sauce.

La Carbonara, piazza Campo de' Fiori 23. ☎ 6864783.

Cuisine: ROMAN. **Reservations:** Recommended. **Bus:** 64.
Prices: Appetizers 8,000–14,000 lire ($4.80–$8.40); main courses 16,000–30,000 lire ($9.60–$18). AE, MC, V.
Open: Lunch Wed–Mon noon–2:30pm; dinner Wed–Mon 6:30–10:30pm.

Contained within an antique palazzetto, at the edge of a square dominated by the evocative statue of Gordano Bruno, the philosopher who was burned at the stake, this amiable trattoria claims to be the home of the original version of spaghetti carbonara. (According to the legend, which is much disputed in other parts of Italy, the forebears of the present owners devised the recipe in the final days of World War II, when American G.I.s donated their K-rations of powdered eggs and salted bacon to the chef. The result is the egg yolk–, cheese–, and bacon-enriched pasta dish that is famous throughout the world.) The dining room features succulent antipasti, grilled meats, fresh and intelligently prepared seasonal vegetables, and—in addition to its famous version of carbonara—several other kinds of pasta. Another pasta specialty is bucatini alla matriciana, a well-flavored chef's version of the traditional tomato sauce made with pancetta (Italian bacon).

Eau Vive, via Monterone 85. ☎ 68801095.

Cuisine: FRENCH/INTERNATIONAL. **Reservations:** Recommended.
Bus: 64 or 78.
Prices: Appetizers 4,000–12,000 lire ($2.40–$7.20); main courses 18,000–25,000 lire ($10.80–$15); fixed-price menus 15,000 lire ($9), 20,000 lire ($12), and 30,000 lire ($18). AE, MC, V.
Open: Lunch Mon–Sat noon–2:30pm; dinner Mon–Sat 8–9:30pm.
Closed: Aug 10–20.

Dining at Eau Vive qualifies as an offbeat adventure. It is run by lay missionaries who wear the dress or costumes of their native countries. In this formal atmosphere, at 10 o'clock each evening, the waitresses chant a religious hymn and recite a prayer. Your gratuity for service will be turned over for religious purposes. Pope John Paul II used to dine here when he was still archbishop of Cracow, and it's a popular place with overseas monsignors on a visit to the Vatican.

Specialties include hors d'oeuvres and frogs' legs. An international dish is featured daily. The restaurant's cellar is well stocked with French wines. Main dishes range from guinea hen with onions and grapes in a wine sauce to couscous. A smooth finish is the chocolate mousse. Under vaulted ceilings, the atmosphere is deliberately kept subdued, and the place settings—with fresh flowers and good glassware—are tasteful. However, some of the most flamboyant members of international society have adopted Eau Vive as their favorite spot. Located on a narrow street in Old Rome, it's hard to find, but it's near the Pantheon.

La Majella, piazza del Teatro di Pompeo 18. ☎ **6864174.**

Cuisine: ABRUZZI. **Reservations:** Recommended for dinner. **Bus:** 62, 64.
Prices: Appetizers 8,000–15,000 lire ($4.80–$9); main courses 12,000–20,000 lire ($7.20–$12). AE, DC, MC, V.
Open: Lunch Mon–Sat 12:30–3pm; dinner Mon–Sat 8pm–midnight.
Closed: Two weeks in Aug.

For many years, La Majella served well-prepared food to a clientele that included Polish Cardinal Karol Wojtyla before his elevation to the papal throne. In 1993 the restaurant moved out of its premises in a small palazzo, because of the encroachment of a nearby museum, and into new premises nearby. Its latest venue lies within a trio of old-fashioned dining rooms in a building a block northeast of the Campo de' Fiori, about a block south of Corso Vittorio Emanuele.

Despite the move, the cuisine changed hardly at all, and includes such Abruzzi mountain food as partridge and venison with polenta, suckling pig, an array of pastas (including pappardelle with rabbit), and roasted lamb with herbs. Fish includes grilled or fried versions of sea bass, flounder, lobster, and shrimp. One especially recommended dish is risotto with zucchini flowers and wild mushrooms.

Le Maschere, via Monte della Farina 29. ☎ **687944.**

Cuisine: CALABRIAN. **Reservations:** Recommended. **Bus:** 26, 44, 60, 70, or 75.
Prices: Appetizers 10,000–15,000 lire ($6–$9); main courses 14,000–25,000 lire ($8.40–$15). AE, DC, MC, V.
Open: Dinner only, Tues–Sun 7:30pm–midnight. **Closed:** Aug 15–Sept 20.

La Maschere, near largo Argentina, and within walking distance of piazza Navona, specializes in the fragrant, often-fiery cookery of Calabria's Costa Viola. That means lots of fresh garlic and wake-up-your-mouth red peppers. The restaurant, decorated in regional artifacts of Calabria, occupies a cellar from the 1600s with small outside tables in summer overlooking a tiny little piazza deep in the heart of Rome. Begin with a selection of antipasti calabresi. There are many different preparations of eggplant. Others prefer the pasta dishes, one made with broccoli, and one flavored with devilish red peppers, garlic, breadcrumbs, and more than a touch of anchovy. The chef also grills meats and fresh swordfish caught off the Calabrian coast. For dessert, finish with a sheep cheese of Calabria or a fresh fruit salad. If you don't want a full meal, you can just visit for pizza and beer.

$ Ristorante del Pallaro, largo del Pallaro 15. ☎ **58801488.**

Cuisine: ROMAN. **Reservations:** Recommended for dinner on weekends. **Bus:** 46, 70, or 492.

Prices: Fixed-price meals 28,000–30,000 lire ($16.80–$18). No credit cards.

Open: Lunch Tues–Sun 1–3pm; dinner Tues–Sun 8–11:30pm.

The cheerful and kindhearted woman in white who emerges with clouds of steam from this establishment's bustling kitchen is the owner, Paola Fazi. With her husband, Giovanni, she maintains a simple duet of very clean dining rooms where price-conscious Romans go for good food at bargain price. No à la carte meals are served, but the fixed-price menus have made the place famous. As you sit down, the first of eight courses will appear, one following the other, until you've had more than your fill. You begin with antipasti, then go on to such dishes as the pasta of the day, which might be spaghetti, rigatoni, or pappardelle. The meat courses include roast veal, white meatballs, or (only on Friday) dried cod. Potatoes and eggplant are offered. For your final courses, you're served mozzarella cheese, cake with custard, and fruit in season. The meal also includes bread, a liter of mineral water, and half a liter of the house wine. On a historical note, the owners claim that the assassination of Julius Caesar occurred on this site, whose foundations were constructed by the ancient Romans.

6   Near St. Peter's

Moderate

Il Matriciano, via dei Gracchi 55. ☎ **3212327.**

Cuisine: ROMAN. **Reservations:** Required, especially for dinner. **Metro:** Lepanto.

Prices: Appetizers 8,000–12,000 lire ($4.80–$7.20); main courses 16,000–22,000 lire ($9.60–$13.20). AE, DC, MC, V.

Open: Lunch daily 12:30–3pm; dinner daily 8–11:30pm. Closed: Aug 2–29 and Wed (Nov–Apr) and Sat (May–Oct).

Il Matriciano is a family restaurant with a devoted set of regulars. Its location near St. Peter's makes it all the more distinguished. The food is good, but it's only regional fare—nothing fancy. The decor, likewise, is kept to a minimum. In summer, try to get one of the sidewalk tables behind a green hedge and under a shady canopy; the luncheon clientele seems to linger a long time. For openers, you might prefer a zuppa di verdura or ravioli di ricotta. The preferred choice, however, is tagliolini con tartufi. From many dishes, I recommend scaloppa alla valdostana, abbacchio (baby lamb) al forno, and tripa (tripe) alla romana. The most obvious specialty of the house is derived from what some experts say is the favorite sauce in the Roman repertoire of cuisine: matriciana sauce. Here, it's prepared with bucatini pasta, and richly flavored with bacon, tomatoes, and basil.

Ristorante Giardinaccio, via Aurelia 53. ☎ **631367.**

> **Cuisine:** MOLISIAN. **Reservations:** Recommended, especially on weekends. **Bus:** 46, 62, or 98.
>
> **Prices:** Appetizers 7,000–14,000 lire ($4.20–$8.40); main courses 20,000–31,000 lire ($12–$18.60). AE, DC, MC, V.
>
> **Open:** Lunch Wed–Mon 12:15–3:30pm; dinner Wed–Mon 7:15–11pm.

This popular restaurant, operated by Nicolino Mancini, is only 200 yards from St. Peter's. Unusual for Rome, it offers Molisian specialties (from one of Italy's provinces). It's rustically decorated in the country-tavern style with dark wood and exposed stone. Flaming grills provide succulent versions of perfectly done quail, goat, and other dishes, but perhaps the mutton goulash would be more adventurous. Many versions of pasta are featured, including taconelle, a homemade pasta with lamb sauce. Vegetarians and others will like the large self-service selection of antipasti.

Ristorante Pierdonati, via della Conciliazione 39. ☎ **68803557.**

> **Cuisine:** ROMAN. **Reservations:** Not required. **Bus:** 64 from Stazione Termini.
>
> **Prices:** Appetizers 10,000–19,000 lire ($6–$11.40); main courses 16,000–30,000 lire ($9.60–$18); set menu 25,000 lire ($15). AE, MC, V.
>
> **Open:** Lunch Fri–Wed noon–3:30pm; dinner Fri–Wed 7–10:30pm. **Closed:** Aug.

Ristorante Pierdonati has been serving wayfarers to the Vatican since 1868. In the same building as the Hotel Columbus (see my hotel recommendation in Chapter 4), this restaurant was the former home of Cardinal della Rovere. Today it's the headquarters of the Knights of the Holy Sepulchre of Jerusalem, and the best restaurant in the gastronomic wasteland of the Vatican area. Its severely classical facade is relieved inside by a gargoyle fountain spewing water into a basin. You'll dine beneath a vaulted ceiling. Try the calves' liver Venetian style, the stewed veal with tomato sauce, or ravioli bolognese. To get really Roman, order the tripe. It can get rather crowded here on days that see thousands upon thousands flocking to St. Peter's.

---

7 Trastevere

Very Expensive

 Alberto Ciarlà, piazza San Cosimato 40. ☎ **5818668.**

> **Cuisine:** SEAFOOD. **Reservations:** Required, especially on weekends. **Bus:** 44, 75, or 170.
>
> **Prices:** Appetizers 18,000–30,000 lire ($10.80–$18); main courses 30,000–60,000 lire ($18–$36). AE, DC, MC, V.
>
> **Open:** Lunch Mon–Sat 12:45–2:30pm; dinner Mon–Sat 8:30pm–12:30am. **Closed:** Two weeks Aug and 10 days in Jan (dates vary).

Alberto Ciarlà is one of the best and most expensive restaurants in Trastevere; in fact, some critics consider it one of the finest restaurants in all of Rome. Contained in a building set into an obscure corner of an enormous square, it serves some of the most elegant fish dishes in Rome. You'll be greeted at the door with a cordial reception and a lavish display of seafood on ice. A dramatically modern decor plays shades of brilliant light against patches of shadow. Specialties include a handful of ancient recipes subtly improved by Signor Ciarlà (an example is the soup of pasta and beans with seafood). Original dishes include a delectable salmon Marcel Trompier, with lobster sauce, and other delicacies feature a well-flavored sushi, spaghetti with clams, ravioli di pesce, and a full array of shellfish. The filet of sea bass is prepared in at least three different ways including an award-winning version with almonds.

Expensive

Sabatini I, piazza Santa Maria in Trastevere 10. ☎ **5812026.**

> **Cuisine:** ROMAN/SEAFOOD. **Reservations:** Recommended. **Bus:** 44, 75, or 170.
>
> **Prices:** Appetizers 14,000–22,000 lire ($8.40–$13.20); main courses 20,000–40,000 lire ($12–$24). AE, DC, MC, V.
>
> **Open:** Lunch daily noon–3pm; dinner daily 8pm–midnight.

Sabatini I, owned by the Sabatini brothers, is one of the most popular dining spots in Rome. At night, piazza Santa Maria—one of the settings used in Fellini's *Roma*—is the center of the liveliest action in Trastevere. The place is very tied to the hustle-bustle of the Trastevere landscape and its memories of the celebrities it used to attract. In summer, tables are placed outside on this charming square, and you can look across at the floodlit golden mosaics of the church on the piazza. If you can't get a table outside, you may be assigned to a room inside under beamed ceilings, with stenciled walls, lots of paneling, and framed oil paintings. So popular is this place that you may have to wait for a table even if you have a reservation. You can choose from a large table of antipasti. Fresh fish and shellfish, especially grilled scampi, may tempt you. The spaghetti with seafood is excellent. For a savory treat, try pollo con peperoni (chicken cooked with red and green peppers). The meal price will rise if you order grilled fish or the Florentine steaks. For wine, try a white Frascati or an Antinori Chianti in a hand-painted pitcher.

Moderate

La Cisterna, via della Cisterna 13. ☎ **5812543.**

> **Cuisine:** ROMAN. **Reservations:** Recommended. **Bus:** 44, 75, or 170.
>
> **Prices:** Appetizers 9,000–13,000 lire ($5.40–$7.80); main courses 15,000–35,000 lire ($9–$21). AE, DC, MC, V.
>
> **Open:** Dinner only, Mon–Sat 7pm–midnight.

La Cisterna lies deep in the heart of Trastevere. Since the 1930s it has been run by the Simmi family, who are genuinely interested in serving only the best as well as providing a good time for all guests. The cistern in the name comes from an ancient well discovered in the cellar, dating from imperial Rome. When the weather's good, you can dine outside at sidewalk tables; if it's rainy or cold, you can select from one of a series of inside rooms decorated with murals, including the *Rape of the Sabine Women*. In summer you can inspect the antipasti—a mixed selection of hors d'oeuvres—right out on the street before going in. Recommended are roasted meat dishes, such as veal, and fresh fish.

Romolo Nella Giardina della Fornarina, via Porta Settimiana 8. ☎ 5818284.

Cuisine: ROMAN. **Reservations:** Recommended at dinner. **Bus:** 23 or 280.

Prices: Appetizers 10,000–13,500 lire ($6–$8.10); main courses 19,000–25,000 lire ($11.40–$15). AE, DC, MC, V.

Open: Lunch Tues–Sun noon–3pm; dinner Tues–Sun 7:30pm–midnight. **Closed:** Aug 5–25.

Romolo is a Trastevere gem established in 1848. You can sit in a Renaissance garden that once belonged to Raphael's mistress, della Fornarina (the baker's daughter), who posed for some of his madonnas. Historically, it's been patronized by everybody from Kirk Douglas to Clare Boothe Luce, although today's celebrities go elsewhere. To begin your meal, try the fettuccine with meat sauce, followed by scaloppine al marsala or deviled chicken. A fresh garden salad is extra. For dessert, try a "charlotte"—a sponge cake lathered with whipped cream and topped by a decorative motif. If the garden isn't in use, you'll like the cozy interior, with its bric-a-brac of copper, wood, and silver.

Inexpensive

Trattoria Vincenzo, via della Lungaretta 173. ☎ 5882876.

Cuisine: SEAFOOD. **Reservations:** Not required. **Bus:** 23.

Prices: Appetizers 3,000–12,000 lire ($1.80–$7.20); main courses 12,000–25,000 lire ($7.20–$15); pizza 7,000–12,000 lire ($4.20–$7.20). AE, DC, MC, V.

Open: Lunch Tues–Sun noon–2:45pm; dinner Tues–Sat 7:30–10:45pm.

Trattoria Vincenzo is surrounded by far more expensive restaurants in the Trastevere district. It serves some of the best prepared dishes—particularly seafoods—in this colorful section of the city. Small and popular (always crowded with flea marketeers at Sunday lunch), the Vincenzo serves a zuppa di pesce, a stew that is as good as the most savory bouillabaisse. Meat items include saltimbocca alla romana (veal with ham and sage). Sample the ravioli di ricotta e spinaci (ravioli with cottage cheese and spinach) or the spaghetti alla carbonara.

8 The Old Ghetto

Expensive

Vecchia Roma, via della Tribuna di Campitelli 18. ☎ **6864604.**

Cuisine: ITALIAN. **Reservations:** Recommended. **Bus:** 64.
Prices: Appetizers 15,000–25,000 lire ($9–$15); main courses 20,000–
31,000 lire ($12–$18.60). AE, DC.
Open: Lunch Thurs–Tues 12:30–4pm; dinner Thurs–Tues 8pm–midnight. **Closed:** Aug 10–25.

Vecchia Roma is a charming, moderately priced trattoria in the heart
of the ghetto (a short walk from Michelangelo's Campidoglio); head
toward the Theater of Marcellus, but turn right at the synagogue.
Movie stars have frequented the place. The room in the back, with a
bas-relief, is popular. The owners are known for their selection of
fresh seafood. The minestrone of the day is made with fresh vegetables
or else you may want to begin with an order of vegetables, such as
spinach. An interesting selection of antipasti is always presented,
including salmon or else a vegetable antipasto. The pastas and risottos
are also excellent, including linguine alla marinara with scampi. A
"green" risotto with porcini mushrooms is invariably good. Excellent
cuts of meat are served, including lamb, which is a specialty of the
chef.

Moderate

Angelino a Tormargana, piazza Margana 37. ☎ **6783328.**

Cuisine: ROMAN. **Reservations:** Not required. **Bus:** 64, 70, 170,
or 710.
Prices: Appetizers 10,000–14,000 lire ($6–$8.40); main courses 14,000–
25,000 lire ($8.40–$15). MC, V.
Open: Lunch Mon–Sat noon–3:30pm; dinner Mon–Sat 7:30–11pm.

Angelino a Tormargana, about three blocks from piazza Venezia, is
housed in Goethe's historic inn. In this setting of old palazzi and
ancient cobblestone squares, you can dine al fresco at tables hedged
with greenery. At night the colored lanterns are turned on. A
somewhat elegant clientele is attracted to the inn, and the atmosphere
is welcoming. The food is in the typical Roman trattoria style—not
exceptionally imaginative, but good for what it is. I recommend the
eggplant parmigiana, followed by chicken with peppers.

Da Giggetto, via del Portico d'Ottavia 21–22. ☎ **6861105.**

Cuisine: ROMAN. **Reservations:** Recommended. **Bus:** 62, 64, 75,
or 170.
Prices: Appetizers 9,000–12,000 lire ($5.40–$7.20); main courses
16,000–21,000 lire ($9.60–$12.60). AE, DC, MC, V.
Open: Lunch Tues–Sun 12:30–3:30pm; dinner Tues–Sun 7:30–
10:30pm. **Closed:** Aug 1–15.

Da Giggetto, in the old ghetto, is a short walk from the Theater of Marcellus. Not only is it right next to ruins, but old Roman columns extend practically to its doorway. The Romans flock to this bustling trattoria for their special traditional dishes. None is more typical than carciofi alla giudia, the baby-tender fried artichokes—this is a true delicacy. The cheese concoction, mozzarella in carrozza, is another delight. Yet another specialty is zucchini flowers stuffed with mozzarella and anchovies. Or else sample fettuccini alla matriciana, shrimps sautéed in garlic and olive oil, tripe, saltimbocca, or codfish.

9 Near the Circus Maximus, the Forum & the Colosseum

Expensive

Alfredo alla Scrofa, via della Scrofa 104A. ☎ 68806163.

Cuisine: ROMAN/INTERNATIONAL. **Reservations:** Recommended. **Metro:** Piazza di Spagna.
Prices: Appetizers 13,000–20,000 lire ($7.80–$12); main courses 18,000–25,000 lire ($10.80–$15). AE, DC, MC, V.
Open: Lunch Wed–Mon 12:30–3pm; dinner Wed–Mon 7:30–11:30pm.

Established in 1925 in a 16th-century building, this restaurant maintains a visitors' autograph book that reads like a retrospective of 20th-century history. Famous clients have included everyone from Mussolini to Ava Gardner, Arthur Miller (who arrived with Marilyn Monroe in 1960), and, in 1993, Tony Curtis. Gold-framed photographs of many of the visitors hang against oak paneling on the walls. Many first-time visitors order the *maestose fettuccine al triplo burro,* where waiters make choreography out of whipping butter and cheese on rolling carts at tableside. The main-course specialties include *filetto di tacchino dorato* (breast of turkey, sautéed in batter and covered with thin slices of Piemontese white truffles); filet mignon Casanova (prepared with red wine, pepper, and foie gras); roasted lamb with potatoes in the Roman style; and saltimbocca.

Alvaro al Circo Massimo, via dei Cerchi 53. ☎ 6786112.

Cuisine: ITALIAN. **Reservations:** Required. **Metro:** Circo Massimo. **Bus:** 15, 90, or 160.
Prices: Appetizers 10,000–16,000 lire ($6–$9.60); main courses 20,000–48,000 lire ($12–$28.80). MC, V.
Open: Lunch Tues–Sun 1–3pm; dinner Tues–Sat 7–11pm. **Closed:** Aug.

Alvaro al Circo Massimo is the closest thing in Rome to a genuine provincial inn. It's at the edge of the Circus Maximus, which brings back memories of *Ben Hur.* The decor is typical of Italian taverns, including corn on the cob hanging from the ceiling and rolls of fat sausages. You can begin with the antipasti or one of the fine pasta dishes, such as fettuccine. Meat courses are well prepared, and there is an array of fresh fish. Other specialties include risotto with seafood; tagliolini with mushrooms and black truffles; roasted turbot with potatoes; and many other kinds of seafood. They are especially well stocked with seafood, exotic seasonal mushrooms, and black truffles. A basket of fresh fruit rounds out the repast. Try to linger longer and make an evening of it—the atmosphere is mellow.

Inexpensive

$ **Abruzzi,** via de Vaccaro 1. ☎ 6793897.
Cuisine: ABRUZZI. **Reservations:** Recommended. **Bus:** 64, 70, or 75.
Prices: Appetizers 3,000–10,000 lire ($1.80–$6); main courses 9,000–18,000 lire ($5.40–$10.80). DC, MC, V.
Open: Lunch Sun–Fri 12:30–3pm; dinner Sun–Fri 7:30–10:30pm.
Closed: Two weeks in Aug (dates vary).

Abruzzi takes its name from a little-explored region east of Rome known for its haunting beauty and curious superstitions. The restaurant is located at one side of piazza SS. Apostoli, just a short walk from piazza Venezia. Many young people have selected this restaurant as their enduring favorite—probably because they get good food here at reasonable prices. The chef is justly praised for his satisfying assortment of cold antipasti; you can make your own selection from the trolley cart. With your beginning, I suggest a liter of garnet-red wine. If you'd like a soup, you'll find a good stracciatella (made with a thin batter of eggs and grated parmesan cheese poured into a boiling chicken broth). A typical main dish is saltimbocca, the amusing name ("jump-in-the-mouth") for tender slices of veal that have been skewered with slices of ham, sautéed in butter, and seasoned with marsala.

Trattoria l'Albanese, via dei Serpenti 148. ☎ 4740777.
Cuisine: ROMAN. **Reservations:** Recommended on weekends.
Metro: Cavour.
Prices: Appetizers 10,000–15,000 lire ($6–$9); main courses 15,000–24,000 lire ($9–$14.40). DC, MC, V.
Open: Lunch Wed–Mon noon–3pm; dinner Wed–Sun 6:30–10:30pm.

For years visitors found it difficult to locate a good, inexpensive restaurant while exploring the center of imperial Rome. Trattoria l'Albanese, however, is a fine choice. It has a garden in the rear where you can order lunch. Sample the cannelloni or ravioli di ricotta. The location is between via Nazionale and via Cavour.

10 On the Outskirts

Monte Testaccio

Checchino dal 1887, via di Monte Testaccio 30. ☎ 5746318.
Cuisine: ROMAN. **Reservations:** Recommended. **Bus:** 27.
Prices: Appetizers 10,000–14,000 lire ($6–$8.40); main courses 12,000–25,000 lire ($7.20–$15). AE, DC, MC, V.
Open: Lunch Tues–Sun 12:30–3pm; dinner Tues–Sat 8–11pm. **Closed:** Aug, one week around Christmas, and Sun at lunch between June and Sept.

In 55 A.D., the Emperor Nero ordered that Rome's thousands of broken amphoras and terra-cotta roof tiles be stacked in a carefully designated pile east of the Tiber, just west of Pyramid and today's Ostia Railway Station. Over the centuries, the mound grew to a height of around 200 feet, then compacted to form the centerpiece for one of the city's most unusual neighborhoods. Eventually, houses were built on the terra-cotta mound, and caves were dug into its mass for the storage of wine and foodstuffs. (A constant temperature of 50 degrees was maintained, thanks to the porosity of the terra cotta, throughout the winter and summer.)

During the 1800s, a local wine shop flourished by selling drinks to the corps of butchers working in the neighborhood's many slaughterhouses. In 1887, the ancestors of the present owners obtained a license to sell food, thus giving birth to the restaurant you'll find on these premises today. Slaughterhouse workers in those days were paid part of their meager salaries with the *quinto quarto* (fifth quarter) of each day's slaughter (i.e., the tail, the feet, the intestines, and the offal), which otherwise had no commercial value. Following many centuries of Roman traditions, Ferminia, the wine shop's cook, somehow transformed these products into the tripe and oxtail dishes that form an integral part of the Roman working-class diet to this day.

Many Italian diners come here to relish these dishes, which admittedly might not be to every foreign visitor's taste. They include rigatone *con pajata* (pasta with small intestines), *coda alla vaccinara* (oxtail stew), *fagiole e cotiche* (beans with intestinal fat), and other examples of *la cocina povera* (food of the poor). Less adventurous and probably more appealing to readers of this guide is the restaurant's array of well-prepared salads, soups, pastas, steaks, cutlets, grills, and ice creams, which the kitchen produces in abundance. The English-speaking staff is helpful and kind, tactfully proposing well-flavored alternatives to a cuisine that, at least in Rome, is by now a well-established legend.

The Appian Way

Hostaria l'Archeologia, via Appia Antica 139. ☎ 788-0494.

> **Cuisine:** ROMAN. **Reservations:** Recommended, especially on weekends. **Bus:** No. 118.
> **Prices:** Appetizers 10,000–16,000 lire ($6–$9.60); main courses 12,000–22,000 lire ($7.20–$13.20). AE, DC.
> **Open:** Lunch Fri–Wed 12:30–3:30pm; dinner Fri–Wed 8–10:30pm.

Hostaria l'Archeologia, on the historic Appian Way, is only a short walk from the catacombs of St. Sebastian. The family-run restaurant is like an 18th-century village tavern with lots of atmosphere, strings of garlic and corn, oddments of copper hanging from the ceiling, earth-brown beans, and sienna-washed walls. In summer, guests dine in the garden out back, sitting under the spreading wisteria. For the chilly months, there are two separate dining rooms on either side of a gravel walkway. The Roman victuals are first-rate; you can glimpse the kitchens from the exterior garden parking lot. Many Roman families visit on the weekend, sometimes with as many as 30 diners in a group.

Of special interest is the wine cellar, excavated in an ancient Roman tomb, where wines dating back to 1800 are kept. You go through an iron gate, down some stairs, and into the underground cavern. Along the way, you can still see the holes once occupied by funeral urns.

11 Specialty Dining

A Tea Room/Brunch

Babington's Tea Rooms, piazza di Spagna 23. ☎ **6786027.**

Cuisine: ENGLISH/MEDITERRANEAN. **Reservations:** Not required.
Metro: Piazza di Spagna.
Prices: Main courses 19,000–35,000 lire ($11.40–$21); brunch 40,000 lire ($24). AE, DC, MC, V.
Open: Wed–Mon 9am–8pm.

When Victoria was on the English throne, an Englishwoman named Anne Mary Babington arrived in Rome and couldn't find a place for "a good cuppa." With stubborn determination, she opened her own tearooms near the foot of the Spanish Steps, and the rooms are still going strong. You can order everything from Scottish scones to a club sandwich to Ceylon tea to American coffee. Brunch is served at all hours.

Breakfast

Bibo Astoria '73, piazza Cola di Rienzo 60. ☎ **3610007.**

Cuisine: INTERNATIONAL/ITALIAN. **Reservations:** Required. **Bus:** 70, 81, 492, or 910.

Frommer's Cool For Kids: Restaurants

Ambasciata d'Abruzzo (see p. 129) This all-you-can eat place is recommended for its lively excitement as much as for its hearty cuisine. Your children can pick and choose what they want from a wide assortment of food.

Il Matriciano (see p. 141) This is a safe, clean, and reasonably priced family restaurant near St. Peter's. It's good country fare—nothing fancy.

McDonald's (see p. 150) Even in Rome, kids get hungry for the Big Mac. They're also offered an array of freshly made salads (far better than most of those back home).

Piedra del Sol (see p. 154) If you kids crave familiar fare from back home, this is the place. A Tex-Mex cuisine is featured, and the location near Piazza di Spagna is most central.

Prices: Appetizers 6,500–13,000 lire ($3.90–$7.80); main courses 8,000–16,000 lire ($4.80–$9.60); sandwiches 5,000–8,500 lire ($3–$5.10). AE, MC, V.

Bibo Astoria '73, at the intersection of piazza del Risorgimento and via Cola di Rienzo, is a bar and restaurant, with both an Italian and international kitchen. It is an especially good choice for breakfast with omelets beginning at 7,000 lire ($4.20). Breakfast is served throughout the day, beginning at 7am in the bar. The cafe is known for its covered winter garden, which is like a veranda. Most visitors come here to order the delectable and savory pizzas that emerge bubbling hot from the ovens—the kitchen even serves pizza during lunch, which is rare in Italy. However, you can also settle for a plate of spaghetti, and no one faints if you ask for just a hamburger. Nothing is fancy here; the service, like the food, is informal. You get good value and you don't need to dress up.

Fast Food

Birreria Viennese, via della Croce 21-22. ☎ **6795569.**

Cuisine: GERMAN/AUSTRIAN. **Reservations:** Not required. **Metro:** Piazza di Spagna.
Prices: Appetizers 8,000–12,000 lire ($4.80–$7.20); main courses 10,000–18,000 lire ($6–$10.80). AE, DC, MC, V.
Open: Thurs–Tues noon–midnight. **Closed:** July 20–Aug 20.

This restaurant was established in 1939 by the same people who own it today, the Jissauf family. Multilingual and charming, they are the descendants of an Austrian father and a South Tyrolean mother who came to Rome to establish this, the most famous German-Austrian restaurant in the city. It has a cozy atmosphere, with rustic Austrian decorations. The kitchen produces all kinds of Middle European dishes, such as Wiener Schnitzel, Hungarian goulash, and overstuffed sausage and sauerkraut. Venison is the most expensive main course. Three kinds of beer on draft are served here, and few diners object to that final meal tab because it's so reasonable. Those with gargantuan appetites ask for the Transylvania plate, with three kinds of meat, served with vegetables, potatoes, even sausage and bacon (for two or more people). There's no need to reserve a table. The location is between the shopping artery, via del Corso, and one of Rome's "living rooms," piazza di Spagna.

McDonald's, piazza di Spagna 46. ☎ **699224000.**

Cuisine: AMERICAN FAST FOOD. **Bus:** 492 from Stazione Termini.
Prices: Big Mac 4,500 lire ($2.70). No credit cards.
Open: Daily 10am–midnight.

This McDonald's practically caused a riot when it was plunked down in the midst of chic boutiques. But today the U.S.-based food emporium has found its place and is popular, even among Romans shopping in the area.

Dining with a View

Il Canto Del Riso, moored in the Tiber, in front of no. 7 Lungotevere dei Millini. ☎ 3220859.

> **Cuisine:** ITALIAN. **Reservations:** Required. **Metro:** Piazza Cavour.
> **Prices:** Appetizers 10,000–18,000 lire ($6–$10.80); main courses 20,000 lire–32,000 lire ($12–$19.20). No credit cards.
> **Open:** Lunch daily 12:30–3pm; dinner daily 7:30pm–midnight. **Closed:** Sun night and all day Mon in winter.

This barge and passenger ship is permanently moored beside one of the quays of the Tiber, a short walk north of the Ponte Cavour. Below decks, you'll find a cozy dining room outfitted with nautical accessories. Many diners prefer to visit here during warm weather, when management expands its premises by setting up tables on the riverside quay. Then, strings of colored lights and potted plants add a festive note, despite the nearby traffic that races along parallel to the edges of the Tiber.

Menu items include veal, lamb, beef, and lots of fish and seafood, especially shrimps, mussels, and clams in tomato-garlic sauce, served as dressings for pastas or as main courses. Also featured are many kinds of risotto, including varieties made with asparagus, artichokes, spinach, and other ingredients favored by vegetarians.

 Les Etoiles, in the Hotel Atlante Star, via Vitelleschi 34. ☎ 6893434.

> **Cuisine:** MEDITERRANEAN. **Reservations:** Required. **Metro:** Ottaviano. **Bus:** 64, 81 or 492.
> **Prices:** Appetizers 15,000–25,000 lire ($9–$15); main courses 22,000–45,000 lire ($13.20–$27). AE, DC, MC, V.
> **Open:** Lunch daily 12:30–2:30pm; dinner daily 7:30–11pm.

Les Etoiles, which means "The Stars," deserves all the stars it received—both for its cuisine and also for its spectacular view of Rome. The restaurant in this previously recommended hotel has been called "the most beautiful rooftop in Italy." At this garden in the sky, you'll have an open window over the rooftops of Rome—a 360° view of landmarks, especially the floodlit dome of St. Peter's. A flower terrace contains a trio of little towers, named Michelangelo, Campidoglio, and Ottavo Colle.

In summer everyone wants a table outside if the weather's right, but in winter almost the same view is possible from tables placed near picture windows. The color and fragrance of a refined Mediterranean cuisine is served here. Such specialties are featured as artichokes filled with risotto and fondue, tagliolini (a form of pasta) served with a ragoût of duck and mushrooms, or lamb flavored with aromatic Roman mint. The creative chef is rightly proud of his many regional dishes, and the service is deluxe, with a wine list some Roman food critics have labeled "exciting."

Ristorante Ulpia, via del Foro Traiano 2. ☎ 6789980.

> **Cuisine:** INTERNATIONAL. **Reservations:** Recommended. **Bus:** 64 or 70.

Prices: Appetizers 13,000–18,000 lire ($7.80–$10.80); main courses 21,000–31,000 lire ($12.60–$18.60). AE, DC, MC, V.
Open: Lunch Mon–Sat noon–3pm; dinner Mon–Sat 7–11pm.

Ristorante Ulpia sits on a terrace above the sprawling excavations of what used to be Trajan's Market, where the produce of much of ancient Rome was bought and sold. Today you can dine by candlelight on the restaurant's sheltered balcony while reflecting on the fate of faded empires. You might also take a look at the interior, where a statue of Ulpia, goddess of the marketplace, seems to complement the fragments of ancient bas-reliefs, copies of Roman frescoes, Etruscan-style balustrades, and fresh flowers. Your meal might include sole meunière, stewed chicken with peppers, or other straightforward, flavorful dishes.

Roof Restaurant, in the Hassler, piazza Trinità dei Monti 6.
☎ **6782651.**
Cuisine: INTERNATIONAL. **Reservations:** Required. **Metro:** Piazza di Spagna. **Bus:** 497 from Stazione Termini.
Prices: Appetizers 28,000–34,000 lire ($16.80–$20.40); main courses 42,000–48,000 lire ($25.20–$28.80). AE, DC, MC, V.
Open: Breakfast daily 7:30am–11am; lunch Mon–Sat noon–3:30pm; dinner Mon–Sat 7:30–11pm; Sun brunch 11:30am–3pm.

This was the first rooftop dining spot to open after World War II. From its covered terrace you'll have one of the finest views of the city, including many of its ancient monuments such as the Spanish Steps and St. Peter's. You can see hundreds of flowery terraces as well as the Villa Borghese and the Pincio gardens. People-watching or celebrity-watching is often a favorite game here. In days of yore, we've spotted the late Richard Nixon and Ted Kennedy dining here (not on the same day!), as well as the late movie director Federico Fellini.

The service is first rate, and the menu is based on what is the best and freshest produce in any given season. Some representative dishes include risotto flavored with squid ink, salt cod, braised sea bass, or rack of lamb flavored with Roman mint and served with artichokes. The cuisine is both traditional and refined—everything given a Mediterranean flavor.

Hotel Dining

Massimo d'Azeglio, via Cavour 18. ☎ **4814101.**
Cuisine: ROMAN. **Reservations:** Recommended. **Metro:** Stazione Termini.
Prices: Appetizers 10,000–20,000 lire ($6–$12); main courses 18,000–30,000 lire ($10.80–$18); fixed-price menus 30,000–40,000 lire ($18–$24). AE, DC, MC, V.
Open: Lunch Mon–Sat 12:30–3pm; dinner Mon–Sat 7–11pm.

Massimo d'Azeglio, in a hotel but with a separate entrance, has dispensed Roman cuisine since 1875. Built near the Stazione Termini, which was a fashionable address in the 19th century, it was named after a famous Savoy-born statesman who helped Garibaldi unify Italy. Today the restaurant is adorned with oil portraits of distinguished Italians. It's run by Angelo Bettoja, whose great-great-grandfather was the founder. Menu items include an excellent version of penne with vodka, trout Cavour (with pine nuts), grilled swordfish, plus an array of grilled meats.

Vegetarian

Antico Bottaro, Passeggiata di Ripetta 15. ☎ **3240200.**

Cuisine: VEGETARIAN. **Reservations:** Recommended. **Metro:** Flaminio.
Prices: Appetizers 12,000–19,000 lire ($7.20–$11.40); main courses 17,000–26,000 lire ($10.20–$15.60). AE, DC, MC, V.
Open: Dinner only, Tues–Sun 8–11:30pm.

Established in the early 1990s, this is the second vegetarian restaurant opened by Rome's most prominent vegetarian guru, Claudio Vannini. (His older, better-known, and somewhat less expensive vegetarian restaurant, Margutta Vegetariano, is recommended separately—see below.) Set within a Renaissance building on a narrow street near piazza del Popolo, Antico Bottaro offers a consciously formal setting, a sense of grandeur, and food items that reflect the agrarian bounty of Italy. Menu items include a seasonally changing selection of risottos and pastas, garnished with asparagus, exotic mushrooms, truffles, and/or a lavish array of herbs; soufflés made with spinach, wild mushrooms, potatoes, or whatever happens to be fresh at the market that day; meatless goulash; carefully prepared crudités; and eggplant parmigiana. The restaurant carries a wide selection of ciders and wines.

Margutta Vegetariano, via Margutta 119. ☎ **6786033.**

Cuisine: VEGETARIAN. **Reservations:** Recommended. **Metro:** Piazza di Spagna.
Prices: Appetizers 10,000–15,000 lire ($6–$9); main courses 17,000–26,000 lire ($10.20–$15.60). AE, DC, MC, V.
Open: Lunch Mon–Sat 1–3pm; dinner Mon–Sat 7:30–10:30pm.
Closed: Two weeks in August.

Established in 1980 by Claudio Vannini, an enthusiast of new-wave thinking and Indian philosophy, and a former friend and neighbor of the late director Federico Fellini, this functioned for many years as one of Rome's few vegetarian restaurants. Partly because of the patronage of Mr. Fellini and his entourage, and partly because of its excellent cuisine, the restaurant quickly became a stylish favorite of Italian film stars and TV personalities. Recent visitors have included Michael Bolton (in 1993), Marcello Mastroianni, and hundreds of less celebrated diners who ignore the traditional riches of Italian cuisine in favor of the high-fiber specials served within. Within an 18th-century building, you can order a wide array of risottos and pastas, herb-enriched soups, mixed salads, a mélange of fried vegetables, meatless goulash, soyburgers, and a selection of soufflés made with potatoes, spinach, or wild mushrooms. Eggplant parmigiana is a perennial favorite. There's also a large selection of wines and ciders. In 1993, Vannini established a second vegetarian restaurant, Antico Bottaro, which is recommended separately (see above).

Late-Night Snacks

Piedra del Sol, Vicolo Rosini 6. ☎ **68736651.**

> **Cuisine:** MEXICAN. **Reservations:** Not necessary. **Metro:** Piazza di Spagna.
>
> **Prices:** Appetizers 9,000–15,000 lire ($5.40–$9); main courses 10,000–20,000 lire ($6–$12). AE, MC, V.
>
> **Open:** Lunch Tues–Sun noon–2:30pm; dinner Tues–Sun 7:30pm–midnight.

Lying two blocks east of the via del Corso of shopping fame, this is the busiest Roman branch of a chain of theme restaurants that today stretches along the peninsula, and which seems to intrigue and sometimes baffle the Italians. Inside, you'll find souvenirs of the Texas-Mexican wars, assorted cacti, and the kinds of desert-inspired artifacts you'd expect in the American southwest. Menu items include frothy margaritas and Mexican beers, fajitas, enchiladas, and nachos, all cooked as they might have been prepared in New Mexico. After the kitchens close down, the bar remains open until 2am.

Picnic Supplies & Where to Eat Them

Although Rome abounds in delicatessens and food stores, with several in every neighborhood, it's much more fun to get the makings for a picnic lunch at one of the open-air daily **food markets** of Rome. The biggest and most plentifully stocked is the one at piazza Vittorio Emanuele, near the Stazione Termini. One of the most characteristic food markets is at the piazza Campo de' Fiori, south of piazza Navona.

Romans prefer to go to **specialty shops** for their supplies instead of a general food market (American-type supermarkets are rare). Cheese, yogurt, and other milk products are sold at a *latteria*. Vegetables are sold at an *alimentari* (actually a small grocery store), and deli-like cold cuts are available at a *salumeria*. For your bread, go to a *panetteria*. For dessert, visit a *pasticceria*, and, if you want something to drink (wine, that is), patronize a *vinatteria*.

The best place for a picnic is the **Villa Borghese,** the only park in the center of Rome, which begins at the top of via Veneto. To picnic here is doing it in style, though you'd be wise to exercise a bit of caution by avoiding the deserted areas and not bringing along a camera or purse.

6

What to See & Do in Rome

WHERE ELSE BUT IN ROME COULD YOU ADMIRE A 17TH-CENTURY colonnade designed by Bernini, while resting against an Egyptian obelisk carried off from Heliopolis while Christ was still alive? Or stand amid the splendor of Renaissance frescoes in a papal palace built on top of the tomb of a Roman emperor? Where else, for that matter, are there vestal virgins buried adjacent to the Ministry of Finance?

Tourists have been sightseeing in Rome for 2,000 years. There is, in fact, almost too much to see, at least for visitors on a typical 20th-century timetable. Would that we were traveling around as our 19th-century forebears did, in a coach with tons of luggage, stopping a month here and a month there. Instead, we swoop down from the sky, or roar up at the train station, and expect to see everything in a few days. Travelers with this approach have met their match in Rome. An absolute minimum of time to see the city with any sort of perspective is five days, and even that's heavy sightseeing. Seven days would be better.

Suggested Itineraries

If You Have 1 Day   Rome wasn't built in a day, and you aren't likely to see it in a day either, but make the most of your limited time. You'll basically have to decide on the legacy of imperial Rome—mainly the Roman Forum, the Imperial Forum, and the Colosseum—or else St. Peter's and the Vatican. Walk along the Spanish Steps at sunset.

If You Have 2 Days   If you elected to see the Roman Forum and the Colosseum, then spend the second day exploring St. Peter's and the Vatican museums (or vice versa).

If You Have 3 Days   Spend your first two days as above. Go in the morning to the Pantheon in the heart of Old Rome, then try to explore two museums after lunch: Castel Sant'Angelo and the Etruscan Museum. (National Museum of Villa Giulia). Have dinner at a restaurant on piazza Navona.

If You Have 5 Days   Spend your first three days as above. On Day 4 head for the environs, notably Tivoli, where you can see the Villa d'Este and Hadrian's Villa. On Day 5 explore the ruins of Ostia Antica, return to Rome for lunch, and visit the Galleria Borghese and Basilica di San Giovanni in Laterano in the afternoon. Go to the Trevi Fountain and toss a coin in to ensure your return to Rome, as you didn't get to see it all.

1   The Top Attractions

In addition to the top attractions in the city itself, there are several places in the environs of Rome worth visiting before leaving this part of the country. It would be a shame to strike out for Naples or Florence without having at least visited Hadrian's Villa and the Villa d'Este, not to mention Palestrina and Ostia Antica (see "Easy Excursions from Rome," Chapter 10).

The Vatican

 St. Peter's, piazza San Pietro. ☎ **6984466.**

As you stand in Bernini's piazza San Pietro (St. Peter's Square), you'll be in the arms of an ellipse; the Doric-pillared colonnade reaches out to embrace the faithful. Holding 300,000 people is no problem for this square.

In the center of the square is an Egyptian obelisk, brought from the ancient city of Heliopolis on the Nile Delta and used to adorn Nero's Circus, which was nearby. Flanking the obelisk are two 17th-century fountains—the one on the right (facing the basilica) by Carlo Maderno, who designed the facade of St. Peter's, was placed there by Bernini himself; the other is by Carlo Fontana.

Inside, the size of this famous church is awe-inspiring—although its dimensions are not apparent at first. Guides like to point out to Americans that the basilica is like two football fields joined together. St. Peter's is said to have been built over the tomb of the crucified saint. Originally, it was erected on the order of Constantine, but the present structure is essentially Renaissance and baroque; it showcases the talents of some of Italy's greatest artists: Bramante, Raphael, Michelangelo, and Maderno.

The detail of gilt, marble, and mosaic is overwhelming, and the basilica is rich in art. The truly devout are prone to kiss the feet of the 13th-century bronze of St. Peter, attributed to Arnolfo di Cambio (at the far reaches of the nave, against a corner pillar on the right). Under Michelangelo's dome is the celebrated "baldacchino" by Bernini, resting over the papal altar. The canopy was created in the 17th century—in part, so it is said, from bronze stripped from the Pantheon. However, analysis of the bronze seems to contradict that.

In the nave on the right (the first chapel) is the best-known piece of sculpture, the *Pietà,* which Michelangelo sculpted while still in his early 20s. In one of the most vicious acts of vandalism on record, a madman screaming "I am Jesus Christ" attacked the *Pietà,* battering the Madonna's stone arm, the folded veil, her left eyelid, and nose. Now restored, the *Pietà* is protected by a wall of reinforced glass.

Much farther on, in the right wing of the transept near the Chapel of St. Michael, rests Canova's neoclassic sculptural tribute to Pope Clement XIII.

In addition, you can visit the sacristy and treasury, filled with jewel-studded chalices, reliquaries, and copes. One robe worn by Pius XII strikes a simple note in these halls of elegance. Later you can make a visit underground to the **Vatican grottoes,** with their tombs—ancient and modern (Pope John XXIII gets the most adulation). They are open daily from 7am to 6pm in summer, daily from 7am to 5pm October to March.

To go even farther down, to the area around St. Peter's tomb, you must apply several days beforehand to the excavations office beneath Arco della Campana to the left of the basilica. You can make your applications Monday through Saturday from 9am to noon and 2 to 5pm. It is reached by passing under the arch to the left of the facade of St. Peter's. For 10,000 lire ($6), you'll take a guided tour of the tombs that were excavated in the 1940s, 23 feet beneath the floor of the church.

The grandest sight is yet to come: the climb to **Michelangelo's dome,** which towers about 375 feet high. Although you can walk up the steps for 5,000 lire ($3), I recommend the elevator for as far as it'll carry you; the cost is 6,000 lire ($3.60).

The dome is open daily from 8am to 6:15pm March to September, and daily from 8am to 4:30pm October to February. You can walk along the roof, for which you'll be rewarded with a panoramic view of Rome and the Vatican.

Note: To be admitted to St. Peter's, women should wear long skirts or pants—anything that covers the knees. Men in shorts are not allowed in, and sleeveless tops are a no-no for either gender.

Private audiences with the pope are very difficult to obtain. Public audiences with the pope are held regularly, usually on Wednesday morning, but the hour of this gathering is likely to vary. Sometimes it's 11am, but it could also be at 10am if it's an especially hot day. In summer, audiences take place in St. Peter's Square. In winter, however, they are held regularly at 11am in the large Paul IV Hall, close to the south side of St. Peter's. Anyone is welcome.

To attend a general audience, you can obtain a free ticket from the office of the Prefecture of the Pontifical Household, which lies at the far reach of the northern colonnade of St. Peter's Square. Hours are 9am to 1pm on Tuesday and from 9am until right before the papal appearance on Wednesday.

Prospective visitors should write to the Prefecture of the Papal Household, 00120 Città del Vaticano (☎ **6982**), indicating their language, the dates of their visit, the number of people in the party, and, if possible, the hotel in Rome to which the cards should be sent by hand on the afternoon preceding the audience. American Catholics, armed with a letter of introduction from their parish priest, should apply to the North American College, via dell'Umiltà 30, 00187 Rome (☎ **6789184**).

In summer the pope appears on Sunday at his summer residence at Castel Gandolfo. He says a few words at noon, prays, and bestows his blessing upon the throng gathered there.

Open: Apr–Sept, daily 7am–7pm; Oct–Mar, daily 7am–6pm.
Bus: No. 23, 30, 32, 49, 51, or 64.

⭐ **The Vatican and the Sistine Chapel,** with entrances to the museums on viale Vaticano. ☎ **69883333.**

In 1929 the Lateran Treaty between Pope Pius XI and the Italian government created Vatican City, the world's smallest independent state.

IMPRESSIONS

As a whole St. Peter's is fit for nothing but a ballroom, and it is a little too gaudy even for that.
—John Ruskin, Letter To The Rev. Thomas Dale, December 1840

This state may be small, but it contains a gigantic repository of treasures from antiquity and the Renaissance housed in labyrinthine galleries. The Vatican's art collection reaches its apex in the Sistine Chapel.

The Vatican museums (a house of museums) comprise a series of lavishly adorned palaces and galleries built over the centuries. The entrance is on viale Vaticano, a long walk around from St. Peter's Square. Visitors can follow one of four itineraries—A, B, C, or D—according to the time they have at their disposal and their special interests. Determine your choice by consulting large-size panels placed at the entrance; then follow the letter- and color-coded signs that mark the itinerary chosen. Facilities for disabled visitors are available.

Obviously, 1, 2, or even 20 trips will not be enough to see the wealth of the Vatican, much less digest it. With that in mind, I've previewed only a representative sampling of masterpieces. A dozen museums and galleries should be inspected.

Pinacoteca (Picture Gallery): After climbing the spiral stairway, keep to the right; this path will take you to the Pinacoteca, where some of the most enduring works of art from the Byzantine to the baroque are displayed. For a break with the Byzantine, see one of the Vatican's finest artworks—the *Stefaneschi Polyptych* (six panels) by Giotto and his assistants. You'll also see the works of Fra Angelico, the 15th-century Dominican monk who distinguished himself as a miniaturist (his *Virgin Enthroned with Child* is justly praised—look for the microscopic eyes of the Madonna).

In the Raphael salon you'll find three paintings by that giant of the Renaissance, including the *Virgin of Foligno* and *The Transfiguration* (completed by assistants following his death). There are also 10 tapestries made by Flemish weavers from cartoons by Raphael. Seek out Leonardo da Vinci's masterful—but uncompleted—*St. Jerome with the Lion,* as well as Giovanni Bellini's *Entombment of Christ.* One of Titian's greatest works, the *Virgin of Frari,* is also displayed. Finally, feast your eyes on one of the masterpieces of the baroque period, Caravaggio's *Deposition from the Cross.*

Egyptian-Gregorian Museum: Review the grandeur of the pharaohs by studying sarcophagi, mummies, statues of goddesses, vases, jewelry, red-granite queens, and hieroglyphics.

Etruscan-Gregorian Museum: With sarcophagi, a chariot, bronzes, urns, jewelry, and terra-cotta vases, this gallery affords remarkable insight into a mysterious people. One of the most acclaimed exhibits is the Regolini-Galassi tomb, unearthed at Cerveteri (see Chapter 10, "Easy Excursions from Rome") in the 19th century. It shares top honors with the *Mars of Todi,* a bronze sculpture that probably dates from the 5th century B.C.

Pius Clementinus Museum: Here you'll find Greek and Roman sculptures, many of them immediately recognizable masterpieces. In the rotunda is a large gilded bronze of Hercules that dates from the time of Christ. Other major works of sculpture are under porticoes

Rome Attractions

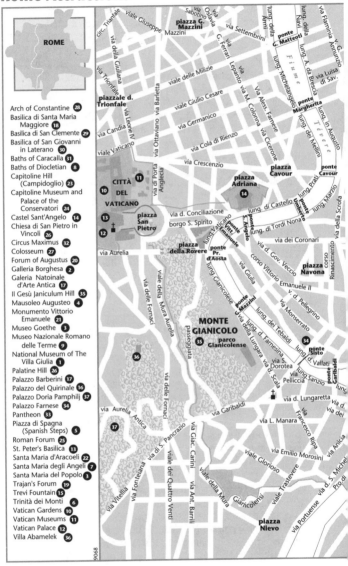

in rooms that open onto the Belvedere courtyard. Dating from the 1st century B.C., one sculpture shows Laocoön and his two sons locked in an eternal struggle with the serpents (the original statue is broken in parts; the completed version nearby is a copy). The incomparable *Apollo of Belvedere* (Roman reproduction of an authentic Greek work from the 4th century B.C.) has become the symbol of classic male

Villa Borghese

viale dell' Uccelliera

Villa Borghese

viale d. Magnolie

viale d. Canonica

viale Giov. Paisiello

via Po

via Salaria

via Savoia

via Nizza

viale Margherita

viale Regina

via Nomentana

viale G. Washington

vle G. Washington

via d. Magnolie

piazza del Popolo

via del Muro Torto

viale del Muro Torto

via Pinciana

corso d'Italia

piazza Fiume

piazza di Alessandria

piazza di Porta Pia

viale d. Policlinico

via di Ripetta

via Trinità d. Monti

via del Corso

via Babuino

piazza Augusto Imperatore

via Tomacelli

via Condotti

piazza di Spagna

via Sistina

via F. Crispi

via d. Due Macelli

via Campania

via Romagna

via Piemonte

via Boncompagni

via Ludovisi

via di Porta Pinciana

via di Quintino Sella

via XX Settembre

via Piave

via Gaeta

via Palestro

via Castro Pretorio

viale Castro Pretorio

via Vittoria

via Borgognona

via Tomacelli

via d. Cupa

via della Vite

via del Tritone

via Vitt.

via S. Basilio

piazza Barberini

via Barberini

via Cernaia

via Volturno

via Vicenza

via Marsala

via Pr

Castro Pretorio

Giardino d. Quirinale

via d. Scuderi

via d. Quirinale

piazza della Repubblica

piazza del Cinquecente

via Napoli

via Torino

Stazione Termini

via dell'Umiltà

via del Corso

via Nazionale

via Milano

via G. Amendola

via F. Turati

via Giolitti

via C. Battisti

via IV Novembre

via Panisperna

via S. Maria Maggiore

via Cavour

MONTE VIMINALE

via Quattro Cantoni

via del Carlo Alberto

via Napoleone III

piazza Vittorio Emanuele II

via Eugenio

via Plebiscito

piazza Venezia

via Giovanni Lanza

via Conte Verde

via Emanuele Filiberto

MONTE CAPITOLINO

via Marcello

via dei Fori Imperiali

via d. Serpenti

via del Monte Oppio

MONTE ESQUILINO

via Merulana

via d. Statuo

lung. d. Cenci

lung. dei Pierleoni

ponte Palatino

via di S. Teodoro

viale del Monte Oppio

parco Traiano

via Labicana

via Rugg. Bonghi

via Mecenate

via Manzoni

Anguillara

Salumi Genovesi

Ripa Grande

lung. Testaccio

via S. Sabina

via A. Magno

ponte Sublicio

via di S. Gregorio

MONTE PALATINO

via del Cerchi

piazza SS. Giovanni e Paolo

via Claudia

MONTE CELIO

via di S. Giovanni in Laterano

via di S. Stefano Rotondo

piazza Giovanni XXII

COLLE AVENTINO

via del Circo Massimo

piazzale Romolo e Remo

piazza di Pta. Capena

via delle Terme

via di S. Erasmo

via di Navicella

via dell'Amba Aradam

via Guido Baccelli

viale Aventino

piazza di Porta Metronia

via Gallia

ponte

Fiume Tevere

via d. S. Prisca

via Anselmo

piazza Albania

Parco di Porta Capena

via Pannonia

beauty. The rippling muscles of the *Torso of Belvedere*, a partially preserved Greek statue (1st century B.C.), reveal an intricate knowledge of the human body that predated Michelangelo by centuries, but equaled his achievements.

Chiaramonti Museum: You'll find a dazzling array of Roman statuary and copies of Greek originals in these galleries, including

The Nile, a reproduction of a long-lost Hellenistic original, and one of the most remarkable pieces of sculpture from antiquity. The statue of Augustus presents him as a regal commander.

Vatican Library: The library is so richly decorated and frescoed that it detracts from its treasures—manuscripts under glass. In the Sistine Salon are sketches by Michelangelo, drawings by Botticelli to illustrate the *Divine Comedy,* and a Greek Bible from the 4th century.

The Stanze of Raphael: While still a young man, Raphael was given one of the greatest assignments of his short life: the decoration of a series of rooms for Pope Julius II, who saw to it that Michelangelo was busy in the Sistine Chapel. In these works Raphael achieves the Renaissance aim of blending classic beauty with realism. In the first chamber, the Stanza dell'Incendio, you'll see much work of Raphael's pupils, but little of the master—except in the fresco across from the window. The figure of the partially draped man rescuing an older comrade (to the left of the fresco) is also Raphael's.

Raphael reigns supreme in the next and most important salon, the Stanza della Segnatura, where you'll find the majestic *School of Athens,* one of the artist's best-known works, which depicts such figures as Aristotle and Plato (even Raphael himself). Another well-known masterpiece, the *Disputà* (Disputation), is across from it. The Stanza d'Eliodoro, also by the master, manages to flatter Raphael's papal patrons (Julius II and Leo X) without compromising his art (although one rather fanciful fresco depicts the pope driving Attila from Rome). Finally, there's the Sala di Costantino, which was completed by his students after Raphael's death.

The Chapel of Nicholas V. The chapel provides an intimate interlude in a field of museums. The chapel was frescoed by the Dominican monk Fra Angelico, probably the most saintly of all Italian painters.

In Their Footsteps

Raphael (1483–1520) This Italian painter and architect (in Italian, Rafaello Sanzio or Santi) created masterpieces that embody the Renaissance ideal of the beauty of the natural form. Born in Urbino, he worked in Florence before coming to Rome in the service of Pope Julius I. By 1514, he'd been appointed chief architect of St. Peter's.

Accomplishments: His most enduring works include the frescoes in the Vatican, but he was equally renowned as a painter of such masterpieces as the *Sistine Madonna,* the *Madonna of the Goldfinch,* and *Marriage of the Virgin.*

Favorite Haunts: Via Porta Settimiani 8 in Rome, the home of da Fornarina (the baker's daughter) who became his mistress. She posed for some of his madonnas.

Resting Place: Rome's Pantheon.

The Borgia Apartments: This apartment, which was frescoed with biblical scenes of Pinturicchio of Umbria and his assistants, was designed for Pope Alexander VI (the famous Borgia pope). The rooms, although generally badly lit, have great splendor and style.

The Collection of Modern Religious Art: This gallery represents American artists' first invasion of the Vatican. Before it opened in 1973, the church limited its purchases to European art, and usually did not exhibit any works created after the 18th century. But Pope Paul VI changed all that. Of the 55 galleries that make up the Collection of Modern Religious Art, at least 12 are devoted solely to American artists. All the works chosen for the museum were judged on the basis of their "spiritual and religious values," but religious groups outside the Vatican are represented as well. Among the American works is Leonard Baskin's five-foot bronze sculpture of *Isaac.* Modern Italian artists, such as de Chirico and Manzù, are also displayed, and there's a special room for the paintings of the French artist Georges Rouault.

The Sistine Chapel: The story of Michelangelo painting the ceiling of the Sistine Chapel was dramatized by Irving Stone in *The Agony and the Ecstasy;* Charlton Heston did the neck-craning in the film version and thus earned a worldwide audience for one of the classic stories of art history. Michelangelo, of course, considered himself a sculptor, not a painter. While in his 30s, he was virtually commanded by Julius II to stop work on the pope's own tomb and to devote his considerable talents to painting ceiling frescoes—an art form of which the Florentine master was contemptuous.

Michelangelo labored for four years over this epic project, which was so physically taxing that it permanently damaged his eyesight. All during the task, he had to contend with the pope's incessant urgings to hurry up; at one point, Julius threatened to topple Michelangelo from the scaffolding—or so Vasari relates.

It is ironic that a project undertaken against the artist's wishes would form his most enduring legend. Glorifying the human body as only a sculptor could, Michelangelo painted nine panels, taken from the pages of Genesis, and surrounded by prophets and sibyls. The most notable panels detail the expulsion of Adam and Eve from the Garden of Eden, and the creation of man—where God's outstretched hand imbues Adam with spirit.

The Florentine master was in his 60s when he began to paint the masterly *Last Judgment* on the altar wall. Again working against his wishes, Michelangelo presents a more jaundiced view of mankind and his fate; God sits in judgment, and sinners are plunged into the mouth of hell.

A master of ceremonies under Paul III, Monsignor Biagio, protested to the pope against the "shameless nudes" painted by Michelangelo, Michelangelo showed he wasn't above petty revenge by painting the prude with the ears of a jackass in hell. When Biagio complained to the pope, Paul III maintained that he had no jurisdiction in hell. However, Daniele de Volterra was summoned to drape clothing over some of the bare figures—thus earning for himself a dubious distinction as a haberdasher.

The restoration of the Sistine Chapel in the 1990s touched off a worldwide debate among art historians. The Sistine Chapel was on the verge of collapse, both from its age and the weather, and restoration has taken years, as restorers used advanced computer analyses in their painstaking and controversial work. They reattached the fresco and repaired the ceiling. No longer dark and shadowy, Michelangelo's frescoes are now bright and pastel. Critics claim that in addition to removing centuries of dirt and grime, a vital second layer of paint was removed as well. Purists argue that many of the restored figures seem flat when compared to the original, which had more shadow and detail. Others in the media have hailed the project for having saved Michalengelo's masterpiece for future generations to appreciate.

On the side walls are frescoes by other Renaissance masters, such as Botticelli, Perugino, Luca Signorelli, Pinturicchio, Cosimo Rosselli, and Ghirlandaio. I'd guess that if these paintings had been displayed by themselves in other chapels, they would be the object of special pilgrimages. But here they have to compete with the artistry of Michelangelo.

The Ethnological Missionary Museum: This museum is an assemblage of works of art and objects of cultural significance from all over the world. The principal route is a half-mile walk through 25 geographical sections, which display thousands of objects covering 3,000 years of world history. The section devoted to China is especially interesting and worthwhile.

Did You Know . . . ?

- Rome has 913 churches.
- Some Mongol khans and Turkish chieftains pushed westward to conquer the Roman Empire after it had ceased to exist.
- Pope Leo III sneaked up on Charlemagne and set an imperial crown on his head, a surprise coronation that launched a precedent of Holy Roman Emperors being crowned by popes in Rome.
- The bronze of Marcus Aurelius, one of the world's greatest equestrian statues, escaped being melted down because the early Christians thought the statue was of Constantine.
- The Theater of Marcellus incorporated a gory realism in some of its stage plays: Condemned prisoners were often butchered before audiences as part of the plot.
- Christians were not fed to the lions at the Colosseum, but in one day 5,000 animals were slaughtered (one about every 10 seconds).

Gregorian Profane Museum: This museum houses a collection of antiquities including Roman sculptures, urns, funereal monuments, sarcophagi, and mosaic floors.

The Vatican Gardens: Separating the Vatican from the secular world on the north and west are 58 acres of lush, carefully tended gardens filled with winding paths, brilliantly colored flowers, groves of massive oaks, and ancient fountains and pools. In the midst of this pastoral setting is a small summer house, the Casino of Pius IV, built for Pope Pius IV in 1560 by Pirro Ligorio.

The Vatican Tourist Office: On the left side of piazza San Pietro, near the Arco delle Campane, is the Vatican Tourist Office (☎ 69884466), open daily from 8:30am to 6:30pm, where you can buy a map of the Vatican and have your questions answered about St. Peter's or the Vatican museums. Tours of the Vatican gardens, which must be arranged in advance, run March to October, Monday through Saturday, at 10am; November to February, tours are conducted only on Tuesday, Thursday, and Saturday, also at 10am. Tickets, which cost 16,000 lire ($9.60) per person, are available here at the tourist office. In summer, arrange tours as far in advance of departure as your schedule permits; the size of the tour group is limited to 33 people, and no reservations are taken on the phone.

A cafeteria is open to visitors from 8:45am to 2:45pm (to 4:45pm from July to the end of September and during Easter week).

Admission: 13,000 lire ($7.80) adults, 8,000 lire ($4.80) children. Free first Sun of each month.

Open: Museums, Oct–June, Mon–Sat 8:45am–1:45pm; July–Sept and Easter week, Mon–Sat 8:45am–4:45pm. Ticket sales stop one hour before closing time. **Metro:** Ottaviano station. **Bus:** No. 23, 30, 32, 49, 51, 64, 70, 81, 490, 492, 495, 907, 990, 991, or 994.

The Roman Forum & Palatine Hill

⭐ **The Roman Forum,** along via dei Fori Imperiali. ☎ 6780782 for information.

When it came to cremating Caesar, raping Sabine women, purchasing a harlot for the night, or sacrificing a naked victim, the Roman Forum was where the action was. Traversed by via Sacra, the Forum was built in the marshy land between the Palatine and the Capitoline Hills. It flourished as the center of Roman life in the days of the republic, before it gradually lost prestige to the Imperial Forum.

Be warned: Expect only fragmented monuments, an arch or two, and lots of overturned boulders. That any semblance of the Forum remains today is miraculous, as it was used for years, like the Colosseum, as a quarry. Eventually it reverted to what the Italians call a *campo vaccino* (cow pasture). But excavations in the 19th century began to bring to light one of the world's most historic spots.

By day, the columns of now-vanished temples and the stones from which long-forgotten orators spoke are mere shells. Bits of grass and weed grow where a triumphant Caesar was once lionized. But at night, when the Forum is silent in the moonlight, it isn't difficult to imagine that vestal virgins still guard the sacred temple fire. (Historical footnote: The function of the maidens was to keep the temple's sacred fire burning—but their own flame under control. Failure to do the latter sent them to an early grave . . . alive!)

You can spend at least a morning wandering through the ruins of the Forum. If you want the stones to have some meaning, you'll have to purchase a detailed plan, as the temples are hard to locate otherwise.

Some of the ruins are more important than others, of course. The best of the lot is the handsomely adorned Temple of Castor and Pollux, erected in the 5th century B.C. in honor of a battle triumph. The Temple of Antonius and Faustina, with its lovely columns and frieze (griffins and candelabra), was converted into the San Lorenzo in Miranda Church.

The senators used to meet and walk on the Curia's marble floors. Diocletian reconstructed the Senate, and it was later transformed into a medieval church. Across from the Curia is the "Lapis Niger," a black marble slab said to be the tomb of Romulus, legendary cofounder of the city (you can go down the stairs).

The Temple of the Vestal Virgins is a popular attraction. Some of the statuary, mostly headless, remains. The Temple of Saturn was rebuilt in the days of the republic in the 1st century B.C.

The Temple of Julius Caesar was ordered constructed by Octavian, in honor of the place where Caesar's body was cremated following his assassination. Rather oddly placed is the Church of Santa Maria Antiqua, with Christian frescoes that go back to the 7th century A.D.

Finally, the two arches are memorable: the Arch of Septimius Severus, erected in A.D. 203 with bas-reliefs, and the Arch of Titus, with much better carving, commemorating a victory in Jerusalem.

Admission: 10,000 lire ($6) adults, free for children under 12 if accompanied by an adult.

Open: June 1–July 15, Mon and Wed–Sat 9am–7pm, Sun and Tues 9am–2pm; May and July 16–Aug 15, Mon and Wed–Sat 9am–6:30pm, Sun and Tues 9am–2pm; Apr 16–30 and Aug 16–31, Mon and Wed–Sat 9am–6pm, Sun and Tues 9am–2pm; Mar 16–Apr 15 and Sept, Mon and Wed–Sat 9am–5:30pm, Sun and Tues 9am–2pm; Feb 16–Mar 15 and Oct, Mon and Wed–Sat 9am–5pm, Sun and Tues 9am–2pm; Nov–Jan 15, Mon and Wed–Sat 9am–4:30pm, Sun and Tues 9am–2pm. Last admission is always one hour before closing. **Closed:** Jan 16–Feb 15. **Metro:** Colosseo station. **Bus:** No. 27, 30, 85, 87, or 88.

The Palatine Hill, a walk uphill from the Roman Forum.

A long walk up from the Roman Forum leads to the Palatine Hill, one of the seven hills of Rome. The Palatine, tradition tells us, was

IMPRESSIONS

Rome, Italy, is an example of what happens when the buildings in a city last too long.
—Andy Warhol, *The Philosophy Of Andy Warhol (From A to B and Back Again)*, 1975

the spot on which the first settlers built their huts, under the direction of Romulus. In later years, the hill became a patrician residential district that attracted such citizens as Cicero. In time, however, the area was gobbled up by imperial palaces, and it drew a famous and infamous roster of tenants, such as Caligula (who was murdered here), Nero, Tiberius, and Domitian.

Only the ruins of its former grandeur remain today, and you really need to be an archeologist to make sense of them, as they are more difficult to understand than those in the Forum. But even if you're not interested in the past, it's worth the climb for the panoramic sweep of both the Roman and Imperial Forums, as well as the Capitoline Hill and the Colosseum.

Of all the ruins to inspect, none is finer than the so-called **House of Livia** (the "abominable grandmother" of Robert Grave's *I Claudius*). Actually, recent archeological research indicates that the house was in fact the "casa" of her husband, Livia used to slip him maidens noted for their discretion. A guard who controls the gate will show you the mythological frescoes reminiscent of those discovered at Herculaneum and Pompeii.

Domitian lived in the Imperial Palace—the **Domus Augustana**—which is an easy walk away, in the virtual heart of the Palatine. In the middle of the once-lavish estate—now stripped to the brick—is a large peristyle with a fountain. Domitian also ordered the building of the Palatine Stadium or **Hippodrome,** below, as well as a once-remarkable structure, the **Palace of Flavil,** which has a triclinium or great hall. When not overseeing real estate construction, Domitian was insuring that his name became immortal in the history of vice.

When the glory that was Rome has completely overwhelmed you, you can enjoy a respite in the cooling **Farnese Gardene,** laid out in the 16th century, which incorporate some of the designs of Michelangelo.

Admission: Your ticket from the Forum will admit you.

Open: Same hours as the Roman Forum (see above). **Metro:** Colosseo station. **Bus:** No. 27, 30, 85, 87, or 88.

The Colosseum & Its Environs

 The Colosseum, piazzale del Colosso. ☎ **7004261.**

In spite of the fact that it's a mere shell, the Colosseum remains the greatest architectural inheritance from ancient Rome. Vespasian ordered the construction of the elliptically shaped bowl, called the Amphitheatrum Flavium, in A.D. 72; it was inaugurated by Titus in A.D. 80 with a many-weeks-long bloody combat between gladiators and wild beasts.

At its peak, under the cruel Domitian, the Colosseum could seat 50,000 spectators. The vestal virgins from the temple screamed for blood, as more and more exotic animals were shipped in from the far corners of the empire to satisfy jaded tastes (lion vs. bear, two humans vs. hippopotamus). Not-so-mock naval battles were staged (the canopied Colosseum could be flooded), in which the defeated combatants might have their lives spared if they put up a good fight. One of the most enduring legends linked to the Colosseum—that is, that Christians were fed to the lions here—is considered to be without foundation by some historians.

Long after it ceased to be an arena to amuse sadistic Romans, the Colosseum was struck by an earthquake. Centuries later it was used as a quarry, and its rich marble facing was stripped away to build palaces and churches.

On one side, part of the original four tiers remain; the first three levels were constructed in Doric, Ionic, and Corinthian styles to lend it variety.

Admission: Street level, free; upper levels, 6,000 lire ($3.60)

Open: June–July 15, Mon–Tues and Thurs–Sat 9am–7pm, Wed 9am–2pm; May and July 16–Aug 15, Mon–Tues and Thurs–Sat 9am–6:30pm, Wed 9am–2pm; Apr 16–30 and Aug 16–31, Mon–Tues and Thurs–Sat 9am–6pm, Wed 9am–2pm; Mar 16–Apr 15 and Sept, Mon–Tues and Thurs–Sat 9am–5:30pm, Wed 9am–2pm; Feb 16–Mar 15 and Oct, Mon–Tues and Thurs–Sat 9am–5pm, Wed 9am–2pm; Nov–Jan 15, Mon–Tues and Thurs–Sat 9am–4:30pm, Wed 9am–2pm; holidays 9am–2pm. **Closed:** Jan 16–Feb 15. **Metro:** Colosseo station.

Arch of Constantine, next to the Colosseum, piazzale del Colosseo.

A highly photogenic memorial, the Arch of Constantine was erected in honor of Constantine's defeat of the pagan Maxentius (A.D. 306). It is a landmark in every way, physically and historically. Physically, it's beautiful, perhaps marred by the aggravating traffic that zooms around it at all hours, but so intricately carved and well preserved that you almost forget the racket of the cars and buses. Many of the reliefs have nothing whatsoever to do with Constantine or his works, but tell of the victories of earlier Antonine rulers—they were apparently lifted from other, long-forgotten memorials.

Historically, the arch marks a period of great change in the history of Rome, and therefore the history of the world. Rome, which had been pagan since the beginning, now had a Christian emperor, Constantine. Converted by a vision on the battlefield, he led his forces to victory and officially ended the centuries-long persecution of the Christians. By Constantine's time, many devout followers of the new religion had been put to death for the sake of their religion, and the new emperor put an end to it. While he did not ban paganism (which survived officially until the closing of the temples more than half a century later), he interceded on an imperial level to stop the persecutions. And by espousing Christianity himself, he began the inevitable development that culminated in the conquest of Rome by the Christian religion. The arch is a tribute to the emperor erected by the Senate in A.D. 315.

Metro: Colosseo station.

Domus Aurea, via Labicana, on the Esquiline Hill.

After visiting the Colosseum, it is also convenient to look at the site of the Domus Aurea, or the Golden House of Nero; it faces the

Colosseum and is adjacent to the Forum. The Domus Aurea, one of the most sumptuous palaces of all time, was constructed by Nero after a disastrous fire swept over Rome in A.D. 64. Not much remains of its former glory, but once the floors were made of mother-of-pearl and the furniture of gold. The area that is the Colosseum today was an ornamental lake, which reflected the grandeur and glitter of the Golden House. The hollow ruins—long stripped of their lavish decorations—lie near the entrance of the Oppius Park.

During the Renaissance, painters, such as Raphael, chopped holes in the long-buried ceilings of the Domus Aurea to gain admittance. Once there, they were inspired by the frescoes and the small "grotesques" of cornucopia and cherubs. The word "grotto" came from this palace, as it was believed to have been built underground. Remnants of these original almost 2,000-year-old frescoes and fragments of mosaics remain. All interiors are currently closed for renovation.

Metro: Colosseo station.

The Capitoline Hill [Campidoglio]

Of the seven hills of Rome, Campidoglio is considered the most sacred—its origins stretch way back into antiquity (an Etruscan temple to Jupiter once stood on this spot). The most dramatic approach to the Capitoline Hill is to walk from piazza Venezia, the center of Rome, to via di Teatro Marcello.

On your left, you can climb the steps designed by Michelangelo. At the top of the approach is the perfectly proportioned square of piazza del Campidoglio, also laid out by the Florentine genius.

Michelangelo positioned the bronze equestrian statue of Marcus Aurelius in the center, but after restoration it was moved inside to be protected from pollution.

One side of the piazza is open; the others are bounded by the **Senatorium** (Town Council), the statuary-filled **Palazzo del Conservatori,** and the **Capitoline Museums** (see "Museums & Galleries," below). The Campidoglio is dramatic at night (walk around to the back for a regal view of the floodlit Roman Forum). On your return, head down the small steps on your right. If you care to climb the other steps adjoining Michelangelo's approach, they'll take you to **Santa Maria d'Aracoeli** (see "Churches," below). **Bus:** No. 46, 89, or 92.

More of Ancient Rome

Castel Sant'Angelo, on the Tiber at largo Castello. ☎ **6875036.**

This overpowering structure, in a landmark position on the Tiber, was originally built in the 2nd century A.D. as a tomb for the emperor Hadrian; it continued as an imperial mausoleum until the time of Caracalla. It is an imposing and grim castle with thick walls and a cylindrical shape. If it looks like a fortress, it should, as that was its function in the Middle Ages (it was built over the Roman walls and linked by an underground passageway to the Vatican, which was

170

much used by the fleeing papacy who escaped from unwanted visitors, including Charles V, during his sack of the city in 1527).

In the 14th century it became a papal residence, enjoying various connections with Boniface IX, Nicholas V, even Julius II, patron of Michelangelo and Raphael. But its legend rests largely on its link with Pope Alexander VI, whose mistress bore him two children—Cesare and Lucrezia Borgia.

Of all the women of the Italian Renaissance, Lucrezia is the only one who commands universal recognition in the Western world; her name is a virtual synonym for black deeds, such as poisoning. But popular legend is highly unreliable: Many of the charges biographers have made against her (such as incestuous involvements with her brother and father) may have been only successful attempts to blacken her name. In addition to being part of an infamous family, she was a patron of the arts and a devoted charity worker, especially after she moved to Ferrara. Her brother, Cesare, of course, is without defense—he was a Machiavellian figure who is remembered accurately as a symbol of villainy and cruel spite.

Today the highlight of the castle is a trip through the Renaissance apartments, which have coffered ceilings and lush decoration. Their walls have witnessed plots and intrigues that make up some of the arch treachery of the High Renaissance. Later, you can go through the dank cells that once rang with the screams of Cesare's victims of torture, such as Astorre Manfredi of Faenza, who was finally relieved of his pain by being murdered.

Perhaps the most famous figure imprisoned here was Benvenuto Cellini, the eminent sculptor and goldsmith, remembered chiefly for his classic, candid *Autobiography.* Cellini kept getting into trouble—murdering people, etc.—but was jailed here on a charge of "peculation" (embezzlement of public funds). He escaped, was hauled back to jail, but was finally freed.

Now an art museum, the castle halls display the history of the Roman mausoleum, along with a wide-ranging selection of ancient arms and armor. Climb to the top terrace for another one of those dazzling views of the Eternal City. The museum can be visited on your way to St. Peter's.

Admission: 8,000 lire ($4.80) for any age.

Open: Daily 9am–1pm. **Bus:** 23, 46, 62, 64, 87, 98, 280, and 910. **Metro:** Ottaviano.

⭐ **The Pantheon,** piazza della Rotonda. ☎ **369831.**

Of all the great buildings of ancient Rome, only the Pantheon ("all the gods") remains intact today. It was built in 27 B.C. by Marcus

IMPRESSIONS

Brickwork I found thee, and marble I left thee! their Emperor vaunted;
'Marble I thought thee, and brickwork I find thee!' the Tourist may answer.
—Arthur Hugh Clough, *Amours De Voyage,* 1849

In Their Footsteps

Lucrezia Borgia (1480–1519) The one woman of the High Renaissance in Italy whose name is known around the world, she was the daughter of Pope Alexander VI. She was said to have been involved in various intrigues, crime, and immorality with her brother, the catlike and sinister Cesare, but the charges were never proven. She was married three times.

Accomplishments: She settled in Ferrara and made that city an artistic and cultural center. Her court attracted poets, artists, and the learned men of her day, including Titian.

Resting Place: The Monastery of Corpus Domini at Ferrara.

Agrippa, and later reconstructed by Emperor Hadrian in the first part of the 2nd century A.D. This remarkable building is among the architectural wonders of the world because of its dome and its concept of space. Byron described the temple as "simple, erect, austere, severe, sublime."

The Pantheon was once ringed with white marble statues of pagan gods, such as Jupiter and Minerva, in its niches. Animals were sacrificed and burned in the center, and the smoke escaped through the only means of light, an opening at the top 27 feet in diameter. The Pantheon is 142 feet wide, 142 feet high. Michelangelo came here to study the dome before designing the cupola of St. Peter's (whose dome is 2 feet smaller than the Pantheon's).

Other statistics are equally impressive. The walls are 25 feet thick, and the bronze doors leading into the building weigh 20 tons each. The temple was converted into a church in the early 7th century.

In the 1860s, the tomb of Raphael was discovered in the Pantheon (fans still bring him flowers). Victor Emmanuel II, king of Italy, was interred here.

Admission: Free.

Open: July–Sept, daily 9am–6pm; Oct–June, Mon–Sat 9am–4pm, Sun 9am–1pm. **Bus:** 64, 170, or 175 to largodi Torre Argentina.

The Appian Way & the Catacombs

Of all the roads that led to Rome, the Appia Antica—built in 312 B.C.—was the reigning leader. It eventually stretched all the way from Rome to the seaport of Brindisi, through which trade with the colonies in Greece and the East was funneled. According to the Christian tradition, it was on the Appian Way that an escaping Peter encountered the vision of Christ which caused him to go back into the city to face subsequent martyrdom.

Along the Appian Way, the patrician Romans built great monuments above the ground, while the Christians met in the catacombs beneath the earth. The remains of both can be visited today. In some dank, dark grottoes (never stray too far from either your party or one of the exposed lightbulbs), you can still discover the remains of early Christian art.

Only someone wanting to write a sequel to *Quo Vadis* would visit all the catacombs. Of those open to the public, the Catacombs of St. Calixtus and those of St. Sebastian are the most important.

The **Tomb of St. Sebastian,** called the Catacombe di San Sebastiano, is at via Appia Antica 136 (☎ **7887035**). Today the tomb of the martyr is in the basilica (church), but his original tomb was in the catacomb that is under the basilica. From the reign of Emperor Valerian to the reign of Emperor Constantine, the bodies of Saint Peter and Saint Paul were hidden in the catacomb. The big church was built here in the 4th century. None of the catacombs, incidentally, is a grotto; all are dug from tufo, a soft volcanic rock. This is the only Christian catacomb in Rome that is always open.

The tunnels here, if stretched out, would reach a length of seven miles. In the tunnels and mausoleums are mosaics and graffiti, along with many other pagan and Christian objects from centuries even before the time of Constantine. Visiting hours are Wednesday through Monday from 9am to noon and 2:30 to 5:30pm, and admission is 8,000 lire ($4.80); children under 10 are admitted free.

The **Catacombs of St. Callixtus,** via Appia Antica 110 (☎ **5136725**), are "the most venerable and most renowned of Rome," according to Pope John XXIII. The founder of Christian archeology, Giovanni Battista de Rossi (1822–1894), called them "catacombs par excellence." They are the first cemetery of the Christian community of Rome, burial place of 16 popes in the 3rd century. They bear the name of St. Callixtus, the deacon whom pope St. Zephyrinus put in charge of them. Callixtus himself was later elected pope (217–222). The cemeterial complex is made up of a network of galleries, stretching for nearly 15 miles. It is structured in five different levels, reaching a depth of about 99 feet (30 meters). There are many sepulchral chambers and some 10,000 tombs. Paintings, sculptures, and epigraphs (with such symbols as the fish, the anchor, and the dove) provide invaluable material for the study of the life and customs of the ancient Christians and the story of their persecutions.

Entering the catacombs, one sees at once the most important crypt, that of the nine popes (three of whom were martyrs). Some of the original marble tablets of their tombs are still preserved. The next crypt is that of St. Cecilia, the patron of sacred music. This early Christian martyr received three ax strokes on her neck, the maximum allowed by Roman law, which failed to kill her outright. She reportedly died after three days of agonizing pain and bleeding. Farther on, the famous Cubicula of the Sacraments can be reached, with 3rd-century frescoes. The catacombs were dug in the middle of the 2nd century up until the middle of the 5th century. They were cemeteries and places of prayers—never private dwellings.

Access to visitors has been improved by well-lighted galleries, providing an underground route through the maze. Admission is

Frommer's Favorite Rome Experiences

Fountain Hopping   Rome abounds in Renaissance and baroque fountains—lavish, theatrical, spectacular—none more so than the Trevi Fountain. They're fed by an abundant freshwater supply. See "The Fountains of Rome" under "The Top Attractions."

The Campidoglio at Night   Climb steps designed by Michelangelo to the back of the square to see a sound-and-light summer spectacle. Suddenly, you hear marching legions, glaring trumpets, rumbling drums—all the sounds needed to convince you that you're back in the days of ancient Rome, with soldiers, soothsayers, and vestal virgins.

Opera at the Baths of Caracalla   In the gigantic ruins of a former Roman bathhouse, open-air opera is presented, none more spectacular than *Aïda*. An army of extras people the stage, and elephants or braces of horses come charging in near curtain time.

Flea-Market Shopping   Every Sunday morning (until 1pm), the flea market of Rome stretches for two miles from Porta Portese to the Trastevere rail station. Barter, bargain, buy, or "window shop"— this array of merchandise, everything from fake antiques to illegally cut tapes, from "oddities" from the attic to portraits of Mussolini, will equal one of the shopping adventures of a lifetime. (Watch your wallet.)

8,000 lire ($4.80) for adults, 4,000 lire ($2.40) for children. Hours are Thursday through Tuesday from 8:30am to noon and 2:30 to 5:30pm in summer; Thursday through Tuesday from 8:30am to noon and 2:30 to 5pm off-season. Take bus 118 from San Giovanni in Laterano, from the Colosseum or from the Baths of Caracalla, or bus 218 from San Giovanni in Laterano to Fosse Ardeatine. Ask the driver to let you off at the Catacombs of St. Callixtus.

Of the Roman monuments, the most impressive is the **Tomb of Cecilia Metella,** on via Appia Antica, within walking distance of the catacombs. The cylindrically shaped tomb honors the wife of one of Caesar's military commanders. Why such an elaborate tomb for such an unimportant person in history? Cecilia Metella happened to be singled out for enduring fame because her tomb remained and the others decayed.

Take bus no. 118, which leaves from near the Colosseum near the Metro station, St. John in Lateran, or Circus Maximus; or no. 218 from St. John in Lateran to Fosse Ardeatine. Ask the driver to drop you at the catacombs.

Piazza di Spagna [Spanish Steps]

The Spanish Steps were the last part of the outside world that Keats saw before he died in a house at the foot of the stairs. The steps— filled, in season, with flower vendors, young jewelry dealers, and photographers snapping pictures of tourists—and the square take their names from the Spanish embassy, which used to have its headquarters here.

At the foot of the steps is a nautically shaped fountain that was designed by Pietro Bernini (Papa is not to be confused with his son, Giovanni Lorenzo Bernini, who proved to be a far greater sculptor of fountains). About two centuries ago, when the foreign art colony was in its ascendancy, the 136 steps were covered with young men and women who wanted to pose for the painters. At the top of the steps is a good view and the 16th-century church of Trinità dei Monti, built by the French, with twin towers. Metro: Piazza di Spagna.

The Fountains of Rome

Rome is a city of fountains—a number of which are of such artistic merit that they're worth a special pilgrimage. Some of the more famous ones are the Four Seasons and Bernini's Triton Fountain at piazza Barberini, but the two that hold the most enduring interest are the Fountain of Trevi and the waterworks at piazza Navona.

⭐ **Piazza Navona,** surely one of the most lavishly baroque sites in all of Rome, is like an ocher-colored gem, unspoiled by new buildings or even by traffic. The shape results from the ruins of the Stadium of Domitian, which lie underneath the present constructions. Great chariot races, some of which were rather unusual, were once held here. In one, for instance, the head of the winning horse was lopped off as he crossed the finish line and carried by runners to be offered as a sacrifice by vestal virgins on top of the Capitoline Hill. In medieval times, historians note that the popes used to flood the piazza to stage mock naval encounters. Today the most strenuous activities are performed by occasional fire-eaters who go through their evening paces before an interested crowd of Romans and visitors.

Beside the twin-towered facade of the **Church of Saint Agnes** (17th century), the piazza boasts several other baroque masterpieces. In the center is Bernini's *Fountain of the Four Rivers,* whose four stone personifications symbolize the world's greatest rivers—the Ganges, Danube, de la Plata, and Nile. It's fun to try to figure out which is which (hint: the figure with the shroud on its head is the Nile, so represented because the river's source was unknown at the time the fountain was constructed). The fountain at the south end, the *Fountain of the Moor,* is also by Bernini and dates from the same period as the church and the *Fountain of the Four Rivers.* The *Fountain of Neptune,* which balances that of the Moor, is a 19th-century addition. During the summer there are outdoor art shows in the evening, but visit during the day—it's the best time to inspect the fragments of the original stadium under a building on the north side of the piazza. If you're interested, walk out at the northern exit and turn left for a block. It's astonishing how much the level of the ground has risen since ancient times.

As you elbow your way through the summertime crowds around the ⭐ **Trevi Fountain** (Fontana di Trevi) at piazza di Trevi, you'll find it hard to believe that this little piazza was nearly always deserted before *Three Coins in the Fountain* brought the tour buses. Today it's a must on everybody's itinerary. Tradition dictates that you throw a coin in the fountain to ensure your return to Rome one day. To do it properly, hold your lire coin in the right hand, turn your back to the fountain, and toss the coin over your shoulder, being careful not to bean anyone behind you.

Actually, this is an evolution of an even older tradition of drinking from the fountain. Nathaniel Hawthorne (1804–1864) in his novel, *The Marble Faun,* wrote that anyone drinking from this fountain's water "has not looked upon Rome for the last time." Because of pollution, no one drank from it for years. After the fountain was restored and was running again in 1994, the water is supposedly pure, owing to an electronic devise that keeps the pigeons at bay. I'd still suggest you skip the "Trevi cocktail" and have a mineral water at a cafe instead.

Pope Urban VIII (1623–1644), a Barberini, asked artists of his day to design the fountain and they did, emerging with a triumphant figure of Neptunus Rex. The figure occupies the main niches of a palace wall, and stands on a shell chariot drawn by winged steeds and led by a pair of tritons. Two allegorical figures in the side niches represent good health and fertility. On one corner of the piazza you'll see an ancient church with a strange claim to fame: In it are the hearts and viscera of several centuries of popes. This was the parish church of the popes when they resided at the Quirinale Palace on the hill above, and for many years each pontiff willed those parts of his body to this church.

Piazza Barberini lies at the foot of several Roman streets, among them via Barberini, via Sistina, and via Veneto. It would be a far more pleasant spot were it not for the considerable amount of traffic swarming around its principal feature, Bernini's ***Fountain of the Triton.*** For more than three centuries, the strange figure sitting in a vast open clam has been blowing water from his triton. Off to one side of the piazza is the clean, aristocratic side facade of the Palazzo Barberini, named for one of Rome's powerful families. The Renaissance Barberini reached their peak when a son was elected pope (Urban VIII). This Barberini pope encouraged Bernini and gave him great patronage.

As you go up via Veneto, look for the small fountain on the right-hand corner of piazza Barberini, which is another of Bernini's works, the small ***Fountain of the Bees.***

2 More Attractions

The Baths of Caracalla

Named for the emperor Caracalla, the **Terme di Caracalla,** via delle Terme di Caracalla 52 (☎ **5758302**), were completed in the early part of the 3rd century. The richness of decoration has faded, and the lushness of these imperial baths can only be judged from the shell of brick ruins that remain.

Viewing the baths during the day is one experience. Even more spectacular, however, is to attend an opera here, perhaps a version of Verdi's *Aïda* (see Chapter 9, "Rome Nights").

Admission costs 6,000 lire ($3.60). From April to September, the hours are Tuesday to Saturday 9am to 6pm, Sunday and Monday 9am to 1pm; October to March, the hours are Tuesday to Saturday 9am to 3pm, Sunday and Monday 9am to 1pm. Take bus no. 90 or 118 from the Stazione Termini.

Janiculum Hill [Gianicolo]

From many vantage points in the Eternal City, the views are magnificent. Scenic gulpers, however, have traditionally preferred the outlook from Janiculum Hill (across the Tiber), not one of the "seven hills" but certainly one of the most visited (and a stopover on many coach tours). The view is seen at its best at sundown, or at dawn when the skies are often fringed with mauve. Janiculum was the site of a battle between Giuseppe Garibaldi and the forces of Pope Pius IX in 1870—an event commemorated today with statuary. Take bus no. 41 from Ponte Sant'Angelo.

The Quirinale

In a wide pink piazza in the heart of Rome stands the palace of the president of Italy. It was the home of the king of Italy until the end of World War II, and before that it was the residence of the pope. The steep marble steps that lead to Santa Maria in Aracoeli on the Capitoline Hill once led to the site of Augustus's Temple of the Sun. The great baths of Constantine also stood nearby, which accounts for some of the fountain statuary. Metro: Barberini.

Cemeteries

See also Section 4, later in this chapter, for details on the Protestant Cemetery.

Pyramid of Caius Cestius, piazzale Ostiense.

Dating from the 1st century B.C., the Pyramid of Caius Cestius, about 90 feet high, looks as if it belongs to the Egyptian landscape. The pyramid can't be entered, but it's fun to circle and photograph. Who was Caius Cestius? A judge of sorts, a man less impressive than his tomb.

Bus: No. 30.

Cimitero Monumentale dei Padri Cappuccini, in the Church of the Immaculate Conception, via Veneto 27.

This cemetery, Rome's most macabre sight, is a short walk from piazza Barberini. You enter from the first staircase on the right of the church, at the entrance to the friary. Guidebooks of old used to rank this sight along with the Forum and the Colosseum as one of the city's top attractions. Qualifying as one of the most horrifying sights in all Christendom, it is a cemetery of skulls and crossbones woven into "works of art." To make this allegorical dance of death, the bones of more than 4,000 Capuchin brothers were used. Some of the skeletons are intact, draped with Franciscan habits. The creator of this chamber of horrors? The tradition of the friars is that it was the work of a French Capuchin. Their literature suggests that the cemetery should be visited keeping in mind the historical moment of its origins, when Christians had a rich and creative cult for their dead, when great spiritual masters meditated and preached with a skull in hand. Those who have lived through the days of crematoriums and other such massacres may view the graveyard differently, but to many who pause to think, this macabre sight of death has a message. It's not for the squeamish.

Admission: 1,000 lire (60¢).

Open: Apr–Sept, daily 9am–noon and 3–6:30pm; Oct–Mar, daily 9:30am–noon and 3–6pm. **Metro:** Piazza Barberini.

Churches

St. Peter's is not the only church you should see in Rome. The city's hundreds of churches—some built with marble stripped from ancient monuments—form a major sightseeing treasure. I've highlighted the best of the lot, including four patriarchal churches of Rome that belong to the Vatican. Others are equally worth viewing, especially one designed by Michelangelo.

Basilica of San Giovanni in Laterano, piazza di San Giovanni 4. ☎ **6986433.**

This church—not St. Peter's—is the cathedral of the diocese of Rome. Catholics all over the world refer to it as their "mother chruch." Originally built in 314 A.D. by Constantine, the cathedral has suffered the vicissitudes of Rome, and was badly sacked and forced to rebuild many times. Only fragmented parts of the baptistery remain from the original structure.

The present building is characterized by its 18th-century facade by Alessandro Galilei (statues of Christ and the Apostles ring the top). A terrorist bomb in 1993 caused severe damage, especially to the facade. Borromini gets the credit (some say blame) for the interior, built for Innocent X. It is said that in the misguided attempt to redecorate, frescoes by Giotto were destroyed (remains believed to have been painted by Giotto were discovered in 1952 and are now displayed). In addition, look for the unusual ceiling, the sumptuous transept, and explore the 13th-century cloisters, with their twisted double columns.

The popes used to live next door at the **Lateran Palace** before the move to Avignon in the 14th century. But the most unusual sight is across the street at the "Palace of the Holy Steps," called the **Scala Sancta.** It is alleged that these were the actual wooden steps that Christ climbed when he was brought before Pilate. These steps are supposed to be climbed only on your knees, which you're likely to see the faithful doing throughout the day.

Admission: Free.

Open: Daily 7am–6pm. **Bus:** No. 91.

Basilica of St. Mary Major [Santa Maria Maggiore], piazza di Santa Maria Maggiore. ☎ **483195.**

This great church, one of the four major basilicas of Rome, was originally founded by Pope Liberius in 358 A.D., then rebuilt by Pope Sixtus III from 432 to 440 A.D. Its campanile, erected in the 14th century, is the loftiest in the city. Much doctored in the 18th century, the church's facade is not an accurate reflection of the treasures inside. The basilica is especially noted for the 5th-century Roman mosaics in its nave, as well as for its coffered ceiling, said to have been gilded with gold brought from the New World. In the 16th century Domenico Fontana built a now-restored "Sistine Chapel." In the following century Flaminio Ponzo designed the Pauline (Borghese) Chapel in the baroque style. The church contains the tomb of Bernini, Italy's most important architect during the flowering of the baroque in the 17th century. Ironically, the man who changed the face of Rome with his elaborate fountains was buried in a tomb so simple it takes a sleuth to track it down (to the right near the altar).

Admission: Free.

Open: Apr–Sept, daily 7am–8pm; Oct–Mar, daily 7am–7pm. **Metro:** Stazione Termini.

San Paolo Fuori le Mura [Basilica of St. Paul Outside the Walls], via Ostiense. ☎ **5410341.**

The Basilica of St. Paul, whose origins go back to the time of Constantine, is the fourth great patriarchal church of Rome. It burned in 1823 and was subsequently rebuilt. This basilica is believed to have been erected over the tomb of St. Paul (St. Peter's was built over the tomb of that saint). Inside, the windows may appear at first to be stained glass, but they are alabaster—the effect of glass is created by the brilliant light shining through. With its forest of single-file columns and its mosaic medallions (portraits of the various popes), this is one of the most streamlined and elegantly decorated churches in Rome. The basilica's single most important treasure is a 12th-century candelabrum, designed by Vassalletto, who is also responsible for the remarkable cloisters—in themselves worth the trip "outside the walls." They contain twisted pairs of columns enclosing a rose garden. The Benedictine monks and students sell a fine collection of souvenirs, rosaries, and bottles of Benedictine. The gift shop is open every day except Sunday and religious holidays.

Admission: Free.

Open: Cloisters, Mon–Sat 9–11:45am; basilica, Mon–Sat 9am–1pm and 3–6pm. **Metro:** San Paolo Basilica. **Bus:** 23, 170, or 673.

Chiesa di San Pietro in Vincoli [Saint Peter in Chains], piazza di San Pietro in Vincoli 4A, off via degli Annibaldi. ☎ **4882865.**

From the Colosseum, head up a "spoke" street, via degli Annibaldi, to a church founded in the 5th century A.D. to house the chains that bound St. Peter in Palestine. The chains are preserved under glass. But the drawing card is the tomb of Julius II, with one of the world's most famous pieces of sculpture, *Moses* by Michelangelo. As readers of Irving Stone's *The Agony and the Ecstasy* know, Michelangelo was to have carved 44 figures for Julius's tomb. That didn't happen, of course, but the pope was given one of the greatest consolation prizes—a figure intended to be "minor" that is now numbered among Michelangelo's masterpieces. Of the stern, father symbol of Michelangelo's *Moses,* Vasari, in his *Lives of the Artists,* wrote: "No modern work will ever equal it in beauty, no, nor ancient either."

Admission: Free.

Open: Mon–Sat 7am–12:30pm and 3:30–6pm, Sun 7–11:45am and 3–7pm. **Metro:** Via Cavour. **Bus:** No. 11, 27, or 81.

Santa Maria degli Angeli, piazza della Repubblica 12. ☎ **4880812.**
On this site, which adjoins the National Roman Museum near the railway station, once stood the "tepidarium" of the 3rd-century Baths of Diocletian. But in the 16th century, Michelangelo—nearing the end of his life—converted the grand hall into one of the most visited churches in Rome. Surely the artist wasn't responsible for "gilding the lily"—that is, putting trompe-l'oeil columns in the midst of the genuine pillars. The church is filled with tombs and paintings, but its crowning treasure is the statue of St. Bruno by the great French sculptor Jean-Antoine Houdon. His sculpture is larger than life and about as real.

Admission: Free.

Open: Daily 7:30am–noon and 4–6:30pm. **Metro:** Piazza della Repubblica.

Basilica di San Clemente, piazza di San Clemente, via Labicana 95. ☎ **7316723.**
From the Colosseum, head up via di San Giovanni in Laterano, which leads to the Basilica of Saint Clement. This isn't just another Roman church—far from it! In this church-upon-a-church, centuries of history peel away like stalks of the fennel that Romans eat for dessert. In the 4th century a church was built over a secular house of the 1st century A.D., beside which stood a pagan temple dedicated to Mithras (god of the sun). Down in the eerie grottoes (which you can explore on your own—unlike the catacombs on the Appian Way), you'll discover well-preserved frescoes from the 1st century through the 3rd century A.D. After the Normans destroyed the lower church, another one was built in the 12th century. Its chief attraction is its bronze-orange mosaic (from that period), which adorns the apse, as well as a chapel honoring St. Catherine of Alexandria (murals are by Masolino de Panicale, who decorated the Brancacci Chapel in the Church of Carmine in Florence in the 15th century).

Admission: Church, free; grottoes, 2,000 lire ($1.20).

Open: Mon–Sat 9am–noon and 3:30–6pm, Sun 10am–12:30pm and 3:30–6:30pm. **Metro:** Colosseo.

Santa Maria in Cosmedin, piazza della Verità 18. ☎ **6781419.**
This charming little church was founded in the 6th century, but subsequently rebuilt—and a campanile was added in the 12th century in the Romanesque style. The church is ever popular with pilgrims drawn not by its great art treasures but by its "Bocca della Verità" or

"Mouth of Truth," a large disk under the portico. According to tradition, it is supposed to chomp down on the hand of liars who insert their paws. According to local legend, a former priest used to keep a scorpion in back to bite the fingers of anyone he felt was lying. In the movie *Roman Holiday,* Gregory Peck put his hand in the *bocca.* But when he pulled it out, his hand had disappeared up his sleeve, causing Audrey Hepburn to scream in shock, fearing he'd lost his hand. On one of my visits to the church, a little woman, her head draped in black, sat begging a few feet from the medallion. A scene typical enough—except this woman's right hand was covered with bandages.

Admission: Free.

Open: Daily 9am–noon and 3–5pm. **Bus:** 57, 95, or 716.

Santa Maria d'Aracoeli, Capitoline Hill. No phone.

Sharing a spot on Capitoline Hill (but unfortunately reached by a long, steep flight of steps different from those leading to piazza del Campidoglio), this landmark church was built for the Franciscans in the 13th century. According to legend, Augustus once ordered a temple erected on this spot, where a sibyl, with her gift of prophecy, forecast the coming of Christ. In the interior of the present building, you'll find a nave and two aisles, two rows with 11 pillars each, a Renaissance ceiling, and a mosaic of the Virgin over the altar in the Byzantine style. If you're sleuth enough, you'll also find a tombstone carved by the great Renaissance sculptor Donatello. The church is known for its Bufalini Chapel, a masterpiece of Pinturicchio, who frescoed it with scenes illustrating the life and death of St. Bernardino of Siena. He also depicted St. Francis receiving the stigmata. These frescoes are considered a highpoint in early Renaissance Roman painting. If you're on the piazza del Campidoglio, you can avoid these steps by crossing the piazza and climbing fewer steps on the far side of the Museo Capitolino.

Admission: Free.

Open: Daily 7am–noon and 4–7pm. **Bus:** 46, 89, or 92.

Museums & Galleries

National Roman Museum [Museo Nazionale Romano], via Enrico de Nicola 79. ☎ **4824181.**

Located near piazza dei Cinquecento, which fronts the railway station, this museum occupies part of the 3rd-century A.D. Baths of Diocletian and a section of a convent that may have been designed by Michelangelo. It houses one of Europe's finest collections of Greek and Roman sculpture and early Christian sarcophagi.

The Ludovisi Collection is the apex of the museum, particularly the statuary of the Gaul slaying himself after he's done in his wife (a brilliant copy of a Greek original from the 3rd century B.C.).

Another prize is a one-armed Greek Apollo. A galaxy of other sculptured treasures include *The Discus Thrower of Castel Porziano* (an exquisite copy); *Aphrodite of Cirene* (a Greek original); and the so-called *Hellenistic Ruler,* a Greek original of an athlete with a lance.

A masterpiece of Greek sculpture, *The Birth of Venus,* is mounted on the Ludovisi throne. The *Sleeping Hermaphrodite* (Ermafrodito Dormiente) is an original Hellenistic statue. Don't fail to stroll through the cloisters, filled with statuary and fragments of antiquity, including a fantastic mosaic.

Admission: 3,000 lire ($1.80).

Open: Tues–Sat 9am–2pm, Sun and holidays 9am–1pm. **Metro:** Piazza della Repubblica.

⭐ **National Museum of Villa Giulia [Etruscan],** piazza di Villa Giulia 4. ☎ **3201500.**

A 16th-century papal palace in the Villa Borghese gardens shelters this priceless collection of art and artifacts of the mysterious Etruscans, who predated the Romans. Known for their advanced art and design, the Etruscans left a legacy of sarcophagi, bronze sculptures, terra-cotta vases, and jewelry, among other items.

If you have time only for the masterpieces, head for Sala 7, which has a remarkable *Apollo* from Veio from the end of the 6th century B.C. (clothed, for a change). The other two widely acclaimed pieces of statuary in this gallery are *Dea con Bambino* (a goddess with a baby) and a greatly mutilated, but still powerful, *Hercules* with a stag. In the adjoining room, Sala 8, you'll see the lions' sarcophagus from the mid–6th century B.C., which was excavated at Cerveteri, north of Rome.

Finally, one of the world's most important Etruscan art treasures is the bride and bridegroom coffin from the 6th century B.C., also dug out of the tombs of Cerveteri (in Sala 9). Near the end of your tour, another masterpiece of Etruscan art awaits you in Sala 33: the *Cista Ficoroni,* a bronze urn with paw feet, mounted by three figures, which dates from the 4th century B.C.

Admission: 8,000 lire ($4.80) adults, free for children under 18.

Open: June–Aug, Tues–Sat 9am–7pm, Sun 9am–1pm; Sept–May, Tues–Sun 9am–2pm. **Bus:** 19 or 30.

⭐ **Galleria Borghese,** piazzale del Museo Borghese, off via Pinciano. ☎ **858577.**

The gallery, housed in a handsome villa, contains some of the finest paintings in Rome; there's a representative collection of Renaissance and baroque masters, along with important Bernini sculpture. Among these is the so-called *Conquering Venus* by Antonio Canova, Italy's greatest neoclassic sculptor. Actually, this early–19th-century work created a sensation in its day, because its model was Pauline Bonaparte Borghese, sister of Napoleon (if the French dictator didn't like to see his sister naked, he was even more horrified at Canova's totally nude version of himself). In the rooms that follow are three of Bernini's most widely acclaimed works *David, Apollo and Daphne* (his finest piece), and finally, *The Rape of Persephone.*

The paintings form a display of canvases almost too rich for one visit. If you're pressed for time, concentrate on three works by Raphael (especially the young woman holding a unicorn in her lap and the *Deposition from the Cross*).

Works of Caravaggio (1569–1609), leader of the realists, are on view, including the *Madonna of the Palafrenieri*. Rubens's favorite theme, the elders lusting after Susanna, is displayed. Titian's *Sacred and Profane Love* is exhibited, along with three other works of his.

After visiting the gallery, you may want to join the Italians in their strolls through the **Villa Borghese,** replete with zoological gardens and small bodies of water. Horse shows are staged at piazza di Siena.

Admission: 4,000 lire ($2.40).

Open: Tues–Sat 9am–2pm, Sun 9am–1pm. **Bus:** 910 from Stazione Termini or 56 from piazza Barberini.

★ **Capitoline Museum and Palace of the Conservatori,** piazza del Campidoglio. ☎ 67102475.

These two museums house some of the greatest pieces of classical sculpture in the world. The **Capitoline Museum,** or Musei Capitolini, was built in the 17th century, based on an architectural sketch by Michelangelo. It originally housed a papal collection that was founded by Sixtus IV in the 15th century.

In the first room is *The Dying Gaul*, a work of majestic skill that brings worldwide instant recognition. It's a copy of a Greek original that dates from the 3rd century B.C. And in a special gallery all her own is *The Capitoline Venus*, who demurely covers herself; this statue was the symbol of feminine beauty and charm down through the centuries (this one is a Roman copy of the Greek original from the 3rd century B.C.). Finally, *Amore* (Cupid) and *Psyche* are up to their old tricks.

The famous equestrian statue of Marcus Aurelius that stood for years in the middle of the piazza was unveiled after a restoration; it had been a victim of pollution. Now it is located in the museum for greater protection. This is the only bronze statue to have survived from ancient Rome, and it was saved only because it had been tossed into the Tiber by marauding barbarians. For centuries after its discovery it was thought to be a statue of Constantine the Great; this mistake protected it further, since Papal Rome respected the memory of the first Christian emperor. It's a well-executed statue even though the perspective is rather odd—it was originally designed to sit on top of a column, hence the foreshortened effect. The emperor's stirrups, by the way, are not missing—they were simply unknown in classical times, and Roman horsemen never used them. The statue is found in a glassed-in room on the street level called Cortile di Marforio; it's a kind of Renaissance greenhouse, surrounded by windows.

The **Palace of the Conservatori** across the way was also based on an architectural plan by Michelangelo. It is rich in classical sculpture and paintings. One of the most notable bronzes—a work of incomparable beauty—is the *Spinario* (the little boy picking a thorn from his foot), a Greek classic that dates from the 1st century B.C. In addition, you'll find *Lupa Capitolina* (Capitoline Wolf), a rare Etruscan bronze that may go back to the 6th century B.C. (Romulus and Remus, the legendary twins that the wolf suckled, were added at a later date). The palace also contains a "Pinacoteca"—mostly paintings from the 16th and 17th centuries. Notable canvases include Caravaggio's *Fortune-Teller* and his *John the Baptist;* the *Holy Family* by Dosso Dossi; *Romulus and Remus* by Rubens; and Titian's *Baptism of Christ.*

Admission: Museum and palace, 10,000 lire ($6) adults and children.

Open: Apr–Sept, Tues–Fri 9am–2pm, Sat 9am–2pm and 8–11pm, Sun 9am–1:30pm; Oct–Mar, Tues and Sat 9am–1:30pm and 5–8pm, Wed–Fri 9am–1:30pm, Sun 9am–1pm. **Bus:** No. 46, 89, or 92.

Galleria Nazionale d'Arte Moderna, viale delle Belle Arti 131. ☎ **3224151.**

The National Gallery of Modern Art is in the Villa Borghese gardens, a short walk from the Etruscan Museum. With its neoclassic and romantic paintings and sculpture, it's a dramatic change from the glories of the Renaissance and the Romans. Its 75 rooms house the largest collection in Italy of 19th- and 20th-century artists, including a comprehensive collection of modern Italian paintings.

Also included are important works of Balla, Boccioni, de Chirico, Morandi, Manzù, Marini, Burri, Capogrossi, and Fontana, and a large collection of Italian optical and pop art.

Look for Modigliani's *La Signora dal Collaretto* and the large *Nudo.* Several important sculptures, including one by Canova, are on display in the museum's gardens. The gallery also houses a large collection of foreign artists, including French impressionists Degas, Cézanne, and Monet, and the postimpressionist van Gogh. Surrealism and expressionism are well represented in works by Klee, Ernst, Braque, Miró, Kandinsky, Mondrian, and Pollock. You'll also find sculpture by Rodin. The collection of graphics, the storage rooms, and the department of restoration can be visited by appointment Tuesday through Friday.

Admission: 8,000 lire ($4.80) adults, free for children 17 and under and those 60 or more.

Open: Tues–Sat 9am–7pm, Sun 9am–1pm. **Bus:** No. 19 or 30.

Palazzo Doria Pamphilj, piazza Grazioli 5. ☎ **6797323.**

Located off via del Corso, the museum offers visitors a look at what it's really like to live in an 18th-century palace. The mansion, like many Roman palaces of the period, is partly leased to tenants (on the upper levels), and there are even shops on the street level, but all this is easily overlooked after you enter the grand apartments of the historical, princely Doria Pamphilj family, which traces its line to before the great 15th-century Genoese admiral Andrea Doria. The regal apartments surround the central court and gallery of the palace.

The 18th-century decor pervades the ballroom, drawing rooms, dining rooms, and even the family chapel. Gilded furniture, crystal chandeliers, Renaissance tapestries, and portraits of family members are everywhere. The Green Room is especially rich in treasures, with a 15th-century Tournai tapestry, paintings by Memling and Filippo Lippi, and a seminude portrait of Andrea Doria by Sebastiano del

Piombo. The Andrea Doria Room is dedicated to the admiral and to the ship of the same name. It contains a glass case with mementos of the great maritime disaster of the 1950s.

Skirting the central court is a picture gallery with a memorable collection of frescoes, paintings, and sculpture. Most important among a number of great works are the portrait of *Innocent X* by Velázquez, called one of the three or four best portraits ever painted; *Salome* by Titian; and works by Rubens and Caravaggio. Notable also are *Bay of Naples* by Pieter Brueghel the Elder and Raphael's portrait of Principessa Giovanna d'Aragona de Colonna (who looks remarkably like Leonardo's *Mona Lisa*). Most of the sculpture came from the Doria country estates; it includes marble busts of Roman emperors, bucolic nymphs, and satyrs. Even without the paintings and sculpture, the gallery would be worth a visit—just for its fresco-covered walls and ceilings.

Admission: Gallery, 10,000 lire ($6); apartments, 5,000 lire ($3).
Open: Tues and Fri–Sun 10am–1pm. **Metro:** Flaminio.

Museo Nazionale del Palazzo di Venezia, via del Plebiscito 118. ☎ **6798865.**

The Museum of the Palazzo Venezia, in the geographic heart of Rome, is the building that served until the end of World War I as the seat of the Austrian embassy. During the Fascist regime (1928–43), it was the seat of the Italian government. The balcony from which Mussolini used to speak to the Italian people was built in the 15th century. It overlooks the 20th-century monument to Victor Emmanuel II, king of Italy, a lush work often compared to a birthday cake and containing the Tomb of the Unknown Soldier. The museum itself, founded in 1916 in a former papal residence, is filled with rooms and halls containing oil paintings, antiques, porcelain, tapestries, ivories, and ceramics. No one particular exhibit stands out—it is the sum total that adds up to a major attraction.

Admission: 8,000 lire ($4.80) adults, free for children under 18.
Open: Tues–Sat 9am–2pm, Sun 9am–1:30pm. **Bus:** 64, 75, 85, or 170.

Galleria Nazionale d'Arte Antica, via delle Quattro Fontane 13. ☎ **4814591.**

The Palazzo Barberini, right off piazza Barberini, is one of the most regal baroque palaces in Rome. It was begun by Carlo Maderno in 1627 and completed in 1633 by Bernini, whose lavishly decorated rococo apartments, called the Gallery of Decorative Art, are on view. The palace houses the Galleria Nazionale.

The bedroom of Princess Cornelia Costanza Barberini and Prince Giulio Cesare Colonna di Sciarra still stands just as it was on their wedding night, and many household objects are displayed in the decorative art gallery. In the chambers, which have frescoes and hand-painted silk linings, you can see porcelain from Japan and Bavaria, canopied beds, and a baby carriage made of wood.

On the first floor of the palace, a near priceless array of paintings includes works that date back to the 13th and 14th centuries, most notably the *Mother and Child* by Simone Martini. Also praiseworthy are paintings by Florentine artists from the 15th century, including art by Filippo Lippi. Some salons display 15th- and 16th-century paintings by such artists as Andrea Solario and Francesco Francia. Il Sodoma has some brilliant pictures here, including *The Rape of the Sabines* and *The Marriage of St. Catherine*. One of the best-known paintings is Raphael's beloved *La Fornarina* of the baker's daughter who was his mistress and who posed for his Madonna portraits. Titian is represented by a portrait of Philip II. Other artists exhibited include Tintoretto, El Greco, and Holbein the Younger. Many visitors come here just to see the incomparable Caravaggios, including *Narcissus*.

Admission: 6,000 lire ($3.60) adults, free for children under 18.

Open: Tues–Sun 9am–7pm. **Metro:** Piazza Barberini.

Museo della Civiltà Romana, piazza Giovanni Agnelli. ☎ **5926135.**

This museum of Roman civilization houses Fiat-sponsored reproductions that recapture life in ancient Rome. Its major exhibition is a plastic representation in miniature of what Rome looked like at the apex of power. You'll see the Circus Maximus, the intact Colosseum, the Baths of Diocletian—and lots more.

Admission: 5,000 lire ($3) adults and children.

Open: Tues–Sat 9am–1:30pm (plus Tues and Thurs 4–7pm), Sun 9am–1pm. **Metro:** Linea B to EUR Fermi.

Museo di Arte Ebraico della Comunità Israelitica de Roma, lungotevere Cenci (Tempio). ☎ **6875051.**

This museum of Hebraic art houses a permanent exhibition of the Roman Jewish community. It contains Jewish ritual objects and scrolls from the 17th to the 19th century as well as copies of tombstones, paintings, prints, and documents that illustrate 2,000 years of Jewish history in Rome. The collection of silver ceremonial objects is important, as is a selection of ancient ceremonial textiles. Documents of Nazi persecution are of exceptional interest.

Admission: 5,000 lire ($3) adults and children.

Open: July–Aug, Mon–Thurs 9:30am–6pm, Fri 9:30am–2pm, Sun 9:30am–noon. Sept–Oct, Mon–Fri 9:30am–2pm, Sun 9:30am–12:30pm. **Bus:** 56 or 60.

Parks & Gardens

The **Villa Borghese** in the heart of Rome covers a landmass of 3 1/2 miles in circumference. One of the most elegant parks in Europe, it was created by Cardinal Scipione Borghese in the 1600s. Umberto I, king of Italy, acquired it in 1902 and presented it to the city of Rome, renaming it Villa Umberto I. However, Romans preferred their old name, which has stuck. A park of landscaped vistas and wide-open "green lungs," the greenbelt is crisscrossed by roads. But you can escape from the traffic and seek a shaded area—usually pine or oak—to enjoy a picnic. In the northeast of the park is a small zoo, and the park is also host to the Galleria Borghese, one of the finest museums of Rome, with many masterpieces by Renaissance and baroque artists.

The **Villa Doria Pamphilj,** behind the Vatican, acquired from Princess Orietta Doria Pamphilj, was opened to the public in 1971. (The princess is descended from the world-famous naval commander Andrea Doria.) The park is about half as large as Central Park in New York, but it's more than twice the size of the Villa Borghese. Villa Pamphilj fills a sad emptiness in the Roman capital by providing some much-needed green space. At one time the park belonged to Pope Innocent X, who planted it with exotic shrubbery, trees, and flowers. Take bus no. 23, 30, 32, 49, 51, or 64.

3 Cool for Kids

Rome has lots of other amusements for children when they tire of ancient monuments, although they're usually fond of wandering around the **Colosseum** and the **Roman Forum** (see "The Top Attractions," above). Many children also enjoy the climb to the top of St. Peter's. The **Fun Fair** (Luna Park), along via delle Tre Fontane (☎ **5925933**), at E.U.R., is one of the largest in Europe. It's known for its "big wheel" at the entrance, and there are merry-go-rounds, miniature railways, and shooting galleries, among other attractions. Admission is free, but you pay for each ride. It is closed Tuesday.

Teatro delle Marionette degli Accettella, performing at the Teatro Mongiovino, via Giovanni Genocchi 16 (☎ **5139405**), has performances for children on Saturday and Sunday (except in August) at 4:30pm. Both adults and children pay 10,000 lire ($6) for tickets.

The **Puppet Theater** on Pincio Square (☎ **8601733**) in the Villa Borghese gardens has performances nearly every day. While there, you might also like to take your children through the park (it's closed to traffic). Children enjoy the fountain displays and the lake, and there are many wide spaces in which they can play. Boats can be hired at the **Giardino del Lago.** A trip to the zoo in Rome is also possible, as it lies in the **Villa Borghese,** at viale del Giardino Zoologico 10 (☎ **3216564**). It's open Monday through Friday from 8:30am to 4pm and Saturday and Sunday from 8:30am to 5pm; admission is 10,000 lire ($6) for adults, free for children. Take bus no. 19 or 30.

At 4pm every day, you can take your child to the **Quirinale Palace,** piazza del Quirinale, the residence of the president of Italy. There's a military band and a parade at that time, as the guards change shifts.

4 Special-Interest Sightseeing

Keats-Shelley Memorial, piazza di Spagna 26. ☎ **6784235.**

At the foot of the Spanish Steps is this 18th-century house where Keats died of consumption on February 23, 1821. "It is like living in a violin," wrote the Italian author Alberto Savinio. The apartment where Keats spent his last months, carefully tended by his close friend Joseph Severn, shelters a museum, with a strange death mask of Keats as well as the "deadly sweat" drawing by Severn and many other mementos of Keats, Shelley, and Byron. For those interested in the full story of the involvement of Keats and Shelley in Italy, a good little book compiled by Neville Rogers is sold on the premises.

Admission: 5,000 lire ($3) adults and children.

Open: June–Sept, Mon–Fri 9am–1pm and 3–6pm; Oct–May, Mon–Fri 9am–1pm and 2:30–5:30pm. **Metro:** Piazza di Spagna.

Protestant Cemetery, via Caio Cestio 6. ☎ **5741900.**

Near St. Paul's station, in the midst of a setting of cypress trees, lies the old cemetery where John Keats was buried. In a grave nearby, Joseph Severn, his "death-bed" companion, was interred beside him six decades later. Dejected, and feeling his reputation as a poet diminished by the rising vehemence of his critics, Keats asked that the following epitaph be written on his tombstone: "Here lies one whose name was writ in water." A great romantic poet Keats certainly was, but a prophet, thankfully not.

Shelley, author of *Prometheus Unbound,* drowned off the Italian Riviera in 1822, before his 30th birthday. His ashes rest alongside those of Edward John Trelawny, fellow romantic and man of the sea. Trelawny maintained that Shelley may have been murdered, his boat overrun by petty pirates bent on robbery. While you're here, you may want to drop in at the neighboring **Pyramid of Caius Cestius** (see "Cemeteries" under "More Attractions," above).

Admission: Free, but a 1,000 lire (60¢) offering is customary, more if you feel generous.

Open: Mar–Sept, Thurs–Tues 8–11:30am and 3:30–5:30pm; Oct–Feb, Thurs–Tues 8–11:30am and 2:30–4:30pm. **Metro:** St. Paul's. **Bus:** 13, 27, or 30.

For the Architecture Enthusiast

At the height of Mussolini's power, he launched a complex of modern buildings—many of them in cold marble—to dazzle Europe with a scheduled world's fair. But Il Duce got strung up, and **EUR**—the area in question—got hamstrung. The new Italian government that followed inherited the uncompleted project and decided to turn it into a center of government and administration. It has also developed into a residential section of fairly deluxe apartment houses. Most of the cold granite edifices fail to escape the curse of "Il Duce moderno," but the small "city of tomorrow" is softened considerably by a man-made lagoon, which you can row across in rented boats.

Italy's great modern architect, Milan-born Pier Luigi Nervi, designed the **Palazzo dello Sport** on the hill. One of the country's most impressive modern buildings, it was the chief site of the 1960 Olympics. Another important structure is the **Palazzo dei Congressi** in the center, an exhibition hall with changing displays of industrial shows that is well worth a stroll. You'll also spot architecture reminiscent of Frank Lloyd Wright, and a building that evokes the design of the United Nations in New York.

For still another look at Mussolini's architectural achievements, head across the river from EUR to the **Foro Italico.** Shades of 1932! This complex of sports stadiums blatantly honors Il Duce. At the entrance to the forum, an obelisk bears the name MVSSOLINI so firmly engraved that to destroy the lettering would be to do away with the monument. It stands defiantly. Visitors on a sunny day walk across the mosaic courtyard with DVCE imbedded repeatedly in the pavement. The big attraction of this freakish site is the "Stadium of Marbles," encircled with 50 marble nude athletes—draped discreetly so as not to offend the eyes of the Golden Madonna on the hill beyond. Take bus no. 1 from piazza della Repubblica.

5 Organized Tours

Because of the sheer volume of artistic riches in Rome, some visitors prefer to begin their stay with an organized tour. While few things can really be covered in any depth on these "overview tours," they are sometimes useful for getting the feel and geography of a complicated city. One of the leading tour operators (among the zillions of possibilities) is **American Express,** piazza di Spagna 38 (☎ **67641**).

One of the most popular tours is a four-hour orientation tour of Rome, which costs 45,000 lire ($27) per person. Times of departure depend on the time of the year. For 50,000 lire ($30), you can go on a Monumental and Religious Rome tour. One four-hour tour takes visitors to the Sistine Chapel and Vatican museums at the cost of 55,000 lire ($33). The major excursion outside Rome is to Tivoli, with its Villa d'Este and Villa Adriana, costing 65,000 lire ($39). You can get farther afield, on a one-day tour to Pompeii, Naples, and Sorrento, at a cost of 140,000 lire ($84) per person. To do this, you'll need a lot of stamina, as the tour departs from Rome at 7am and returns after 11pm to your hotel. Less taxing might be the abbreviated version, visiting only Naples and Pompeii. Priced at 120,000 lire ($72) per person, it departs from Rome at 7am and returns around 8:30 or 9pm the same day.

6 Sports & Recreation

Sports

SOCCER Soccer (*calcio*) is one of the three or four all-consuming passions of thousands of Romans. Rome boasts two intensely competitive teams, Lazio and Roma, which tend to play either against each other or against visiting teams from other parts of the world every Sunday afternoon. Matches are held at the **Stadio Olimpico,** Foro Italico dei Gladiatori (☎ **36851**), originally built by Mussolini as a nationalistic (Fascist) statement. Thousands of tickets are sold during the two or three hours before each game. The players usually take a break during June, July, and August, beginning the season with something approaching pandemonium in September.

Recreation

BIKING The traffic is murderous, and the pollution might make your head spin, but there are quiet times (early morning and Sunday) when a spin beside the Tiber or through the Borghese gardens might prove highly appealing. It's highly advisable to wear a helmet when bicycling, even if the local Vespa riders don't.

Bike-rental concession stands are found at the following Metro stops: piazza del Popolo, largo San Silvestro, largo Argentina, piazza di Spagna, and viale della Pineto in the Villa Borghese.

BOWLING   One of the city's largest bowling complexes, whose hordes of participants provide a spectacle almost more interesting than the game itself, lies at **Bowling Roma,** viale Regina Margherita 181 (☎ **8551184**), off via Nomentana.

GOLF   Rome boasts several golf courses, which will usually welcome members of other golf clubs. Each, of course, will be under the greatest pressure on Saturday and Sunday, so as a nonmember it would be best to schedule your arrival for a weekday.

One of the capital's best courses, with a clubhouse set within a villa built during the 1600s and fairways designed by Robert Trent Jones, is the **Country Club Castelgandolfo,** via Santo Spirito 13, Castelgandolfo (☎ **9313084**). An older, more entrenched, and probably more prestigious course is the **Circolo del Golf Roma,** via Acqua Santa 3 (☎ **7803407**), about $8^1/2$ miles from the center of Rome. Near the Appian Way, about 12 miles from the center of town, lies the Olgiata Golf Club, largo Olgiata 15, off via Cassia (☎ **3789141**).

HORSEBACK RIDING   The most convenient of Rome's several riding clubs is the **Associazione Sportiva Villa Borghese,** via del Galoppatoio 23 (☎ **3606797**). Other stables are in the **Circolo Ippico Olgiata,** largo Olgiata 15 (☎ **3788792**), near Cassia, and the **Società Ippica Romana,** via dei Monti della Farnesina 30 (☎ **3966214**). Tack and equipment are English style.

JOGGING   Not only does jogging provide a moving view of the city's monuments, but it might improve your general health as well. Beware of the city's heat, however, and be alert to speeding traffic. Several possible itineraries include the park of the **Villa Borghese,** where the series of roads and pathways, some of them beside statuary, provide a verdant oasis within the city's congestion. (Keep your wits about you and exercise caution here though.) The best places to enter the park are at piazza del Popolo or at the top of via Veneto. The **Cavalieri Hilton,** via Cadlolo 101, Monte Mario (☎ **35091**), offers a jogging path (measuring a third of a mile) through the trees and flowering shrubs of its landscaping. The grounds that surround the Villa Pamphilij contain three running tracks, although they might either be locked or in use by local sports teams during your exercise period. Certain roads beside the Tiber might provide an almost uninterrupted stretch for runners. A final possibility, not recommended for jogging after dark, is the rounded premises of the **Circus Maximus.** Built by the ancient Romans, and now reduced to dust and grandiose rubble, it contains a footpath inside its ruined walls, and an outward perimeter (ringed with roaring traffic) that measures about a half mile.

SWIMMING   One of the busiest all-year pools is the **Roman Sport Center,** via del Galoppatoio 33 (☎ **3201667**), which lies adjacent to the parking lot on the grounds of the Villa Borghese. Open to the public, it contains two large swimming pools, squash courts, a gym, and saunas. In another part of town, the **Piscina della Rose,** viale America (☎ **5926717**), is an Olympic-size pool open to the public (and crowded with teenagers and *bambini*) between June and September. More sedate, set in lushly landscaped gardens, and open to nonresidents, is the pool in the resort-inspired premises of the **Cavalieri Hilton,** via Cadlolo 101 (☎ **35091**).

TENNIS   The best tennis courts are at private clubs many of which are within a handful of suburbs. Players are highly conscious of proper tennis attire, so be prepared to don your most sparkling whites and your best manners. One of the city's best-known clubs is the **Tennis Club Parioli,** largo Uberto de Morpurgo 2, via Salaria (☎ **86200882**). Hours are daily from 8am to noon only.

7

Strolling Around Rome

IT WOULD BE IDEAL IF YOU COULD TAKE EACH OF THE WALKING TOURS, BUT
visitors with very limited time might want to concentrate only on
ancient Rome, in which case you should take Walking Tour 1 of
Imperial Rome and Walking Tour 2 of the Roman Forum & Palatine Hill.

Yet it would be a shame to miss the treasures you'll see by taking
Walking Tour 3 and Walking Tour 4. These two tours cut through
the monumental heart of the city, visiting such landmarks as the
piazza del Popolo, the Spanish Steps, and the Trevi Fountain, where
you can toss a coin into the waters to guarantee your return visit to
Rome, at least according to tradition.

Visitors with an extra day or so may also want to take Walking
Tour 5 and Walking Tour 6, which explore the district of Trastevere
and the part of Rome that was built along the Tiber.

Except for the Vatican, St. Peter's, and two or three major museums, many visitors find that strolling along the streets of Rome is far
more interesting and enlightening than visiting the interiors of many
attractions.

Walking Tour 1
Imperial Rome

Start   Colosseum.
Finish   Circus Maximus.
Time   2 hours.
Best Time   Any sunny day.
Worst Time   Rush hours—morning or early evening.

Even in the days of the republic, the population explosion was a
problem. Julius Caesar saw the overcrowding and began to expand,
starting what were known as the Imperial Forums in the days of the
empire. After the collapse of Rome and during the Dark Ages, the
Forums were lost to history, buried beneath layers of debris. Mussolini
set out to restore the grandeur of Rome by reminding his compatri-
ots of their glorious past.

Take the Metro to the Colosseo stop for the:

1. **Colosseum,** a good starting point, as you get your bearings
   with the traffic at piazza del Colosseo. The Colosseum is
   the greatest monument of ancient Rome, and visitors are
   invariably impressed with its size and majesty. Either visit it
   now or return for a longer visit later.

   With your back to the Colosseum, begin your walk
   up the:

2. **via dei Fori Imperiali,** keeping to the right side of the
   street. It was Mussolini who ordered Roman workers to cut
   through the years of debris and junky buildings to carve out
   this boulevard, which links the Colosseum to piazza
   Venezia. Excavations began at once, and much was

Walking Tour—Imperial Rome

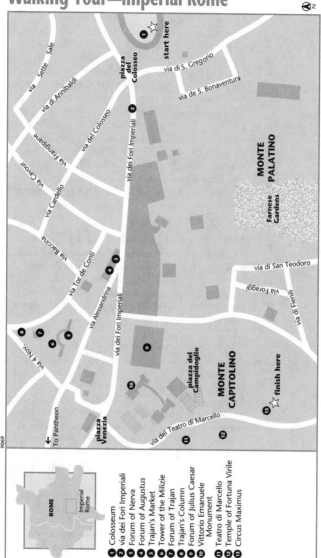

MONTE PALATINO

Farnese Gardens

via di S. Gregorio

via de S. Bonaventura

via di San Teodoro

MONTE CAPITOLINO

piazza del Campidoglio

piazza Venezia

start here

finish here

↓ To Pantheon

via di Annibaldi

via Sette Sale

via del Colosseo

via Frangipane

via Cavour

via Cardello

via Baccina

via Tor de Conti

via Alessandrina

via dei Fori Imperiali

via 4 Nov.

via del Teatro di Marcello

via Foraggi

via di Fienili

piazza del Colosseo

ROME

Imperial Rome

1 Colosseum
2 via dei Fori Imperiali
3 Forum of Nerva
4 Forum of Augustus
5 Trajan's Market
6 Tower of the Milizie
7 Forum of Trajan
8 Trajan's Column
9 Forum of Julius Caesar
10 Vittorio Emanuele Monument
11 Teatro di Marcello
12 Temple of Fortuna Virile
13 Circus Maximus

revealed. Today the boulevard is one of the most intriguing
walks in Rome. All the Imperial Forums (Fori) can be seen
from street level.

The ruins across the street are what's left of the
colonnade that once surrounded the Temple of Venus and
Roma. Next to it, you'll see the back wall of the Basilica of

Constantine. Shortly, you'll come to a large outdoor restaurant, where via Cavour joins the boulevard you're on.

Just beyond the small park across via Cavour are the remains of the:

3. Forum of Nerva, built by the emperor whose two-year reign (A.D. 96–98) followed that of the paranoid Domitian. The Forum of Nerva is best observed from the railing that skirts it on via dei Fori Imperiali. You'll be struck by just how much the ground level has risen in 19 centuries. The only really recognizable remnant is a wall of the Temple of Minerva with two fine Corinthian columns. This forum was once flanked by that of Vespasian, which is now completely gone. It's possible to enter the Forum of Nerva from the other side, but you can see it just as well from the railing.

Refueling Stop

Bar Martini, piazza del Colosseo 3, stands on a hill behind the landmark Colosseum. Have your coffee or cool drink outside at one of the tables and absorb one of the world's greatest architectural views: that of the Colosseum itself. The bar even serves a low-cost *menu turistico* for 16,000 lire ($9.60) if you're in the district for lunch. Service is daily from 8:30am to midnight.

The next forum you approach is the:

4. Forum of Augustus, built before the birth of Christ to commemorate the emperor's victory over the assassins Cassius and Brutus in the Battle of Philippi (42 B.C.). Fittingly, the temple that once dominated this forum—and whose remains can still be seen—was that of Mars Ultor, or Mars the Avenger. In the temple once stood a mammoth statue of Augustus, which has unfortunately completely vanished. Like the Forum of Nerva, you can enter the Forum of Augustus from the other side (cut across the wee footbridge).

Continuing along the railing, you'll see the vast semicircle of:

5. Trajan's Market, via Quattro Novembre 95 (☎ **67102070**), whose teeming arcades stocked with merchandise from the far corners of the Roman world long-ago collapsed, leaving only a few ubiquitous cats to watch after things. The shops once covered a multitude of levels, and you can still wander around many of them. In front of the perfectly proportioned semicircular facade— designed by Apollodorus of Damascus at the beginning of the 2nd century—are the remains of a great library, and fragments of delicately colored marble floors still shine in the sunlight between stretches of rubble and tall grass. While the view from the railing is of interest, Trajan's

Market is worth the descent below street level. To get there, follow the service road you're on until you reach the monumental Trajan's Column on your left, where you turn right and go up the steep flight of stairs that leads to via Nazionale. At the top of the stairs, about half a block farther on the right, you'll see the entrance to the market.

From April to September, it is open Tuesday through Saturday from 9am to 1:30pm, and also on Tuesday in the afternoon from 4 to 7pm; Sunday hours are 9am to 1pm. From October to March, it operates Tuesday through Saturday from 9am to 1:30pm and on Sunday from 9am to 1pm. Admission is 3,750 lire ($2.30) for adults and half price for children.

Before you head down through the labyrinthine passageways, you might like to climb the:

6. **Tower of the Millizie,** a 12th-century structure that was part of the medieval headquarters of the Knights of Rhodes. The view from the top (if it's open) is well worth the climb. From the tower, you can wander through the ruins of the market and admire the sophistication of the layout and the sad beauty of the bits of decoration that still remain. When you've examined the brick and travertine corridors, head out in front of the semicircle to the site of the former library; from here, scan the retaining wall that supports the modern road and look for the entrance to the tunnel that leads to the:

7. **Forum of Trajan (Foro Traiano),** entered on via Quattro Novembre near the steps of via Magnanapoli. Once through the tunnel, you'll emerge in the most beautiful of the Imperial Forums, designed by the same man who laid out the adjoining market. There are many statue fragments and pedestals that bear still-legible inscriptions, but more interesting is the great Basilica Ulpia, whose gray marble columns rise roofless into the sky. You wouldn't know it to judge from what's left, but the Forum of Trajan was once regarded as one of the architectural wonders of the world. Constructed between 107 and 113 A.D., it was designed by the Greek architect Apollodorus of Damascus.

Beyond the Basilica Ulpia is:

8. **Trajan's Column,** already mentioned, which is a hearty survivor of ancient times, with intricate bas-relief sculpture depicting Trajan's victorious campaign (although from your vantage point you'll only be able to see the earliest stages). The emperor's ashes were kept in a golden urn at the base of the column. If you're fortunate, someone on duty at the stairs next to the column will let you out there. Otherwise, you'll have to walk back the way you came.

The next stop is the:

9. **Forum of Julius Caesar,** the first of the Imperial Forums. It lies on the opposite side of via dei Fori Imperiali, the last

set of sunken ruins before the Victor Emmanuel Monument. While it's possible to go right down into the ruins, you can see everything just as well from the railing. This was the site of the Roman stock exchange, as well as of the Temple of Venus, a few of whose restored columns stand cinematically in the middle of the excavations.

From here, retrace your last steps until you're in front of the white Brescian marble monument around the corner on piazza Venezia, where the:

10. **Vittorio Emanuele Monument** dominates the piazza. The most flamboyant landmark in Italy, it was constructed in the late 1800s to honor the first king of Italy. It has been compared to everything from a frosty birthday cake to a Victorian typewriter. An eternal flame burns at the Tomb of the Unknown Soldier. The interior of the monument has been closed to the public for many years.

Keep close to the monument and walk to your left, in the opposite direction from via dei Fori Imperiali. You might like to pause at the fountain that flanks one of the monument's great white walls and splash some icy water on your face. There is another fountain just like this one on the other side of the monument, and they're both favorite spots for tired visitors. Stay on the same side of the street, and just keep walking around the monument. You'll be on via del Teatro Marcello, which takes you past the twin lions that guard the sloping stairs and on along the base of Capitoline Hill.

Keep walking along this boulevard until you come to the:

11. **Teatro di Marcello**, on your right. You'll recognize the two rows of gaping arches, which are said to be the models for the Colosseum. Julius Caesar is the man credited with starting the construction of this theater, but it was finished many years after his death (in 11 B.C.) by Augustus, who dedicated it to his favorite nephew, Marcellus. You can stroll around the 2,000-year-old arcade, a small corner of which has been restored to what presumably was the original condition. Here, as everywhere, there are numerous cats stalking around the broken marble.

The bowl of the theater and the stage were adapted many centuries ago as the foundation for the Renaissance palace of the Orsini family. Walk around the theater to the right. The other ruins belong to old temples. Soon you'll walk up a ramp to the street, and to the right is the Porticus of Octavia, dating from the 2nd century B.C. Note how later cultures used part of the Roman structure without destroying its original character. There's another good example of this on the other side of the theater. There you'll see a church with a wall, which completely incorporates part of an ancient colonnade.

Returning to via del Teatro Marcello, keep walking away from piazza Venezia for two more long blocks, until you come to piazza Bocca della Verità. The first item to notice in this piazza is the rectangular:

12. **Temple of Fortune Virile.** You'll see it on the right, a little off the road. Built a century before the birth of Christ, it's still in relatively good condition. Behind it is another temple, dedicated to Vesta. Like the one in the forum, it is round, symbolic of the prehistoric huts where continuity of the hearthfire was a matter of survival.

About a block to the south, you'll pass the facade of the church of Santa Maria in Cosmedin, set on the piazza Bocca della Verità. Even more noteworthy, a short walk to the east, is the:

13. **Circus Maximus,** whose elongated oval proportions and ruined tiers of benches might remind visitors of the setting for *Ben Hur.* Today a formless and dusty ruin, the victim of countless raids upon its stonework by medieval and Renaissance builders, the remains of the once-great arena lie directly behind the church. At one time 250,000 Romans could assemble on the marble seats, while the emperor observed the games from his box high on the Palatine Hill.

The circus lies in a valley formed by the Palatine Hill on the left and the Aventine Hill on the right. Next to the Colosseum, it was the most impressive structure in ancient Rome, located certainly in one of the most exclusive neighborhoods. Emperors lived on the Palatine, while the great palaces of patricians sprawled across the Aventine, which is still a rather nice neighborhood. For centuries, the pomp and ceremony of imperial chariot races filled this valley with the cheers of thousands.

When the dark days of the 5th and 6th centuries fell on the city, the Circus Maximus seemed a symbol of the complete ruin of Rome. The last games were held in 549 on the orders of Totilla the Goth, who had seized Rome in 546 and established himself as emperor. He lived in the still-glittering ruins on the Palatine and apparently thought that the chariot races in the Circus Maximus would lend credence to his charade of empire. It must have been a pretty miserable show, since the decimated population numbered something like 500 when Totilla captured the city. The Romans of these times were caught between Belisarius, the imperial general from Constantinople, and Totilla the Goth, both of whom fought bloody battles for control of Rome. After the travesty of 549, the Circus Maximus was never used again, and the demand for building materials reduced it, like so much of Rome, to a great dusty field.

To return to other parts of town, head for the bus stop adjacent to Santa Maria in Cosmedin Church, or walk the

length of the Circus Maximus to its far end and pick up the
Metro to Stazione Termini.

Walking Tour 2
The Roman Forum & the Palatine Hill

Start   Via Sacra.
Finish   Orti Farnesiani.
Time   2½ hours.
Best Time   Any sunny day.
Worst Time   When the place is overrun with tour groups.

THE ROMAN FORUM   The entrance to the Roman Forum is
off via dei Fori Imperiali, right at the intersection with via Cavour.
Take the Metro to the Colosseo stop.

As you walk down the ramp from the entrance, you'll be heading
for the via Sacra, the ancient Roman road that ran through the Forum, connecting the Capitoline Hill to your right, with the Arch of
Titus (1st c. A.D.), way off to your left. During the Middle Ages when
this was the *campo vaccino* and all these stones were underground,
there was a dual column of elm trees connecting the Arch of Titus,
off to your left, with the Arch of Septimius Severus (A.D. 200) to your
right. Arriving at the via Sacra, turn right. The random columns on
the right as you head toward the Arch of Septimius Severus belong
to the:

1. Basilica Emilia, formerly the site of great meeting halls and
   shops all maintained for centuries by the noble Roman
   family who gave it its name. At the corner nearest the
   Forum entrance are some traces of melted bronze
   decoration that fused to the marble floor during a great fire
   set by invading Goths in A.D. 400.
       The next important building is the:
2. Curia, or Senate house—it's the large brick building on the
   right that still has its roof. Romans had been meeting on
   this site for centuries before the first structure was erected,
   and that was still centuries before Christ. The present
   building is the fifth (if one counts all the reconstructions
   and substantial rehabilitations) to stand on the site. Legend
   has it that the original building was constructed by an
   ancient king, with the curious name of Tullus Hostilius.
   The tradition he began was a noble one indeed, and our
   present legislative system owes much to the Romans who
   met in this hall. Unfortunately the high ideals and inviolate
   morals that characterized the early republican senators gave
   way to the bootlicking of imperial times, when the Senate
   became little more than a rubber stamp. Caligula, who was
   only the third emperor, had his horse appointed to the
   Senate (it was a life appointment), which pretty much sums
   up where the Senate was by the middle of the 1st century A.D.

Walking Tour
Roman Forum & Palatine Hill

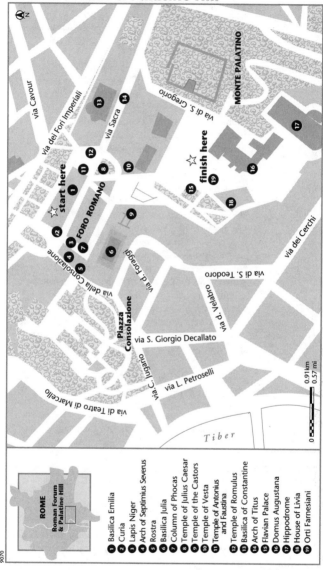

Z

MONTE PALATINO

via Cavour

via dei Fori Imperiali

via Sacra

via di S. Gregorio

start here ☆

FORO ROMANO

finish here

☆

via della Consolazione

via d. Foraggi

Piazza Consolazione

via S. Giorgio Decallato

via C. Jugario

via L. Petroselli

via di Teatro di Marcello

via d. Velabro

via di S. Teodoro

via di Cerchi

Tiber

0.91 km
0.57 mi

0

ROME
Roman Forum & Palatine Hill

❶ Basilica Emilia
❷ Curia
❸ Lapis Niger
❹ Arch of Septimius Severus
❺ Rostra
❻ Basilica Julia
❼ Column of Phocas
❽ Temple of Julius Caesar
❾ Temple of the Castors
❿ Temple of Vesta
⓫ Temple of Antonius and Faustina
⓬ Temple of Romulus
⓭ Basilica of Constantine
⓮ Arch of Titus
⓯ Flavian Palace
⓰ Domus Augustana
⓱ Hippodrome
⓲ House of Livia
⓳ Orti Farnesiani

9070

The building was a church until 1937, when the Fascist government tore out the baroque interior and revealed what we see today. The original floor of Egyptian marble and the tiers that held the seats of the senators have miraculously survived. In addition, at the far end of the great chamber we can see the stone on which rested the fabled golden statue of Victory. Originally installed by Augustus, it was finally disposed of in the late 4th century by a fiercely divided Senate, whose Christian members convinced the emperor that it was improper to have a pagan statue in such a revered place.

Outside, head down the Curia stairs to the:

3. **Lapie Niger,** the remains of black marble blocks that reputedly mark the tomb of Romulus. They bask today under a corrugated roof. Go downstairs for a look at the excavated tomb. There's a stone here with the oldest Latin inscription in existence, which unfortunately is nearly unintelligible. All that can be safely assumed is that it genuinely dates from the Rome of the kings. Remember, they disappeared in a revolution in 509 B.C.

Across from the Curia, the:

4. **Arch of Septimius Severus,** was dedicated at the dawn of the troubled 3rd century to the last decent emperor who was to govern Rome for some time. The friezes on the arch depict victories over Arabs and Parthians by the cold but upright Severus and his two dissolute sons, Geta and Caracalla. Severus died on a campaign to subdue the unruly natives of Scotland at the end of the first decade of the 3rd century. Rome unhappily fell into the hands of young Caracalla, chiefly remembered today for his baths.

Walk around to the back of the Severus arch, face it, and look to your right. There amid the rubble can be discerned a semicircular stair that led to the famous:

5. **Rostra,** the podium from which dictators and caesars addressed the throngs of the Forum below. One can just imagine the emperor, shining in his white toga, surrounded by imperial guards and distinguished senators, gesticulating grandly like one of the statues on a Roman roofline. Later emperors didn't have much cause to use the Rostra; they made their policies known through edict and assassination instead.

Now, facing the colonnade of the Temple of Saturn, once the public treasury, and going to the left, you'll come to the ruins of the:

6. **Basilica Julia,** again little more than a foundation. The basilica gets its name from Julius Caesar, who dedicated the first structure in 46 B.C. Like many buildings in the Forum, the basilica was burned and rebuilt several times, and the last structure dates from those shaky days after the Gothic invasion of 410. Throughout its history, it was used for the hearing of civil court cases, which were conducted in the pandemonium of the crowded Forum, open to anyone who happened to pass by. The building was also reputed to be particularly hot in the summer, and it was under these sweaty and unpromising circumstances that Roman justice, the standard of the world for a millennium, was meted out.

Walking back down the ruined stairs of the Basilica Julia and into the broad area whose far side is bounded by the Curia, you'll see the:

7. **Column of Phocas.** Probably lifted from an early structure in the near vicinity, this was the last monument to be erected in the Roman Forum, and it commemorates the Byzantine emperor Phocas's generous donation of the Pantheon to the pope of Rome, who almost immediately transformed it into a church.

Now make your way down the middle of the Forum nearly back to the ramp from which you entered. The pile of brick with the semicircular indentation that stands in the middle of things was the:

8. **Temple of Julius Caesar,** erected some time after the dictator was deified. Judging from the reconstruction, it was quite an elegant building. As you stand facing the ruins, with the entrance to the Forum on your left, you'll see on your right three columns belonging originally to the:

9. **Temple of the Castors.** This temple perpetuated the legend of Castor and Pollux, who appeared out of thin air in the Roman Forum and were observed watering their horses at the fountain of Juturna (still visible today), just as a major battle against the Etruscans turned in favor of Rome. Castor and Pollux, the heavenly twins—and the symbol of the astrological sign Gemini—seem a favorite of Rome.

The next major monument is the circular:

10. **Temple of Vesta,** wherein dwelt the sacred flame of Rome, and the Atrium of the Vestal Virgins. A vestal virgin was usually a girl of good family who signed a contract for 30 years. During that time, she lived in the ruin we're standing in right now. Of course, back then it was an unimaginably rich marble building with two floors. There were only six vestal virgins during the imperial period, and even though they had the option of going back out into the world at the end of their 30 years, few did. The cult of Vesta came to an end in 394, when a Christian Rome secularized all its pagan temples. A man standing on this site before then would have been put to death immediately.

Stand in the atrium with your back to the Palatine and look beyond those fragmented statues of former vestals to the:

11. **Temple of Antonius and Faustina.** It's the building with the freestanding colonnade just to the right of the ramp where you first entered the Forum. Actually, just the colonnade dates from imperial times; the building behind is a much later church dedicated to San Lorenzo.

After you inspect the beautifully proportioned Antoninus and Faustina temple, head up via Sacra away from the entrance ramp toward the Arch of Titus. Pretty soon, on your left, you'll see the twin bronze doors of the:

12. **Temple of Romulus.** It's the doors themselves that are really of note here—they're the original Roman doors, and swing on the same massive hinges they were originally mounted on in A.D. 306. In this case, the temple is not dedicated to the legendary cofounder of Rome, but to the son of its builder, the emperor Maxentius, who gave Romulus his name in a fit of antiquarian patriotism. Unfortunately for both father and son; they competed with a general who deprived them of their empire and lives. That man was Constantine, who, while camped outside Rome during preparations for one of his battles against Maxentius, saw the sign of the Cross in the heavens with the insignia IN HOC SIGNO VINCES (In This Sign Shall You Conquer). Raising the standard of Christianity above his legions, he defeated the (pagan) emperor Maxentius and later became the first Christian emperor.

   At the time of Constantine's victory (A.D. 306), the great:

13. **Basilica of Constantine** (marked by those three gaping arches up ahead on your left) was only half finished, having been started by the unfortunate Maxentius. However, Constantine finished the job and affixed his name to this, the largest and most impressive building in the Forum. To my taste, the more delicate, Greek-influenced temples are more attractive, but you have to admire the scale and the engineering skill that erected this monument. The fact that portions of the original coffered ceiling are still intact is amazing. The basilica once held a statue of Constantine so large that his little toe was as wide as an average man's waist. You can see a few fragments from this colossal thing—the remnants were found in 1490—in the courtyard of the Conservatory Museum on the Capitoline Hill. As far as Roman emperors went, Christian or otherwise, ego knew no bounds.

   From Constantine's basilica, follow the Roman paving stones of via Sacra to the:

14. **Arch of Titus,** clearly visible on a low hill just ahead. Titus was the emperor who sacked the great Jewish temple in Jerusalem, and the bas-relief sculpture inside the arch shows the booty of the Jews being carried in triumph through the streets of Rome, while Titus is crowned by Victory, who comes down from heaven for the occasion. You'll notice in particular the candelabrum, for centuries one of the most famous pieces of the treasure of Rome. In all probability, the treasure now lies at the bottom of the Busento River in the secret tomb of Alaric the Goth.

   THE PALATINE HILL   When you've gathered your strength in the shimmering hot sun, head up the Clivus

Palatinus, the road to the palaces of the Palatine Hill. With your back to the Arch of Titus, it's the road going up the hill to the left.

It was on the Palatine Hill that Rome first became a city. Legend tells us the date was 753 B.C. The new city originally consisted of nothing more than the Palatine, which was soon enclosed by a surprisingly complex wall, remains of which can still be seen on the Circus Maximus side of the hill. As time went on and Rome grew in power and wealth, the boundaries were extended and later enclosed by the Servian Wall. When the last of the ancient kings was overthrown (509 B.C.), Rome had already extended onto several of the adjoining hills and valleys. As republican times progressed, the Palatine became a fashionable residential district. So it remained until Tiberius—who, like his predecessor, Augustus, was a bit too modest to really call himself "emperor" out loud— began the first of the monumental palaces that were to cover the entire hill.

It's difficult today to make sense out of the Palatine. The first-time viewer might be forgiven for suspecting it to be an entirely artificial structure built on brick arches. Those arches, which are visible on practically every flank of the hill, are actually supports that once held imperial structures. Having run out of building sites, the emperors, in their fever, simply enlarged the hill by building new sides on it. The road goes only a short way, through a small sort of valley filled with lush, untrimmed greenery. After about five minutes (for slow walkers), you'll see the ruins of a monumental stairway just to the right of the road. The Clivus Palatinus turns sharply to the left here, skirting the monastery of San Bonaventura, but we'll detour to the right and take a look at the remains of the:

15. Flavian Palace. As you walk off the road and into the ruins, you'll be able to discern that there were once three rooms here, but it's really impossible for anyone but an archeologist to comprehend quite how splendid these rooms were. The entire Flavian Palace was decorated in the most lavish of colored marbles, sometimes inlaid with precious silver. The roofs were, in places, even covered with gold. Much of the decoration survived as late as the 18th century, when the greedy duke of Parma removed most of what was left. The room closest to the Clivus Palatinus was called the Lararium and held statues of the divinities that protected the imperial family. The middle room was the grandest of the three. It was the imperial throne room, where sat the ruler of the world, the emperor of Rome. The far room was a basilica, used for court functions, such as audiences with the emperor. This part of the palace was used entirely for ceremonial functions. Adjoining these

three rooms are the remains of a spectacularly luxurious peristyle. You'll recognize it by the hexagonal remains of a fountain in the middle. Try, if you can, to imagine this fountain surrounded by marble arcades, planted with mazes, and equipped with mica-covered walls. On the opposite side of the peristyle from the throne rooms are several other great reception and entertainment rooms. The banquet hall was here, and beyond it, looking over the Circus Maximus, are a few ruins of former libraries. Although practically nothing remains except the foundations, every now and again you'll catch sight of a fragment of colored marble floor, in a subtle pattern.

The imperial family lived in the:

16. **Domus Augustana,** the remains of which lie toward the Circus Maximus, and slightly to the left of the Flavian Palace. The new building that stands here—it looks old to us, but in Rome it qualifies as a new building—is a museum (usually closed). It stands in the absolute center of the Domus Augustana. In the field adjacent to the Stadium well into the present century stood the Villa Mills, a gingerbread Gothic villa of the 19th century. It was quite a famous place. Owned by a rich Englishman who came to Rome from the West Indies, Villa Mills was the scene of many fashionable soirees in Victorian times, and it's interesting to note, as H. V. Morton pointed out, that the last dinner parties that took place on the Palatine Hill were given by an Englishman.

Heading across the field parallel to the Clivus Palatinus, you come to the north end of the:

17. **Hippodrome,** or Stadium of Domitian. The field was apparently occupied by parts of the Domus Augustana, which in turn adjoined the enormous stadium. The stadium itself is worth examination, although sometimes it's difficult to get down inside it. The perfectly proportioned area was usually used for private games, staged for the amusement of the imperial family. As you look down the stadium from the north end, you can see, on the left side, the semicircular remains of a structure identified as Domitian's private box. I'll note at this point that some archeologists claim the "stadium" was actually an elaborate sunken garden, and perhaps we'll never know exactly what it was.

The aqueduct that comes up the wooded hill used to supply water for the Baths of Septimius Severus, whose difficult-to-understand ruins lie in monumental piles of arched brick at the far end of the stadium.

Returning to the Flavian Palace, leave the peristyle on the opposite side from the Domus Augustana and follow the signs for the:

18. **House of Livia.** They take you down a dusty path to your left, to the entrance. Although legend says that this was the house of Augustus's consort, it actually was Augustus's all along. The place is notable for some rather well-preserved murals showing mythological scenes. But more interesting is the aspect of the house itself—it's smallish, and there never were any great baths or impressive marble arcades. Augustus, even though he was the first emperor, lived simply compared to his successors. His wife, Livia, was a fiercely ambitious aristocrat who divorced her own husband to marry the emperor (the ex-husband was made to attend the wedding, incidentally) and according to some historians was the true power behind Roman policy between the death of Julius Caesar and the ascension of Tiberius. She even controlled Tiberius, her son, since she had engineered his rise to power through a long string of intrigues and poisonings.

    After you've examined the frescoes in Livia's parlor, head up the steps that lead to the top of the embankment to the north. Once on top, you'll be in the:

19. **Orti Farnesiani,** the 16th-century addition of a Farnese cardinal. They are built on the top of the Palace of Tiberius, which, you'll remember, was the first of the great imperial palaces to be put up. It's impossible to see any of it, but the gardens are cool and nicely laid out. You might stroll up to the promontory above the Forum and admire the view of the ancient temples and the Capitoline heights off to the left.

    When you've seen this much, you've seen the best of the Forum and the Palatine. To leave the archeological area, you should now continue through the Orti Farnesiani, keeping the Forum on your left. Soon you'll come to a stairway that leads to the path from the Arch of Titus. There is an exit just behind the arch, but since it's usually closed, you'll probably have to exit up the ramp you entered by.

Walking Tour 3
From Piazza Barberini to Piazza del Popolo

Start   Piazza Barberini.
Finish   Piazza del Popolo.
Time   2 leisurely hours.
Best Time   Any sunny day.
Worst Time   Rush hours—morning or late-afternoon.

1. **Piazza Barberini** (also the Metro stop) lies at the foot of several important Roman streets: via Barberini, via Sistina, via delle Quattro Fontane, and via del Tritone. It would be

a far more pleasant spot were it not for the considerable amount of traffic swarming around its principal feature, Bernini's Fontana del Tritone (Triton Fountain). Day and night for more than three centuries, the strange figure sitting in a vast open clam has been blowing water from his triton. Nearby is the aristocratic side facade of the Palazzo Barberini.

As you start up via Veneto directly north of the square, look for the small fountain on the right corner of piazza Barberini. There you'll see another of Bernini's many works, the small Fontana delle Api or "Fountain of the Bees." At first they look more like flies, but they are the bees of the Barberini, the crest of that powerful family complete with the crossed keys of St. Peter above them (the crossed keys were added to a family crest when a son was elected pope).

Before you survey the attractions of via Veneto, you might stop first at the:

2. **Cimitero Monumentale del Padri Cappuccini,** in the Church of the Immaculate Conception, via Veneto 27, a short walk from piazza Barberini, where the bones of 4,000 monks have been artistically arranged in various geometric and representational patterns. There is, appropriately, a design that shows the "grim reaper" amid a sea of skulls and thighbones. You'll find it just below the church.

After leaving the church, the posh, tree-lined:

3. **Via Veneto** awaits you. It doesn't look as elegant as it did in the 1950s when it reached its peak. Those *La Dolce Vita* days are gone.

Via Veneto makes a large S-curve, and just where it straightens out for the last time, you'll see the swank U.S. Embassy, whose consular division is in a rose-colored palace where the queen of Italy once lived. From the embassy on up to the Aurelian Wall are the chicest of the cafes, which still carry on a thriving business despite the depletion of the celebrity roster. These cafes, with their brightly colored umbrellas and awnings, are perfectly designed for people-watching. They straddle the sidewalk, and there's no way to stroll up via Veneto without going through the middle of half a dozen of them.

The end of via Veneto brings you to a number of plush hotels and Harry's Bar.

Refueling Stops

At the top of via Veneto, **Harry's Bar,** at no. 148, is everybody's perennial favorite. The IBF—International Bar Flies—are here in constant attendance. You can enjoy a drink or a complete meal, depending on your taste and pocketbook. The most famous cafe along the boulevard is

Walking Tour
From Piazza Barberini To Piazza Del Popolo

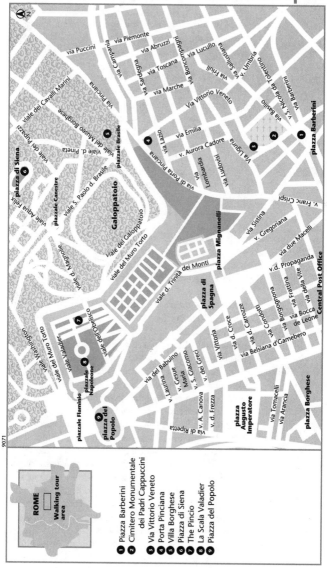

N

via Puccini · via Piemonte
via Abruzzi
via Campania · via Sardegna · via Toscana · via Boncompagni · via Lucullo
via Marche
via Vittorio Veneto
viale dei Cavalli Marini
via Pincana
via Lazio
via Emilia
viale del Museo Borghese
viale d. Pineta
piazzale Brasile
v. Aurora Cadore
via di Porta Pinciana
viale di Brasile
viale S. Paolo d. Brasile
Galoppatolo
viale del Galoppatolo
viale del Muro Torto
piazzale Canestre
viale Aqua Felix
piazza di Siena
viale dei Pupazzi
viale di Magnolie
viale del Muro Torto
viale Valadier
viale Washington
viale dell'Obelisco
piazzale Flaminio
piazzale Napoleone
piazza del Popolo
via Puccini
via Sallustiana
via Friuli
V. Umbria
v. S. Nicolao del Tolentino
via Basilio
via Vitt. del Tolentino
piazza Barberini
v. Franc Crispi
via Sistina
via Gregoriana
via due Macelli
v.d. Propaganda
via Frattina
via della Vite
via Sistina
piazza Mignanelli
piazza di Spagna
piazza di Trinità dei Monti
via Borgognona
via Condotti
via Bocca de Leone
Central Post Office
via d. Croce
via d. Carozze
via Belsiana d'Carnebero
via Vittoria
via del Babuino
v. Laurina
v. Gesu Maria
v. S. Giacomo
v. del Greci
via A. Canova
v.d. Frezza
via di Ripetta
piazza Augusto Imperatore
via Tomacelli
via Arancia
piazza Borghese
Via Ludovisi
Via Lombardia
Via Ludovisi
Via Lazio

1 Piazza Barberini
2 Cimitero Monumentale dei Padri Cappuccini
3 Via Vittorio Veneto
4 Porta Pinciana
5 Villa Borghese
6 Piazza di Siena
7 The Pincio
8 La Scala Valadier
9 Piazza del Popolo

ROME
Walking tour area

9071

Caffè de Paris, via Veneto 90 (see "Rome Nights," Chapter 9).

Right in front of you is the hulking brickwork of the Aurelian Wall, begun in A.D. 271. The gate however, is a bit newer.

4. **Porta Pinciana** derives its name from the Pincian Hill. It
was built in A.D. 546 by the Byzantine general Belisarius,
who was, at the time, seeking to assert the rule of Eastern
Rome over the fallen capital of Western Rome. The city
was in a shambles after more than a century of barbarian
assaults, which had looted it of nearly all its ancient
treasure. The last emperor of the West had long fallen (A.D.
476), and the pope was the real power in Rome. Even the
pope was gone, however—most of the population had fled
the city as a result of the constant upheaval. The leader of
the Goths was Totilla, and though he initially defeated
Belisarius, Belisarius won in the end, eventually laying the
dead Goth at the feet of his emperor in Constantinople.

   While Belisarius was building the Pincian Gate, the
land just outside was the sometime campground of Totilla.
All traces of the Goths have long ago been smoothed away,
and today we see a perfectly exquisite (albeit well-used)
17th-century country estate, with the addition of modern
roads. It is today the:

5. **Villa Borghese,** one of the most magnificent parks and
gardens in Europe. The land was developed by Cardinal
Scipione Borghese, a high churchman belonging to another
of Rome's mighty families. In later years a Borghese prince
was to marry Napoleon's sister, Pauline. The most striking
feature of Villa Borghese (aside from the palace, whose
museum is described in Chapter 6) are its trees—stark and
eerie looking, their trunks rising some 50 or more feet into
the air without a single branch, only to burst forth in an
evergreen canopy high above. Few activities are quite as
pleasant as a slow stroll through Villa Borghese on a sunny
afternoon, pausing to admire carefully planned
17th-century vistas, ornamental fountains, and stately trees.

   From the Pincian Gate, cross the street and bear right
down the path through the trees. Soon you'll see the
equestrian statue of King Umberto I. That statue faces the:

6. **Piazza di Siena,** through a bit of intermediate territory.
The piazza is a perfect oval ring, lined with elegant pines—
a fine place for a picnic if you have time. Beyond the road
at the far end of the piazza lies another section of the park
whose iron fence you'll have to follow (to the left) for a
while. Turn right at the gate and walk straight in. Soon
you'll come to a delightful small lake, complete with Greek
temple and rental rowboats.

   Retrace your steps to the road and turn right. A walk
the equivalent of several blocks brings you to another tract
of gardening, this one dating from the 19th century.

7. **The Pincio** stands on the summit of the Pincian Hill on
the ancient site of the gardens of Lucullus. This formal
garden was laid out by Napoleon's architect, Valadier.
There are almost as many busts here as there are trees—

almost all with new noses, since it seems a favorite sport to chip off the old marble ones. The main attraction of the Pincio is a wide terrace that overlooks the city from a vantage point high above piazza del Popolo. From the ornate balustrade, there's a fine view across the Tiber that includes the wooded slopes of Monte Mario and the Janiculum with the white dome of St. Peter's in between. It's a most romantic view, especially at sunset.

And for an evening stroll take:

8. La Scala Valadier, the stairs to the right that lead down the hill, past several fountains lit with golden-orange lights at night, until finally you arrive below at the:

9. Piazza del Popolo. Aside from the Pincio, this exquisitely balanced piazza is the only Roman reminder of the once-considerable influence of Napoleon. Valadier chose the sites for the central fountain, the flanking semicircular retaining walls, and the hillside of fountains. The matching baroque churches on either side of the Corso date from the 17th century. Like every part of Rome, this piazza has a long history. It was also a part of Lucullus's estate—a lavish one—and later was the burial site of several emperors, Nero among them. The area was supposedly haunted by that imperial ghost until a medieval pope tore down the tomb and consecrated the site. The obelisk is thousands of years old. It originally was Roman booty from the Egyptian city of Heliopolis and once stood in the Circus Maximus. It's surrounded today by four marble lions, carved with the initials of 19th-century tourists. At night, the thin sheets of water from the lions' mouths are illuminated by spotlights hidden in the marble basins below. A fashionable meeting place these days, piazza del Popolo boasts two sidewalk cafes—Canova, and the much better known Rosati—which are ideal for watching expensive Italian cars full of rich Italians doing expensive things.

There are buses from piazza del Popolo straight down the Corso to piazza Venezia and other points in town.

Walking Tour 4
The Spanish Steps to Quirinale

Start   Scalinata di Spagna.
Finish   Quirinale.
Time   2 hours.
Best Time   Sunday morning.
Worst Time   Rush hours—morning and afternoon.

1. The Scalinata di Spagna (Spanish Steps) and the adjoining piazza di Spagna both take their name from the Spanish embassy, which occupied a palace here during the 19th century. The Spanish, however, had nothing to do

with the construction of the steps. The steps were built by the French and lead to the French church in Rome, Trinità dei Monti, and that's why they're called "Scala della Trinità dei Monti." There is nothing Spanish in their real Italian name; "Spanish Steps" is just an easy way of referring to them in English. The twin-towered church behind the obelisk at the top of the steps is early 16th century. The steps themselves are early 18th century. The French are in the church to this day, and the adjoining Villa Medici is now a French school.

The Spanish Steps are at their best in spring, when the many flights are filled with flowers. You'll see a wide variety of types of people, most of them young, sitting around here anytime of the year. In the fall and winter, the population is much sparser, with only an occasional Roman soaking up a few of the sun's warming rays. It is a rare visitor who hasn't sat for a while on one of the landings—there's one every 12 steps—perhaps to read a letter from home or observe the other sitters. It's interesting to note that in the early 19th century the steps were famous for the sleek young men and women who lined the travertine steps flexing muscles and exposing ankles in hopes of attracting an artist and being hired as a model. The Barcaccia fountain at the foot was designed by Bernini's father at the end of the 16th century.

There are two nearly identical houses at the foot of the steps on either side. One is the home of Babington's Tea Rooms (see the "Refueling Stop," below); the other was the house where the English romantic poet John Keats lived— and died.

2. The Keats-Shelley Memorial, at piazza di Spagna 26, has been bought by English and American contributors and turned into a museum. The rooms where Keats lived are chock-full of mementos of the poet.

Refueling Stop

Babington's Tea Rooms, piazza di Spagna 23, were opened in 1893 by Miss Anne Mary Babington, and this place has been serving homemade scones and muffins— along with a "good cuppa"—ever since, based on her original recipes. Celebrities and thousands upon thousands of tourists have stopped off here. Prices are high, however.

In the past, the piazza di Spagna area was a favorite of English lords, who rented palaces hereabouts and parked their coaches on the streets. Americans predominate in the 20th century, especially since the main office of American Express is right on piazza di Spagna and dispenses all those letters (and money) from home. There's a street called:

3. via della Croce that intersects the northern end of piazza di Spagna perpendicularly from the left. Follow this street for

Walking Tour
The Spanish Steps To Quirinale

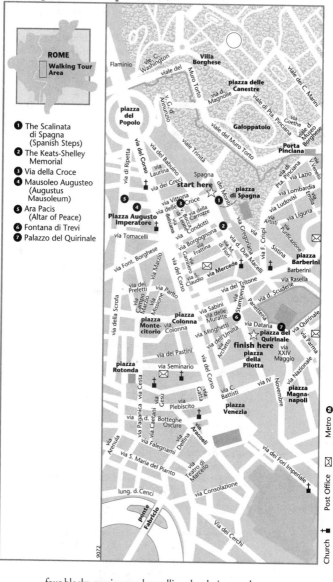

ROME
Walking Tour Area

1. The Scalinata di Spagna (Spanish Steps)
2. The Keats-Shelley Memorial
3. Via della Croce
4. Mausoleo Augusteo (Augustus Mausoleum)
5. Ara Pacis (Altar of Peace)
6. Fontana di Trevi
7. Palazzo del Quirinale

Metro **M**

Post Office ✉

Church ✝

four blocks, passing vendors selling the choicest and most expensive fruit in town between parked cars, and small workrooms filled with dust where old men are repairing 16th-century gilt frames, until you come to via del Corso. Continue straight across the Corso, where the street takes a sharp turn to the left. At the first intersection, turn right, and across the piazza is your next stop, the:

4. **Mausoleo Augusteo (Augustus Mausoleum)**. This seemingly indestructible pile of bricks along via di Ripetta has been here for 2,000 years, and will probably remain for another 2,000. Like the larger tomb of Hadrian across the river, this was once a circular, marble-colored affair with tall cypress trees on the earth-covered dome. Many of the emperors of the 1st century had their ashes deposited in golden urns inside this building, and it was probably because of the resultant crowding that Hadrian decided to construct an entirely new tomb for himself. The imperial remains stayed intact until the 5th century, when invading barbarians smashed the bronze gates and stole the golden urns, probably emptying the ashes on the ground outside. The tomb was restored in the 1930s. You cannot enter, but you can walk around and look inside.

   Across via di Ripetta, the main street on the far side of the tomb, is an airy glass-and-concrete building right on the banks of the Tiber at Ponte Cavour. Within it is one of the treasures of antiquity, the:

5. **Ara Pacis (Altar of Peace)**, built by the Senate during the reign of Augustus as a tribute to that emperor and the peace he had brought to the Roman world. On the marble walls can be seen portraits of the imperial family—Augustus, Livia (his wife), Tiberius (Livia's son and the successor to the emperor), even Julia (the unfortunate daughter of Augustus, exiled by her father for her sexual excesses). The altar was reconstructed from literally hundreds of fragments scattered in museums for centuries. A major portion came from the foundations of a Renaissance palace on the Corso. The reconstruction—quite an architectural adventure story in itself—was executed by the Fascists during the 1930s. Pacis (☎ **7102071**) is open on Tuesday and Wednesday and Friday through Sunday from 9am to 1:30pm. From April through September, it is also open in the afternoon on Tuesday and Saturday from 4 to 7pm. Admission is 3,750 lire ($2.30).

   Continuing south, take via del Corso, a shopping artery leading to piazza Colonna, and its Marcus Aurelius Column, which dominates the piazza. Here is the Palazzo Chigi, official residence of the Italian prime minister, and the Bernini-designed Palazzo di Montecitorio, east of the Italian legislature, the Chamber of Deputies (closed to the public).

   From via del Corso, walk up the right side of via del Tritone and then follow the signs to the:

6. **Fontana di Trevi**. At piazza di Trevi, the Trevi Fountain is the most famous one in all of Rome. Tourists come here to toss coins in the fountain, which according to legend, ensures their return to Rome. Supplied by water from the

Acqua Vergine aqueduct, it was based on the design of Nicolo Salvi, and completed in 1762.

On one corner of the piazza, you'll see an ancient church with a strange claim to fame. In it are contained the hearts and viscera of several centuries of popes. This was the parish church of the popes when they resided at the Quirinale Palace on the hill above, and for many years each pontiff willed those parts of his body to the church.

To reach the Quirinale, take via Lucchesi from the church for two blocks where it intersects with via Doloria. Turn left and straight ahead you'll see the steps to the:

7. **Palazzo del Quirinale.** At the top of the stairs, you'll be in a wide pink piazza, piazza del Quirinale, with the palace of the president of Italy on your left. Until the end of World War II, the palace was the home of the king of Italy, and before that it was the residence of the pope. In antiquity, this was the site of Augustus's Temple of the Sun. The steep marble steps that lead to Santa Maria d'Aracoeli on the Capitoline Hill once led to that temple. The great baths of Constantine also stood nearby, and that's the origin of some of the fountain statuary.

From here, your closest public transportation is on via Nazionale, reached by taking via della Consulta between piazza della Consulta and the little park.

Walking Tour 5

Trastevere

Start   Isola Tiberina.

Finish   Piazza Santa Maria in Trastevere.

Time   2 hours.

Best Time   Daylight hours during weekday mornings, when the outdoor food markets are open, or early on a Sunday, when there's very little traffic.

Worst Time   After dark.

Not until the advent of the Fellini films (whose grotesqueries seemed to reflect many of the scenes you're likely to see in this neighborhood) did Trastevere emerge as a world-famous district of Rome. Set on the western bank of the Tiber, away from the bulk of Rome's most-visited monuments, Trastevere (whose name translates as "across the Tiber") seems a world apart from the ethics, mores, and architecture of the rest of Rome. (Its residents have traditionally been considered less extroverted and more suspicious than the Romans across the river.)

Because only a fraction of Trastevere has been excavated, it remains one of Rome's most consistently unchanged medieval neighborhoods, despite a trend toward gentrification. Amply stocked with dimly lit and very ancient churches, crumbling buildings angled above streets barely wide enough for a single Fiat, and highly articulate inhabitants who have stressed their independence from Rome for many centuries, the district is one of the most consistently colorful districts of the Italian capital.

Be warned that street crime, pickpockets, and purse snatchers seem more plentiful here than in Rome's more frequently visited neighborhoods, so leave your valuables behind, and be alert to what's going on around you.

Your tour begins on the tiny but historic:

1. **Isola Tiberina.** Despite its location in the heart of Rome, it has always been considered a refuge for the sick, and a calm and sun-flooded backwater. The oldest bridge in Rome, the Ponte Fabricio, built in 62 B.C., connects the island to the Tiber's northern bank. The church at the island's eastern end, San Bartolomeo, was built during the 900s by the Holy Roman Emperor Otto III, although dozens of subsequent rebuildings have removed virtually everything from the original structure. The complex of buildings at the island's western end contain the hospital of Fatebenefratelli, whose foundations and traditions date back to the ancient world. (The ancient world associated the island with the healing powers of the God Aesculapius, son of Apollo.)

   Walk south along the bridge (Ponte Cestio) that connects the island to the western bank of the Tiber. After crossing the raging traffic, which runs parallel to the riverbanks, continue south for a few steps. Soon, you'll reach the:

2. **Piazza Piscinula.** Named after the Roman baths ("piscina") that once flowed here, the square contains the tiny but ancient Church of San Benedetto, whose facade was rebuilt in a simplified baroque style during the 1600s. It's classified as the smallest Romanesque church in Rome and supposedly is built on the site where St. Benedict, founder of the Benedictine order, lived as a boy. Directly opposite the church rises the intricate stonework of the Casa dei Mattei. Occupied during the Renaissance by one of the city's most powerful and arrogant families (the Mattei), it was abondoned by them as unlucky after several of its members were murdered during a brawl at a family wedding held inside. In reaction, the family moved to more elegant quarters across the Tiber.

   Exit from the piazza's northwest corner, walking west along either the narrow via Gensola or the somewhat wider via della Lungaretta. Within about two jagged blocks, you'll reach a pair of interconnected squares, the:

3. **Piazza Sidney Sonnino** (named after the Italian minister of Foreign Affairs during World War I) and the **piazza Belli.** In the latter stands a statue commemorating Giuseppe Gioacchino Belli (1791–1863), whose more than 2,000 satirical sonnets (written in Roman dialect) on Roman life have made him a particular favorite of the

Walking Tour—Trastevere

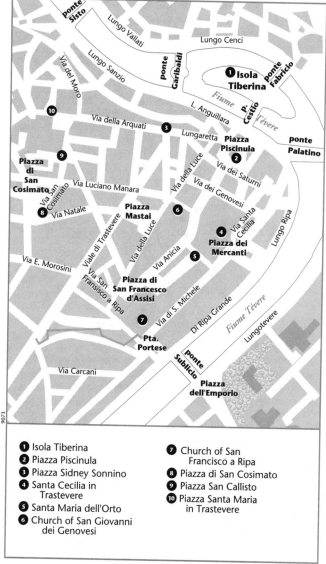

1 Isola Tiberina
2 Piazza Piscinula
3 Piazza Sidney Sonnino
4 Santa Cecilia in Trastevere
5 Santa Maria dell'Orto
6 Church of San Giovanni dei Genovesi

7 Church of San Francisco a Ripa
8 Piazza di San Cosimato
9 Piazza San Callisto
10 Piazza Santa Maria in Trastevere

uninhibited and sometimes pugnacious Trasteverans. From one edge of the piazza rise the 13th-century walls of the Torre degli Anguillara and the not-very-famous church of St. Agatha, while on the southern edge rise the walls of the Church of San Crisogono. Founded in the 500s, and rebuilt in the 1100s (when its bell tower was added), it contains stonework and mosiacs, which merit a visit to its interior.

Now, cross the traffic-clogged viale di Trastevere, and head southeast into a maze of narrow alleyways defined as either the viale San Crisogono or the via dei Genovesi. Traverse both via della Luce and via Anicia (which was named after the family that produced the medieval leader Pope Gregory the Great), then look to your right at the high walls and ancient masonary of:

4. **Santa Cecilia in Trastevere.** (To reach its entrance, continue walking another block, then turn right onto via Santa Cecilia, which soon funnels into piazza dei Mercanti.) A cloistered and still-functioning convent, with a fine garden, Santa Cecilia contains a difficult-to-visit fresco by Cavallini within its inner sanctums, and a more easily visited church containing a white marble statue of the saint herself. The church is built on the reputed site of her long-ago palace and contains sections dating from the 12th to the 19th century.

St. Cecilia, who proved of enormous importance in the history of European art as a symbol of the struggle of the early church, was a Roman aristocrat—and one of the wealthiest women in Rome—condemned for her faith by a Roman prefect around 300 A.D. According to legend, her earthly body proved extraordinarily difficult for Roman soldiers to slay, affording the saint ample opportunity to convert bystanders to the Christian cause.

Refueling Stop

About a half-dozen cafes lie near this famous church. Any of them will serve frothy cups of cappuccino, tasty sandwiches, ice cream, and drinks.

After your refreshment, take the opportunity to wander randomly down three or four of the narrow streets outward from the piazza dei Mercanti. Of particular interest might be via del Porto, which stretches south to the Tiber. A port—the largest within Rome—once flourished at this street's terminus (Porto di Ripa Grande). During the 1870s redesign of the riverfront, when the embankments were added, the port was demolished.

Returning to piazza dei Mercanti, walk southeast along via di San Michele, then turn right onto via Madonna dell'Orto. The baroque church you'll see there is:

5. **Santa Maria dell'Orto,** which was originally founded by the vegetable gardeners of Trastevere during the early 1400s., when the district provided most of the green vegetables for the tables of Rome. Famous for the obelisks that decorate its corniches (added in the 1760s) and for the baroque gilding inside, it's one of the district's most traditional churches.

A few steps later, turn right on via Anicia. At no. 12, on your left-hand side, lies the:

6. **Church of San Giovanni dei Genovesi.** Built during the 1400s for the community of Genoa-born sailors who labored at the nearby port, it contains a tranquil garden, which may or may not be visited according to the whim of the gatekeeper. Now, retrace your steps on the via Anicia, heading south. The street funnels into piazza di San Francesco d'Assisi. On your left, notice the ornate walls of the:

7. **Church of San Francisco a Ripa.** Built in the baroque style, and attached to a medieval Francisan monastery, the church contains a statue by Bernini. Crafted in the mannerist style, and depicting Ludovica Albertoni, it is the last known work Bernini ever sculpted, and supposedly one of his most mystically transcendental.

   Exit from piazza di San Francesco d'Assisi. After traversing the feverish traffic of viale di Trastevere, take the first left onto a tiny street with a long name, via Natale del Grande Cardinale Merry di Val. Its name is sometimes shortened to simply "via Natale," if it's marked at all on your map. This funnels into:

8. **Piazza di San Cosimato,** known for its busy food market, which operates every weekday from early morning until around noon. On the north side of the square lies the awkwardly charming church of San Cosimato, sections of which were built around 900 A.D., and which is closed to the public.

   Exit from the piazza's north side, heading up via San Cosimato (its name might not be marked). This will funnel into the:

9. **Piazza San Callisto.** Much of the real estate surrounding this square, including the 17th-century Palazzo San Callisto, belongs to the Vatican. The edges of this piazza will almost imperceptibly flow into one of the most famous squares of Rome, the:

10. **Piazza Santa Maria in Trastevere.** The Romanesque church that lends the piazza its name (Santa Maria in Trastevere) is probably the most famous building in the entire district. Originally built around 350 A.D. and considered one of the oldest churches in Rome, it sports a body added around 1100 and an entrance and portico that were added in the 1840s. The much restored mosiacs on both the facade and within the interior, however, date from around 1200. Its sense of timelessness is enhanced by the much-photographed octagonal fountain in front and the hundreds of pigeons.

Refueling Stop

Try one of the many cafes that line this famous square. Though any would be suitable, a good choice might be **Café Bar di Marzio,** piazza di Santa Maria in Trastevere

14B, where rows of tables, both inside and out, offer an engaging view of the ongoing carnival of Trastevere.

Walking Tour 6
The Tiber & Via Giulia

Start   Via della Conciliazione (Piazza Pia).
Finish   Palazzo Spada.
Time: 2 hours, not counting a tour of the Castel Sant'Angelo and a visit to the Palazzo Spada.
Best Time   Early and mid-mornings.
Worst Time   Afternoon, several of the monuments along the way close early.

The thread that unifies this tour is the river that has transported food, wine, building supplies, armies, looted booty from other parts of Europe, and such famous personages as Cleopatra and Mussolini into Rome. Slower and less powerful than many of Italy's other rivers (such as the mighty Po which irrigates the fertile plains of Lombardy and the north), the Tiber varies, depending on the season, from a sluggish ribbon of sediment-filled water only four feet deep to a 20-foot-deep torrent capable of flooding the banks that contain it.

The last severe flood to destroy Roman buildings occurred in 1870. Since then, civic planners have built mounded barricades high above its winding banks, a development that has diminished the river's visual appeal. The high embankments, as well as the roaring traffic arteries that parallel them, obscure views of the water throughout most of the river's trajectory through Rome. In any event, the waters of the Tiber are so polluted that many modern Romans consider their concealment something of a benefit.

Begin your tour at the westernmost end of Rome's most sterile and impersonal boulevard, the:

1. **via della Conciliazione (piazza Pia).** Its construction required the demolition of a series of medieval neighborhoods between 1936 and 1950, rendering it without challenge the most disliked avenue in Rome. Conceived by Mussolini as a monumental preface to the faraway dome of St. Peter's Basilica, it will allow a view from afar of the monumental dome of Christendom's most famous church, St. Peter's Basilica.

   Walk east toward the massive and ancient walls of the:

2. **Castel Sant'Angelo.** Originally built by the emperor Hadrian in 135 A.D., as one of the most impressive mausoleums in the ancient world, it was adapted for use as a fortress, a treasure vault, and a pleasure palace for the Renaissance popes. Visit its interior, noting the presence near the entrance of architectural models showing the castle at various periods of its history. Note the building's plan (a circular tower set atop a square foundation), and the dry moats (used today for impromptu soccer games by

neighborhood urchins), which long ago were the despair of many an invading army.

After your visit, walk south across one of the most ancient bridges in Rome,:

3. **Ponte Sant'Angelo.** The trio of arches in the river's center is basically unchanged since the bridge was built around 135 A.D.; the arches that abut the river's embankments were added late in the 19th century as part of the above-mentioned flood-control program. On December 19, 1450, so many pilgrims gathered on this bridge (which at the time was lined with wooden buildings) that about 200 of them were crushed to death. Today, the bridge is reserved exclusively for pedestrians, since vehicular traffic was banned in the 1960s. On the southern end of the bridge is the site of one of the most famous executions of the Renaissance, the:

4. **Piazza San Angelo.** There, in 1599, Beatrice Cenci and several members of her family were beheaded on orders of Pope Clement VIII. Their crime? Plotting the successful death of their very rich and very brutal father. Their tale later inspired a tragedy by Shelley and a novel by a 19th-century Italian politician named Francesco Guerrazzi.

From the square, cut southwest for two blocks along via Paola (crossing the busy traffic of corso Vittorio Emmanuele in the process) onto the:

5. **Via Giulia.** Laid out during the reign of Pope Julius II (1503–13), its straight edges were one of Renaissance Rome's earliest examples of urban planning. Designed to facilitate access to the Vatican, it was the widest, straightest, and longest inner-city street in Rome at the time of its construction. Its edges housed the 16th-century homes of such artists as Raphael, Cellini, Borromini, and the architect Sangallo. Today, the street is lined with some of the most spectacular antiques stores in Rome. At the terminus of via Paola, the first building on via Giulia you're likely to see is the soaring dome of the:

6. **Chiesa di San Giovanni dei Florentini (The Florentine Church)**, designated as the premier symbol of the city of Florence within papal Rome. Its design is the result of endless squabblings between such artistic rivals as Sansovino, Sangallo, and Maderno, each of whom added embellishments of his own. Michelangelo had submitted a design for the church, although his drawing did not prevail during the initial competition. Although most of the building was completed during the 1620s, Lorenzo Corsini added the facade during the 1700s.

Now, walk in a southeasterly direction along via Giulia, making special note of houses set at no. 82 (built in the 1400s, it was offered by Pope Julius II to the Florentine community); no. 85 (the land it sits on was originally owned by Raphael); and no. 79 (built in 1536 by the architect Sangallo as his private home, it was later snapped up by a relative of Cosimo de' Medici).

Within less than three short blocks, on the northwest corner of vicolo del Cefalo, rises the symmetrical bulk of the:

7. **Palazzo Sacchetti.** Completed by Vasari in the mid-1500s, it was built by the Sacchetti family, a Florence-based family of bankers and merchants who moved to Rome after they lost an epic power struggle with the Medicis. Continue walking south along via Giulia for another block. After you traverse via Bresciani, you'll notice the imposing walls of a historic building, which will also serve as a good place to take a break.

Refueling Stop

Visit the bar of the **Cardinal Hotel,** via Giulia 62 (entrance on via Bresciani). Some of the stones used to build it were pillaged from the Roman Forum during the 1500s. Originally intended as a *palazzo* for dispensation of justice by the popes, its design underwent alterations by Bramante and a battalion of other architects. Today, it reeks of history as well as a sampling of historic relics and stonework, and a color scheme that is uncompromisingly and stridently red. The hotel's bar serves drinks and coffee in a subdued ambience, which tired pedestrians appreciate.

After your refueling stop, continue walking south along via Giulia. On your right rises the baroque facade of the unpretentious:

8. **Church of San Biagio.** Although its front was added in the early 1700s, it's considered one of the oldest churches in Rome, rebuilt from an even earlier model around 1070. Considered the property of an Armenian Christian sect based in Venice, the church is named after an early Christian martyr (St. Biagio), a portion of whose throat is included among the sacred objects inside.

Walk another short block south along via Giulia. Between via del Gonfalone and vicolo della Scimia are the barred windows of what was originally built early in the 19th century as a:

9. **Prison for Minors.** This, along with another nearby building (at no. 52 via Giulia, a few blocks to the south, which was built during the mid-1600s) incarcerated juvenile delinquents, political prisoners, debtors, common rogues, and innocent victims of circumstance for almost a hundred years. During its Industrial Revolution heyday, armed guards supervised all comings and goings along this section of via Giulia.

Turn right onto vicolo della Scimia, and descend toward the Tiber. On your left, at no. 18, is a building used

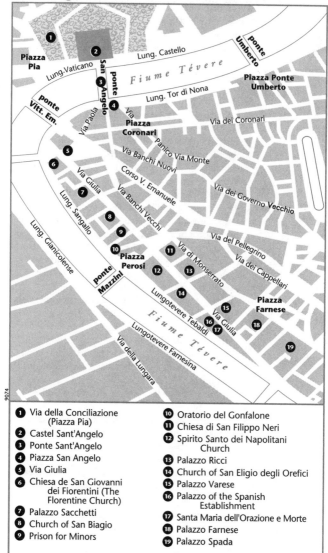

1 Via della Conciliazione
   (Piazza Pia)
2 Castel Sant'Angelo
3 Ponte Sant'Angelo
4 Piazza San Angelo
5 Via Giulia
6 Chiesa de San Giovanni
   dei Fiorentini (The
   Florentine Church)
7 Palazzo Sacchetti
8 Church of San Biagio
9 Prison for Minors
10 Oratorio del Gonfalone
11 Chiesa di San Filippo Neri
12 Spirito Santo dei Napolitani
   Church
13 Palazzo Ricci
14 Church of San Eligio degli Orefici
15 Palazzo Varese
16 Palazzo of the Spanish
   Establishment
17 Santa Maria dell'Orazione e Morte
18 Palazzo Farnese
19 Palazzo Spada

since the early 1500s as a guildhall for the flag-bearers of
Rome:

10. **Oratorio del Gonfalone.** The guild of flag-bearers had, by
the time this building was constructed, evolved into a
charitable organization of concerned citizens and a rather
posh social and religious fraternity. The frescoes inside were
painted in 1573 by Zuccari. Restored during the early

1980s, they today form a backdrop for the concerts held inside. The building is usually open Monday to Saturday from 9:30am to noon.

Walk to the very end of vicolo della Scimia and make a hard left onto vicolo Prigioni, which will eventually lead back to via Giulia.

At this point, as you continue to walk south along via Giulia, you'll notice a swath of trees and a curious absence of buildings flanking the corner of the via Moretta. In 1940, Mussolini ordered the demolition of most of the buildings along via Moretta for the construction of a triumphal boulevard running from east to west. His intention—which was never fulfilled—was the linking together of the nearby Ponte Mazzini with corso Vittorio Emmanuele. One building that suffered was the:

11. **Chiesa di San Filippo Neri,** whose baroque facade sits near the above-mentioned corner. Originally funded during the early 1600s by a wealthy but ailing benefactor in hopes of curing his gout, the church retains only its facade. The rest of the building was demolished. Where choirs once sang and candles burned during masses, there now exists a market for the sale of fruits and vegetables.

Within about another block to the south, on your right, rises the bulk of the:

12. **Spirito Santo del Napolitani Church.** Once one of the headquarters of the Neapolitan community in Rome, the version you see today was a product of a rebuilding during the 1700s, although parts of the foundation were originally built during the 1300s.

Slightly farther to the south, at no. 146 via Giulia, rises the:

13. **Palazzo Ricci,** one of the many aristocratic villas that once flanked this historic street. For a better view of its exterior frescoes, turn left from via Giulia into piazza Ricci to admire this building from the rear.

Returning to via Giulia, walk south for a block, then turn right onto via Barchetta. At the corner of via di San Eligio, notice the:

14. **Church of San Eligio degli Orefici,** which was originally designed, according to popular belief, by Raphael in 1516. Completed about 60 years later, it was dedicated to (and funded by) the city's gold and silversmiths. Return to via Giulia and notice, near its terminus, the:

15. **Palazzo Varese,** via Giulia 16, built as an aristocratic residence in the Tuscan style; and, at via Giulia 151, the:

16. **Palazzo of the Spanish Establishment.** Built in anticipation of the 1862 visit of Elizabeth, queen of Spain, for the occasion of her charitable visit to Rome, it was designed by Antonio Sarti. Continue walking south along via Giulia, past the faded grandeur of at least another

half-dozen *palazzi*. These will include Palazzo Cisterno, circa 1560, at no. 163; Palazzo Baldoca/Muccioli/Rodd, circa 1700, at no. 167; and Palazzo Falconieri, circa 1510, at no. 1.

Opposite the corner of via dei Farnesi rise the walls of one of the most macabre buildings in Rome, the church of:

17. **Santa Maria dell'Orazione e Morte.** Built around 1575, and rebuilt about 160 years later, it was the property of an order of monks whose job it was to collect and bury the unclaimed bodies of the indigent. Notice the depictions of skulls decorating the church's facade. During the Renaissance, underground chambers lined with bodies led from the church to the Tiber, where barges carried the bodies away. Though these vaults are not open to the public, the church's interior decoration carries multiple reminders of the omnipresence of death.

After exiting the church, notice the covered passageway arching over via Giulia. Built in 1603, and designed by Michelangelo, it connected the:

18. **Palazzo Farnese,** whose rear side rises to your left, with the Tiber and a series of then-opulent gardens and villas that no longer exist. The Palazzo Farnese, built between 1514 and 1589, was designed by Sangallo, Michelangelo, and others, and was considered astronomically expensive at the time of its construction. Its famous residents have included a 16th-century member of the Farnese family, Pope Paul III, Cardinal Richelieu, and the former Queen Christina of Sweden, who moved to Rome after abdicating her throne. During the 1630s, when the building's heirs could not afford to maintain it, the palace became the site of the French embassy, a function it has served ever since. It is closed to the public. For the best view of the Palazzo Farnese, cut west from via Giulia along any of the narrow streets (via Mascherone or via dei Farnesi would do nicely) to reach piazza Farnese.

To the southwest is a satellite square, piazza Quercia, at the southern corner of which rises the even more spectacular exterior of the:

19. **Palazzo Spada,** Capo di Ferro 3. Built around 1550 for Cardinal Gerolamo Capo di Ferro, and later inhabited by the descendants of several other cardinals, it was sold to the Italian government in the 1920s. Its richly ornate facade, covered as it is in high-relief stucco decorations in the mannerist style, is considered the finest of any building from 16th-century Rome. Although the State Rooms are closed to the public, the richly decorated courtyard and a handful of galleries are open.

8

Shopping A to Z

Rome offers shoppers temptations of every kind. This section will try to give you focus so that when you feel the urge to shop, which sometimes overcomes even the most stalwart of visitors, you'll be ready. You may well find charming shops and stores offering excellent value as you venture off the beaten track; what follows here is a description of certain streets known throughout Italy for their elegant shops. Be forewarned: The rents on these famous streets is very high, and some of those costs will almost certainly be passed on to the consumer. Nonetheless, a stroll down some of these streets usually presents a cross section of the most sought-after wares in Italy.

Cramped urban spaces and a sophisticated sense of taste has encouraged most Italian stores to elevate the boutique philosophy to its highest levels. Lack of space usually restricts an establishment's goods to one particular style, degree of formality, or mood. So browse at will, and let the allure of the shop window (particularly when shopping for fashions) communicate the mood and style of what you're likely to find inside.

Caveat: I won't pretend that Rome is Italy's finest shopping center (Florence, Venice, and Milan are), nor that its shops are unusually inexpensive—many of them aren't. But even on the most elegant of Rome's thoroughfares, there are values mixed in with the costliest items.

Also, as mentioned earlier in the book, many times you'll find that the street numbers start on one side of the street, run all the way down that side in sequence, then change sides and run all the way back; so, no. 500 is sometimes across the street from no. 1.

1 The Shopping Scene

Bring your pocket calculator with you and keep in mind that stores are often closed between 1 and 4pm (check listings in this chapter for hours of individual stores).

SHIPPING Shipping can be a problem, but—for a price—an object, no matter how fragile or elaborate, can be packed, shipped, and insured. For major purchases, you should buy an all-risks insurance policy to cover damage or loss in transit.

Since these policies can be expensive, check into whether using your credit card to make your purchase will provide automatic free insurance. Shipping from reputable stores or shipping companies is, of course, recommended.

TAX REBATES ON PURCHASES IN ITALY Visitors to Italy are sometimes appalled at the high taxes and add-ons that seem to influence so many of the bottom-line costs of going to Italy. Those taxes, totaling as much as 19% to 35% for certain goods, apply to big-ticket purchases of more than 525,000 lire ($315) but can be refunded if you plan ahead and perform a bit of sometimes tiresome paperwork. When you make your purchase, make sure to get a receipt from the vendor. When you leave Italy, find an Italian Customs agent at the point of your exit from the country. The agent will want to see the item you've bought, confirm that it is physically leaving Italy, and stamp the vendor's receipt.

You should then mail the stamped receipt (keeping a photocopy for your records) back to the original vendor. The vendor will, sooner or later, send you a check representing a refund of the tax you paid at the time of your original purchase. Reputable stores view this as a matter of ordinary paperwork and are very businesslike about it. Less honorable stores might lose your receipts. It pays to deal with established vendors on purchases of this size.

Major Shopping Streets

Via Borgognona   It begins near piazza di Spagna, and both the rents and the merchandise are chic and very, very expensive. Like its neighbor, via Condotti, via Borgognona is a mecca for wealthy, well-dressed shoppers from around the world. Its architecture and its storefronts have retained their baroque or neoclassical facades.

Via Condotti   Easy to find because of its beginning at the base of the Spanish Steps, it is the most posh upper-bracket shopping street in Rome. Even the incursion in recent years of a sampling of less elegant stores hasn't diminished the allure of this street as a consumer's playground for the rich and the very, very rich. Its landmark coffeehouse, the **Antico Caffè Greco,** via Condotti 86 (☎ **6791700**) is where the district's gossip probably travels faster than anywhere else in Rome.

Via Frattina   It runs parallel to via Condotti, and begins at piazza di Spagna. Part of its length is closed to traffic. The concentration of shops is denser, although some claim that its image is slightly less chic and prices are less expensive than those you'll find on via Condotti. Via Frattina is usually thronged with shoppers who appreciate the lack of motor traffic.

Via del Corso   It doesn't attempt the stratospheric image (or prices) of via Condotti or via Borgognona, and its styles tend to be aimed at younger consumers. There are, however, some gems scattered amid the shops selling jeans and sporting equipment. This street was lucky enough to have most of its automobile traffic diverted for some of its length. The most interesting shops are on the section of this street nearest the fashionable cafes of the piazza del Popolo.

Via Sistina   Beginning at the top of the Spanish Steps, and running from that point (the Trinità dei Monti) into piazza Barberini, via Sistina's shops are small, stylish, and based on the personalities of their owners. Pedestrian traffic is not as dense as it is on the other streets on this list.

Via Francesco Crispi   Most shoppers reach this street by following via Sistina one long block from the top of the Spanish Steps. Within a block of the intersection of these streets lie several shops well-suited for unusual and not very expensive gifts.

Via Nazionale   Its layout reeks of 19th-century grandeur and ostentatious beauty, but its traffic is horrendous and crossing it involves a good sense of timing and a strong understanding of Italian driving patterns. It begins at piazza della Repubblica (with its great Fountain of the Naiads in front of the Baths of Diocletian) and runs down almost to the 19th-century monuments of the piazza Venezia. There is an abundance of leather stores—more reasonable than in many other parts of Rome—many different apartment buildings, and a welcome handful of stylish boutiques.

Via Veneto and Via Barberini   Evocative of *La Dolce Vita* fame and (now-diminished) fortunes, via Veneto is filled these days with luxury hotels and cafes and an array of relatively expensive stores selling shoes, gloves, and leather goods. Although it's considered a desirable address by day, this street can be rough at night (muggings), and motor traffic is always both dense and noisy.

Best Buys

The Italian aesthetic has probably exerted more power on the definition of beauty for Westerners than that of any other culture, and because of the Italians' consummate skill as manufacturers and designers, it is no surprise that consumers from all over the world flock to Italy's shops, trade fairs, and design studios to see what's new, hot, and salable back home.

Most obvious is **fashion,** which since World War II has played a major part in the economy of Milan, whose entrepreneurs view Rome as a principal distribution center. There are literally hundreds of famous designers for both men and women, most of whom make eminently stylish garments. Materials include silks, leathers, cottons, synthetics, and wools, often of the finest quality.

Italian design influences everything from typewriter keyboards to kitchen appliances to furniture. The Italian studios of Memphis-Milan and Studio Alchimia are two of the leaders in this field, and many of their products (and many copies of their products by derivative companies) are now highly visible in machines and furnishings throughout the world. Many of Italy's new products and designs can be previewed by reading a copy of *Domus,* a monthly magazine that reports, with photographs, on many different aspects of the country's design scene.

Food and wine never go out of style, and many gourmets bring home to North America the gastronomic products that somehow always taste better in Italy. Many Roman shops sell chocolates, pastries, liqueurs, wines, and limited-edition olive oils. Be alert to restrictions in North America against importing certain food products. Italian wines, of course, include many excellent vintages, and bottles of liqueurs (which are sometimes distilled from herbs and flowers) make unusual gifts.

The **glassware** of Italy (and especially of Venice) is famous throughout the world and sold all over Rome. Shipping is a problem, but for a price, any object—no matter how fragile or elaborate—can be packed, shipped, and insured.

The **porcelain** of Italy is elegant and sought after, but I personally prefer the hand-painted rustic plates and bowls of thick-edged **stoneware.** Done in strong and clear glazes, and influenced by their rural origins, the bowls and plates are often used at the most formal dinners for their originality and style. The **tiles** and **mosaics** of Italy are virtually without equal in the world, whether used individually as drink coasters or decorative ornaments, or in groups set into masonry walls.

Lace was, for many years, made in convents by nuns. Venice became the country's headquarters. Handmade Italian lace is exquisite and justifiably expensive, crafted into a wide array of tablecloths, napkins, clothing, and bridal veils. Beware of machine-made imitations, although with a bit of practice you'll soon be able to recognize the shoddy copies.

Paper goods, stationery, elegantly bound books, prints, and engravings are specialties of Italy. The engravings you find amid stacks of dozens of others will invariably look stately when hanging—framed—on a wall back home.

Fabrics, especially silk, are made near Lake Como, in the foothills of the Italian Alps. Known for their supple beauty and their ability to hold color for years (the thicker the silk, the more desirable), these silks are rivaled only by the finest of India, Thailand, and China. Their history in Italy goes back to the era of Marco Polo, and possibly much earlier.

Finally, Rome is the home to a **religious objects** industry. Centered in Rome around the streets near the Church of Santa Maria Sopra Minerva are dozens of shops selling pictures, statues, and reliefs of most of the important saints, the Madonna, Jesus, and John the Baptist.

2 Shopping A to Z

Antiques

Some visitors to Italy come for its treasure trove of salable antiques alone. But long gone are the postwar days when you found priceless treasures for pocket change. The values of almost all antiques have risen to alarming levels as increasingly wealthy Europeans have outbid one another in frenzies of acquisitive lust. You might remember that any antiques dealer who risks the high rents of central Rome to open an antiques store is probably acutely aware of the value of almost everything ever made, and will probably recognize anything of value long before his or her clients. Beware of fakes, insure anything you buy and have shipped, and for larger purchases, keep your paperwork in order for your eventual tax refund.

If you love to shop for antiques, one street you should frequent is **via dei Coronari.** Buried in an ancient section of the Campo Marzio (Renaissance Rome), via del Coronari is an antiquer's dream: There are more than 40 antiques stores within the four blocks, literally lined with inlaid secretaries, gilded consoles, vases, urns, chandeliers, breakfronts, marble pedestals, chaises, refectory tables, candelabra—you name it. The entrance to the street lies just north of piazza Navona. Turn left outside the piazza, past the excavated ruins of Domitian's Stadium, and the street will be just ahead of you.

Galleria Coronari, via dei Coronari 59. ☎ **6869917.**

Galleria Coronari is a desirable shop that might be used as a starting point to browsing through many other shops nearby. Many of its antiques are nostalgia-laden-bric-a-brac, small enough to fit into a suitcase, including jewelry, dolls, paintings, and ornate picture frames from the 19th century. Also represented is furniture from the 18th, 19th, and early 20th centuries, and such oddities as a completely furnished dollhouse, accurate even down to the miniature champagne bottles in the miniature pantry. Open Monday 3:30 to 7:30pm, Tuesday to Saturday 10am to 1pm and 3:30 to 7:30pm.

Art

Aldo Di Castro, via del Babuino, 71. ☎ **6794900.**

Aldo di Castro is one of the largest dealers of antique prints and engravings in Rome. You'll find rack after rack of depictions of everything from the Colosseum to the Pantheon, each evocative of the best architecture in the Mediterranean world, priced between $25 and $1,000, depending on the age and rarity of the engraving. Open Monday 3:30 to 7:30pm, Tuesday to Saturday 10am to 1pm and 3:30 to 7:30pm.

Galleria d'Arte Schneider, rampa Mignanelli 10. ☎ **6784019.**

Located a few steps from one of the ramps leading into the side of the Spanish Steps, near the Hassler Hotel, this is one of the best-established and most enduring art galleries in Rome. Established in 1953 by Robert Schneider, an American-born professor of languages and an art connoisseur, it specializes in lesser-known sculpture and paintings by Italians or foreign residents of Rome. Among the artists whose work has been promoted early in their careers by this gallery are Dimitre Hadzi, George d'Almeida, Paolo Buggiani, and Mirko Balsedella. Surprisingly, within the world of Italian art galleries, the frequently changing inventories here are considered relatively affordable, ranging in price from 1,000,000 lire ($600) to 10,000,000 lire ($6,000). The building that contains the gallery, incidentally, was designed in the 19th century by a Danish sculptor to serve as a refuge for artists ever after. Today, the day-to-day operations of the gallery are conducted by Mr. Schneider's charming wife, Dolores. Open Monday through Saturday from 4:30 to 7:30pm (closed for part of August).

Giovanni B. Panatta Fine Art Shop, via Francesco Crispi 117. ☎ **6795948.**

In business since 1890, this store is up the hill toward Villa Borghese. Here, you'll find excellent prints in color and black-and-white, covering a variety of subjects from 18th-century Roman street scenes to astrological charts. Also, there is a good selection of reproductions of medieval and Renaissance art—attractive and reasonably priced as well. Open Monday 3:30 to 7:30pm, Tuesday through Saturday 9:15am to 1pm and 3:30 to 7:30pm.

Beauty Salons

Sergio Valente Beauty Center, via Condotti 11. ☎ **6794515.**

This place offers every cosmetic indulgence—hair styling, coloring, scalp treatments, facials, manicures, massages, and sauna—in bright, luxurious surroundings. English is spoken. Open Tuesday to Saturday 9:30am to 6pm.

Bookstores

Economy Book And Video Center, via Torina 136. ☎ **4746877.**

Catering to the expatriate English-speaking communities of Rome, this bookstore sells only English-language books (both new and used, paperback and hardcover), greeting cards, and videos. Staffed by British, Australian, or American workers, it lies about a block from the piazza della Repubblica Metro station, and bus lines no. 64 and 70. In summer, it's open Monday to Friday 9:30am to 7:30pm and Saturday 9:30am to 1:30pm. In winter, it's open Monday 3 to 7:30pm, and Tuesday through Saturday 9:30am to 7:30pm.

The Lion Bookshop, via del Babuino 181. ☎ **3225837.**

The Lion Bookshop is the oldest English-language bookshop in town, specializing in literature, both American and English. It also sells children's books and photographic volumes on both Rome and Italy. In a branch called The Lion Two, via della Fontanella 7 (☎ **3613037**) a vast choice of English-language videos is for sale or rent. The stores are open Monday through Saturday from 9:30am to 1:30pm and 3:30 to 7:30pm (closed in August).

Rizzoli, largo Chigi 15. ☎ **6796641.**

Rizzoli has one of the largest collections of Italian-language books in Rome. If your native language happens to be French, English, German, or Spanish, the endless shelves of this large bookstore will have a section to amuse, enlighten, and entertain you. Open Monday 2:30 to 7:30pm, Tuesday to Saturday 9am to 2pm and 2:30 to 7:30pm.

Department Stores

Coin, piazzale Appio 15. ☎ **7080020.**

This bustling, workaday store is a Roman staple, known for carrying almost everything. Its selection of clothing is very large. Open Monday 4 to 8pm, Tuesday to Saturday 9am to 1pm and 4 to 8pm.

La Rinascente, piazza Colonna, via del Corso 189. ☎ **6797691.**

This upscale department store offers clothing, hosiery, perfume, cosmetics, and other goods. It also has its own line of clothing (Ellerre) for men, women, and children. This is the largest of the Italian department store chains, and its name is seen frequently on billboards and newspaper ads throughout the country. Open Monday 2 to 7:30pm, Tuesday to Saturday 9:30am to 7:30pm.

Standa, corso Francia 124. ☎ **3338719**.

Standa could not be considered stylish by any stretch of the imagination, but some visitors find it enlightening to wander—just once—through the racks of department-store staples to see what an average Italian household might accumulate. Other branches are at corso Trieste 200; via Trionfale (without number); via Cola di Rienzo 173; viale Regina Margherita (without number); and viale Trastevere 60. Open Monday 3:30 to 7:30pm, Tuesday to Saturday 9am to 1pm and 2:30 to 7:30pm (all branches).

Upim, piazza Santa Maria Maggiore. ☎ **736658**.

Even more unassuming than Standa, Upim will sell you the full line of practical department-store necessities that you may have forgotten to bring from home. Other branches lie at via Alessandria 160; via Nazionale 211; and via del Tritone 172. Open Monday 1 to 7:30pm, Tuesday to Saturday 9am to 7:30pm (all branches).

Discount Shopping

Certain stores that can't move their merchandise at any price often consign their unwanted goods to discounters. In Italy, the original labels are usually still inside the garment (and you'll find some very chic labels strewn in with mounds of garments bearing less enviable names). Know in advance, however, that these garments couldn't be sold at higher prices in more glamorous shops, and some garments are either the wrong size, the wrong "look," or have a stylistic mistake.

Discount System, via del Viminale 35. ☎ **4746545**.

Discount System sells men's and women's wear by many of the big names (Armani, Valentino, Nino Cerruti, Fendi, and Krizia). Even if an item isn't from a famous designer, it often belongs to a factory that produces some of the best quality Italian fashion. However, don't give up hope: if you find something you like, know that it will be priced at around 50% of its original price tag in its original boutique, and it just might be a cut-rate gem well worth your effort. Open on Monday from 3:30 to 7:30pm and Tuesday through Saturday from 9:30am to 1pm and 3:30 to 7:30pm.

Eyeglasses

La Barbera, via Barberini 74. ☎ **483628**.

This place has been in business since 1837 and has a substantial reputation in the field of optical equipment. The store also carries a full spectrum of related wares: cameras, films, binoculars, opera glasses, and microscopes. You can have prescription glasses reproduced in 48 hours. For those once-fashionable hangouts on via Veneto and piazza del Popolo, take a look at Barbera's collection of sunglass frames—more than 5,000 varieties. Open Tuesday to Saturday 9am to 1pm and Monday to Saturday 3:30 to 7:30pm.

232

Shopping A to Z Fashion

Fashion

FOR MEN

Angelo, via Bissolati 34. ☎ **4741796.**

Angelo is a custom tailor for discerning men and has been featured in such publications as *Esquire* and *GQ.* He employs the best cutters and craftspeople, and his taste in style and design is impeccable. Custom shirts, suits, dinner jackets, even casual wear, can be made on short notice. A suit, for instance, takes about eight days. If you haven't time to wait, Angelo will ship anywhere in the world. Open Monday to Friday 9:30am to 1pm and 3:30 to 7:30pm.

Carlo Palazzi, via Borgognona 7E. ☎ **6789143.**

Housed in a 16th-century palazzo near the Spanish Steps, this shop will create or refurbish a man's wardrobe with beautiful suits and shirts, either off-the-rack or custom-made. Amid the antique/modern decor and sculptures, there is also a wide selection of knitwear, ties, belts, and whatever else a discerning man wears. Open Monday 3:30 to 7:30pm, Tuesday to Saturday 9:30am to 1pm and 3:30 to 7:30pm. In July and August, closed Saturday afternoon instead of Monday morning.

Emporio Armani, via del Babuino 119. ☎ **6796898.**

This store stocks relatively inexpensive menswear crafted by the couturier who has dressed perhaps more stage and screen stars than any other designer in Italy. The designer's more expensive line—sold at sometimes staggering prices that are nonetheless sometimes 30% less expensive than what you'd pay in the United States—lies a short walk away, at Giorgio Armani, via Condotti 77 (☎ **6991460**). Hours of both branches are Monday from 3 to 7pm, Tuesday through Friday from 10am to 7pm, and Saturday from 9am to 7pm.

Gianfranco Ferré, via Borgognona 6. ☎ **6797445.**

This is the outlet for his world-famous men's line. Although small, the shop is packed with quality items in menswear. The staff of young men advertise the products by wearing the latest in Ferré designs. Everything from T-shirts (even they are very expensive) to silk suits is sold here. Open Monday to Thursday 9:30am to 1pm and 3:30 to 7:30pm, Friday and Saturday 9:30am to 7:30pm.

Gianni Versace Uomo, via Borgognona 36. ☎ **6795292.**

This is the biggest Roman outlet for the famous designer's menswear line of daring clothes. The outlet also sells household items such as dishes and pillows. Open Monday 3:30 to 7:30pm, Tuesday to Saturday 9am to 1:30pm and 3:30 to 7:30pm.

Ribot, via Veneto 98A. ☎ **483485.**

Ribot, in front of the Excelsior Hotel, offers silk neckties and Ribot exclusive cashmeres; all Etrolines lines, including suits, jackets, and sportswear; plus elegant and conservative shoes by Church's of London. Open on Monday from 3:30 to 7:30pm and Tuesday through Saturday from 9:30am to 1:30pm and 3:30 to 7:30pm.

Valentino, via Mario de' Fiori 22. ☎ **6783656.**

This is a swank emporium for the men's clothing of the acclaimed designer. Here you can become the most fashionable man in town, but only if you can afford those high prices. Valentino's women's haute couture is sold around the corner, in an even bigger showroom at via Bocca di Leone 15 (☎ **6795862**). Open Monday 3 to 7pm, Tuesday to Saturday 10am to 7pm (both stores).

FOR WOMEN

Benetton, via Condotti 19. ☎ **6797982.**

Despite the gracefully arched ceiling and its prized location, this branch of the world-wide sportswear distributor charges about the same prices as branches at less glamorous addresses. Famous for woolen sweaters, tennis wear, blazers, and the kind of outfits you'd want to wear on a private yacht, this company has suffered (like every other clothier) from inexpensive copies of its designs. The original, however, is still best for guaranteed quality. Open Monday 3:30 to 7:30pm, Tuesday to Saturday 9:30am to 7:30pm.

Gianfranco Ferré, via Borgognona 42B. ☎ **6790050.**

Here you'll find the women's line for this famous designer whose clothes have been called "adventurous." Open Monday 3:30 to 7:30pm, Tuesday to Saturday 9:30am to 1:30pm and 3:30 to 7:30pm.

Givenchy, via Borgognona 21. ☎ **6784058.**

This is the Roman headquarters of one of the great designer names of France, Givenchy, a company known since World War I for its couture. In its Roman branch, the company emphasizes ready-to-wear garments for stylish women with warm Italian weather in mind. Open on Monday from 3 to 7pm and Tuesday through Saturday from 10am to 7pm.

Max Mara, via Frattina 48, at largo Goldoni. ☎ **6793638.**

Max Mara is considered one of the best outlets in Rome for women's clothing. The fabrics are appealing and the alterations are free. Open Monday 3:30 to 7:30pm, Tuesday to Saturday 10am to 2pm and 3:30 to 7:30pm.

Pancani, via Sistina 117. ☎ **4881434.**

Catering to affluent women and their admirers, Pancani is one of those rare boutiques where a team of seamstresses and tailors is stationed on the premises for last-minute alterations and changes. Most of the garments are designed as evening wear. Many are crafted from silk, some from cashmere, and most exude a kind of dignified and/or slinky noctural appeal that many women (and men) find very appealing. Most of the garments are handmade. If you decide to drop in, notice the fanciful ceiling fresco by Roman artist Novella Parigini. Open on Monday from 3:30 to 7:30pm and Tuesday through Saturday from 9:30am to 1pm and 3:30 to 7:30pm.

Renato Balestra, via Sistina 67. ☎ **6795424.**

Rapidly approaching the stratospheric upper levels of Italian fashion is Renato Balestra, whose women's clothing exudes a light-hearted elegance. This branch carries a complete line of the latest Balestra ready-to-wear designs for women. The company's administrative headquarters and the center of its couture department is nearby, at via Ludovici 35 (☎ **4821723**), although advance appointments are recommended there. It's probably advisable to stop into the via Sistina branch for an idea of the designer's style before launching yourself into a dialogue with Balestra's couture department, if only to save costs. Both outlets are open Monday from 3 to 7pm, Tuesday through Friday 10am to 7pm, and Saturday 9am to 7pm.

Vanilla, via Frattina 37. ☎ **6790638.**

This boutique for women offers an unusual collection of sometimes offbeat items, including handmade, elaborately decorated sweaters and imaginative accessories. Open Monday 3:30 to 7:30pm, Tuesday to Saturday 9:30am to 7:30pm.

SPORTSWEAR FOR MEN & WOMEN

Oliver, via del Babuino 61. ☎ **6798314.**

Specializing exclusively in sportswear for women or men, this is the least expensive line of clothing offered by the otherwise chillingly expensive designer Valentino. Clothing is easy to wear, and casually stylish, with warm-weather climates in mind. Open on Monday from 3 to 7pm, and Tuesday through Saturday from 10am to 7pm.

FOR CHILDREN

Baby House, via Cola di Rienzo 117. ☎ **3214291.**

Baby House offers what might be the most label-conscious collection of children's and young people's clothing in Italy. With an inventory of clothes suitable for children and adolescents to age 15, they sell clothing by Valentino, Bussardi, and Laura Biagiotti, whose threads are usually reserved for adult, rather than juvenile, playtime. Open on Monday from 3:30 to 7:30pm and Tuesday through Saturday from 9am to 1pm and 3:30 to 7:30pm.

Benetton, via Condotti 19. ☎ **6797982.**

Benetton isn't as expensive as you might expect. This store is the outlet for children's clothes (from infants to age 12) of the famous sportswear manufacturer. You can find rugby shirts, corduroys and jeans, and accessories in a wide selection of colors and styles. Open Monday 3:30 to 7:30pm, Tuesday to Saturday 10am to 7:30pm.

The College, via Vittoria 52. ☎ **6784073.**

The College has everything you'll need to make adorable children more adorable. Part of the inventory of this place is reserved for adult men and women, but the majority is intended for the infant and early adolescent offspring of the store's older clients. This establishment maintains another branch at via Condotti 47 (☎ **6787737**), which sells only clothes for women, not for children or men. Both branches maintain the same hours—Monday 3:30 to 7:30pm, Tuesday to Saturday 9:30am to 1pm and 3:30 to 7:30pm.

Food

Castroni, via Cola di Rienzo 196. ☎ **6874383.**

This place carries a bountiful array of unusual foodstuffs from throughout the Mediterranean. If you want herbs from Apulia, peperoncino oil, cheese from Val d'Aosta, or that strange brand of balsamic vinegar whose name you can never remember, Castroni will probably have it. Large, old-fashioned, and filled to the rafters with the abundance of agrarian Italy, it also carries certain foods considered exotic in Italy but commonplace in North America, such as taco shells and corn curls. Open Monday to Saturday 8:30am to 2pm and 3:30 to 8pm.

Gifts

Anatriello del Regalo, via Frattina 123. ☎ **6789601.**

This store is known for stocking an inventory of new and antique silver, some of it among the most unusual in Italy. All of the new items are made by Italian silversmiths, in designs ranging from the whimsical to the severely formal and dignified. Also on display are antique pieces of silver from England, Germany, and Switzerland. Open Monday 3:30 to 7:30pm; Tuesday through Saturday 9am to 1pm and 3:30 to 7:30pm.

A. Grispigni, via Francesco Crispi 59. ☎ **6790290.**

This store has a large assortment of leather-covered boxes, women's purses, compacts, desk sets, and cigarette cases. Many items are inlaid with gold, including Venetian wallets and Florentine boxes. Open Monday 3:30 to 7:30pm, Tuesday to Saturday 9:30am to 1pm and 3:30 to 7:30pm.

Lembo, Via XX Settembre 25A. ☎ **4883759.**

Lembo is a good place to find such gifts as crystal, china, glassware, and sterling. It's loaded with inventories. Open Monday through Friday from 9am to 7:30pm and on Saturday from 9am to 2pm and 3:30 to 7:30pm.

Hats

Borsalino, via IV Novembre 157B. ☎ **6794192.**

This millinery is chock-full of rakish hats reminiscent of the 1930s. The most famous hatmaker of all of Italy—the world, even—offers all sorts of other styles, too, for both women and men. The store also sells ultra-well-made trousers and suits. Open Monday 3:30 to 8pm, Tuesday to Saturday 9am to 1pm and 3:30 to 8pm.

Jewelry

Since the ancient Romans imported amethysts and pearls from the distant borders of their empire, and since the great trading ships of Venice and Genoa carried rubies and sapphires from Asia, the Italians have always collected jewelry. That is still true today, as can be seen by the dozens of jewelry stores throughout Rome. Styles range from the most classically conservative to neo-punk-rock frivolous and part of the fun is shopping for styles you might never have considered to be truly your own.

Bulgari, via Condotti 10. ☎ **6793876.**

Bulgari is the capital's most prestigious jeweler and has been since the 1890s. The shop window, on a conspicuously affluent stretch of via Condotti, is a bit of a visual attraction in its own right. Bulgari designs combine classical Greek aesthetics with Italian taste. Over the years Bulgari has followed changes in style, yet clings to tradition as well. Prices range from "affordable" to "the sky is the limit." Open Monday from 3 to 7pm and Tuesday through Saturday from 10am to 7pm.

E. Fiore, via Ludovisi 31. ☎ **4819296.**

In this store near via Veneto, you can choose a jewel and have it set according to your specifications. Or make your selection from a rich assortment of charms, bracelets, necklaces, rings, brooches, corals, pearls, and cameos. Also featured are elegant watches, silverware, and goldware. Fiore also does expert repair work on your own jewelry and watches. Open Monday 3:30 to 7:30pm, Tuesday to Saturday 9am to 1pm and 3:30 to 7:30pm; closed in August.

Federico Buccellati, via Condotti 31. ☎ **6790329.**

One of the best gold- and silversmiths in Italy, Federico Buccellati sells neo-Renaissance creations that will change your thinking about the way gold and silver are designed. Here you will discover the Italian tradition and beauty of handmade jewelry and hollowware whose principles sometimes hark back to the designs of Renaissance goldmaster Benvenuto Cellini. Open Tuesday to Saturday 10am to 1:30pm and 3 to 7pm.

Leather

Italian leather is among the very best in the world, and at its best can attain butter-soft textures more pliable than cloth. You'll find hundreds of leather stores in Rome, many of them excellent.

Cesare Diomedi Leather Goods, via Vittorio Emanuele Orlando 96–97. ☎ **4884822.**

Located in front of the Grand Hotel, this store offers one of the most outstanding collections of leather goods in Rome. And leather isn't all you'll find in this small, two-story shop with a winding staircase. There are many other distinctive items, such as small gold cigarette cases and jeweled umbrellas, that make this a good stopping-off point for that last gift. Upstairs is a wide assortment of elegant leather luggage and accessories. Open Monday 3:30 to 7:30pm, Tuesday to Saturday 9am to 1pm and 3:30 to 7:30pm.

Elena, via Sistina 81. ☎ **6781500.**

Elena is a lesser-known leather store, selling well-made wallets and bags for women. Although its goods might not carry the name recognition of other vendors in this neighborhood, its prices are sometimes commensurately lower. Incidentally, it does not sell shoes. Open on Monday from 3:30 to 7:30pm and Tuesday through Saturday from 10:30am to 7:30pm.

Fendi, via Borgognona 36A-39. ☎ **6797641.**

The House of Fendi is mainly known for its leather goods, but it also has furs, stylish purses, ready-to-wear clothing, and a new men's line of clothing and accessories. Gift items, home furnishings, and sports accessories are also sold here, all emblazoned with an "F." Open Monday 3:30 to 7:30pm, Tuesday to Saturday 9:30am to 7:30pm; closed Saturday afternoon July through September.

Gucci, via Condotti 8. ☎ **6790405.**

Gucci, of course, is a legend. An established firm since 1900, it sells high-class leather goods, such as suitcases, handbags, wallets, shoes, and desk accessories. It also has departments complete with elegant men's and women's wear, including tailored shirts, blouses, and dresses, as well as ties and scarves of numerous designs. *La bella figura* is alive and well at Gucci, and prices have never been higher. Among the many temptations is Gucci's own perfume. Open Monday 3 to 7pm, Tuesday to Saturday 10am to 7pm.

Pappagallo, via Francesco Crispi 115. ☎ **6783011.**

This is a suede and leather factory; the staff at this "parrot" makes their own goods here, including bags, wallets, and suede coats. The quality is fine too, and the prices are most reasonable. Open Monday 3:30 to 7:30pm, Tuesday to Saturday 9am to 1pm and 3:30 to 7:30pm.

Lingerie

Brighenti, via Frattina 7–8. ☎ **6791484.**

Brighenti sells strictly *lingerie di lusso*, or perhaps better phrased, *haute corseterie*. The shop is amid several famous neighbors on the previously recommended via Frattina. Open Monday 3:30 to 7:30pm, Tuesday to Saturday 9am to 1pm and 3:30 to 7:30pm; closed August.

Cesari, via del Babuino 195. ☎ **3613451.**

Cesari is a respected shop set next to the piazza del Popolo, selling lingerie, plus skillfully embroidered linens, towels, and handkerchiefs. Open Monday from 3:30 to 7:30pm, Tuesday through Saturday from 9am to 1pm and 3:30 to 7:30pm.

Tomassini di Luisa Romagnoli, via Sistina 119. ☎ **4881909.**

This place offers delicately beautiful lingerie and negligées, all the original designs of Luisa Romagnoli. Most of the merchandise sold here is of shimmery Italian silk; others, to a lesser degree, are of fluffy cotton or frothy nylon. Highly revealing garments are sold either ready-to-wear or custom-made. Open on Monday from 3:30 to 7:30pm and Tuesday through Sunday from 9am to 1pm and 3:30 to 7:30pm.

Liquors

Ai Monasteri, piazza delle Lune 76. ☎ **68802783.**

Italy produces a staggering volume of wines, liqueurs, and after-dinner drinks, and here is one of the city's best selections. It offers a treasure trove of liquors (including liqueurs and wines), honey, and herbal teas made in monasteries and convents all over Italy. You can buy excellent chocolates and other candies here as well. The shop will ship some items home for you. You make your selections in a quiet atmosphere, reminiscent of a monastery, just two blocks from Bernini's Fountain of the Four Rivers in piazza Navona. Open Monday to Wednesday and Friday and Saturday 9am to 1pm and 4:30 to 7:30pm, Thursday 9am to 1pm.

Markets

At the sprawling **open-air flea market** of Rome held every Sunday morning, every peddler from Trastevere and the surrounding Castelli Romani sets up a temporary shop. The vendors are likely to sell merchandise ranging from secondhand paintings of madonnas (the Italian market is glutted with these) to termite-eaten Il Duce wooden medallions (many of the homes of the lower-income groups still display likenesses of the murdered dictator), to pseudo-Etruscan hairpins, to bushels of rosaries, to 1947 television sets, to books printed in 1835. Serious shoppers can often ferret out a good buy. If you've ever been impressed with the bargaining power of the Spaniard, you haven't seen anything till you've viewed an Italian.

Go to the flea market in Trastevere, near the end of viale Trastevere (bus no. 75 to Porta Portese), then walk a short distance to via Portuense. By 10:30am the market is full of people. Some of the vendors get there as early as midnight to get their choice space. As you would at any street market, beware of pickpockets. Open Sunday 7am to 1pm.

Mosaics

Savelli, via Paolo VI no. 27. ☎ **68307017.**

This company specializes in the manufacture and sale of mosaics, an art form as old as the Roman Empire itself. Many of the objects displayed in the company's gallery were inspired by ancient originals discovered in thousands of excavations throughout the Italian peninsula, including those at Pompeii and Ostia. Others, especially the floral designs, depend on the whim and creativity of the artists. Objects include tabletops, boxes, and vases. The cheapest mosaic objects begin at around $125, and are unsigned products crafted by students at a school for artists which is partially funded by the Vatican. Objects made in the Savelli workshops that are signed by the individual artists (and that tend to be larger and more elaborate) range from $500 to as much as $25,000. The outlet also contains a collection of small souvenir items such as keychains and carved statues. Open Monday through Saturday from 9am to 6:30pm and on Sunday from 9:30am to 1:30pm.

Religious Art

Anna Maria Guadenzi, piazza della Minerva 69A. ☎ **6790431.**

Set in a neighborhood loaded with purveyors of religious art and icons, this shop claims to be the oldest of its type in Rome. If you collect depictions of the Mother of Jesus, paintings of the saints, exotic rosaries, chalices, small statues, or medals, you can feel secure knowing that thousands of pilgrims have spent their money here before you. Whether you view its merchandise as a devotional aid or as bizarre kitsch, this shop has it all. Open Monday 3:30 to 7:30pm, Tuesday to Saturday 9am to 1pm and 3:30 to 7:30pm; closed August 10 to 30.

Shoes

Bruno Magli, via Veneto 70A. ☎ **4884355.**

Bruno Magli offers dressy footwear for both sexes. There is another store at via del Gambero (without number; ☎ **6793802**). Open Monday 3:30 to 7:30pm, Tuesday to Saturday 9:30am to 1pm and 3:30 to 7:30pm (both stores).

Dominici, via del Corso 14. ☎ **3610591.**

An understated facade a few steps from piazza del Popolo shelters an amusing and lighthearted collection of men's and women's shoes in a rainbow variety of vivid colors. The style is aggressively young-at-heart, and the children's shoes are adorable. Open Monday 3:30 to 8pm, Tuesday to Saturday 9:30am to 1pm and 3:30 to 8pm.

Fragiacomo, via Condotti 35. ☎ **6798780.**

Here you can buy shoes for both men and women in a champagne-colored showroom with gilt-touched chairs and big display cases. Open Monday 3:30 to 7:30pm, Tuesday to Saturday 9:30am to 1:30pm and 3:30 to 7:30pm.

Lily Of Florence, via Lombardia 38 (off via Veneto). ☎ **4740262.**

This famous Florentine shoemaker now has a shop in Rome, with the same merchandise which made the outlet so well known in the Tuscan capital. Colors come in a wide range, the designs are stylish, and leather texture is of good quality. Shoes for both men and women are sold here, and American sizes are a feature. Open Monday through Saturday from 9:30am to 7:30pm.

Raphael Salato, via Veneto 104. ☎ **484677.**

This shop, near the Excelsior Hotel, is where the style-conscious woman goes for the latest in shoe fashions. The selection of unusual and well-crafted shoes is wide. In addition, Raphael Salato stocks an exclusive line of children's shoes, plus bags and leather fashions. Open Monday 3:30 to 7:30pm, Tuesday to Saturday 9:30am to 1:30pm and 3:30 to 7:30pm.

Salvatore Ferragamo, via Condotti 73–74. ☎ **6798402.**

Salvatore Ferragamo sells elegant and fabled footwear, plus women's clothing and accessories, ties and ready-to-wear in an atmosphere full of Italian style. The name became famous in America when such screen stars as Pola Negri and Greta Garbo began appearing in Ferragamo shoes. From June 15 through September 15, hours are Monday through Friday from 3:30pm to 7:30pm and on Saturday from 9:30am to 1:30pm. From September 16 to June 14, hours are Monday from 3:30 to 7:30pm and Tuesday through Saturday from 9:30am to 7:30pm.

Silver

Fornari, via Frattina 71–72. ☎ **6792524.**

Fornari has been providing fine silver to an international clientele since the 1930s. The via Frattina showroom consists of two floors, where one can see the precision-crafted items that have earned this establishment the reputation of being the finest silversmith in Rome. Elegant silver trays and boxes, complete tea services, small gift items, handsome silver table settings, and many fine antique pieces, as well as modern gift items, are on display and can be shipped anywhere in the world. It's fun to browse around and inspect the objects in elegantly curved brass-and-glass cases. In addition, the store has added a whole section of dishes and glassware, which includes everything that might be on a bride's and groom's wish list. Open Monday 3:30 to 7:30pm, Tuesday to Saturday 10am to 7:30pm.

Toys

La Città Del Sole, via della Scrofa 65. ☎ **6875404.**

This is the largest and best-stocked of any of the stores within this nationwide chain. It has toys ranging from simple and inexpensive to very complicated, including puzzles that will challenge children's gray matter and drive their parents crazy. Also for sale are such rainy-day distractions as miniature billiard tables and tabletop golf sets. Open Monday 3 to 8pm, Tuesday to Saturday 10am to 7:30pm.

Wines

Buccone, via Ripetta. ☎ **3612154.**

This is an historic wine shop, right near piazza del Popolo. Its selection of wines and gastronomic specialties is considered among the finest in Rome. Open Monday through Saturday from 8:30am to 1:30pm and 3:30 to 8pm.

Enoteca Rocchi, via Alessandro Scarlatti 7. ☎ **8551022.**

Rocchi carries one of Rome's largest selection of wines and liqueurs. The staff will ship your purchases anywhere. Open Monday to Saturday 8:30am to 2pm and 4:30 to 8pm; closed August.

Trimani Il Wine Bar, via Goito 20. ☎ **4469661.**

Trimani, established in 1821, sells wines and spirits from Italy, among other offerings. Purchases can be shipped to your home. It collaborates with the Italian wine magazine, *Gambero Rosso,* organizing some lectures about wine where devotees can improve their knowledge and educate their tastebuds. Open Monday through Saturday from 8:30am to 1:30pm and 3:30 to 8pm.

9

Rome Nights

WHEN THE SUN GOES DOWN, LIGHTS ACROSS THE CITY BATHE PALACES, ruins, fountains, and monuments in a theatrical white light. There are few things quite as pleasurable as a stroll past the solemn pillars of old temples, or the cascading torrents of Renaissance fountains glowing under the blue-black sky. Of the fountains, the *Naiads* (piazza della Repubblica), the *Tortoises* (piazza Mattei), and, of course, the *Trevi* are particularly alluring. The **Capitoline Hill** is panoramically lit at night. Behind the Senatorial Palace is a fine view of the **Roman Forum.** If you're staying across the Tiber, **piazza San Pietro** (in front of St. Peter's Basilica) is particularly impressive at night, when the tour buses and crowds have departed. And a combination of illuminated architecture, Renaissance fountains, and, frequently, sidewalk stage shows and art expositions is at **piazza Navona.** If you're ambitious and have a good sense of direction, try exploring the streets west of piazza Navona, which look like a stage set when they're lit at night.

There are no inexpensive nightclubs in Rome, so be duly warned. Another important warning: During the peak of summer, usually in August, many nightclub proprietors lock their doors and head for the seashore. Others close at different times each year, so it's hard to keep up to date. Always have your hotel check to see if a club is operating before you make a trek to it. Furthermore, many of the legitimate nightclubs, besides being expensive, are frequented by hookers plying their trade.

But remember that for many Romans, a night on the town means dining late at a trattoria. The local denizens like to drink wine and talk after their meal, even when the waiters are putting chairs on top of empty tables.

For information about events in Rome, pick up a copy of *This Week in Rome,* which is distributed free at the tourist office and often is available at hotel reception desks. It spotlights seasonal entertainment and documents events of special interest.

Even if you don't speak Italian, you can generally follow the listings of special events and evening entertainment featured in *La Repubblica,* one of the leading Italian newspapers. *TrovaRoma,* a special weekly entertainment supplement—good for the coming week—is published in this paper on Thursday.

1 The Performing Arts

Rome has an active cultural life, and music is its forte. The list of famous personalities from this city is overwhelming—just think of such composers as Verdi, Paganini, Rossini, Scarlatti, Vivaldi; the conductor Muti; and, of course, the opera star Pavarotti.

Major Performing Arts Companies

Rome's premier cultural venue is the **Teatro dell'Opera** (see below), where standards may not be as high as at Milan's legendary La Scala, but where performances are stellar nevertheless. Even more spectacular operas are staged at the **Termi di Caracalla** (see below). The outstanding local troupe is the **Rome Opera Ballet** (see below).

Rome doesn't have a major center for classical music concerts, although performances of the most important orchestra, the **RAI Symphony Orchestra,** most often take place at the RAI Auditorium as well as at the Academy of St. Cecilia (see below).

Rome is also a major stopover for international stars. Rock headliners often perform at **Stadio Flaminio** (☎ 391239), **Foro Italico** (☎ 36865625), and at two different places in the EUR, the **Palazzo della Civiltà del Lavoro** and the **Palazzo dello Sport** (☎ 5925107). Most of the concerts are at the Palazzo dello Sport.

Instead of trying to call these venues, contact a ticket agent, **Orbis,** piazza Esquilino 37 (☎ 4827403), which not only will let you know what's happening in Rome at the time of your visit, but will also sell you a ticket to the performance. The Orbis box office is open Monday through Friday from 9:30am to 1pm and 4 to 7:30pm, Saturday 10am to 1pm.

Classical Music

Academy Of St. Cecilia, via della Conciliazione 4. ☎ **6780742.**

Concerts given by the orchestra of the Academy of St. Cecilia usually take place at piazza di Villa Giulia, site of the Etruscan Museum, from the end of June to the end of July; in winter they are held in the concert hall on via della Conciliazione. Take bus no. 30.

Tickets: 20,000–45,000 lire ($12–$27) for symphonic music, 20,000–35,000 lire ($12–$21) for chamber music.

Teatro Olimpico, piazza Gentile da Fabriano. ☎ **3234890.**

Large and well-publicized, this echoing stage hosts a widely divergent collection of singers, both classical and pop, who perform according to a schedule that sometimes changes at the last minute. Occasionally, the space is devoted to chamber orchestras or orchestral visits from foreign countries.

Tickets: 20,000–80,000 lire ($12–$48), depending on the event.

Opera

⭐ **Teatro dell'Opera,** piazza Beniamino Gigli 2. ☎ **481601.**

If you're in the capital for the opera season, usually from November to May, you may want to attend a performance at the historic Rome Opera House, located off via Nazionale. The sale of tickets begins 2 days before a performance is scheduled. Nothing is presented here in August.

Tickets: 26,000–160,000 lire ($15.60–$96) opera; 15,000–18,000 lire ($9–$10.80) ballet; 20,000–50,000 lire ($12–$30) symphonic concerts.

⭐ **Terme di Caracalla,** via delle Terme di Caracalla. ☎ **4811601.**

When the Romans stage something, they like it to be of epic quality. At the Baths of Caracalla, you can attend summer performances of grand opera, usually from the first of July to the middle of August.

Sponsored by the Rome Opera House, the season is likely to include Verdi's *Aïda*, the best selection for employing the grandeur of the setting. *Aïda* ends with a smash—the celebrated "double scene," when the floodlit upper part represents the Temple of Vulcan, the part underneath, the tomb. And for sheer unrivaled Cecil B. de Mille, it's worth seeing the phalanx of trumpeters enter in the second act playing the "Grand March"; they are followed by Egyptian troops with banners, chariots, Ethiopian slaves, dancing girls—a spectacular crescendo.

Tickets are on sale at the Teatro dell'Opera (see above). If you don't mind taking along a pair of binoculars, you can buy an unreserved seat.

Tickets: 30,000–65,000 lire ($18–$39) opera; 25,000–50,000 lire ($15–$30) ballet.

Ballet & Dance

Performances of the **Rome Opera Ballet** are given at the Teatro dell'Opera (see above). The regular repertoire of classical ballet is supplemented by performances of internationally acclaimed guest artists, and Rome is on the agenda for major troupes from around the world, ranging from the United States to Russia. Major performances are at the Teatro dell'Opera, but watch for announcements in the weekly entertainment guides to Rome about other venues, including Teatro Olimpico or even open-air ballet performances. Both modern (such as the Alvin Ailey dancers) and classical dance troupes appear frequently in Rome. Check the entertainment guides to see what's happening at the time of your visit.

Dinner Theater

Fantasie di Trastevere, via di Santa Dorotea 6. ☎ **588-1671.**

In this unusual place, you'll be instantly immersed in the bravura and gaiety of uninhibited Roman nightlife. The setting is the "people's theater," where the famous actor, Petrolini, made his debut. You dine on hearty regional cuisine while you're entertained by folksingers and musicians performing in provincial attire. Some of their songs are old Roman and Neapolitan favorites; others are esoteric. Expect to pay 75,000 lire ($45) for a full meal. If you visit for a drink, the first one will cost 30,000 lire ($18). Some two dozen folk singers and musicians in regional costumes perform, making it a festive affair. The theater is open Monday through Saturday from 8 to 11pm, and the folklore show, featuring both Roman and Neapolitan favorites, is presented from 9:30 to 10:30pm.

2   The Club & Music Scene

Nightclubs

Arciliuto, piazza Monte Vecchio 5. ☎ **6879419.**

One of the most romantic candlelit spots in Rome is reputedly the former studio of Raphael. Guests enjoy a musical salon ambience, listening to both a guitarist and lutist. The evening's presentation also includes Neapolitan love songs, old Italian madrigals, even current hits from New York's Broadway or London's West End. The setting and atmosphere are intimate. Highly recommended, it is hard to find, but it's within walking distance of piazza Navona. Open Monday to Saturday from 10pm to 1:30am.

Admission (including one drink): 35,000 lire ($21); subsequent drinks 15,000 lire ($9). **Closed:** July 20–Sept 5.

La Cabala/The Blue Bar/Hostaria dell'Orso, via dei Soldati 25. ☎ 6864221.

These premises were once the most talked-about evening venue of Rome, attracting elegant Italians and well-heeled foreigners throughout the 1950s and 1960s. Today, the spotlight has shifted to other venues, although many Romans continue to view the place with affection and nostalgia. The setting is a 14th-century palazzo, near piazza Navona, which began its life as a simple inn. Clients who have used its dining and/or overnight facilities through the ages have included Dante, Rabelais, Montaigne, Goethe, and thousands of other, less well-documented scholars and pilgrims.

Today, the establishment contains three separate areas: In the cellar, The Blue Bar is a moody but mellow enclave featuring cocktails and music from two pianists and a guitarist. On street level is a formal restaurant serving international cuisine, the Hostaria dell'Orso, charging 25,000 to 35,000 lire ($15–$21) for appetizers and 45,000 to 65,000 lire ($27–$39) for main courses. One floor above street level is La Cabala, a disco that attracts a well-dressed, over-25 crowd. Some clients visit all three areas during a night on the town, although no one will mind if you decide to visit only the disco or only the bar. The restaurant serves dinner only, Monday through Saturday 7:30pm to midnight. The Blue Bar and La Cabala are open Monday through Saturday 10:30pm to 3 or 4am, depending on business. All three floors are closed on Sunday. If you plan to dine here, reservations are recommended.

Admission: In Blue Bar, first drink 35,000 lire ($21); subsequent drink 20,000 lire ($12). In La Cabala, first drink 30,000 lire ($18), subsequent drink 20,000 lire ($12).

Divina, via Romagnosi 11A. ☎ 3611348.

The aptly named Divina is a chic rendezvous, a relaxing piano bar where you just might end up spending the evening. Many people still come here looking for Gil's, a famous club that once stood on

Major Concert & Performance Halls	
Rome Opera House (Teatro dell'Opera)	☎ 481601
Terme di Caracalla	☎ 4811601
Academy of St. Cecilia	☎ 3234890
Teatro Olimpico	☎ 3234890

this spot and has gone down in Roman nightlife history. What you get today is a romantic evening in one of several small rooms lined with mirrors. It's open Tuesday through Saturday from 11pm to either 4 or 5am. *Note:* It's important to call for a reservation, as some nights are by invitation only, at which time you can't get in unless you're a "friend of the club" (frequent patron).

Admission (including one drink): Tues–Thurs 35,000 lire ($21), Fri–Sat 40,000 lire ($24).

Gilda, via Mario de' Fiori, 97. ☎ 6784838.

Gilda is noted as an adventurous combination of nightclub, disco, and restaurant, and for the glamorous acts it books. Past performances have included Diana Ross and splashy, Paris-type revues, often with young women from England and the United States. Everyone from Prince Albert of Monaco to Sylvester Stallone has shown up here. The artistic direction assures first-class shows, a well-run restaurant, three bars, and latest disco music played between the live musical acts. The restaurant features Italian and international cooking, with meals costing from 85,000 lire ($51). The restaurant is open Tuesday to Saturday 9:30pm to 3:30am, and the nightclub is open Tuesday to Saturday 10:30pm to 3:30am.

Admission (including one drink): 35,000 lire ($21) Sun–Thurs, 40,000 lire ($24) Fri–Sat.

Cabaret

Da Ciceruacchio, via del Porto 1. ☎ 5806046.

Located on piazza dei Mercanti, this restaurant was once a sunken jail—the ancient vine-covered walls date from the days of the Roman Empire. Folkloric groups are presented throughout the evening, especially singers of Neapolitan songs, accompanied by guitars and harmonicas—a rich repertoire of oldtime favorites, some of them with bawdy lyrics. Featured here are charcoal-broiled steaks and chops, along with lots of local wine. Bean soup is a specialty. The grilled mushrooms are another good opening, as is the spaghetti with clams. For a main course, I'd recommend scampi with curry or charcoal-broiled meats. You can dine here Tuesday through Sunday from 8pm to midnight for 40,000–65,000 lire ($24–$39).

Da Meo Patacca, piazza dei Mercanti 30. ☎ 58331086.

Da Meo Patacca, in Trastevere, would certainly have pleased Barnum and Bailey. On a gaslit piazza from the Middle Ages, it serves bountiful self-styled "Roman country" meals to flocks of tourists. The atmosphere is one of extravaganza—primitive, colorful, theatrical in a carnival sense. It's good fun if you're in the mood. From the huge open-spit oven and the charcoal grill, many hastily turned out platters are served. Downstairs is a vast cellar with strolling musicians and singers. The restaurant has a tavern theme and is decked out with wagon wheels, along with garlands of pepper and garlic. And many offerings are as adventurous as the decor: wild boar, wild hare, and quail; but there are also corn on the cob, pork and beans, thick-cut sirloins, and chicken on a spit. Come here for the general fun and entertainment—not for refined cuisine. Expect to spend 60,000 lire ($36) and up for a meal here. In summer, you can dine at outdoor tables. It's open daily from 8 to 11:30pm.

Jazz, Soul & Funk

Alexanderplatz, via Ostia 9. ☎ 3729398.

At Alexanderplatz, a leading jazz club, you can hear jazz (not rock) Monday to Saturday from 9pm to 2am. Entrance is free, and the price of your evening of listening pleasure depends on what you have to drink. A whisky costs from 10,000 lire ($6). There is also a restaurant, with a good Italian kitchen, which serves everything from pesto alla genovese to gnocchi alla romana. A full meal begins at 38,000 lire ($22.80).

Big Mama, vicolo San Francesco a Ripa 18. ☎ 5812551.

Big Mama is a hangout for jazz and blues musicians where you're likely to meet the up-and-coming jazz stars of tomorrow. But sometimes the big names appear as well. The entrance fee, therefore, depends on what's being presented. Drinks range from 5,000 to 21,000 lire ($3–$12.60). Closed July through September, the club is open nightly from 9pm to 1:30am.

   Admission: 20,000 lire ($12) one-time membership card, plus 10,000–30,000 lire ($6–$18) cover, depending on the act.

Fonclea, via Crescenzio 82A. ☎ 6896302.

Fonclea offers live music every night—Dixieland, rock, and rhythm and blues. This is basically a cellar jazz establishment that attracts a cross spectrum of Roman life. The music starts at 10:30pm and usually lasts until 12:30am. The club is open nightly from 8pm to 2:30am (on Friday and Saturday it stays open until 3:30am). There's also a restaurant that features grilled meats, salads, and crêpes. A meal starts at 35,000 lire ($21), but if you want dinner it's best to reserve a table, as the club becomes crowded after 10:30pm. Drinks run 7,000–10,000 lire ($4.20–$6). Closed July and August.

   Admission: 10,000 lire ($6) except Sun–Thurs, when it's free between 8 and 9pm.

Music Inn, largo dei Fiorentini 3. ☎ 6544934.

The Music Inn is considered among the leading jazz clubs of Rome. Some of the biggest names in jazz, both European and American, have performed here. It's open Thursday through Sunday from 8:30pm to 1am. Closed in August.

   Admission (including one drink): 35,000 lire ($21).

Notorious, via San Nicolà de Tolentino 22. ☎ 4746888.

Notorious really isn't. It's one of the most popular discos of Rome, and the music is always recorded. Some of the most beautiful people of Rome show up in these crowded confines, often in their best disco finery. But show up late—it's more fashionable. It's open Tuesday through Sunday from 11pm to 4am.

   Admission (including one drink): 35,000 lire ($21).

Saint Louis Music City, via del Cardello 13A. ☎ **4745076.**

This is another leading jazz venue. In large, contemporary surroundings, it doesn't necessarily attract the big names in jazz; what you get instead are young and sometimes very talented groups beginning their careers. Many celebrities have been known to patronize the place. Soul and funk music are performed on occasion. You can also enjoy meals at a restaurant on the premises, which cost 35,000 lire ($21) and up. Drinks range from 6,000 to 10,000 lire ($3.60 to $6). It's open Tuesday through Sunday from 9pm to 2am.

Admission: 10,000 lire ($6), including club membership.

Veleno, via Sardegna 27. ☎ **493583.**

Veleno ("Poison") is a Roman nightlife oddity, lying off via Veneto and north of piazza Barberini. In their fashionable finery, Romans show up here to enjoy dance music, including rap, soul, and funk. It's also been a favorite on the celebrity circuit. Open Tuesday to Sunday 10pm to 4am.

Admission (including one drink): Men, 22,000 lire ($13.20) Tues–Thurs, 32,000 lire ($19.20) Fri–Sat; women, free.

Gay Clubs

Angelo Azzuro, via Cardinal Merry del Val 13. ☎ **5800472.**

Angelo Azzuro is a gay "hot spot," deep in the heart of Trastevere, which is open Friday, Saturday, and Sunday from 11pm to 4am. No food is served, nor is live music presented. Men dance with men to recorded music, and women are also invited to patronize the club. Friday is for women only. Saturday and Sunday nights are reserved for gay men only. After the drink requirement is met (see below), subsequent libations cost 8,000 lire ($4.80) each.

Admission (including an obligatory first drink): 20,000 lire ($12).

L'Alibi, via Monte Testaccio 44. ☎ **5743448.**

L'Alibi, in the Testaccio sector, away from the heart of Rome, is a year-round venue on many a gay man's agenda. The crowd, however, tends to be mixed, both Roman and international, straight and gay, male and female. One room is devoted to dancing. It's open Tuesday through Sunday from 11pm to 5am. Take bus no. 20N or 30N from largo Argentina near the Piramide. Drinks run 10,000 lire ($6).

Admission: Tues–Thurs and Sun 10,000 lire ($6); Fri 15,000 lire ($9); Sat 20,000 lire ($12).

The Hangar, via in Selci 69. ☎ **4881397.**

Established in 1984 by an expatriate, Louisiana-born American, John, and his Italian partner, Gianni, this is probably the premier gay bar in Rome. It's set on one of Rome's oldest streets, adjacent to the Roman Forum in the house on the site of the palace inhabited by Emperor Nero's deranged wife, Messalina. (Her ghost is rumored to still inhabit the premises.) Each of the establishment's two bars contains its own independent sound system.

Women are welcome any night except Monday, when videos and entertainment for gay men are featured. The busiest nights are

Saturday, Sunday, and Monday, when as many as 500 patrons cram inside. Beer costs from 5,000 lire ($3); whisky from 8,000 lire ($4.80). It's open Wednesday through Monday from 10:30pm to at least 4am, and often later. The Hangar is closed during three weeks in August.

Admission: Free.

Joli Coeur, via Sirte 5. No phone.

Open only on Saturday nights, from 11pm until around 5am, this bar caters only to gay women. A fixture in the city's lesbian nighttime scene, it attracts women from around Europe during its very limited opening hours. Information about Joli Coeur (which translates as "Pretty Heart") is offered at The Hangar (see above), because of the difficulties in reaching Joli Coeur directly. After the obligatory first drink (see below), subsequent libations cost from 6,000 lire ($3.60) each.

Admission (including the first drink): 15,000 lire ($9).

3   The Cafe & Bar Scene

It seems there is nothing Romans like to do better than sit and talk over their favorite beverage—usually wine or coffee. So it is not surprising that there is a variety of places in which you, too, can enjoy these pleasures.

Cafes

VIA VENETO

The most famous of the cafes of Rome are on via Veneto. While they line the streets from piazza Barberini all the way to the Pincian Gate, the best are near the latter landmark. The most famous of these are Harry's Bar and the Caffè de Paris.

This area, once exclusive and expensive—now only expensive—is still a much-visited part of town, with stores selling jewels and airline tickets.

Those old enough to remember the 1950s may recall Marcello Mastroianni fighting off the paparazzi in *La Dolce Vita.* You'll probably spend at least one night on the via Veneto. Few visitors want to miss it.

Caffè de Paris, via Veneto 90. ☎ **4885284.**

Caffè de Paris rises and falls in popularity, depending on the decade. In the 1950s it was a haven for the fashionable; it is now a popular restaurant in summer where you can occupy a counter seat along a bar or a table inside. However, if the weather's right, the tables spill right out onto the sidewalk and the passing crowd walks through. Coffee costs from 6,000 lire ($3.60) if you sit outside. Open Thursday to Tuesday 8am to 1am.

Harry's Bar, via Veneto 148. ☎ **484643.**

Harry's Bar is the choicest watering spot along this gilded street. It has no connections with the world-famous Harry's Bars in Florence, Venice, Paris, and other cities. In many respects, the Roma Harry's is the most elegant of them all, with tapestry walls, elaborate wood paneling, curvy plastering, and sconces.

You can have excellent, but outrageously priced, food here as well, taking your meal in summer (if you prefer) at one of the sidewalk tables. In back is a small dining room, which serves some of the finest food in central Rome; meals go for 60,000–80,000 lire ($36–$48). A whisky costs 10,000–12,000 lire ($6–$7.20). The bar is open Monday through Saturday from 11:30am to 1:30am; closed August 1–10.

PIAZZA DEL POPOLO

The fashion-conscious denizens of Rome, known as the *bella gente,* or Beautiful People, are seldom seen on the via Veneto anymore. Instead some of them make a point to be seen (especially after midnight) in piazza del Popolo. There is an element of excitement in the air here—the feeling that something interesting is just about to happen. The little outdoor tables of the two leading sidewalk cafes sprawl far and wide. They're surrounded by expensive Italian sports cars, elegant women with German accents, and men in leather pants.

Café Rosati, piazza del Popolo 4–5. ☎ **3611418.**

The most chic place to go for a drink has been in business since 1923. Originally it was more or less an ice-cream parlor. Light food items are available, but most people order a drink, a beer, or a dish of ice cream. You can sit out front at one of the tables spreading into the piazza. Low, growling Maseratis cruise slowly by while young Italian men in silk shirts hang from the car windows, eyeing sleek blondes. There is a constant stream of expensive automobiles cruising by Rosati at night.

Drinks are more expensive, of course, if you select a table. But who wants to stand at the bar?

Whisky at a table costs from 11,000 lire ($6.60); coffee at a table costs 6,000 lire ($3.60). Open daily 7:30am to 1am (closed Tuesday from November through March).

Canova Café, piazza del Popolo. ☎ **3612231.**

Although the management has filled the interior of this cafe with boutiques selling expensive gift items, which include luggage and cigarette lighters, many Romans still consider this the place to be on piazza del Popolo. The Canova has a sidewalk terrace for pedestrian-watching, plus a snack bar, a restaurant, and a wine shop inside. In summer, you'll have access to a quiet courtyard whose walls are covered with ivy and where flowers grow in terra-cotta planters. Expect to spend 1,100 lire (70¢) for a coffee at the stand-up bar. If ordered at a table, coffee costs 6,000 lire ($3.60). A meal is offered for around 38,000 lire ($22.80). Food is served daily from noon to 3:30pm and 7 to 11pm, but the bar is open daily from 7am to midnight or 1am. It's closed Monday from November to April.

TRASTEVERE

Just as piazza del Popolo lured the chic crowd from via Veneto, several cafes in Trastevere, across the Tiber, threaten to do the same for Popolo. Fans who saw Fellini's *Roma* know what piazza Santa Maria, deep in the heart of Trastevere, looks like. The square—filled with milling throngs in summer—is graded with an octagonal fountain and a church dating from the 12th century. On the piazza, despite a certain amount of traffic, children run and play, and occasional spontaneous guitar fests are heard when the weather's good.

Café-Bar di Marzio, piazza di Santa Maria in Trastevere 158. ☎ 5816095.

This warmly inviting place, which is strictly a cafe (not a restaurant), has both indoor and outdoor tables at the edge of the square with the best view of its famous fountain. Whisky begins at 11,000 lire ($6.60), and a coffee goes for 3,000 lire ($1.80). It's open Tuesday through Saturday from 7am to 2:30am.

NEAR THE PANTHEON

Despite the allures of Trastevere, many visitors to the Eternal City now view piazza della Rotonda, across from the Pantheon, reconstructed by the emperor Hadrian in the first part of the 2nd century A.D., as the "living room" of Rome. (It is also much easier to get to, and there always seem to be more taxis available than in the narrow streets of somewhat remote Trastevere.) The neighborhood around the Pantheon (which many visitors consider their favorite building anywhere in Europe) is especially popular on a summer night.

Caffè Sant'Eustachio, piazza Sant'Eustachio 82. ☎ 6861309.

Strongly brewed coffee might be considered one of the elixirs of Italy, and many Romans will walk many blocks for what they consider a superior brew. One of the most talked-about espresso shops, Sant'Eustachio, is on a small square near the Pantheon, where the city water supply comes from a source outside Rome that the emperor Augustus funneled in with an aqueduct in 19 B.C. Rome's most experienced judges of espresso claim that the water plays an important part in the coffee's flavor, although steam forced through ground Brazilian coffee roasted on the premises has an effect as well. Purchase a ticket from the cashier for as many cups of coffee as you want, and leave a small tip of 100 lire (10¢) for the counterman when he gives you your receipt. Coffee costs 1,200 lire (70¢) to stand, 3,000 lire ($1.80) at a table. Open Tuesday to Sunday 8:30am to 1am, Saturday 9:30am to 1:30am.

Di Rienzo, piazza della Rotonda 8–9. ☎ 6869097.

This is the most desirable cafe here, and in fair weather you can sit at one of the sidewalk tables (if you can find one that's available). In cooler weather you can retreat inside the elegant cafe, whose walls are inlaid with the same type of marble found on the floor of the Pantheon. Menu specialties include risotto with artichokes, spaghetti with seafood, and crespelle alla ricotta e spinaci. You can also order piazzas. Coffee costs 4,000 lire ($2.40); a complete meal goes from

35,000 lire ($21) and up. The restaurant is open Wednesday to Monday 11am to midnight; the bar, Wednesday to Monday 7am to 1:30am.

ON THE CORSO

Café Alemagna, via del Corso 181. ☎ **6789135**.

Alemagna is a monumental cafe usually filled with busy shoppers. On the premises are just about every kind of dining facility a hurried resident of Rome could want, including a stand-up sandwich bar with dozens of selections available from behind a glass case, a cafeteria, and a sit-down area with waiter service. The decor includes high coffered ceilings, baroque wall stencils, glove lights, crystal chandeliers, and black stone floors. Pastries start at 1,500 lire (90¢), coffee at 1,000 lire (60¢). It's open daily from 7am to 10pm.

NEAR THE SPANISH STEPS

⭐ **Antico Caffè Greco**, via Condotti 86. ☎ **6791700**.

This cafe has been reputed for many years to be both the place of origin and the relay point for much of the gossip of Rome's most glamorous shopping district. This spot is considerably older than the other cafes mentioned; in fact, it has been serving drinks in its front-room bar since 1760. Over the years it has attracted such notables as Goethe, Stendhal, and D'Annunzio. Lying half a block from the foot of the Spanish Steps, it still retains a 19th-century atmosphere. The waiters wearing black tailcoats seat you at small marble tables. Beyond the carved wooden bar are four or five small, elegant rooms, whose walls are covered with silk and hung with oil paintings in gilded frames. The house specialty is a paradiso, made with lemon and orange, costing 9,000 lire ($5.40), and light sandwiches are also available. A cup of cappuccino costs 7,500 lire ($4.50) if you're seated. The cafe is open Monday through Saturday from 8am to 9pm, but closed for two weeks in August (days vary).

NEAR PIAZZA COLONNA

Giolitti, via Uffici del Vicario 40. ☎ **6991243**.

For devotees of *gelato* (addictively tasty ice cream), Giolitti is one of the city's most popular nighttime gathering spots; in the evening, it's thronged with strollers with a sweet tooth. To satisfy that craving, try a whipped-cream–topped Giolitti cup of gelato. The ice cream costs from 3,000 lire ($1.80) and up. Some of the sundaes look like Vesuvius about to erupt. If you sit at a table and order one, the cost is from 6,000 lire ($3.60). During the day, good-tasting snacks are also served.

Many people take gelato out to eat on the streets, while others enjoy it in the post-Empire splendor of the salon inside. You can have your "coppa" from 7am to 2am Tuesday to Sunday. There are many excellent, smaller *gelateria* throughout Rome, wherever you see the cool concoction advertised as *produzione propria* (homemade).

NEAR PIAZZA NAVONA

Bar della Pace, via della Pace 3–5. ☎ **6861216.**

Bar della Pace, located near piazza Navona, has elegant neighbors, such as Santa Maria della Pace, a church with sybils by Raphael and a cloister designed by Bramante. The bar dates from the beginning of this century, with wood, marble, and mirrors forming its decor. It's open Tuesday through Sunday from 3pm to 2:30am. A whisky begins at 11,000 lire ($6.60).

Hemingway, piazza delle Coppelle 10. ☎ **68804135.**

Hemingway is hidden behind a discreet door off one of the most obscure piazzas in Rome. Inside, the owners have re-created a 19th-century decor beneath soaring vaulted ceilings that shimmer from the reflection of various glass chandeliers. An interior room repeats in scarlet what the first room did with shades of emerald. Evocations of a Liberty-style salon are strengthened by the sylvan murals and voluptuous portraits of reclining odalisques. Assorted painters, writers, and creative dilettantes occupy the clusters of overstuffed armchairs and listen to classical music. Drinks cost from 18,000 lire ($10.80). Open Monday to Saturday 9am to 3am; closed August 9 to 19.

Wine Bars

The fermented fruits of the vine have played a prominent role in Roman life since the word "bacchanalian" was first invented (and that was very early indeed).

Enoteca Fratelli Roffi Isabelli, via della Croce 76. ☎ **6790896.**

This is one of the best places to taste the wines of Italy. A stand-up drink within its darkly antique confines might be the perfect ending to a visit to the nearby Spanish Steps. Set behind an unflashy facade, this place is the best repository in this chic shopping district for Italian wines, brandies, and grappa. You can opt for a postage-stamp table in back or else stay at the bar with its impressive display of wines, which are stacked on shelves in every available corner. A glass of wine costs 3,000–10,000 lire ($1.80–$6); grappa costs from 5,500 lire ($3.30). Open Monday to Saturday 11am to 12:30am.

Irish Pubs

The two most popular Irish pubs in Rome draw mostly English-speaking expatriates. You can always see a cluster of disoriented local teenagers here and there, but their Italian is drowned in the sea of English, Scottish, Irish, Canadian, Australian, and sometimes American accents. If you want to mingle with people who speak your language (albeit with an unfamiliar accent), try one of these places. Both near piazza Santa Maria Maggiore, they may be a little difficult to find, but once you've found one, someone will direct or even walk with you to the other.

Druid's Den, via San Martino Monto 28. ☎ **4880258.**

The popular Druid's Den is open daily from 6pm to 12:30am. Here, while enjoying a pint of beer at 7,000 lire ($4.20), you can listen to

Irish music and dream of Eire. A group of young Irishmen one night even did the Irish jig in front of the delighted Roman spectators. The "den" is near piazza Santa Maria Maggiore and the train station.

Fiddler's Elbow, via dell'Olmata 43. ☎ **4872110.**

Fiddler's Elbow, near piazza Santa Maria Maggiore and the railway station, is reputedly the oldest pub in the capital. It's open Tuesday through Sunday from 4:30pm to 12:15am; a pint of Guinness is 7,000 lire ($4.20). Sometimes, however, the place is so packed you can't find room to drink it.

---

4 Movies

Pasquino, vicolo del Piede 19, piazza Santa Maria in Trastevere. ☎ **5803622.**

This is a small theater showing English-language films of rather recent vintage. Phone the theater if you want to know what's playing. It's on a little street, just a block from piazza Santa Maria in Trastevere. In fact, it makes quite a pleasant evening to catch a show at Pasquino, then have a drink or cappuccino afterward at one of the cafes on the square, where you can admire the village atmosphere, the fine architecture, and the scene around the fountain. Tickets to the theater cost 7,000 lire ($4.20). There are usually four screenings daily between 4 and 11pm. Take bus no. 56 or 60 from via Veneto or 170 from Stazione Termini.

10

Easy Excursions from Rome

Rome is surrounded by a countryside that has delighted Romans and foreigners for hundreds of years. The attractions are varied—beaches, ancient temples, Renaissance palaces—and all are within easy trip distance. While I have outlined means of public transportation below, here's where a rental car really comes in handy. (See Chapter 3 for information on renting a car.)

Unless you're rushed beyond reason, allow at least three days for taking a look at the attractions in the environs of Rome.

1   Tivoli

20 miles E of Rome

GETTING THERE • By Bus   Take Metro Linea B to the end of the line, the Rebibbia Station. After exiting the station, catch an Acotral bus the rest of the way to Tivoli. Generally buses depart about every 20 minutes. Service is daily from 5:30am to 11pm, a one-way ticket costing 2,300 lire ($1.40).

• By Car   Expect about an hour's drive with traffic on the via Tiburtina.

ESSENTIALS   The area code is 0774. For tourist information, go to piazza Garibaldi (☎ 21249).

An ancient town, Tivoli has origins that probably predate those of Rome itself. At the height of the empire, "Tibur," as it was called, was a favorite retreat for the rich. Horace, Catullus, Sallust, Maecenas, and a few emperors (notably Hadrian) maintained lavish villas here near the woods and waterfalls. It was popular enough to warrant a Roman road, the via Tiburtina, whose modern descendant funnels trucks and tour buses into today's Tivoli. During the Middle Ages, Tivoli achieved a form of independence, which was to last through its rise in fortunes during the Renaissance. This latter period saw real-estate investment by several of the wealthier princes of the church, especially Cardinal Ippolito d'Este. By the late 19th century, Tivoli had been incorporated into the new kingdom of Italy, and its former privileges of independence passed into history.

What to See & Do

★ **Villa Adriana [Hadrian's Villa]**, via di Villa Adriana. ☎ 0774/530203.

Below the foothills on which Tivoli is built lies a gently sloping plain, the site of the Villa Adriana, built in A.D. 135. Today the ruins cover slope after slope of the rolling terrain, fully 180 acres of villa. Hadrian was a widely traveled and highly cultured man; he was also something of an amateur architect, and he personally designed a large part of the villa. It was built as a heaven on earth in which to spend a long and luxurious retirement surrounded by a court that numbered in the hundreds. Having traveled extensively as a general, Hadrian had seen much of the world, and he sought to re-create in his villa at Tibur those sights that most pleased him. Hadrian did not wish to build replicas of just rooms, or even palaces he had seen: He reconstructed entire valleys complete with the temples that had made them famous (the Canopus on the estate is one example). Much of the ruin is readily recognizable, and it's easy to wander around the hot baths and the cold baths and experience a real sense of the villa as it once was. In addition to the Poekile, the Lyceum, the valley of Tempe (named after a vale in Thessaly), the Academy, and the Canopus (a replica of a sacred canal linking the Nile to the Temple of Serapis), there was even an Inferno. (This last attraction is in an olive grove lying in a portion of the villa that hasn't yet been excavated, so it's hard to visit.)

Hadrian didn't live long enough to enjoy the full pleasure he expected from the villa; he died of a painful and undiagnosed illness three years after its completion. Legend has it that he was able to perform miracles on his deathbed—restoring sight to the blind and that sort of thing.

Admission: 8,000 lire ($4.80) adults, free for children.

Open: Daily 9am–sunset (about 7:30pm in Apr–Oct, 4pm in Nov–Mar). **Bus:** No. 2 or 4 from the center of Tivoli to the villa gateway.

⭐ **Villa d'Este,** piazza Trento, viale delle Centro Fontane. ☎ **0774/22070.**

Villa d'Este was named after the 16th-century cardinal who transformed it from a government palace (it had been built in the 13th century as a Benedictine convent) into a princely residence that remained in the cardinal's family until 1918.

The 16th-century frescoes and decorations of the place are attractive, but unexceptional. The garden on the sloping hill beneath is another story—a perfect fairy tale of the Renaissance, using water as a medium of sculpture, much the way the ancients used marble—there are fountains in every imaginable size and shape. Pathways are lined with 100 fountains, and stairs are flanked with cascades on either side. There are fountains you can walk under, fountains you can walk over, and long reflecting pools with surreal trees in between. The fountains have names—*Owl and Bird,* the *Oval Fountain, Fountain of Glass*—and in centuries past, might possibly have concealed practical jokes. The Renaissance aristocracy were immensely amused by a shot of water in someone else's eye.

Admission: 10,000 lire ($6) adults and children.

Open: Feb–Oct, daily 9am–6:30pm; Nov–Jan, daily 9am–4pm. **Transportation:** The bus from Rome stops right near the entrance (see "Getting There," above).

Villa Gregoriana, largo Sant'Angelo. ☎ **0774/21249.**

The gardens were built by Pope Gregory XVI in the 19th century. Whereas the Villa d'Este dazzles with artificial glamour, the Villa Gregoriana relies on nature. At one point on the circuitous walk carved along a slope, visitors stand and look out onto the most spectacular waterfall (Aniene) at Tivoli. The trak to the bottom of the banks of the Annio is studded with grottoes, and balconies open onto

Easy Excursions From Rome

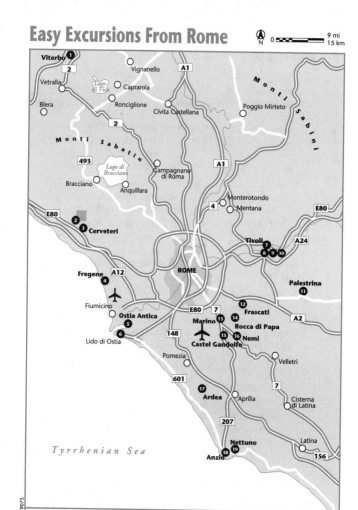

the chasm. From one of the belvederes is a panoramic view of the Temple of Vesta on the hill. The only problem is that if you do make the full journey, you may need to summon a helicopter to lift you back up again (the climb is fierce).

Admission: 3,000 lire ($1.80) adults and children.

Open: Daily 9am–1 hour before sunset. **Transportation:** The bus from Rome stops near the entrance (see "Getting There," above).

Where to Dine

Albergo Ristorante Adriano, via di Villa Adriana 194.
☎ **0774/535028.**

Cuisine: ITALIAN. **Reservations:** Not required. **Bus:** No. 2 or 4 from Tivoli.
Prices: Appetizers 9,000–16,000 lire ($5.40–$9.60); main courses 16,000–25,000 lire ($9.60–$15); fixed-price lunch 30,000 lire ($18); fixed-price dinner 50,000–60,000 lire ($30–$36). AE, DC, MC, V.
Open: Lunch daily 12:30–2:30pm; dinner Mon–Sat 8–10pm.

This place might be the perfect stopover before or after you visit Hadrian's Villa. At the bottom of the villa's hill, in a stucco-sided building a few steps from the ticket office, it offers terrace dining under plane trees in summer or indoor dining in a high-ceilinged room with terra-cotta walls, neoclassical moldings, and Corinthian pilasters painted white Roman menus include roast lamb, saltimbocca, homemade pastas, a variety of veal dishes, deviled chicken, a selection of salads and cheeses, and simple desserts.

Le Cinque Statue, via Quintillio Varo 1. ☎ **0774/20366.**

Cuisine: ROMAN. **Reservations:** Recommended. **Bus:** The bus from Rome stops nearby (see "Getting There," above).
Prices: Appetizers 8,000–10,000 lire ($4.80–$6); main courses 16,000–25,000 lire ($9.60–$15). DC, MC, V.
Open: Lunch Sat–Thurs 12:30–3pm; dinner Sat–Thurs 7:30–10pm.
Closed: Aug 15–Sept 7.

This comfortable restaurant is maintained by a single hard-working Italian family, who prepare an honest and unpretentious cuisine without a lot of fuss and bother. Everything is accompanied by the wines of the hill towns of Rome. Begin with a pastiche of mushrooms, or make a selection from their varied antipasti offerings. Try rigatoni with fresh herbs, tripe fried Roman style, or a mixed fry of brains and vegetables. All the pasta is freshly made on the premises. They also have a wide variety of ice creams and fruits.

2 Palestrina

23 miles E of Rome

GETTING THERE • By Bus Buses leave every 30 to 45 minutes during the day from Rome; departures are from via Castro Pretorio (take the Metro to the stop at Castro Pretorio to catch the bus). It takes about an hour to reach Palestrina.

• **By Car** Take either via Prenestina (a much less trafficked roadway than the via Tiburtina), or the Autostrada (A2), getting off at Valmontana; the latter route is much quicker.

ESSENTIALS The area code is 06.

Like Tibur, ancient Preneste (as Palestrina was called) was a superb holiday spot. It was the favorite of Horace and Pliny, and even Hadrian, who maintained a villa here.

What to See & Do

The town was really known for the great **Temple of Fortuna Primigenia,** which covered most of the hill where Palestrina stands today. In its inner sanctum was an oracle, to which thousands journeyed regularly from Rome over the ancient stone road. As it was the fashion for emperors to enlarge and beautify temples and public facilities, the Temple of Fortuna grew to gigantic proportions. However, it fell into rapid decay at the end of the 4th century, when pagan temples were ordered closed by the Christian imperial government. During the Middle Ages it was a stronghold for a string of families—the physical situation on top of Mount Ginestro was perfect—the last of which, the Barberini, erected a palace at the summit of the temple. The vast sanctuary was almost forgotten until World War II, when allied bombers made runs on Palestrina and uncovered the ruins with exploding bombs.

Today Palestrina consists of a modern town at the foot of Mount Ginestro, the excavated levels of the temple on the slopes above, the Palazzo Barberini at the highest point of the temple, and a tangle of medieval streets on the crown of the mountain.

Museo Nazionale Archeologico di Palestrina, Palazzo Barberini. ☎ **06/9558100.**

The Barberini museum houses a collection of Etruscan artifacts, a mosaic of the Nile at flood from the Fortuna sanctuary (an intricate piece on the top floor of the museum), and a view of the surrounding countryside that certainly makes you feel like a Renaissance prince or princess.

Admission: 8,000 lire ($4.80) adults and children.

Open: Nov–Feb, Tues–Sun 9am–4pm; Mar, Tues–Sun 9am–5pm; Apr, Tues–Sun 9am–6pm; May, Tues–Sun 9am–6:30pm; June–Aug, Tues–Sun 9am–7:30pm; Sept, Tues–Sun 9am–5:30pm; Oct, Tues–Sun 9am–5pm. **Directions:** Follow signposts from the center to the top of the town.

Where to Stay & Dine

Albergo Stella and Restaurant Coccia, piazza della Liberazione 3, Palestrina, 0036 Roma. ☎ **06/9538172.** Fax 06/9573360. 28 rms (all with bath), 2 suites. TEL

Rates: 50,000 lire ($30) single; 75,000 lire ($45) double; 100,000 lire ($60) suite. Breakfast 7,000 lire ($4.20) extra. AE, DC, V. **Parking:** Free.

A buff-colored contemporary hotel and restaurant, this is in the commercial district of town on a cobblestone square filled with parked cars, trees, and a small fountain. The lobby is done in warm colors and contains curved leather couches and autographed photos of local sports heroes.

The restaurant, serving a zesty Roman cuisine, is sunny, filled with a cluttered kind of modernity. Meals cost from 35,000 lire ($21). There is a small bar where you might have an apéritif. The bar and restaurant are open daily noon to 3pm and 7 to 9pm.

3   Castelli Romani

The name means "Roman castles," which they're not. The castelli are really a series of little hill towns, grouped on mountain slopes around two lakes. Some are extremely ancient, and all have been popular as holiday retreats at least since the days of the Roman Empire. The best way to visit the castelli is with a car, especially since many of the towns don't have enough to keep you occupied for more than an hour or so. Without a car, you will have to take one of the many buses serving the castelli leaving from the Subaugusta Metro stop, and this takes a lot of time.

Marino

Marino is the closest to Rome (only 15 miles), it's about 4¹/₂ miles off via Appia Nuova quite near Ciampino Airport. Much of Marino's original charm has fallen victim to modern builders, but the town is still the place to go each October, during the grape harvest. At that time, the town's fountains are switched from water to wine, and everyone can drink for free.

Rocca di Papa

This is the most attractive of the hill towns, and it lies only some 6 miles from Marino. The best road if you're driving is 217 to the junction with 218, where you make a left turn. Before the intersection, you'll be high on a ridge above Lake Albano—the views of the lake, the far woods, and the papal palace of Castel Gandolfo on the opposite mountain are superb. Just before Rocca di Papa is the entrance to the toll road to Monte Cavo. A temple of Jove once stood on top of this mountain, and before that, the tribes of the area met with King Tarquin (the Proud) before Rome was a republic. Atop the mountain is a restaurant with reasonable prices and a panoramic view of the surrounding Alban Hills and hill towns. Down below, Rocca di Papa is a tangle of old streets and churches. A legend of dubious origin claims that Hannibal once camped just below the town in a wooded hollow.

Nemi

From Rocca di Papa, it's only a short drive to this tiny town clinging to a woody precipice above the lake of the same name. The ancient Romans knew these parts well. A temple to Diana once stood in the valley and the lake was called her "looking glass." If October is the time for Marino, May is the ideal time for Nemi, when a festival is held in honor of the local strawberries.

WHAT TO SEE & DO

Looking from any of the balconies in Nemi, you'll see what looks like an airplane hangar in the valley right by the lakeshore. This unprepossessing building has the important-sounding name of **Museo delle Navi Romane,** via di Diana (☎ **06/9368140**), and until the last war it held remains of two luxurious barges that floated in the lake during the reign of Caligula (assassinated A.D. 41). The boats, which were fitted out lavishly with bronze and marble, were sunk during the reign of Claudius (he succeeded the insane Caligula), and were entirely forgotten until Mussolini drained the lake in the 1930s. The barges were found, set up in a lakeside museum, and remained as a wonder of ancient Rome until the Nazis burned them (out of spite) during their retreat from Rome and environs in World War II. Admission costs 8,000 lire ($4.80) for adults, free for children under 18 and those over 60. It's open daily 9am to 2pm. To reach the museum, unless you're driving, you have to walk from the center of Nemi toward the lake.

The 15th-century **Palazzo Ruspoli,** a baronial estate, is the focal point of Nemi, but the hill town itself invites exploration—particularly the alleyways the local denizens call streets and the houses with balconies jutting out over the slopes. While darting through the Castelli Romani, try to time your schedule for lunch in Nemi.

WHERE TO DINE

La Taverna, via Nemorense 13. ☎ 06/9368135.

Cuisine: INTERNATIONAL. **Reservations:** Required.

Prices: Appetizers 8,000–10,000 lire ($4.80–$6); main courses 16,000–21,000 lire ($9.60–$12.60). AE, DC, MC, V.

Open: Lunch Thurs–Tues 12:30–2pm; dinner Thurs–Tues 9–10pm.

Offering a large array of the dishes of the region, as well as a rustic atmosphere, La Taverna is worth the trouble it takes to get there. In April the *fragole* (wild strawberries) signs go out. Spring is also the time to order pappardelle e sugo de lepre (large noodles with hare sauce), worthy of the goddess of the hunt. Otherwise try fettuccine with mushrooms. For a main dish, I suggest the chef's specialty, *arrosto di abbacchio e maiale* (it consists of both a pork chop and grilled lamb). Fresh fish is also featured. If you want to have a Roman feast, accompany your main dish with large roasted mushrooms, priced according to size, and a small fennel salad. To top off the galaxy of goodies, it's traditional to order Sambucca, a clear white drink like anisette, "with a fly in it." The "fly," of course, is a coffee bean—usually three of them—which you suck on for added flavor.

En Route to Castel Gandolfo

The road to Gandolfo leads us through a few "worth a visit" towns on the way. **Genzano,** on the other side of Lake Nemi, has views of the countryside and a 17th-century palace that belonged to the Sforza-Cesarini.

Ariccia is an ancient town that sent representatives to meet with Tarquin the Proud on top of Monte Cavo 2,500 years ago. After many centuries of changing hands, especially between medieval and Renaissance families, it has taken on a suburban look. The palace in the middle of town is still private and belongs to the Chigi family.

Albano practically adjoins Castel Gandolfo. It has a long history—this is the reputed site of Alba Longa, the so-called "mother city" of Rome, but it's quite built up in a modern way today. Trains going to Albano leave from Stazione Termini in Rome.

Castel Gandolfo

Now we come to the summer residence of the pope. The papal palace, a 17th-century edifice designed by Carlo Maderno, stands practically on the foundations of another equally regal summer residence, the villa of the emperor Domitian. Unfortunately, the palace, the gardens, and the adjoining Villa Barberini can't be visited. You'll have to content yourself with the piazza out front with its church and fountain by Bernini.

4 Frascati

13 miles SE of Rome

GETTING THERE • By Bus   Acotral buses leave from the Anagnina Station at the end of Metro Linea A in Rome. Service is about every 30 minutes daily from 5am to 10:30pm, a one-way ticket costing 1,500 lire (90¢).

• By Car   From the ring road around Rome (its southeast section), head southeast along the 215.

ESSENTIALS   The area code is 06. Tourist information is available at piazza Marconi 1 (☎ 9420331).

Frascati is the best-known hill town of them all, lying out on the via Tuscolana. Some 1,073 feet above sea level, Frascati is celebrated for its white wines. Golden vineyards cover the surrounding northern slopes of the outer crater ring of the Alban Hills. From its lofty perch, you'll see a panoramic view of the countryside and the other small towns.

At one time Frascati was the most chic mountain resort for Roman society, as wealthy patricians erected villas here, with elaborate gardens and high-spouting fountains. Later the town belonged mainly to the papacy. From that period dates the most important villa, the **Villa Aldobrandini,** via Massala (☎ 9420331), which owes part of its look to Maderno, the designer of the facade of St. Peter's. To visit the gardens, which are open Monday to Saturday from 9am to 1pm, go to the tourist office (see above). Tickets are issued free.

About three miles past the villa, motorists can reach **Tuccolo,** a spot known to the ancients with an amphitheater dating from the 1st century B.C. From here, you'll enjoy one of the most-photographed views in all the castelli.

Villa Torlonia, bombed in World War II, has been converted into a public park, known for its Theater of the Fountains with dramatic water displays.

WHERE TO DINE

Cacciani Restaurant, via Armando Diaz 13. ☎ 9420378.

Cuisine: ROMAN. **Reservations:** Required on weekends.

Prices: Appetizers' 12,000–20,000 lire ($7.20–$12); main courses 18,000–28,000 lire ($10.80–$16.80). AE, DC, MC, V.

Open: Lunch Tues–Sun 12:30–3pm; dinner Tues–Sun 7:30–10:30pm.
Closed: Jan 7–17 and Aug 16–25.

Cacciani is the choicest restaurant in Frascati, where the competition has always been tough (Frascati foodstuffs once attracted Lucullus, the epicurean). A large, modern restaurant in the center of town, with a terrace commanding a view of the valley, Cacciani has drawn such long-ago celebrities as Clark Gable. The kitchen is exposed to the public. To get you started, I recommend the pasta specialties, such as fettuccine (flat noodles) or rigatoni alla vaccinara (oxtail in tomato sauce). For a main course, the baby lamb with a special sauce of white wine and vinegar is always reliable. There is a large choice of wines, which are kept in a cave under the restaurant.

5   Ostia

16 miles SW of Rome

GETTING THERE • By Metro   Take the Metro Linea B to the Magliana station, costing 700 lire (40¢) for a one-way ticket. At Magliana, change to the Lido train (no extra ticket necessary but hold onto your original stub). From there it's about a 20-minute ride to the Ostia Antica stop. From the station, it's only a short walk to the excavations.

• By Car   Drive out the via Ostiense heading for route 8 (signposted Lido di Roma Ostia).

ESSENTIALS   The area code is 06.

Ostia was the port of ancient Rome and a city in its own right. The currents and uneven bottom of the Tiber prevented Mediterranean shipping from going farther upstream, so merchandise was transferred to barges for the remainder of the trip, Ostia's fate was tied closely to that of the empire. At the peak of Rome's power, the city had 100,000 inhabitants—hard to imagine looking at today's ruins. Ostia was important enough to have had a theater (still standing in reconstructed form), numerous temples and baths, great patrician houses, and a large business complex. Successive emperors enlarged and improved the facilities, notably Claudius and Trajan, but by the time of Constantine (4th century), the tide was turning. The barbarian sieges of Rome in the 5th century spelled the end of Ostia.

Without the empire to trade with and Rome to sell to, the port quickly withered, reverting within a few centuries to a malarial swamp without a trace of Roman civilization. The excavations, still only partial, were started by the papacy in the 19th century, but the really substantial work took place between 1938 and 1942 under the Mussolini government.

Today a visit to ◆ **Ostia Antica,** viale dei Romagnoli 717 (☎ **5650022**), is one of the most history-laden afternoons you can spend near Rome. It's relatively secluded, and the ruins invite discovery. There are picnic spots beside fallen columns and near old temple walls, and it's even easy to reach (see "Getting There," above). While you're there be sure to see the **museum,** which has a fine collection of statuary that was found in the ruins. Entrance to the grounds is 10,000 lire ($6), free for those 17 or under. From March through September, hours are daily from 9am to 7pm; from October through February, daily from 9am to 5pm.

The history of **Lido di Ostia,** the congested beachfront, goes back only to 1926, when the first highway linking Rome to the coast was built. Prior to that, it was a malaria-ridden waste, unvisited and unwanted. Because it is so easy to reach by Metro, the beach crowds can and do get quite heavy on weekends.

My recommendation is that you don't join them—at any time. One Roman journalist recently wrote: "The notorious beaches here are dangerous to your health. Don't go near the murky, polluted waters unless it's your custom to swim in the canals of Venice."

Confine your swimming to hotel pools or public swimming pools in the Rome area; or, better yet, head for one of the beach resorts along any of the Italian coastlines. A good beach recommendation near Rome is Fregene (see below).

6 Fregene

23 miles W of Rome

GETTING THERE • By Train   Take a Civitavecchia-bound train from the Stazione Termini in Rome to Fregene, which is the first stop along the route. There are frequent departures.

• By Bus   A bus marked Fregene leaves from the Lepanto Metro stop in Rome, taking passengers into the center of the resort.

• By Car   Take the via Aurelia, which you can pick up behind St. Peter's and the Vatican. Once past the outskirts, the road is excellent and toll free.

ESSENTIALS   The **area code** is 06.

Politically under Roman jurisdiction, Fregene lies on the coastline north of the Tiber and is known for its fields of pine trees. The land in the late 1600s belonged to the Rospigliosi, one of Rome's powerful families, and Clement IX, a Rospigliosi son who became pope, planted a forest $2^1/_2$ miles long and 2,624 feet across. Three hundred years later we have the pines of Fregene.

The forest was planted to protect the inland areas from the sea winds, which damaged crops, but today they form a scenic background for a collection of posh villas and a golden-sand beach. Although most of the beach has been divided by concessionaires (with more promising results than at Lido di Ostia), there are various slivers of free beach within walking distance of the bus stop. In addition to the beach, large areas of the pine forest have been preserved as a park, making for some really good walks.

Where to Stay & Dine

La Conchiglia, lungomare di Ponente 4, Fregene, 00050 Roma.
☎ and fax 06/6685385. 36 rms (all with bath). A/C TV TEL
Rates (including full board): 140,000–160,000 lire ($84–$96) per
person. AE, DC, MC, V. **Parking:** Free.

La Conchiglia means "the shellfish" in Italian—an appropriate name
for this hotel and restaurant right on the beach, with views of the
water and of the pine trees. Its circular lounge is painted white, with
built-in curving wall banquettes that face a cylindrical fireplace with
a raised hearth. A resort aura is created by the large green plants. The
bar in the cocktail lounge, which faces the terrace, is also circular.
The guest rooms are comfortable and well furnished, and some
contain minibars.

It's also possible to stop by for a meal, and the food is good. Try,
for example, spaghetti with lobster and grilled fish. Many excellent
meat dishes are offered. Meals start at 45,000 lire ($27). The
restaurant's in the garden, shaded by bamboo. Oleander flutters in
the sea breezes. The restaurant is open daily from 1 to 3pm and 8 to
10pm.

7 Anzio & Nettuno

About 44 miles S of Rome

GETTING THERE • By Bus   Acotral buses in Rome leave from
the EUR-Fermini station which can be reached by taking Metro Linea
B to its termination. Buses leave daily from 5:30am to 10pm, taking
30 minutes and costing 4,300 lire ($2.60) for a one-way ticket.

• By Car   Motorists can visit Ostia Antica in the morning, then
Anzio and Nettuno in the afternoon. Go west on via Ostiense until
you reach Route 8, which you take to the coast. Once at Lido di Ostia,
you can head south along Route 41 to Anzio.

ESSENTIALS   The area code for both towns is 06. Tourist
information is available in Anzio at riviera Zanardelli 3–5
(☎ **9846119**).

The two towns of Anzio and Nettuno are peaceful seaside resorts
today, but to many Americans and English they conjure up wartime
memories. On January 22, 1944, an Allied amphibious task force
landed the U.S. VI Corps at both towns, as a prelude to the liberation
of Rome. Fighting against terrific odds, the Allies lost many lives.

The Italian government presented 77 acres in **Nettuno** to the
United States for a cemetery; the graves are not only of those who
died on the beaches of Anzio and Nettuno (where holidaymakers now
revel), but are also of those who were killed in the Sicilian campaign.

The fields of Nettuno contain 7,862 American dead—39% of
those originally buried (the others have been returned home by their
relatives). In Nettuno, a Graves Registry office helps visitors locate

the markers of particular servicemen. The neatly manicured fields are peppered with crosses and stars of David, and 488 headstones mark the graves of the unknown. The cemetery is open daily from 8am to 6pm.

In **Anzio,** you can visit the British cemetery filled with war dead. One memorial to B. J. Pownell, a gunner in the Royal Artillery, seems to symbolize the plight of all the young men who died on either side. "He Gave the Greatest Gift of All: His Unfinished Life." Gunner Pownell was struck down on January 29, 1944. He was 20 years old.

Anzio was the birthplace of both Nero and Caligula. Many wealthy Romans once erected villas here at the port said to have been founded by Antias, the son of Circe and Odysseus. In the ruins of Nero's fabulous villa, the famous statue of Apollo Belvedere was discovered.

8 Cerveteri & Tarquinia

As Livy's Trojans landed in ancient Italy, so did the Etruscans. Who were they? We still don't know, and the many inscriptions they left behind—mostly on graves—are no help since the Etruscans' language has never since been deciphered. We deduce the date of their arrival on the west coast of Umbria at around 800 B.C. (See "History" in Chapter 1 for more information on the Etruscans.)

Two former strongholds of the Etruscans can be visited today, Cerveteri and Tarquinia. (For Etruscan museums in Rome, see the Vatican's Etruscan Museum and the Etruscan Museum of Villa Giulia, both in Chapter 6.)

Cerveteri ──────────────────

28 miles NW of Rome

GETTING THERE • By Car   The best way to reach Cerveteri is by car. Head out via Aurelia, northwest of Rome, for a distance of 28 miles.

• By Public Transportation   Take Metro Line A in Rome to the Lepanto stop. From via Lepanto, you can take an Acotral coach to Cerveteri; the trip takes about one hour and costs 3,800 lire ($2.30). Once at Cerveteri, it's a 1 1/4-mile walk to the necropolis. Just follow the signs that point the way.

ESSENTIALS   The area code is 06.

───────────────────────────

Cerveteri is older than Rome and stands on the site of a major Etruscan stronghold called Caere. If you drive there, you'll pass through the rolling hills of the Roman countryside. You'll eventually see the city's medieval walls up in the hills on your right; on the left are the modern towers of Ladispoli, a rapidly growing seaside town.

WHAT TO SEE & DO

It's the Etruscan heritage that brings visitors to Cerveteri today, for while the Caere of the living has long vanished, the Caere of the dead still exists in a relatively good state of preservation. Next to their city, the Etruscans built their major **Necropolis of Cerveteri,** a city of tombs. Most of the circular, dome-shaped graves date from the 7th century B.C., and several have been found completely intact, untouched since their doors were sealed 2,600 years ago. The necropolis lies on the other side of a small valley from the medieval battlements, and it's still surrounded by grape fields. There is no sound here except the rather ghostly moans of the wind in the pine trees. Only a portion of the necropolis is excavated, but it's quite extensive. You can climb in and out of the tombs, which are decorated inside as Etruscan homes were. Note the absence of the arch, an architectural innovation of the later Romans. The necropolis is open May through September, Tuesday to Sunday from 9am to 6pm (in other months 9am to 4pm); closed Monday. Admission is 8,000 lire ($4.80) for adults and children.

Many of the treasures in the Villa Giulia in Rome came from Caere, and many other priceless pieces of that distant culture are on display at the **Museo Nazionale Cerite,** piazza Santa Maria Maggiore (☎ **9550003**). It contains a rare collection of Etruscan pottery, among other exhibits. The museum is housed in Ruspoldi Castle, with its ancient walls and crenellations. It is open daily Tuesday through Sunday, May through September, from 9am to 4pm; off-season, Tuesday through Sunday, 9am to 2pm. Admission is free.

When you're through visiting the necropolis and the museum, it's pleasant to stroll around the twisting lanes of the town, pausing perhaps at the battlements to survey the vastness of the countryside. The Tyrrhenian Sea glitters in the sunshine, and Ladispoli rises like a dream city on the shore.

Tarquinia

60 miles NW of Rome

GETTING THERE • By Train As for public transportation, the train is the preferred choice; a *diretto* train from the Stazione Termini takes 50 minutes.

• By Bus Eight buses a day leave from the via Lepanto stop in Rome for the two-hour trip to the neighboring town, Barriera San Giusto, which is 1 1/2 miles from Tarquinia. Bus schedules are available at the tourist office (see below). In Rome, call **856384** for information.

• By Car Take via Aurelia outside Rome, and continue on the autostrada toward Civitavecchia. Bypass Civitavecchia and continue another 13 miles north until you see the exit signs for Tarquinia.

ESSENTIALS The area code is 0766. Tourist information is available at the tourist office at piazza Cavour (☎ **856384**), 1 1/2 miles from Tarquinia.

An even more striking museum is at Tarquinia, near Civitavecchia, which was the port of Rome in the days of Trajan. The situation of

Tarquinia is commanding, with a view of the sea. It is medieval in appearance, with its fortifications and nearly two dozen towers.

WHAT TO SEE & DO

The ✖ **Tarquinia National Museum,** piazza Cavour (☎ 856036), is housed in the Gothic-Renaissance Palazzo Vitelleschi, dating from 1439. It displays a large number of sarcophagi and Etruscan exhibits removed from the nearby necropolis. But the reason people drive all the way up here from Rome is to see a pair of winged horses, removed from the fronton of a temple. This work by an unknown artist numbers among the great masterpieces of Etruscan art ever discovered. The museum is open May through October, Tuesday through Sunday from 9am to 7pm, and 9am to 2pm in the off-season, and charges 8,000 lire ($4.80) admission.

The same ticket you purchased to enter the museum also admits you to the **Etruscan Necropolis** (☎ 856308), the leading sightseeing attraction of Tarquinia. You can reach the grave sites by taking a bus at the Barriera San Giusto and getting off at the Cimitero stop. Or else it's about a 20-minute walk from the museum. Inquire at the museum for directions.

The most important tombs here are chambers hewn out of rock containing well-preserved paintings. Actually, the necropolis covers more than $2^{1}/_{2}$ miles of windswept ground, with hundreds upon hundreds of tombs—not all of which have been visited by the *tombaroli,* or grave robbers. A guide shows you the most important tombs. The paintings give an intimate glimpse of the daily life of the Etruscans, including their customs, beliefs, and religion. One of the tombs most popular with tourists dates from the 5th century B.C. Paintings there depict guests at a banquet, lying on beds, waited on by naked ephebes. Colors include red and pale pink from iron oxide, blue from the dust of lapis lazuli, and black from charcoal. Hours are Tuesday to Sunday from 9am to 6pm (until 2pm November through March).

9 Viterbo

61 miles N of Rome

GETTING THERE • By Bus and Train   From Rome take the Metro Linea A to Flaminio. At the Flaminio station, follow signs pointing to Roma Nord station. Once there, purchase a combined rail and bus ticket to Viterbo, costing 5,300 lire ($3.20) one way. The train takes you to Saxa Rubra in just 15 minutes. At Saxa Rubra, take an Acotral bus for $1^{1}/_{2}$ hours to Viterbo. Especially if you're trying to see Viterbo on a day trip, it might be worth the extra money to take a taxi from Saxa Rubra the remainder of the way.

• **By Car**   Take Autostrada 2 north to the Orte exit.

ESSENTIALS   The area code is 0761. Tourist information is at piazzale dei Caduti 16 (☎ 304795).

The 2,000 years that have gone into the creation of the city of Viterbo make it one of the most interesting day-trips from Rome. While it traces its history back to the Etruscans, the bulk of its historical architecture dates from the Middle Ages and the Renaissance, when the city was a residence—and hideout—for the popes. The old section of the city is still surrounded by thick stone walls that once protected the inhabitants from papal (or antipapal, depending on the situation at the time) attacks.

What to See & Do

The only way to see Viterbo properly is on a **walking tour** of the medieval town, wandering through the narrow cobbled streets and pausing in front of the antiquity-rich structures. Piazza del Plebiscito, dominated by the 15th-century town hall, impresses one with the fine state of preservation of Viterbo's old buildings. The courtyard and fountain in front of the town hall and the 13th-century governor's palace are favorite meeting places for townfolk and visitors alike.

Just down via San Lorenzo is **piazza San Lorenzo,** the site of Viterbo's cathedral, which sits atop the former Etruscan acropolis. The **Duomo,** dating from 1192, is a composite of architectures, from its pagan foundations to its Renaissance facade to its Gothic bell tower. Next door is the 13th-century **Palazzo Papale,** built as a residence for the pope, but also serving as a hideout when the pope was in exile. It was also the site of three papal elections. The exterior staircase and the colonnaded loggia combine to make up one of the finest examples of civil Roman architecture from the Gothic period.

The finest example of medieval architecture in Viterbo is the **San Pellegrino Quarter,** reached from the piazza San Lorenzo by a short walk past the piazza della Morte. This quarter, inhabited by working-class Viterboans, is a maze of narrow streets, arched walkways, towers, steep stairways, and ornamental fountains.

Worth a special visit is the **Convent of Santa Maria della Verità,** dating from 1100. The church contains 15th-century frescoes by Lorenzo da Viterbo, student of Piero della Francesca.

Villa Lante, Bagnaia. ☎ **288008.**

The English author Sacheverell Sitwell called Villa Lante, located in Bagnaia, a suburb of Viterbo, "the most beautiful garden in Italy"; indeed, it is a worthy contender with Villa d'Este at Tivoli for that title. Water from Monte Cimino flows down to the fountains of the villa, running from terrace to terrace until it reaches the central pool of the regal garden, with statues, stone banisters, and shrubbery. Two symmetrical Renaissance palaces make up the villa. The estate is now partly a public park, which is open during the day. The gardens that adjoin the villa, however, can only be visited on a guided tour. (The gatekeeper at the guard house will show you through, usually with a group that has assembled.) The interiors of the twin mansions can't be visited without special permission.

Admission: 30-minute garden tour, 4,000 lire ($2.40).

Open: May–Aug, Tues–Sun 9am–7:30pm; Mar–Apr and Sept–Oct, Tues–Sun 9am–5:30pm; Nov–Feb, Tues–Sun 9am–4pm. **Bus:** No. 6 from Viterbo.

Parco dei Mostri [Park Of The Monsters], villa delle Meraviglie, Bomarzo. ☎ **924029.**

About eight miles east of Bagnaia at Bomarzo lies the Park of the Monsters, which Prince Vicino Orsini had built in a deep valley, and which is overlooked by the Orsini Palace and the houses of the village. On the other side of the valley are stone cliffs. Prince Orsini's park, Bosco Sacro (Sacred Wood), is filled with grotesque figures carved from natural rock. The figures probably date from about 1560 (Annibale Caro, a Renaissance poet, refers to them in a letter he wrote in 1564). They rise mysteriously from the wild Latium landscape, covered with strangling weeds and moss. Nature and art have created a surrealistic fantasy; the Mouth of Hell (an ogre's face so big that people can walk into its gaping mouth), a crude Hercules slaying an Amazon, nymphs with butterfly wings, a huge tortoise with a statue on its shell, a harpy, a mermaid, snarling dogs, lions, and much, much more. If you need to refresh yourself after the excursion to the edge of madness, you'll find a snack shop near the entrance.

Admission: 10,000 lire ($6) adults, 6,000 lire ($3.60) children under 7.

Open: Daily 8am–dusk. **Bus:** No. 6 from piazza Martiri d'Ungheria in Viterbo.

Where to Dine Nearby

Instead of dining at Viterbo, I suggest a detour to La Quercia, less than two miles from the medieval center of Viterbo. (La Quercia, incidentally, is the seat of the Basilica of the Madonna of Quercia, with a cloister by Bernini, a bell tower by Sangallo, and a ceramic portal by della Robbia.)

Aquilanti, via del Santuario 4. ☎ **0761/341911.**

Cuisine: ITALIAN. **Reservations:** Recommended. **Bus:** No. 6 from Viterbo.

Prices: Appetizers 12,000–25,000 lire ($7.20–$15); main courses 18,000–30,000 lire ($10.80–$18). AE, DC, MC, V.

Open: Lunch Wed–Mon noon–3pm; dinner Wed–Mon 7:30–10pm.

Aquilanti is the best place to eat in the area. The dining room, with a view of an Etruscan burial ground, does not disappoint those seeking good-quality Italian fare. Specialties include fettuccine allo stennarello, ravioli de ricotta e spinaci all'etrusca, plus vitella (veal) alla montanera, as well as a fabulous array of fruits and vegetables. The wine is from Orvieto.

Appendix

A Basic Vocabulary

English	Italian	Pronunciation
Good morning or Good afternoon	**Buongiorno**	bwohn-*djor*-noh
Good evening	**Buona sera**	*bwohn*-ah *say*-rah
Good night	**Buona notte**	*bwohn*-ah *noht*-tay
How are you?	**Come sta?**	*koh*-may *stah?*
Very well	**Molto bene**	*mohl*-toh *bay*-nay
Thank you	**Grazie**	*grah*-tsyeh
Good-bye	**Arrivederci**	ah-reev-ay-*dehr*-chee
Please	**Per piacere**	payr pyah-*chay*-ray
Yes	**Si**	see
No	**No**	noh
Excuse me	**Scusi**	*skoo*-zee
Where is? . . . the station	**Dov'è? . . . la stazione**	doh-*vay?* . . . lah stah-tsee-*oh*-nay
a hotel	**un albergo**	oon-ahl-*bayr*-goh
a restaurant	**un ristorante**	oon rees-toh-*rahn*-tay
the toilet	**il gabinetto**	eelga-bee-*neht*-toh
To the right	**A destra**	ah *dess*-trah
To the left	**A sinistra**	ah see-*nee*-strah
Straight ahead	**Avanti**	ah-*vahn*-tee
How much is it?	**Quanto costa?**	*kwahn*-toh *koh*-stah?
The check, please	**Il conto, per piacere**	eel *kohn*-toh, payr pya-*chay*-rey
When?	**Quando?**	*kwahn*-doh?
Yesterday	**Ieri**	ee-*yeh*-ree
Today	**Oggi**	*ohd*-djee
Tomorrow	**Domani**	doh-*mah*-nee
Breakfast	**Colazione**	koh-lah-*tzyoh*-nay

English	Italian	Pronunciation
Lunch	**Pranzo**	prahn-tsoh
Dinner	**Cena**	*chay*-nah
What time is it?	**Che ore sono?**	kay *oh*-ray *soh*-noh?
What day is it today?	**Che giorno è oggi?**	kay *djor*-noh ay *ohd*-djee?
Monday	**Lunedì**	loo-nay-*dee*
Tuesday	**Martedì**	mahr-tay-*dee*
Wednesday	**Mercoledì**	mehr-koh-lay-*dee*
Thursday	**Giovedì**	djoh-vay-*dee*
Friday	**Venerdì**	vay-nehr-*dee*
Saturday	**Sabato**	*sah*-bah-toh
Sunday	**Domenica**	doh-*may*-neek-ah

Numbers

1 **uno** (*oo*-noh)
2 **due** (*doo*-ay)
3 **tre** (tray)
4 **quattro** (*kwah*-troh)
5 **cinque** (*cheen*-kway)
6 **sei** (say)
7 **sette** (*set*-tay)
8 **otto** (*oht*-toh)
9 **nove** (*noh*-vay)
10 **dieci** (*dyay*-chee)

20 **venti** (*vayn*-tee)
30 **trenta** (*trayn*-tah)
40 **quaranta** (kway-*rahn*-tah)
50 **cinquanta** (cheen-*kwan*-tah)
60 **sessanta** (sehs-*sahn*-tah)

70 **settanta** (seht-*tahn*-tah)
80 **ottanta** (oh-*tahn*-tah)
90 **novanta** (noh-*vahn*-tah)
100 **cento** (*chayn*-toh)
1,000 **mille** (*meel*-lay)

B   Italian Menu Savvy

Abbacchio Roast haunch or shoulder of lamb baked and served in a casserole and sometimes flavored with anchovies.

Agnolotti A crescent-shaped pasta shell stuffed with a mixture of chopped meat, spices, vegetables, and cheese; when prepared in rectangular versions, the same combination of ingredients is identified as ravioli.

Amaretti Crunchy, very sweet, almond-flavored macaroons.

Anguilla alla veneziana Eel cooked in sauce made from tuna and lemon.

Antipasti Succulent tidbits served at the beginning of a meal (before the pasta), whose ingredients might include slices of cured meats, seafood (especially shellfish), and what critics sometimes claim is the most succulent collection of cooked and seasoned vegetables in the Italian repertoire. Typical examples might include: *carciofi alla guidia* (flattened and deep-fried baby artichokes), *carciofi sott' olio* (artichoke hearts in olive oil), *funghi trifolati* (mushrooms with garlic, anchovies, and lemon), *gamberi al fagiolino* (shrimp with white beans), and *prosciutto con melone* (melon garnished with slices of raw cured ham).

Aragosta Lobster.

Arrosto Roasted meat.

Baccalà Dried and salted codfish.

Baccalà alla vicentina Codfish simmered in a broth of milk, onions, anchovies, parsley, and (sometimes) cinnamon.

Bagna cauda Hot and well-seasoned sauce heavily flavored with anchovies, designed for dipping raw vegetables; literally translated as "hot bath."

Bistecca alla fiorentina Florentine-style steaks, coated before grilling with olive oil, pepper, lemon juice, salt, and parsley.

Bocconcini Veal layered with ham and cheese, and fried.

Bollito misto Assorted boiled meats served on a single platter.

Braciola di maiale Pork chop.

Bresaola Air-dried spiced beef.

Bruschetta Toasted bread, heavily slathered with butter and garlic and topped with tomatoes.

Bucatini Hollow, coarsely textured spaghetti.

Busecca alla milanese Tripe (beef intestines) flavored with herbs and vegetables.

Cabretto ripieno al forno Oven-roasted stuffed baby goat.

Cacciucco all livornese Seafood stew.

Calzone Pizza dough rolled with the chef's choice of sausage, tomatoes, cheese, etc., then baked into a kind of savory turnover.

Cannelloni Tubular dough stuffed with meat, cheese, or vegetables, then baked in a creamy white sauce.

Cappellacci alla ferrarese Pasta stuffed with pumpkin.

Cappelletti Small ravioli ("little hats") stuffed with meat or cheese.

Carciofi Artichokes.

Carpaccio Thin slices of raw cured beef, sometimes in a piquant sauce.

Cassatta alla siciliana A richly caloric dessert combining layers of sponge cake, sweetened ricotta cheese, and candied fruit, bound together with an icing of chocolate buttercream.

Cervello al burro nero Brains in black-butter sauce.

Cima alla genovese Baked filet of veal rolled into a tube-shaped package containing eggs, mushrooms, and sausage.

Coppa Cured morsels of pork filet encased in sausage skins, served in slices.

Costoletta alla milanese Veal cutlet dredged in breadcrumbs, fried, and sometimes flavored with cheese.

Cozze Mussels.

Fagioli White beans.

Fave Fava beans.

Fegato alla veneziana Thinly slived calves' liver fried with salt, pepper, and onions.

Fettuccine Flat noodles.

Focaccia Ideally, concocted from potato-based dough left to rise slowly for several hours, then garnished with tomato sauce, garlic, basil, salt, and pepper drizzled with olive oil; similar to a high-pan, deep-dish pizza most popular in the deep south, especially Bari.

Fontina Rich cow's-milk cheese.

Frittata Italian omelet.

Fritto misto A deep-fried medley of whatever small fish, shellfish, and squid are available in the marketplace that day.

Fusilli Spiral-shaped pasta.

Gelato (produzione propria) Ice cream (homemade).

Gorgonzola One of the most famous blue-veined cheeses of Europe; strong, creamy, and aromatic.

Gnocchi Dumplings usually made from potatoes *(gnocchi alla patate)* or from semolina *(gnocchi alla romana)*, often stuffed with combinations of cheese, spinach, vegetables, or whatever combinations strikes the chef's fancy.

Granita Flavored ice, usually with lemon or coffee.

Insalata di frutti di mare Seafood salad (usually including shrimp and squid) garnished with pickles, lemon, olives, and spices.

Involtini Thinly sliced beef, veal, or pork, rolled, stuffed, and fried.

Lasagne An oven-baked pasta dish which incorporates thin layers of green *(lasagne verde)* or white dough alternating with sausage or ground meat, grated cheese, and white sauce; in certain regions this dish is laced with ricotta.

Minestrone A rich and savory vegetable soup usually sprinkled with grated parmesan cheese and studded with noodles.

Mortadella Mild pork sausage, fashioned into large cylinders and served sliced; probably the closest thing in Italy to the U.S. concept of lunchmeat, "bologna."

Mozzarella A nonfermented cheese, made from the fresh milk of a buffalo (or, if unavailable, from a cow), boiled and then kneaded into a rounded ball, served fresh.

Mozzarella con pomodori Fresh tomatoes with fresh mozzarella, basil, pepper, and olive oil.

Nervetti A northern Italian antipasto concocted from chewy pieces of calves' foot or shin.

Ossobuco Beef or veal knuckle slowly braised until the cartilage is tender, and then served with a highly flavored sauce.

Pappardelle alle lepre Pasta with rabbit sauce.

Pancetta Herb-flavored pork belly, rolled into a cylinder and sliced.

Panettone Sweet yellow-colored bread baked in the form of a brioche.

Panne Heavy cream.

Pansotti Pasta stuffed with greens, herbs, and cheeses, usually served with a walnut sauce.

Parmigiano Parmesan, a hard and salty yellow cheese usually grated over pastas and soups but also eaten alone; also known as *granna.*

Peperoni Green, yellow, or red sweet peppers.

Pesci al cartoccio Fish baked in a parchment envelope with onions, parsley, and herbs.

Pesto A flavorful green sauce concocted from basil leaves, cheese, garlic, marjoram, and (if available) pine nuts.

Piccata al marsala Thin escalope of veal braised in a pungent sauce flavored with marsala wine.

Piselli al prosciutto Peas with strips of ham.

Pizza Italy's most popularized culinary export, it's probably the dish most immediately associated with Italy. Specific varieties include: *capricciosa* (its ingredients depend on the whim of the chef and can vary widely depending on his or her culinary vision and the ingredients at hand), *margherita* (incorporates tomato sauce, cheese, fresh basil, and memories of the first queen of Italy, Marguerite di Savoia, in whose honor it was first concocted by a Neapolitan chef), *napoletana* (includes ham, capers, tomatoes, oregano, cheese, and the distinctive taste of anchovies), *quattro stagione* (translated as "four seasons" because of the array of fresh vegetables in it, it also contains ham and bacon), and *siciliana* (contains black olives, capers, and cheese).

Pizzaiola A process whereby something (usually a beefsteak) is covered in a tomato-and-oregano sauce.

Polenta Thick porridge or mush made from cornmeal flour.

Polenta de uccelli Assorted small birds roasted on a spit and served with polenta.

Polenta e coniglio Rabbit stew served with polenta (see above).

Pollo alla cacciatore Chicken with tomatoes and mushrooms cooked in wine.

Pollo alla diavola Highly spiced grilled chicken.

Ragù Meat sauce.

Ricotta A soft and bland cheese, often used in cooking, made from cow's or sheep's milk.

Rigatoni Large macaroni designed with ridges to more effectively absorb sauce.

Risotto Italian rice.

Risotto alla milanese Rice with saffron and wine.

Salsa verde "Green sauce," made from capers, anchovies, lemon juice and/or vinegar, and parsley.

Saltimbocca Veal scallop layered with prosciutto and sage; its name literally translates as "jump in your mouth," a reference to its tart and savory flavor.

Salvia Sage.

Scaloppina alla valdostana Escalope of veal stuffed with cheese and ham.

Scaloppine Thin slices of veal coated in flour and sautéed in butter.

Semifreddo A frozen dessert; usually ice cream with sponge cake.

Seppia Cuttlefish (a kind of squid); its black ink is used for flavoring in certain sauces for pasta, and also in risotto dishes.

Sogliola Sole.

Spaghetti A long, round, thin pasta, variously served: *alla bolognese* (with ground meat, mushrooms, peppers, etc.), *alla carbonara* (with bacon, black pepper, and eggs), *al pomodoro* (with tomato sauce), *al sugo/ragù* (with meat sauce), and *alle vongole* (with clam sauce).

Spiedino Pieces of meat grilled on a skewer over an open flame.

Strangolaprete Small nuggets of pasta, usually served with sauce; the name is literally translated as "priest-choker."

Stufato Beef braised in white wine with vegetables.

Tagliatelle Flat egg noodles.

Tiramisù Richly caloric dessert containing layers of triple-crème cheeses and rum-soaked sponge cake.

Tonno Tuna.

Tortelli Pasta dumplings stuffed with ricotta and greens.

Tortellini Rings of dough stuffed with minced and seasoned meat and served either in soups or as full-fledged pasta covered with sauce.

Trenette Thin noodles served with pesto sauce and potatoes.

Trippe alla fiorentina Beef tripe (intestines).

Vermicelle Very thin spaghetti.

Vitello tonnato Cold sliced veal covered with tuna-fish sauce.

Zabaglione/zabaione Egg yolks whipped into the consistency of a custard, flavored with marsala, and served warm as a dessert.

Zampone Pig's trotter stuffed with spicy seasoned pork, boiled and sliced.

Zuccotto A liqueur-soaked sponge cake, molded into a dome and layered with chocolate, nuts, and whipped cream.

Zuppa inglese Sponge cake soaked in custard sauce and rum.

C Glossary of Architectural Terms

Ambone A pulpit, either serpentine or simple in form, erected in an Italian church.

Apse The half-rounded extension behind the main altar of a church; Christian tradition dictates that it be placed at the eastern end of an Italian church, the side closest to Jerusalem.

Atrium A courtyard, open to the sky, in an ancient Roman house; the term also applies to the courtyard nearest the entranceway of an early Christian church.

Baldacchino (also ciborium) A columned stone canopy, usually placed above the altar of a church; spelled in English as baldachin or baldaquin.

Basilica Any rectangular public building, usually divided into three aisles by rows of columns; in ancient Rome, this architectural form was frequently used for places of public assembly and law courts; later, Roman Christians adapted the form for many of their early churches.

Caldarium The steam room of a Roman bath.

Campanile A bell tower, often detached, of a church.

Capital The top of a column, often carved and usually categorized into one of three different orders: Doric, Ionic, or Corinthian.

Castrum A carefully planned Roman military camp, whose rectangular form, straight streets, and systems of fortified gates quickly became standardized throughout the Roman Empire; modern cities that began as Roman camps and that still more or less maintain their original forms include Chester (England), Barcelona (Spain), and such Italian cities as Lucca, Aosta, Como, Brescia, Florence, and Ancona.

Cavea The curved row of seats in a classical theater; the most prevalent shape was that of a semicircle.

Cella The sanctuary, or most sacred interior section, of a Roman pagan temple.

Chancel Section of a church containing the altar.

Cornice The decorative flange that defines the uppermost part of a classical or neoclassical facade.

Cortile Courtyard or cloisters ringed with a gallery of arches or lintels set atop columns.

Crypt A church's main burial place, usually located below the choir.

Cupola A dome.

Forum The main square, and principal gathering place, of any Roman town, usually adorned with the city's most important temples and civic buildings.

Duomo Cathedral.

Grotesques Carved and painted faces, deliberately ugly, used by everyone from the Etruscans to the architects of the Renaissance; they are especially amusing when set into fountains.

Hypogeum Subterranean burial chambers, usually of pre-Christian origins.

Loggia Roofed balcony or gallery.

Lozenge An elongated four-sided figure which, along with stripes, was one of the distinctive signs of the architecture of Pisa.

Narthex The anteroom, or enclosed porch, of a Christian church.

Nave The largest and longest section of a church, usually devoted to sheltering and/or seating worshipers, and often divided by aisles.

Pietra dura Richly ornate assemblage of semiprecious stones mounted on a flat decorative surface, considered to have been perfected during the 1600s in Florence.

Pieve A parish church.

Portico A porch, usually crafted from wood or stone.

Pulvin A four-sided stone that serves as a substitute for the capital of a column, often decoratively carved, sometimes into biblical scenes.

Putti Plaster cherubs whose chubby forms often decorate the interiors of baroque chapels and churches.

Stucco Colored plaster composed of sand, powdered marble, water, and lime, either molded into statuary or applied in a thin, concretelike layer to the exterior of a building.

Telamone Structural column carved into a standing male form; female versions are called *caryatids.*

Thermae Roman baths.

Transenna Stone (usually marble) screen separating the altar area from the rest of an early Christian church.

Travertine Known as the stone from which ancient and Renaissance Rome was built, it's known for its hardness, light coloring, and tendency to be pitted or flecked with black.

Tympanum The half-rounded space above the portal of a church, whose semicircular space usually showcases a sculpture.

Index